Numerous Meanings:
The Meaning of English Cardinals
and the Legacy of Paul Grice

Current Research in the Semantics/Pragmatics Interface

Series Editors:
K.M. Jaszczolt, University of Cambridge, UK
K. Turner, University of Brighton, UK

Other titles in this Series:

TURNER (ed.)	The Semantics/Pragmatics Interface from Different Points of View
JASZCZOLT	Discourse, Beliefs and Intentions: Semantic Defaults and Propositional Attitude Ascription
GEURTS	Presuppositions and Pronouns
JASZCZOLT (ed.)	The Pragmatics of Propositional Attitude Reports
PEETERS (ed.)	The Lexicon-Encyclopedia Interface
PAPAFRAGOU	Modality: Issues in the Semantics-Pragmatics Interface
LEEZENBERG	Contexts of Metaphor
NÉMETH & BIBOK (eds.)	Pragmatics and the Flexibility of Word Meaning
BRAS & VIEU (eds.)	Semantic and Pragmatic Issues in Discourse and Dialogue
GUTIÉRREZ-REXACH	From Words to Discourse: Trends in Spanish Semantics and Pragmatics
PEREGRIN (ed.)	Meaning: The Dynamic Turn
NEW! **DOBROVOL'SKIJ** **& PIIRAINEN**	Figurative Language: Cross-cultural and Cross-linguistic Perspectives
WEDGWOOD	Shifting the Focus: From Static Structures to the Dynamics of Interpretation

---

NEW!

KAMP & PARTEE (eds.)   **Context-Dependence in the Analysis of Linguistic Meaning**

Does context and context-dependence belong to the research agenda of semantics - and, specifically, of formal semantics? Not so long ago many linguists and philosophers would probably have given a negative answer to the question. However, recent developments in formal semantics have indicated that analyzing natural language semantics without a thorough accommodation of context-dependence is next to impossible. The classification of the ways in which context and context-dependence enter semantic analysis, though, is still a matter of much controversy and some of these disputes are ventilated in the present collection. This book is not only a collection of papers addressing context-dependence and methods for dealing with it: it also records comments to the papers and the authors' replies to the comments. In this way, the contributions themselves are contextually dependent.

In view of the fact that the contributors to the volume are such key figures in contemporary formal semantics as Hans Kamp, Barbara Partee, Reinhard Muskens, Nicholas Asher, Manfred Krifka, Jaroslav Peregrin and many others, the book represents a quite unique inquiry into the current activities on the semantics side of the semantics/pragmatics boundary.

Audience

Researchers and students of linguistics, philosophy of language, computational science and logic.

For further information on the CRiSPI series including sample chapters and details of how to submit a proposal go to:
www.elsevier.com/locate/series/crispi

NUMEROUS MEANINGS: THE MEANING OF ENGLISH CARDINALS AND THE LEGACY OF PAUL GRICE

Bert Bultinck
Antwerp University Association, Belgium

2005

ELSEVIER

Amsterdam – Boston – Heidelberg – London – New York – Oxford
Paris – San Diego – San Francisco – Singapore – Sydney – Tokyo

ELSEVIER B.V.
Radarweg 29
P.O. Box 211, 1000 AE
Amsterdam, The Netherlands

ELSEVIER Inc.
525 B Street
Suite 1900, San Diego
CA 92101-4495, USA

ELSEVIER Ltd.
The Boulevard
Langford Lane, Kidlington,
Oxford OX5 1GB, UK

ELSEVIER Ltd.
84 Theobalds Road
London WC1X 8RR
UK

First edition 2005

Library of Congress Cataloging in Publication Data
A catalog record is available from the Library of Congress.

British Library Cataloguing in Publication Data
A catalogue record is available from the British Library.

ISBN: 0-08-044557-8
ISSN: 1472-7870

⊗ The paper used in this publication meets the requirements of ANSI/NISO Z39.48-1992 (Permanence of Paper).
Printed in The Netherlands.

Current Research in the Semantics/Pragmatics Interface (CRiSPI)

The aim of this series is to focus upon the relationship between semantic and pragmatic theories for a variety of natural language constructions. The boundary between semantics and pragmatics can be drawn in many various ways; the relative benefits of each gave rise to a vivid theoretical dispute in the literature in the last two decades. As a side effect, this variety has given rise to a certain amount of confusion and lack of purpose in the extant publications on the topic. This series provides a forum where the confusion within existing literature can be removed and the issues raised by different positions can be discussed with a renewed sense of purpose. The editors intend the contributions to this series to take further strides towards clarity and cautious consensus.

CONTENTS

ACKNOWLEDGEMENTS

The research for this book was funded by the Fund for Scientific Research – Flanders (FWO-Vlaanderen).

I would like to thank my supervisor Johan van der Auwera for the many useful comments he made on earlier versions of this text. He guided me through the truth-conditional universe of meaning and did not stop me from leaving it when I considered it wise to do so. Eventually, though, I had to admit it is not such a bad place after all. The discussions we have had during the past three and a half years have been inspired by his feeling for clarity, logical argument and, most of all, efficiency.

I would also like to thank Jan Nuyts and Jef Verschueren, my two advisors. Jan encouraged me to think through the use-theoretical perspective on meaning. Our occasional but often intense conversations (usually on the phone) always proved enlightening and motivating. Jef introduced me to deconstructive paradigms in the theory of meaning, and made me realize the extreme flexibility of processes of meaning generation. I would also like to thank Louis Goossens for introducing me to linguistics in general and to data-oriented research in particular.

A number of other people have also commented on earlier versions of this work. I would like to single out Andreas Ammann and Frank Brisard. Both have made many astute suggestions, especially concerning the empirical part of the thesis. Andreas succeeds in combining Teutonic insight and meticulousness with being a really nice guy. Frank mixes rhetorical flamboyancy with intellectual generosity. It is always stimulating (as well as good fun) to disagree with him.

At the University of Antwerp (UIA), I enjoyed the stimulating discussions with Luc Herman and Geert Lernout. I also had thought-provoking conversations with Jürgen Jaspers and Helena Taelman. I would like to thank Geert Buelens, Dirk Van Hulle and Kurt Vanhoutte for their comments on my linguistic work, but especially for being around. When I started working at UIA it soon became clear that they were going to be gentle colleagues, but in the meantime they have become the best of friends. Without them, life at UIA, and elsewhere, would be much less exciting.

In the often tumultuous and always overcrowded headquarters of the Center for Grammar, Cognition and Typology, I enjoyed the conversations with and logistic support of Ludo Lejeune, as well as the company of Iza Kopczynska and Li Renzhi and the discussions with Andrej Malchukov, while at the secretariat, Lus van den Bossche, Gilberte Maerschalk and especially Jef Beckers provided the additional logistic help I needed.

At home, my friends were always ready to listen to what must have seemed extra-terrestrial stories about the meaning of English cardinals: Mark and Wendy, Steven and Sofie, Stefaan and Cil, Koen F, Kenneth and Sigrid, Lieven, Ruud, Koenraad, and Koen vdW. This is probably also the right place to thank Steffen for BGW. I would also like to thank the Yang crowd (Tom, Piet, Inge, Jeroen, Jürgen, Daniël, Marc, Sascha, Stéphane, Belle and Harold), the Finnegans Cake club (Kurt and Alex), the militants of the censorship project (Dirk and Pieter), the militant *par excellence* (Gie), and the militant of the people (Tom N) for distraction and encouragement.

At my mother's place, my family gave me the reassuring feeling that I can fall back on them. I hope the inspiring memories of my father will never fade.

Most of all I would like to thank Katleen for her support during the writing process of the thesis, for her help with the editing, and for her patience, vitality and love in general. She is, and will remain, of absolute value.

CONVENTIONS

Examples from the British National Corpus are indicated as follows:

(85)   <B3J 2772> With an irritated raise of the eyebrows, he called to Renee who
was observing the group from the other end of the bar, and made the request.
Renee shot a disapproving glance at Knocker and began preparing her drink.
Nigger turned his attention to Yanto and Billy. "What about you **two**."

The formulae at the beginning of the examples are references used by the British National
Corpus, indicating the source text (cf. Burnard 1995). The relevant instance of *two* in these
BNC-examples is printed in bold type (often there is more than one instance of *two* in the
excerpt). These examples from the BNC will be called "solutions". If no such formula is
present, the example has a different origin (i.e., either borrowed from other authors or a
constructed example). I have preserved the original state of the BNC material. This means
that I have not added or removed punctuation, nor have I corrected spelling mistakes or typos
in the solutions.

References to linguistic elements are in italics, references to meanings are between single
quotation marks (as in "*two* means 'two' and not 'at least two'", or as in "the 'at least' meaning
of *two*"), "scare quotes" are double, and new / borrowed terms are also between double
quotation marks. Italics are also used for stress. Underlining is used for focus. In the labels of
the various analyses of cardinals (as in "the 'at least' meaning, as opposed to the 'exactly'
analysis"), single quotes are used.

Horn scales are represented as follows:
<Strongest element, Weakest element>

The symbol I used for logical conjunction is ∧ and the one for disjunction is ∨.

This study only concerns the English cardinal numerals. Whenever the term "numerals" is
used, I refer to the cardinal numerals (and not to the ordinal numerals).

1

Introduction

In linguistics, numerals have been investigated from very different angles. A considerable number of studies have analyzed typological properties of numeral systems cross-linguistically (Szemerényi 1960, Greenberg 1978, Gvozdanovic 1992), often focusing on the different "base numbers" of various counting systems (Menninger 1970 [1958], Hammerich 1966, Ifrah 1998 [1994]), while other cross-linguistic work has emphasized the internal structure of numeral sequences (Hurford 1975, Corbett 1978), or their relative frequency (Dehaene and Mehler 1992). Sometimes, this kind of research has also considered ethnological claims in relating specific number systems to different ways of conceptualizing reality (Saxe 1982, Saxe and Posner 1983, Ifrah 1998 [1994], Brysbaert, Fias and Noël 1998). Generative grammars for the English numeral system have been written (Hurford 1975, 1987). Besides more general surveys of the number concept (Brainerd 1979, Kitcher 1984), psycholinguists, starting from the seminal work of Piaget (Piaget 1952), have been interested in the processing of numbers (Dehaene 1992) and have devoted much attention to children's acquisition of number and number words (Gelman and Gallistel 1978, Brainerd 1982, Ginsburg 1983, Wynn 1992). Still others have proposed an "internal syntax" of the English number system (Peters 1980), have examined the scope relations of numerals (Landman 1998), or have suggested interesting reasons why the same set of numbers is used in coins and bills throughout the world (Pollmann and Jansen 1996).

In general, I will not be concerned with any of these approaches, even though they may occasionally be of tangential importance, in which case I will elaborate upon them. This study is set up as a description of the *meaning* of English cardinal numbers, and will delve into what is probably still one of the most influential semantico-pragmatic analyses of quantifiers in general, and numerals in particular: the (neo-) Gricean[1], scalar account of English numerals. Besides having been the most popular semantic description of numerals during the last three decades, this perspective on numerals throws light on the *status quo* of research into the semantics-pragmatics interface, and, hence, of research into the

---

[1] I use the term "neo-Gricean" in a relatively broad sense: to some extent, every analysis of the English cardinals that relies on Grice's maxims can be called "neo-Gricean". I do not distinguish between "post-Gricean" and "neo-Gricean", as the degree of affinity with Grice's original analyses is very hard to measure.

conceptualization of "meaning" in general. In the analysis, I will demonstrate that the neo-Gricean account suffers from methodological insecurity and as a consequence postulates highly non-conventional meanings of numerals as their "literal meaning", that it confuses the level of lexical semantics with that of utterances and that it cannot deal with a large number of counter-examples. I will propose an alternative account of the meaning of English cardinals and the ways in which their interpretation can be influenced by other linguistic elements.

In the early seventies, Laurence Horn (1972) started to use numerals as examples in more or less "radical" pragmatic programs. "Radical pragmatics" was conceived as a scientific project to simplify semantic descriptions as much as possible, by relegating as much as possible of the meaning of a linguistic element or an entire utterance to pragmatics. Sadock writes:

> The big idea in radical pragmatics is that many of what were conceived of as essentially inexplicable structural facts of language are really reflections of the fact that natural language is used by real speakers in real contexts to accomplish real goals. The hope is that by taking into account the appropriate aspects of the use of expressions, the structure becomes otiose and can be dispensed with in explaining the primary linguistic datum, namely, that a certain expression can be used on a certain occasion with a certain effect. (Sadock 1984:141)

Due to their apparent semantic simplicity, numerals proved an ideal and very elucidating example of how speakers could modify word meanings, simply by using them. As the variety of meanings expressed by numerals is rather limited, the relationship between those meanings received more attention. The almost exclusive (and often unacknowledged) focus of neo-Griceans on cardinality uses of numerals reduced the number of positions even more drastically. The question of which meanings are "semantic" and which should be relegated to the "pragmatic" sphere became the central consideration. Numerals were often appropriated for theoretical purposes and the independent investigation of their meaning became subordinate to their integration into a wider framework that tried to account for the relationship between language and use, sentence meaning and speaker meaning, semantics and pragmatics. This led to highly counter-intuitive meaning postulates, but at the same time this "annexation" now serves as an excellent limiting case, foregrounding where and how "radical pragmatics" went wrong. They constitute a prism that offers today's linguist an iridescent history of one of the most fascinating, if often misconstrued, topics in contemporary meaning research: the conversational implicatures.

This study consists of two main bodies, although they are attached to each other with a well-nigh umbilical cord. To entertain the same metaphor, the question of the meaning of numerals came to life only within that theoretical framework. Hardly anyone seemed interested in the meaning of English numerals outside the neo-Gricean context. I contend that this is one of the reasons why neo-Gricean analysis has been able to postulate flaringly counter-intuitive "literal meanings" for numerals for such a long time (at least from 1972 to 1992, the point at which Larry Horn gave in to his critics (Horn 1992), but see Levinson (2000) for contemporary rehabilitations). Given the history of the philosophy of language (from Frege over Russell to Grice), with its marked interest in mathematics and logic (and the attempt to reduce the former to the latter), and its truly fundamental influence on pragmatics as a burgeoning discipline, it is not coincidental that numerals were picked out as semantic guinea pigs. Their fate was doomed accordingly.

In this analysis, I will first explore and evaluate the development of the Gricean program and the various alternatives to it, and then I will embark on a corpus analysis of numerals themselves. The choice for a corpus analysis follows directly from dissatisfaction with the neo-Gricean methodology and results. The theoretical first part will provide the more general motivation for this methodological choice. Furthermore, the dual structure reflects the relative importance of both parts: while it is clear that the investigation of the meaning of English numerals becomes more fascinating when it is related to its place in the history of Gricean pragmatics (and this link certainly was the original trigger for this investigation), I will not make the same mistake as the neo-Griceans and limit myself to a description of how numerals can be fitted into the neo-Gricean picture. I will therefore analyze the meaning of English cardinals relatively independently of the neo-Gricean claims: the corpus analysis will try to describe the ways in which numerals are used in the English language as exhaustively as possible. This means that I will also look at uses of numerals that have been ignored by neo-Gricean accounts, and especially at uses that are less than fully "cardinal", in the sense that the typical 'numerosity' meaning is not the most prominent meaning expressed by these uses. Nevertheless, the results will primarily function as the basis of my critique of the neo-Gricean account. Eventually, the corpus analysis will lead to the defense of an "absolute value" analysis of the semantics of English cardinals, which is essentially different from the numerous other proposals that have been suggested in the past three decades of the "cardinal debate".

2

THE GRICEAN THEORY OF IMPLICATURE

2.0. INTRODUCTION

An evaluation of the way in which numerals are treated in the neo-Gricean paradigm must be based upon a detailed survey of the history of the Gricean approach to meaning in general. Only then can Gricean analyses of numerals be fully understood. I will devote a significant part of this study to a critical reconstruction of its evolution.

As mentioned, the project of Gricean pragmatics is spurred by an overarching tendency to make as many generalizations as possible, in order to simplify semantics as much as possible. As a consequence, numerals themselves have often been used only as an example; in many cases they did not even figure explicitly in the discussion of general mechanisms and principles. However, the application of these principles to a meaning account of numerals is nearly always explicitly or implicitly understood. Indeed, numerals are often not distinguished from the larger class of quantifiers, but they are nevertheless assumed to behave similarly. In Grice's original lectures on "logic and conversation" (Grice 1989 [1967], 1975) the emphasis is on natural language counterparts of formal, logical devices. As far as quantifiers are concerned, this means that the prime examples are the natural language counterparts of the logical existential and universal quantifiers, namely *some* and *all*. Grice himself does not use numerals to make his case. It is only in the work of Larry Horn (1972) that numerals become part of the Gricean canon, to remain so until the present day, be it with considerably more reservations (cf. Levinson 2000:90, but cf. Krifka 1999 and Allan 2001 for unambiguous support of Horn's original 1972 analysis). This means that in the following discussion, the relevance of the theoretical discussions for the meaning analysis of numerals will often be only indirect. This does not mean, however, that some of the sections are of minor importance for the description of number words: the Gricean program is a package-deal, and all of the theoretical topics that will be considered eventually influence the conceptualization of number words as well. Theoretical criticism aimed at separate elements of the general Gricean program always recoils on the meaning construal of numerals.

A concise summary of the most important elements of the (neo-)Gricean line on numerals will introduce the topics, which I will subsequently deal with one by one, in separate sections. The traditional Gricean view is that English cardinal numbers have an 'at least' semantics. It follows that the literal meaning of (1) is 'Mary has at least three children'.

(1)   Mary has three children.

However, neo-Griceans assume that when numerals are used in utterances they usually have an 'exactly'-reading. They claim that (1) is usually, in "normal circumstances", interpreted as 'Mary has exactly three children', no more, no less. According to the neo-Gricean paradigm, this reading is arrived at via a pragmatic process, which takes the linguistically determined 'at least' semantics as input. This pragmatic overlay rests on a number of general insights. According to Grice, rational linguistic (and non-linguistic) communication is steered by one fundamental principle and a number of maxims. Together, these account for specific pragmatic effects, which Grice called "conversational implicatures". The Cooperative Principle (CP) captures the assumption that speakers and hearers are cooperative communicators. They will contribute to the conversation as is required by the general goal of the conversation (this goal is consensually accepted by the communicators). Besides the very general Cooperative Principle, the second important rule for the analysis of numerals (and for all "scalar" phenomena, a term coined by Horn 1972) is the first submaxim of Quantity (Q1), which stipulates that participants should make their contribution as informative as is required. The process that turns the semantic 'at least' meaning into a pragmatic 'exactly'-reading crucially relies on this Quantity-maxim: if the speaker had been in the position to make a stronger claim, he should have done so (otherwise he would have been less informative than required by the current purposes of the exchange). In the case of (1), if the speaker had been in the position to say that Mary has four children, he should have done so. Since he hasn't, the hearer can assume that the speaker did not intend to communicate that Mary has more than three children. Combined with the 'at least' semantics of *three*, this results in an 'exactly'-reading: 'at least three' (semantics) + 'not more than three' (pragmatics, the so-called "implicature") = 'exactly three'. The major advantage of seeing this 'exactly'-reading as a pragmatic meaning is that it gives a ready explanation as to why it is possible to "cancel" the implicature, without creating a contradiction. This is indicated by the term "cancelability" or "defeasibility".

(2)   Mary has three children, in fact she has four.

This is different with entailments (propositions that follow logically from another proposition; i.e., if A is an entailment of B, then A is true in every world in which B is true) are considered "semantic" in nature and cannot be canceled.

(3)   *John went to the cinema and bought a ticket, but in fact he didn't buy a ticket.

This is, in a nutshell, and with limited usage of the Gricean jargon, the neo-Gricean account of the meaning of numerals. As already mentioned, the attraction of this kind of explanation is that it can cover a wide range of ostensibly very different phenomena by means of a limited number of rules and mechanisms. Moreover, the whole schema is based on a unified perspective on meaning, which regards speaker intentions as fundamental.

In the literature, this analysis has been scrutinized from a number of different perspectives. One fundamental question is whether the Gricean maxims are the only principles of conversation. In other words: is Grice's list correct and exhaustive and are the maxims indeed universal? What are they based on? Various attempts have been made to reduce the maxims to some more general maxims. Another central question asks for the kinds of arguments that support an account in terms of implicature. Related to this is the discussion about "tests" for implicatures: how can we be sure that a certain meaning is an implicature rather than part of the semantics of the item in question? How do implicatures interact with other types of meaning effects, such as presuppositions and entailments? And what does it mean to say that implicatures are "defeasible"? This has eventually led to a wider discussion about the division of "meaning" in general: how do implicatures fit in the general division of meaning relations like monosemy, polysemy, ambiguity, vagueness and underdetermination? On another level, there is the more basic question whether there are alternatives to the semantics-pragmatics distinction. Also, the differences between Grice's distinctions between the so-called "particularized" and "generalized" conversational implicatures and the notions "what is said" and "what is implicated" are spelt out.

Furthermore, within the context of the logical properties of natural language - the context in which the whole discussion about implicatures originally arose - it is natural to investigate the interaction of implicatures with negation and other logical operators. The relationship between the Aristotelian Square of Oppositions and linguistic phenomena has also been a matter of debate. Next, much effort has gone into attempts to formalize the generation of implicatures. One crucial question in this debate is the status and the properties of the so-called scales: what does it mean to say that numerals are "scalar" (cf. 2.2.3.1. below)? This attempt at formalization further relies on an accurate and manageable construal of "cotext" (defined as the linguistic elements that are present in the context of an utterance, e.g. the influence of modal expressions on the interpretation of numerals), discourse structure (including intonational hints), extra-linguistic "context" and their effects. Several attempts have been made to make the influence of discourse and context properties more visible. Moreover, the various kinds of implicatures (conventional implicatures, clausal and scalar conversational Q-implicatures, but also implicatures induced by maxims other than Grice's Quantity-maxim) have been ordered according to relative importance. Other researchers have stressed that Grice's extremely ambitious and truly generalizing original project has fragmented into analyses of very local and highly item-specific phenomena. Finally, to return to the question of numerals in this larger debate, people have wondered whether numerals are indeed prototypical scalars and why neo-Griceans have started from an 'at least' semantics. Gricean accounts have been developed that nonetheless do not start from 'at least' meanings. Specific characteristics of numerals (in terms of "roundness", "lexical incorporation" and their mathematical usage) have been pointed out.

I will group these questions into two major chapters: the relatively short first chapter will be devoted to a discussion of the theory of implicatures in general, while the larger second chapter will focus on the consequences of this program for the analysis of English numerals. It will also discuss how other paradigms have dealt with English cardinals. The second part will discuss the general outlines of Grice's maxims and his Cooperative Principle; it will also point out the relationship with Grice's ideas about meaning and the concept "literal meaning". I will go back to Grice's original texts and try to pinpoint the explicit and less explicit objectives of Grice's project. Because Grice's texts on implicatures are often reduced to a survey of principles and maxims, it might be refreshing to try to indicate the underlying motivations that guide his general project. These texts offer much more than a groundbreaking analysis of conversational phenomena; they have firmly established a way of thinking about meaning. Moreover, I will deal with the concept of implicatures, focusing on the "working-out schema", the various subdistinctions within the concept of implicature, the relationship with the notion "entailment", and an appreciation of the importance of "tests" for conversational implicatures. The various attempts at formalization will be covered, mainly focusing on the concept of "scales" and the projection problems, while I will also locate the place of logic in the development of the Gricean paradigm.

The part concerning the specific analysis of numerals will list and discuss the most central phenomena that have been used as examples to underscore the importance of the Gricean theory. The different positions with respect to the meaning of numerals will be evaluated (the neo-Gricean analysis, the semantic description in terms of ambiguity, the influence of "focus", and the underdeterminacy thesis). This will immediately lead us into the next part, in which the Gricean theory will be confronted with a corpus analysis of English numerals, which have often been considered to be one of the core cases of generalized conversational implicatures (cf. Kempson 1986:80).

The literature on the Gricean theory of conversation is enormous. As will be indicated, many of the arguments for and against the theory that will be used here can also be found in various other critiques of the theory. In this theoretical discussion, I have tried to concentrate on those arguments, remarks and (neo-)Gricean tendencies that are relevant for the analysis of English cardinals. My main intention is to clarify my position with respect to the general claims of the theory of conversation and the much more specific claims regarding English cardinals. However, I believe that the methodological decision to criticize the Gricean analysis of numerals by means of a corpus study is new in the field. The theoretical discussion that follows should also be read as a defense of that method.

2.1. IMPLICATURES ACCORDING TO PAUL GRICE

2.1.1. Meaning

Before discussing the details of Grice's maxims of conversation, it is necessary to mention Grice's ideas about meaning in general. The two theories for which Grice is most famous, the "theory of conversation" and the "theory of meaning", are often kept separate (Neale 1992:511). Grice himself hardly ever explicitly points at connections between these two strands of his thinking. Nevertheless, the connection between them can and must be made. Stephen Neale even suggests that Grice's "theory of conversation" can be seen as a component of the "theory of meaning" (Neale 1992:514). As is well known, Grice's influential theory of meaning (most famously defended in his short 1957 paper called "Meaning"), eventually redefines meaning in terms of intentions. This ultimately psychological perspective allows Grice to analyze the simple expression "A meant$_{NN}$ something by x" (Grice 1989

[1957]:220)[1], where the subscript "NN" stands for "non-natural meaning", a concept devised by Grice to distinguish two sorts of uses of the verb *mean* (the "natural" sense includes uses such as *those spots mean measles,* and can be loosely associated with the Peircean concept of "index" (Peirce 1991 [1867]) as opposed to non-natural meaning exemplified in *those three rings on the bell (of the bus) mean that the bus is full,* which can be linked to Peirce's definition of "symbol" (Peirce 1991 [1867])[2]). According to Grice *A* meant$_{NN}$ *something by x* is roughly equivalent to "*A* intended the utterance of *x* to produce some effect in an audience by means of the recognition of this intention" (Grice 1989:220)[3].

The technicalities of this definition are not important for this discussion, but it must be clear that whenever Grice talks about meanings, these meanings can be ultimately reduced to speaker intentions. Because much of what will follow will hinge on the notion of "conventionality", it is important to emphasize that Grice distinguished between two uses of *mean*: the first is used when we talk about *someone* meaning something by a linguistic structure *x* (this is the sense of *meaning* captured in the definition in the previous paragraph), the second is used when we simply talk about linguistic structures that mean something. Crucially, Grice considers the second sense to be derivative of the first. In other words, the meaning of a word or a sentence is based on the intentions with which people standardly use that word or sentence:

> It seems to me, then, at least reasonable and possibly even mandatory, to treat the meaning of words, or of other communication vehicles, as analyzable in terms of features of word users or other communicators; nonrelativized uses of "meaning$_{NN}$" are posterior to and explicable through relativized uses involving reference to word users or communicators. More specifically, what sentences mean is what (standardly) users of such sentences mean by them; that is to say, what psychological attitudes toward what propositional objects such users standardly intend [...] to produce by their utterance. (Grice 1989:350)

This demonstrates that according to Grice a statement indicating a meaning of a linguistic structure should always be reducible to a statement about a specific speaker intention or a disjunction of statements about speaker intentions. Moreover, it is important that the meaning of linguistic structures is characterized as what speakers *standardly* mean by them. Unfortunately, Grice does not really attempt to define this "standard" in a minimally precise way. In what follows, I will assume that the "conventionality" of a meaning can be identified with the degree to which this meaning can *standardly* be said to be expressed by a linguistic structure. In the discussion of Grice's analysis of *or,* I will try to make this notion of "conventionality" more precise.

---

[1] Throughout the text, I will refer to the (slightly revised) 1989 edition of Grice's work. See Neale (1992) for critical evaluation of the revisions made to the original texts.

[2] Grice himself referred to the distinction between "natural" and "conventional" signs (Grice 1989:215).

[3] Various alternatives and amendments to this definition have been proposed, by Grice himself and others. Grandy and Warner (1986) and Neale (1992) provide good overviews of the evolution of Grice's original definition of meaning in terms of intentions.

2.1.2. Logic and conversation

One of the most important strands in Grice's thinking is the differentiation of types of meaning. Especially the distinction between conventional meaning and non-conventional meaning has proved very influential[4]. In what follows, I will introduce Grice's basic insights concerning meaning and conversation in the context of this distinction between conventional meaning and non-conventional / non-literal / non-truth-conditional / implicated meaning, because this perspective will allow us to focus on the essential problem for the analysis of English cardinals: how did Grice and his followers tackle the "meaning analysis"[5] of numerals and why did they do it the way they did? I will concentrate on Grice's two most important texts on implicatures, the lecture called "Logic and conversation" and the one called "Further notes on logic and conversation", with occasional references to some of Grice's other texts. It will appear that Grice's project not only attempts to explain how non-conventional meanings of linguistic elements can be derived from conventional ones, but that it also aims to reconcile the ways in which logical operators are used in logic with the ways in which linguistic elements - which are alleged to be natural language counterparts of these logical operators - are used in everyday conversation. My main claim will be that while Grice's analysis is convincing as far as the explanation of the non-conventional meaning of utterances is concerned, his claim that the "conventional meaning" of the so-called natural language counterparts of logical operators can be equated with the "meaning" of these logical operators is highly problematic.

2.1.2.1. Formalists and informalists

The influence of logic on Grice's writings on conversation must be seen in the context of a long tradition. Already in the seventeenth century, Gottfried Wilhelm Leibniz remarked:

---

[4] Grice's writings have also had an important influence on the status of "literal meaning". To a large extent, the current status of the concept of literal meaning in linguistics has been determined by Grice's lectures on implicatures. Whereas in earlier times a distinction between "proper/current" language and metaphorical, derivative or simply imprecise language was also present (at least since Aristotle's *Poetics*, cf. Leezenberg 1995:33-34), the two-level system that classifies meaning as either literal or non-literal meaning had not yet been extended to such a wide range of phenomena. Grice not only continued the dichotomy between metaphorical and non-metaphorical language, but he extended it to the widest range of phenomena of language use. The way he made this point - the arguments he used, the evidence he adduced and the more general concerns he had - has proved decisive for the further history of the concept of literal meaning. But even though Grice's influence on the two-level system can hardly be overestimated, he rarely used the term "literal meaning" in his writings. At one place he seems to use "literal" as a synonym of "nonderivative" (Grice 1989:48); at other times he uses the term "standard meaning" (Grice 1989 [1957]:216), but most often he uses the term "conventional meaning" or "conventional force". His use of the term "conventional meaning" is such that it can be freely exchanged with the term "literal meaning", although "literal meaning" is more often used to contrast with metaphorical meaning, while "conventional meaning" refers to a particular assumption about the conventionality of language, while this is much less explicit in the term "literal meaning". At least at one point Grice himself clearly links "literalness" with "what is said", and "what is said" is closely associated with "conventional meaning" (Grice 1989: 25).

[5] This somewhat artificial compound is used as a neutral term to indicate the analysis of the meaning of a linguistic item in general. It has the advantage that it does not express a commitment with respect to the semantic or pragmatic status of the meaning discussed.

Natural languages are useful to reason, but are subject to innumerable equivocations, nor can be used in a manner which allows us to discover errors in an argument by retracing our steps to the beginning and to the construction of our words – as if errors were simply due to solecisms or barbarisms. (Leibniz qtd. in Eco 1995:280)

This assumption has lived on in the works of many philosophers of language as well as in much of the linguistic literature. It is one of the most important motivations for the bi-planar approach of meaning, in which "semantic" meaning is distinguished from "pragmatic" meaning. Grice, in particular, locates this assumption with what he calls the "formalist group" (Grice 1989:22-23): these people are convinced of the superiority of formal systems (especially logic) over natural language. Their project eventually leads to the construction of an ideal language, in which truth-values of statements can be rigidly determined. Even though Grice does not list any names, Eco (1995) does: besides G.W. Leibniz, also Francis Bacon, Gottlob Frege, the "first" Ludwig Wittgenstein, and Rudolf Carnap, together with a number of other Logical Positivists (cf. Récanati 1979) complained about the inferiority of natural languages. Most of them proposed a project involving the construction of a "better language", one way or another.

The other group, the "informalists", argues that the formalization of language advocated by the formalists, is unduly oriented towards scientific uses of language. They contend that natural language has a "logic" of its own, which is different from and sometimes incompatible with logic as we know it. This point of view is associated with such philosophers and linguists as (the later) Wittgenstein (Wittgenstein 1972 [1953]:§101-108), and Ordinary Language Philosophers such as J.L. Austin and P. Strawson. It has become the standard opinion in much of current pragmatic theory, if the relationship between logic and communication is addressed there at all. Nevertheless, the equivalence relationships and the inferential mechanisms that can be discerned in logic still provide a source of inspiration for semantic and pragmatic theories.

Grice himself does not want to choose sides; in fact he claims that the divergence between logical operators like ∨ or ~ and items of everyday language like *or* or *not* does not exist. It is because people have not been attentive to the "nature and importance of the conditions governing conversation" (Grice 1989:24) that this divergence has been postulated. Grice's analysis is an explicit attempt to reconcile logic and language, not by building bridges between the two disciplines (e.g. by using mapping relations, or translational schemata as an interface), but by postulating some sort of logical substructure, within natural language itself. Exaggerating only slightly, one could say that instead of arguing that natural language is imperfect, vague or imprecise, he suggests that natural language is as precise as logic, as long as it is not used. As soon as sentences are used, however, the senses are no longer controlled by the semantics of the language, but are transformed via the system of conversational implicatures. Even though Grice contends that these implicatures are also, to some extent, controllable (they are supposed to be "calculable", even if Grice himself allows for a certain "indeterminacy" (Grice 1989:39-40)), it is clear that the "departures" of the "literal meaning" of words and sentences can be manifold.

2.1.2.2. Maxims and implicatures

What exactly are implicatures? The general purpose of Grice's lectures on "logic and conversation" is to demonstrate how "the conditions governing conversation" modify the meaning of linguistic items, and thus to show how logic and conversation, language and language use, can be reconciled. The first example Grice gives is that of a conversation between A and B, who are talking about a mutual friend C. Asked how C is getting on in his new job, B answers:

(4)   Oh quite well, I think; he likes his colleagues, and he hasn't been to prison yet.

Grice argues: "I think it is clear that whatever B implied, suggested, meant, etc., in this example, is distinct from what B said, which was simply that C had not been to prison yet" (Grice 1989:24). A first definition of implicature is a negative one: implicated meanings are those meanings that are part of the "meaning" of an utterance but not part of "what is said". The latter is assumed to be a concept that is intuitively clear, but Grice explicitly affirms that "what is said" is "closely related to the conventional meaning of the words (the sentence) he has uttered" (Grice 1989:25). Grice suggests that these implicatures can be described, expected and calculated on the basis of the following general "rules" of conversation:

> <u>Cooperative Principle</u>: Make your conversational contribution such as is required, at the stage at which it occurs, by the accepted purpose or direction of the talk exchange in which you are engaged.
> <u>Maxims of Quantity</u>:
> Q1: Make your contribution as informative as is required (for the current purposes of the exchange).
> Q2: Do not make your contribution more informative than is required.
> <u>Maxims of Quality</u>: Try to make your contribution one that is true.
> QL1: Do not say what you believe to be false.
> QL2: Do not say that for which you lack adequate evidence.
> <u>Maxim of Relation</u>: Be relevant.
> <u>Maxims of Manner</u>: Be perspicuous.
> M1: Avoid obscurity of expression.
> M2: Avoid ambiguity.
> M3: Be brief (avoid unnecessary prolixity).
> M4: Be orderly.
> (Grice 1989:26-27)

The first is an overarching principle; the other four are more specific rules. Grice emphasizes that these principles are not only descriptions of how people actually behave: he claims that it is *reasonable* for us to follow the standard type of conversational practice as captured by the maxims. These maxims can be construed as general guidelines for the production and interpretation of meaning, and the concept of conversational implicatures is one example of how these maxims help us to (re)construct the meaning of an utterance and differentiate the different "types" of meanings. The typical neo-Gricean example with numerals is the interpretation of *three* in

(5)   Joan has three children.

as 'exactly three': if the speaker knew that Joan has more than three children, he or she should have said so; otherwise he or she would not have been fully cooperative in the sense that he or she has not made the contribution as informative as is required (Q1). But we presume that the speaker is cooperative (and, in Grice's opinion, it is rational to presume that, because it is rational for the speaker to follow the Cooperative Principle) and that is why we conclude that the speaker was not in the position to say that Joan has more than three children because he would be lying (and thereby violating the Quality1-maxim). Grice himself did not use examples with numerals, but he did provide numerous examples with natural language counterparts of logical operators like *or* and *if ...then.* He also listed a number of ways in which language users may behave with respect to these rules: speakers may follow or violate them, they can "opt out", or they may "flout" them, i.e. "blatantly fail to fulfill them" (Grice 1989:30). The most important of these "attitudes" towards the maxims are no doubt the cases in which the speakers merely observe the maxims or those in which they flout them. An example of the latter is when somebody says

(6)   Miss X produced a series of sounds that corresponded closely with the score of "Home Sweet Home".

when saying

(7)   Miss X sang "Home Sweet Home".

would be much more perspicuous. The flouting of the maxim of manner triggers the implicated meaning that Miss X was singing very badly.

Grice also presents a list of six "features" which characterize implicatures. The first and most important feature refers to the "cancelability" of implicatures. Implicatures are canceled when the "extra" meaning that is arrived at through the mechanisms of the Cooperative Principle and the maxims (either by observing them or flouting them) is not retained as part of the meaning of the linguistic expression: "it may be explicitly canceled, by the addition of a clause that states or implies that the speaker has opted out, or it may contextually be canceled, if the form of utterance that usually carries it is used in a context that makes clear that the speaker is opting out" (Grice 1989:39). To return to the example:

(8)   Joan has three children, in fact she has four.

is an example of an explicit cancellation of the implicated 'exactly' meaning. This cancelability can distinguish implicatures from conventional meanings, because conventional meanings can normally not be canceled: ??*I saw a man, in fact I did not.* Second, implicatures are "non-detachable": implicatures are triggered by the meaning of the utterance, not by the manner in which this meaning is expressed. If we replace the linguistic trigger of the implicature with another linguistic element that has the same meaning, the implicature should be preserved. Ironical utterances provide typical examples of this non-detachability. If we say of someone who is very ugly

(9)   He's so handsome.

the ironic interpretation, which is implicated due to the flouting of the maxim of quality, is preserved when we say

(10)   He's gorgeous.

The third feature is the non-conventionality of implicatures: by definition, implicatures are not part of the conventional meaning of the linguistic element in question (be it a lexical element or an utterance). The three other features are the fact that implicatures are capable of being "worked out" (this is referred to as the "calculability" of implicatures), the fact that implicatures are not carried by "what is said", but by the saying of it and the indeterminacy of implicatures (an utterance may yield a "disjunction" of specific explanations that are all compatible with the observance or flouting of the cooperative principle and the maxims). The latter implies that implicatures are vague, and according to Grice, this fits the facts: "if the list of these [explanations] is open, the implicatum will have just the kind of indeterminacy that many actual implicata do in fact seem to possess" (Grice 1989:40).

A final distinction concerns the generality of implicatures. Grice makes a crucial distinction between particularized conversational implicatures and generalized conversational implicatures (the so-called "GCIs"). It is especially the latter type that will be of interest to us, because the implicatures that are claimed to be attached to uses of numerals are generalized ones, not particularized. This means that it is not the case that particular features of the context are responsible for the implicature, but that the 'exactly' implicature of a numeral like *two* is normally carried by saying *two*. This "normally" means that the implicatures are present by default, when no special (contextual) circumstances obtain. Whereas

(11)   There is a garage around the corner.

may trigger the implicature that the speaker thinks that there might be petrol in that garage when it is uttered as a reply to someone else's uttering

(12)   I am out of petrol.

this cannot be a GCI, because special circumstances have to obtain to trigger that implicature. In other words, (11) does not by default trigger the implicature that you might find petrol there. But the utterance of a sentence containing the quantifier *some* usually will carry the implicature 'not all': in the utterances

(13)   Some were invited to the party.

(14)   Some were having a drink.

some will be typically interpreted as 'not all', and this is, according to Grice and the neo-Griceans, a GCI of the use of *some*.

Returning to Grice's attention for the logical tradition and the distinction between meaning and use that will guide Grice throughout his writings on implicature, the next three subsections will illustrate this tendency by focusing on specific analyses. One involves the conventional implicature that Grice associates with *therefore*, the others with conversational implicatures linked with *or* and indicative conditionals.

2.1.2.3. Rescuing logic in conversation (1): therefore
Conventional implicatures, which are associated with items such as *but, therefore, moreover*, take a middle position between "implicatures" and "conventional meaning", because they are regarded as conventionalized, but in spite of this do not belong to "what is said". The concept of "conventional implicature" is confusing because it explicitly prevents the reader to equate "implicature" with "non-conventionality", a conclusion which could be reached on the basis of the definition of "implicature" that Grice gave in his discussion of "what is said". Apparently, there are aspects of conventional meaning that are not part of "what is said".

The concept of "conventional implicature" has not been picked up by very many neo-Gricean or other researchers of meaning. Even though he does suggest that the term is relevant, Levinson writes that "[i]n a sense conventional implicature is not a very interesting concept - it is rather an admission of the failure of truth-conditional semantics to capture all the conventional content or meaning of natural language words and expressions" (Levinson 1983:128). But as Levinson's evaluation shows, the concept is relevant for a good understanding of Grice's general project.

The example of conventional implicature that Grice provides is the relation of consequence inherent in the utterance

(15)   He is an Englishman; he is, therefore, brave.

He claims that the speaker who utters such a statement "has certainly committed [himself], by virtue of the meaning of [his] words, to its being the case that his being brave is a consequence of (follows from) his being an Englishman" (Grice 1989:25). Nevertheless, Grice claims that the speaker has not "*said* (in the favored sense)" (Grice 1989:25 - emphasis in the original) that there is a relation of consequence between the fact that "he" is an Englishman and the fact that "he" is brave. What could Grice mean by saying that a certain meaning has been "indicated, and so implicated" (Grice 1989:25) but not "said (in a favored sense)", in which the favored sense was stipulated on the same page as what is "closely related to the conventional meaning of the words (the sentence)" a person has uttered (Grice 1989:25). The relation of consequence associated with *therefore* is a conventional implicature, but it is not part of what was said, while "what is said" is defined in terms of "conventional meaning". It is conventional, but, then again, not really.

Nevertheless, this confusion turns out to be enlightening, in the sense that it reveals Grice's intentions. There does not seem to be a good reason to deny that the meaning of *therefore* is in fact the indication of a relationship of consequence between two states-of-affairs. In fact, when Grice paraphrases his example in terms of "what is said", the word *therefore* seems to have no meaning (meaning being narrowly construed as "what is said") except for the conjunction expressed by *and*:

> But while I have said that he is an Englishman, and said that he is brave, I do not want to say that I have *said* (in the favored sense) that it follows from his being an Englishman that he is brave, though I have certainly indicated, and so implicated, that this is so. (Grice 1989:25)

The conclusion must be, even though Grice never makes this explicit, that the relation of consequence expressed by *therefore* is not part of what is said, because in Grice's opinion *therefore* is first and foremost a conjunction, which can be translated in logical terms, while the relationship of consequence expressed by *therefore* cannot be captured by a logical counterpart very easily. Grice accepts the statement *He is an Englishman* as a straightforward part of what is said, just like *He is brave*: these two utterances and the conjunction can be easily linked to a propositional form, something to the effect of $E(x) \wedge B(x)$, in which (x) is a variable, which can have the value *he*, E for *is an Englishman* and B for *is brave*. Apparently, Grice considered none of traditional logic's "formal devices" for connecting propositions to be a good expression of the relationship of consequence expressed by *therefore*[6]. It seems that Grice found it impossible to categorize it under the label "what is said", but had to invent a somewhat makeshift category, the category of conventional implicature.

Further evidence for this can be found in his discussion of the feature of "nondetachability", a feature that is neither a necessary nor a sufficient condition for implicatures, but which, as we have seen, is listed by Grice as one of the characteristics of implicatures. The "non-detachability" of implicatures refers to the fact that implicatures are triggered by the meaning of the utterance, not by the manner in which this meaning is expressed. If we replace the linguistic trigger of the implicature with another linguistic element that has the same meaning, the implicature should be preserved. Grice notes that "reliance on this feature is effective primarily for distinguishing between certain conventional implicatures and nonconventional implicatures" (Grice 1989:44). This implies that "conventional implicatures" such as the one associated with *therefore*, should be detachable. That means that it must be possible to find another way of saying the same thing which lacks the implicature. Even though also here Grice does not really make his intentions explicit, in the case of *therefore* the only thing that Grice could have had in mind as "another way of saying the same thing" is, of course, *and*: this does not have the implicature linked with *therefore* (the relation of consequence), but, in Grice's opinion it should "say the same thing"[7].

---

[6] This is rather surprising, since *therefore* could very well be considered a natural language counterpart of the logical relationship of consequence, one of the fundamental notions in logic.

[7] In a later lecture, Grice refined the notion of "what is said", contrasting it with "what is conventionally meant". The latter implies "(i) that when U [utterer] uttered X, the meaning of X included "*p" and (ii) that part of what U meant when he uttered X was that p" (Grice 1989:121; "*" is short for "mood", indicative or imperative). This does not change the fact that the conventional meaning is taken as the basis of "what is said".

In his discussion of *therefore*, there is a good example of how Grice seems to yield to the temptation of saving logic by devising concepts that are only motivated by the desire to ... save logic. Other than the conversational implicatures, which are instrumental in the explanation of how words and sentences can acquire non-conventional meanings (besides trying to rescue the logical meaning of operators), the concept of conventional implicatures shows how Grice sometimes creates relatively artificial concepts to establish logical meanings as part of the linguistic meaning of specific lexical items.

2.1.2.4. Rescuing logic in conversation (2): or

Another example of the same tendency concerns Grice's discussion of *or*. This example is more directly relevant for the analysis below, because it is one of the few examples of a generalized conversational implicature that Grice works out elaborately, and the neo-Gricean analysis of numerals is based on these generalized conversational implicatures. Moreover, in his discussion of *or* he explicitly confronts his own description of the meanings of *or* with theoretical alternatives to his position. Many of Grice's other examples are only discussed in so far as they exemplify how implicatures are triggered, or what general characteristics implicatures have. In his discussion of *or*, however, Grice focuses on how the different meanings that can be attributed to different uses of *or* can be distinguished from, and related to, each other. His discussion of *or* differs from his discussion of *therefore* in that the concept of "conventional implicature" seems to be created mainly for the reconciliation of logical meaning and linguistic meaning, while the concept of conversational implicature is also meant to capture the intuitive difference between conventional and non-conventional meanings of utterances.

In his analysis, he rightly observes that when someone utters *A or B*, this is often interpreted as meaning more than just 'A∨B' (the logical counterpart of the linguistic utterance). The utterance is often taken to mean that the speaker has a non-truth-functional reason for accepting A∨B. This boils down to the fact that *A or B* often implicates that the speaker does not know which of the options, A or B, is true. If he or she does know which of the disjuncts is true (or if he knows that both are true), he has a truth-functional reason for accepting A∨B. In the context of a treasure hunt, for instance, the speaker can say to his or her children:

(16)   The prize is either in the garden or in the attic.

Normally, sentences such as these implicate that the speaker does not know which of the disjuncts is true. The speaker of (16) will normally be assumed to have implicated that he or she does not know which of the two options is true. Grice uses his treasure hunt example to show that this "extra" meaning (the fact that the speaker has non-truth-functional reasons for asserting the disjunction) is not part of the conventional meaning of the utterance. It can be followed by the utterance *I know that because I know where I put it, but I'm not going to tell you*, which cancels the implicature, namely the interpretation that the speaker does not know where the prize is. Grice's general analysis of these meanings of *or* can be summed up as follows: the "logical" meaning of *or*, i.e. '∨', is selected as "what is said" by *or*. As some uses of *or* seem to express more than this logical meaning, this meaning has to be accounted for as well. The extra meaning can be identified with what Grice calls "having non-truth-functional grounds for asserting *A or B*", and Grice accounts for both meanings by using his concept of "generalized conversational implicature". He derives the extra meaning from the logical meaning by referring to general conversational principles.

In my opinion, there are two problems with this line of reasoning. First, Grice uses a vague concept of "conventional meaning", which allows him to equate the "conventional meaning" of linguistic items with the way they operate in logical systems. Second, Grice does not seem to allow the influence of frequency effects on the determination of the "conventional" meaning of a linguistic item.

With respect to the first problem, it is remarkable that Grice does not start his analysis with a survey of the ways in which *or* can be used. Clearly, however, he needs to base his analysis on such a survey to decide what the "weak" sense of *or* could be, because this weak sense should be shared by all senses of *or* that are to be derived through the maxims. In other words, Grice does not have the data necessary for promoting the logical 'v' meaning to the status of conventional meaning of *or*: in principle, it is possible that there is an even more general sense of *or*, which can function as "what is said" by *or*. Moreover, there could be uses of *or* that cannot be derived from the logical meaning. Grice does not motivate his decision to take 'v' as "what is said" by *or*. An analysis of the uses of *or*, which is neutral with respect to the tenets of Gricean meaning analysis, and which is certainly also independent of logical concerns, should precede Grice's account of how these uses can be related with each other. This does not necessarily exclude that Grice is right in selecting the logical meaning as the conventional meaning of *or*, but at least the decision to take this meaning as "what is said" by *or* would have an empirical foundation. Even though Grice is using his analysis of *or* as an example of how his two-step explanation of meaning can simplify the semantics by relegating non-semantic meanings to the pragmatic realm, he does not make clear how the semantic analyst can determine what is the semantic meaning of a linguistic item. His analysis presupposes that the conventional meaning of an item like *or* is already given, but nowhere does he indicate how this meaning was found. Grice simply picks out two interpretations of *or* and labels them "the weak sense" and "the strong sense". However, when we want to analyze the meanings of linguistic elements, we must have a picture of how they are used, and this picture is preferably as complete as possible: we cannot determine directly what the "conventional meaning" of an item is without looking at the ways in which it is used. When the data that are available to us indicate a wide range of uses, and when we decide to analyze the meaning of the item in question by means of Gricean implicatures, then we have to decide which meaning qualifies for the status of "conventional" meaning, because that is what "what is said" is based on. And "what is said" will function as the starting point for the Gricean analysis. As long as we do not have that information, we cannot even start investigating the relationships between specific meanings of a linguistic element. In a short passage, Atlas has hinted at the same problem:

> The claims for the explanatory power of Gricean principles of conversational inference rest upon a highly convincing if vague account of the *relationship* between the *conventional meaning* of the *implicans*, its conversational role, and the resulting implicata. But for words and sentences the theory posits *conventional meanings* that

are controversial, while seeming to assume that the adequacy of such posits of conventional word/sentence-meaning can never be tested directly, but -- and this is a truism in the theory -- only by their contribution to the speaker's utterance-meaning of words and sentences uttered in contexts of actual use. The theory's great success is its convincing explanation of how and what speakers are understood to mean when patently they do *not* mean what their words conventionally do [...] But how much *can* this kind of theory tell us about the *actual* conventional meanings of English expressions? (Atlas 1979:270; emphases in the original)

The second problem is that even if there is an exhaustive survey of all possible uses of a linguistic item (in this case *or*), this will not enable the researcher to determine the conventional meaning of a linguistic item, because he or she will not know the relative "weight" of these different meanings. In other words, it is not enough to know all the "types" of meanings a linguistic item may have, we also need information about the number of "tokens" of each type. An example of this is related to the connector *or*: not only does *or* often "implicate" that there are non-truth-functional reasons in play, but it is well-known that there are two interpretations of *or*, namely "exclusive" *or* (in which *A or B* is true when A is true, B is true, but not when both A and B are true) and "inclusive" *or* (in which *A or B* is also true when A *and* B are true). Now, an analysis of the "conventional" meaning of *or* calls for an investigation of the frequency with which *or* is used in its exclusive sense and when it is used in its inclusive sense. If it turns out that, e.g. the inclusive meaning of *or* is much less frequent than the exclusive one, this is an argument for selecting the exclusive meaning of *or* as the literal or conventional meaning of *or* and - following Grice's mechanism - also for selecting it as the starting point for the analysis of all the meanings of *or*[8].

As argued in the previous paragraph, Grice does not supply a rigid methodology for making that decision. The only criterion he does seem to give is that we have to select a meaning that fits Grice's working-out schema. In other words, the choice of the conventional meaning of an item depends on how we can derive the other senses under discussion from that more basic sense. But this reduces semantic analysis to a rather sterile intellectual puzzle: Grice tries to demonstrate the analytic value of his explanation in terms of a conventional meaning, which is the basis of "what is said", and an implicated meaning, which builds upon "what is said", by providing examples of how non-conventional senses can be derived from a conventional sense. But in his argument the determination of "what is said" crucially depends on whether the selected meaning can function as the starting point of his two-level system! In other words, Grice's system lacks an independent criterion to select a certain meaning as the conventional meaning of a particular linguistic item or utterance. Frequency might be suggested as an example of such a criterion. It is independent of Grice's implicature theory, but it is perfectly compatible with it: if we accept that the conventional meaning of an item should be a meaning that is shared by as many of the uses of a linguistic item as possible -

---

[8] Of course, it is always possible that the different meanings of one linguistic item are completely unrelated, in which a "homonymy" analysis would be the natural analysis. For my purposes, however, this is not immediately relevant, because I focus on the distinction between "conventional meaning" and "conversational implicature". I will not go into the debate concerning the precise status of "homonymy", "polysemy", "ambiguity" and "vagueness" (cf. Geeraerts 1993, van der Auwera 1999 for discussion).

which seems an intuitively plausible definition of "conventionality" - this conventional meaning can still function as the starting point for the derivation of implicatures based on that conventional meaning[9]. Moreover, by identifying the conventional meaning of an item with its most frequent meaning, we can ground the semantic analysis of language in language use.

This becomes especially clear when we take a closer look at the options that Grice considers with respect to the relationship between the two meanings of *or* recognized by Grice (the logical one and the one in which non-truth-functional grounds are involved). In the first option the strong sense of *or* is taken as the "conventional" meaning, which is then "weakened", namely by using it loosely, or "in a relaxed" way (Grice 1989:45). This means that we derive the weaker, semantically simpler sense from the stronger, semantically richer sense. But Grice argues that such an analysis runs into trouble: according to Grice, an utterance like

(17)   If the prize is either in the garden or in the attic, Johnny will find it first.

and other "cancellation cases" can hardly be said to use *or* in a loose way. Moreover, "speaking loosely" does not really apply to the utterance in which *or* is used in a weak sense. As Grice puts it, we may say that someone is speaking loosely if someone says *Macbeth saw Banquo* when he or she actually means that Macbeth hallucinated and did not really *see* Banquo, because the speaker would speak "under license" from other participants. This "license" can be withdrawn when someone objects to this "loose" way of speaking. But this is different from the treasure hunt example, because nobody would complain if someone used *or* without having non-truth-functional reasons to use it: "not even a stickler for correct speech could complain about the utterance (in the described circumstances [i.e. the one indicated by the cancellation phrase]) of *The prize is either in the garden or in the attic*" (Grice 1989:45).

The second option discussed by Grice is the account in which *or* has two senses. Crucially, Grice does not endorse this line of reasoning because, in his opinion, the strong sense of *or* would have to occur in "a reasonably wide range of linguistic settings" (Grice 1989:45) in order to qualify as a "separate" sense, which it does not. This is one of the places in which Grice himself seems to refer to frequency as a criterion for conventionality, but he does not emphasize its importance. Actually, he seems to refer to the range of contexts in which a certain linguistic item has a certain meaning, rather than the frequency with which that item expresses a certain meaning. Moreover "a reasonably wide range of settings" is more vague than the "frequency" criterion for conventionality, which implies that the conventional meaning of an item should be shared by as many uses (tokens) of the item as possible. His main argument against the account in which *or* has two senses, however, is different. In attacking this position, he mainly refers to the generality of his working-out schema of

---

[9] It is important to stress that with the phrase "as many uses as possible" I do not refer to the number of types of uses, but to all tokens of a linguistic item. Moreover, I should emphasize that this criterion of "conventionality" only applies to those meanings of a linguistic item that can be explained by the Gricean mechanism, and not to meanings that are traditionally described in terms of ambiguity or vagueness. Otherwise, this would allow the conventional meaning of *bank* to be 'thing' or 'entity', because *bank* can mean 'financial institution' as well as 'raised ground along the edge of a river' and the only thing that qualifies as a "meaning shared by most uses" of *bank* would probably be something as vague as 'entity'.

implicatures, which applies to the derivation of the strong sense of *or* from the weaker one: "We might try to convince the strong theorist that if *or* is to be regarded as possessing a strong sense as well as a weak one, the strong sense should be regarded as derivative from the weak one" (Grice 1989:46). It is of course this analysis that Grice wants to propose as the correct analysis. He shows how it is possible to derive the strong meaning from the weak one via the maxim of quantity: if the speaker had used *or* when he or she has truth-functional reasons for uttering *A or B* (e.g., if he or she knew that A is true), then this utterance would have been less informative than simply uttering *A*. But because one may assume, due to the Cooperative Principle, that the speaker is as informative as is required, we may also assume that when the speaker utters *A or B* he or she has non-truth-functional reasons for uttering *A or B*.

What is important is not, however, how Grice accounts for this strong meaning of *or*, but the fact that he uses the explanatory force of this reasoning as an argument against the second option, namely the option in which *or* has two meanings, side by side. The attempt to convince the "strong theorist" that his analysis is wrong, and that Grice's analysis by means of the maxims of conversation is correct, is based on the fact that the only two meanings of *or* that are recognized by Grice actually fit the general mechanism that Grice wants to demonstrate. While Grice uses these meanings of *or* as an example of how his "implicature" analysis is superior to an analysis of *or* in terms of ambiguity or even polysemy[10] (in which the two meanings of *or* are both accepted as non-derived meanings), he decides which of the two meanings is part of "what is said" and which is the generalized conversational implicature, on the basis of the theory he wants to demonstrate. The absence of an independent criterion of conventionality leads to circularity.

Naturally, Grice's account has two important attractions: it is intuitively clear that some meanings that can be attributed to utterances are not part of "what is said" in these utterances, and his account can be generalized to many other phenomena. Moreover, the position of the strawman who seems to defend an analysis in terms of ambiguity is not attractive at all: it is hard to imagine how 'having non-truth-functional reasons for uttering the disjunction' could be the full semantic load of one of the two meanings of *or* under consideration. In most, if not all uses of *or*, the other "logical" meaning will be present as well. Most importantly, Grice's analysis of *or* also succeeds in simplifying semantics. Grice refers to what he calls "Modified Occam's Razor": "Senses are not to be multiplied beyond necessity" (Grice 1989:47). If this principle is accepted, then Grice's account of *or* is clearly superior to an account in terms of polysemy, because the latter assigns two meanings to *or*, while Grice only needs one "conventional" meaning, and derives the other meaning from this conventional meaning via his conversational principles. I hope to have made clear, however, that the point I would like to make is not one concerning the correct analysis of *or*, but a more general one about Grice's methodology.

In general, there are three different points of attention in Grice's text: the explanation of how linguistic elements with a conventional meaning can also express other meanings, the simplification of semantics (with Modified Occam's Razor as a guideline), and the

---

[10] "Ambiguity" can be defined as a type of semantic polyfunctionality: when a word has two meanings, it is "ambiguous". Polysemy is a subtype of ambiguity, in the sense that polysemous words have two meanings that are synchronically related.

establishment of logical meanings as the conventional meaning of natural language counterparts of logical operators. While I have elaborated on all three points, I have only attacked the validity of the latter.

There is one other aspect of Grice's analysis of *or* that is problematic, however. The discussion of *or* is not only important because it shows the problematic status of "conventional meaning" or "what is said" in Grice's account of implicatures, but it also shows how easily Grice shifts from the meanings of sentences / utterances to the meaning of lexical elements. While it is certainly true that many sentences containing *or* as a disjunctive coordinator of two clauses *A* and *B* can be interpreted as expressing that the speaker has non-truth-functional reasons for uttering *A or B*, it does not follow that this meaning should be attached to the word *or*, not as part of the conventional meaning of *or*, not as part of "what is said" by *or*, and not as a generalized conversational implicature of *or*. The transition that Grice makes from the observation that utterances containing *or* often have a meaning that is not exhaustively captured by the meaning of the corresponding logical operator, to a description of how different meanings of *or* can be related to each other is highly problematic. It is generally accepted that words have meanings; it is also accepted that utterances can have meanings that cannot be derived directly from the combination of these lexical meanings, and some of these meanings are probably best explained through Gricean mechanisms. But it is highly doubtful whether this allows one to "relocate" these implicated meanings from their original source (the utterance) back to the meaning of the word that is held responsible for triggering this implicated meaning. This is, however, what Grice and very many neo-Griceans seem to do: GCIs are typically assigned to the use of a single lexical element, while they are always part of interpretations of entire utterances. Grice himself made it very explicit that conversational implicatures are triggered by the use of linguistic elements, by "saying what is said". In that perspective, it is rather odd that Grice sometimes talks of implicatures as if they are to be assigned to the use of words rather than to the utterances in which these words occur. This confusion between the meaning of a word and the meaning of an utterance containing that word is not very surprising: it is sometimes very difficult to isolate the meaning of a word from the meaning of the utterances in which it occurs, especially when coordinators such as *or* are involved. But it follows from Grice's own theory that when meanings are analyzed as implicatures, this meaning should not be assigned to the word itself, but to the utterance in which it occurs.

2.1.2.5. *Rescuing logic in conversation (3):* if ... then

Probably the most explicit example of how the Gricean program is driven by logical concerns can be found in the fourth of the William James lectures, the one on "indicative conditionals". The problem is the following: how can it be that the equivalent of "the material condition" in natural language usually carries an extra meaning, namely what Grice calls the Indirectness Condition: "that there are non-truth-functional grounds for accepting p⊃q" (Grice 1989:58)? Grice argues: "The thesis to be examined, then, is that in standard cases to say "if p then q" is to be conventionally committed to (to assert or imply in virtue of the meaning of "if") both the proposition that p⊃q and the Indirectness Condition"[11] (Grice 1989:58). I will not go into the specifics of Grice's analysis. I simply mention this text as yet another example of how his project is guided by logical concerns. I will not repeat the comments we made with respect to Grice's analysis of *or*: his analysis of the *if ... then* construction also suffers from the lack of an independent criterion of "conventionality". Again, Grice does not start from an independent survey of the ways in which *if ... then* is used, but simply adopts the "logical" meaning as the starting point for his analysis.

I would like to point out one new element, however: in his analysis of *if ... then* the importance of truth conditions comes to the fore. Whereas truth conditions are generally seen as an integral part of Grice's theory, it is only in his discussion of *if ... then* that he emphasizes their importance. In his discussion of *or* it was not always clear whether the logical meaning of *or* was considered to be "what is said" by *or*, or whether it was simply the "conventional meaning" of *or*, but in this discussion, Grice unambiguously claims: "The conventional meaning of a conditional is given by a specification of the truth-conditions assigned by truth-tables to the material conditional." (Grice 1989:77). This truth-conditional[12] perspective on meaning will be inherited and stressed by many followers of Grice. Grice himself seems to attach more importance to the non-cancelability and the detachability of conventional meanings, but it is clear that for Grice the conventional meaning is preferably not only a "logical" meaning, but also a truth-conditional one.

2.1.2.6. Conclusion
In the "Logic and conversation" lectures, Grice tries to achieve three goals. The most important goal is the explanation of how words and utterances can express meanings that are not part of their conventional meanings. Grice proposes that an important group of these extra meanings are "implicatures", meanings which can be attributed to the use of a word or a sentence on the basis of four maxims of conversation, which the speaker is supposed to observe. The presumption that the speaker will observe the four maxims is expressed in the Cooperative Principle. Implicatures can be triggered by observing the maxims as well as by "flouting" (blatantly failing to fulfil) them. There are two kinds of implicatures: the conventional implicatures (associated with items such as *therefore*) and the conversational implicatures. It is the latter type that receives most attention; the former is rather hard to define and seems a somewhat *ad hoc* category. The class of conversational implicatures is also divided into two subclasses: the particularized and the generalized conversational implicatures. The particularized conversational implicatures crucially rely on specific contextual conditions; the generalized conversational implicatures are triggered by the use of specific linguistic items in "normal" or "default" circumstances.

---

[11] Note the ambiguous use of "conventional": the rest of Grice's text will be devoted to a demonstration of how this extra sense is precisely *not* part of the conventional meaning of *if ... then...* , but why it should be considered a conversational implicature. Grice recognizes that the Indirectness Condition is somehow conventional, but still decides to call it a conversational implicature (as a consequence of the maxim of quantity), even if one of the defining characteristics of conversational implicatures is their unconventionality.

[12] In this passage, as in some others, "truth-conditionality" may be replaced with "truth-functionality", because Grice often seems to make the stronger, truth-functional claim. For our purposes, however, the fact that truth-conditionality is involved will suffice. I will argue that it is this truth-conditional view that underlies many of the counter-intuitive semantic postulates of Grice and neo-Griceans.

The decision to view specific meanings as implicatures rather than as part of the conventional content of a linguistic element helps Grice to attain his second goal: the simplification of semantics. By relegating meanings that can be construed as implicatures to the pragmatic domain, the semantics of a word or sentence can be simplified considerably. In general, Grice's Modified Occam's Razor suggests that a meaning should only be considered as part of the conventional meaning of an item when it is not possible to derive it from the conventional meaning as an implicature. Grice also mentions that a conventional meaning should be carried by an item in a reasonably wide range of linguistic settings, but he does not check whether the meanings he considers to be "conventional" indeed meet that requirement. In his discussion of indicative conditionals Grice also suggests that this conventional meaning is a truth-conditional one.

The third objective of "Logic and conversation" is, as the title indicates, the reconciliation of logical meanings and linguistic meanings. Grice situates his own position in between the position of the "formalists" and that of the "informalists": he wants to preserve the logical meanings of logical operators as part of the conventional meaning of the natural language counterparts of these operators. Therefore, he adopts the logical meaning of items as *or* and *if ... then* as their conventional meaning. Other meanings that are expressed by these linguistic items are derived as implicatures, via the maxims of conversation.

Grice's general analysis is convincing with respect to the first two goals: the derivation of implicatures can indeed account for a number of non-conventional meanings of words and sentences, which we would be reluctant to consider as part of the conventional meaning of these words or sentences. The idea to reduce the semantic load of an item as much as possible is in some cases more problematic (if Grice's description of conventional meaning is supposed to be psychologically plausible, it may very well be that the rigid version of Modified Occam's Razor has to be abandoned), but it is clear that at least some meanings that are attached to uses of some linguistic elements should not be included into the semantics of that item. Grice's third goal, however, is highly problematic. The emphasis on logical meanings leads to questionable claims with respect to the conventional meaning of specific items. Grice does not provide a theory-independent criterion for deciding which of the meanings is to be considered as the conventional one, and he also fails to take the frequency of meanings into account. The strong connection between the "conventionality" of a meaning of a linguistic item and the frequency with which this item expresses this meaning is thereby ignored. Moreover, Grice does not always distinguish between the lexical level and the utterance level. This causes implicatures of utterances to be reinterpreted as part of the meaning of lexical items:

2.2. IMPLICATURES ACCORDING TO NEO-GRICEANS AND CRITICS

After the presentation of the general framework of Grice's conversational implicatures, it is time to look at the various amendments that have been added to the original theory. Grice's theory of conversation has been very successful and has been readily integrated in the rapidly expanding canon of linguistic pragmatics, to the point that the theory of implicatures is now known as a fundamental part of "classical pragmatics". Nevertheless, numerous researchers have tried to correct, supplement or replace it by new principles and maxims. I will mention the most important proposals in what follows. More directly relevant, however, are the vivid discussions concerning the various classifications that have been suggested to distinguish different "kinds" of meanings. The dialogue between proponents of the different perspectives has been recently revived and is currently one of the most hotly debated topics in semantics / pragmatics. Attention will be devoted to the difference between entailments and implicatures, the importance of truth conditions, and the concepts "enrichment", "completion" and "underdeterminacy". Next, the ways in which the features that Grice proposed as characteristics of implicatures have been turned into tests, how these tests have been evaluated and criticized, and what other tests have been proposed will be dealt with. Moreover, also the various attempts at formalization will be discussed, and in particular Horn's concept of "scales" and Gazdar's "bucket theory" will be evaluated. Finally, the way in which the influence of truth conditions on the theory of conversation has been continued in neo-Gricean work will have light shed on it.

2.2.1. Versions of the conversational principles and their indeterminacy

Horn (1984, 1989, 1990) sketches the evolution of Grice's maxim of Quantity, which he regards as one of the fundamental principles of his theory of conversation. He quotes John Doyle (described as a "proto-Grice"), who formulated a principle similar to Grice's Quantity maxim: "what can be understood without being said is usually, in the interest of economy, not said" (Doyle 1951:382, qtd. in Horn 1990:460). As mentioned by Horn, also Strawson (1952:178-179) and Fogelin (1967:22) have formulated a version of Grice's maxim, and Grice himself has ventured at least two versions of his first Quantity maxim. More important than the genesis of the Q1-maxim is Horn's proposal to reduce three of Grice's four maxims to just two: The Q principle, "make your contribution sufficient", and the R-principle, "make your contribution necessary". This is a simplification of Grice's original proposal: the Q-principle covers Grice's first maxim of Quantity and the last two submaxims of Manner (concerning brevity and order), while the R-principle is meant to capture the maxim of Relation, the second submaxim of Quantity and the first two submaxims of Manner (concerning obscurity and ambiguity). The maxim of Quality is considered to be irreducible. The Q and the R principles are conceived of as opposing forces that are extremely general in nature: "The functional tension between these two antinomic principles governs not just the determination of implicatures but a wide range of linguistic phenomena, from lexical change to politeness strategies, from periphrastic causatives to logical double negation, from euphemism to the interpretation of pronouns and gaps" (Horn 1990:465). He also refers to Zipf's principles of "auditor's economy" and "speaker's economy" to relate his Gricean maxims to more general principles of human communication: the first refers to the fact that the hearer needs sufficient information to understand what the speaker is saying; the second implies that the speaker does not want to give more information than necessary, because of a general principle of "least effort" (Zipf 1949).

Atlas and Levinson (1981) and Levinson (1987, 2000) reduce Grice's maxims to just three principles as well, and these are also based on apparently more fundamental "heuristics".

In the latest version, these are called the Q-heuristic ("What isn't said, isn't"), the I-heuristic ("what is expressed simply is stereotypically exemplified") and the M-heuristic ("what's said in an abnormal way isn't normal") (Levinson 2000:35-39). The Q-heuristic can be related to Grice's Q1-maxim ("make your contribution as informative as is required") rather directly, but especially the second heuristic, the I-heuristic, needs to be clarified. Levinson remarked that Grice's conversational principles could lead to the wrong results: the conjunctive meaning of *and* in *Bill turned the key and the engine started* is normally "strengthened" to a "temporal" and even "causal" interpretation. In the line of Grice's Q1-maxim, however, the speaker should be as informative as required: if he wanted to express a "temporal" or a "causal" relationship between the fact that Bill turned the key and the fact that the engine started, he or she should have made this explicit, by saying *and then* or using *since Bill turned the key, the engine started*. The speaker did not do this, so we may conclude that he did not want to express this. But this is the wrong result: *and* often does convey a temporal or a causal relationship. Therefore, Levinson proposes a principle of informational strengthening, in which the informative content of an utterance may be strengthened to the stereotypical interpretation: the utterance *Bill turned the key and the engine started* stereotypically refers to a situation in which the engine started after and because of the turning of the key. This principle is based on an "apparatus" of other principles: the "maxims of relativity" ("don't bother to say what is non-controversial" and "Hear what is said as consistent with what is non-controversial"), the "convention of non-controversiality" ((i) "it is non-controversial that referents and situations have stereotypical properties" and (ii) "the existence of what a sentence is 'about' is non-controversial") and, finally, the "principle of informativeness" ("The 'best' interpretation of an utterance is the most informative one consistent with what is non-controversial") (Levinson 1987:66). The I-heuristic is meant to explain a number of different interpretation strategies, such as more specific interpretations of lexical items that have a general meaning (e.g., the interpretation of genitives as in *John's book*, which can mean 'the book John wrote', 'the book John read' etc.), stereotypical inferences (e.g., when *the secretary* is typically taken to refer to a woman) or so-called "bridging" inferences, in which a link is provided between two utterances, which is not explicitly expressed (e.g., in the utterances *It was a great party. The DJ was awesome and the people were gorgeous.* "the DJ" and "the people" are assumed to have been at the party). A constraint on the strengthening of information (which Levinson relates to Grice's Q2-maxim) is provided by the opposing Q-heuristic, but also by the M-heuristic: only those utterances that can be considered as the typical linguistic means for expressing that content can be strengthened to the prototype. The M-heuristic expresses the complement, namely: whenever a marked linguistic structure is used, do not strengthen it to the stereotype, but interpret it as referring to a non-stereotypical situation. For instance, if someone uses the word *whitish*, it should be interpreted as referring to a non-stereotypical type of white.

The third notable variant of Grice's original framework is provided by Sperber and Wilson's Relevance Theory (Sperber and Wilson 1986, 1995, Wilson and Sperber 1988, 1992, Carston 1998a,b). Sperber and Wilson reduce Grice's maxims to one general principle of Relevance, which is a cognitive principle that says that the relevance of an utterance is a function of, on the one hand, the "contextual effects" the utterance has in the given circumstances, and, on the other hand, the "cost of effort" to process the utterance. Every linguistic utterance comes with a "presumption of its own optimal relevance" (Sperber and Wilson 1995:158), and "optimal relevance" can be described by the two following definitions:

> (a) The set of assumptions **I** which the communicator intends to make manifest to the addressee is relevant enough to make it worth the addressee's while to process the ostensive stimulus.
> (b) The ostensive stimulus is the most relevant one the communicator could have used to communicate **I**. (Sperber and Wilson 1995:158)

An "ostensive" kind of behavior is defined as "behaviour which makes manifest an intention to make something manifest" (Sperber and Wilson 1995:49). Relevance Theory is actually much more than a reformulation of some of Grice's insights, it is meant as an outline of "the system used by human beings in spontaneous inference, and in normal utterance comprehension in particular" (Sperber and Wilson 1995:94) and has specific psychological ambitions, which ultimately lead to the presentation of a "cognitive architecture". This has never been one of the explicit concerns of Grice, but Relevance Theory is certainly meant to capture Gricean phenomena as well, and Grice's work is explicitly mentioned as an important source of inspiration. Just like Levinson, Sperber and Wilson remark that Grice's theory of conversation is consistent with many different interpretations of a certain utterance. While it is true that this "indeterminacy" is compatible with the way in which communication actually develops (the same utterance can indeed be used to convey many things), Sperber and Wilson feel that one should at least try to give an explanation of why normally one specific interpretation is selected: what Grice's theory fails to show is "that on the same basis, an equally convincing justification could not have been given for some other interpretation that was not in fact chosen" (Sperber and Wilson 1995:37). Relevance Theory aims to explain this by referring to their economic principle of relevance: of all possible inferences (i.e. interpretations of an utterance that are not encoded by that utterance; an "implicature" is a kind of inference), the hearer will select that interpretation that has most contextual effects and least processing costs.

With respect to the formulation of the conversational maxims, these three alternatives can be considered as the most important proposals in the relatively short neo-Gricean history. Various other researchers have provided smaller corrections of the original framework, or have given alternative versions of some of Grice's maxims: e.g. Harnish's maxim of Quantity-Quality ("Make the strongest relevant claim justifiable by your evidence" (Harnish 1976:362))[13] and Gazdar's attempt at a formalization of the maxims, which also triggered some alternative formulations (Gazdar 1979:43-52)[14]. Of all these alternatives, Sperber and Wilson's is certainly the most drastic change. More specifically, the "working-out" schema that was first proposed by Grice is replaced by the much simpler weighing up of pros

---

[13] Matsumoto (1995) redefines the Q1-maxim in a similar way: "Make your contribution as informative (strong) as possible" (Matsumoto 1995:23). See Green (1995) for a critique of this "volubility" interpretation of Grice's original Quantity maxim.

[14] I have not mentioned the work by Ducrot (1972, 1973), Anscombre (1975) and Anscombre and Ducrot (1976, 1978), because they seem to have developed a different type of conversational theory, and not merely a version of Grice's theory. I will come back to their work when I will discuss the history of neo-Gricean numerals.

(contextual effects) and cons (processing costs) of a certain interpretation. The original schema runs as follows:

> (i) the speaker has said that *p*
> (ii) there's no reason to think the speaker is not observing the maxims, or at least the co-operative principle
> (iii) in order for the speaker to say that *p* and be indeed observing the maxims or the co-operative principle, the speaker must think that *q*
> (iv) the speaker must know that it is mutual knowledge that *q* must be supposed if the speaker is to be taken to be co-operating
> (v) the speaker has done nothing to stop me, the addressee, thinking that *q*
> (vi) therefore the speaker intends me to think that *q*, and in saying that *p* has implicated *q*
> (adapted from Levinson 1983:113-114)[15]

Relevance Theory does not rely on the knowledge of specific maxims as this working-out schema does; there is often even a suggestion that the principle of relevance (which says that an act of ostensive communication communicates a presumption of relevance) is not something that speakers "know" at all: "Communicators and audience need no more know the principle of relevance to communicate than they need to know the principles of genetics to reproduce" (Sperber and Wilson 1995:162).

This short and non-exhaustive survey is meant to make clear at least two things: one, many researchers of communication have adopted Grice's original line of thinking; two, many have tried to change important aspects of the original theory, but at the moment, there is not a single reformulation that is generally accepted. With respect to the first point, it is evident that Grice has been very influential in reshaping thought about communication. Sperber and Wilson's identification of the "coding-decoding mode" and the "inferential mode" helps to make this point manifest. They define a code as "a system which pairs messages with signals, enabling two information-processing devices (organisms or machines) to communicate" (Sperber and Wilson 1995:3-4)[16], and distinguish it from an inferential mechanism, which "starts from a set of premises and results in a set of conclusions which follow logically from, or are at least warranted by, the premises" (Sperber and Wilson 1995:12-13). With the aid of these concepts, it is easier to understand why Grice's proposals are so important: in a sense, Grice's most important achievement is not the list of conversational principles for which he is famous, but the distinction between a code model and an inferential mechanism, and the realization that both should be part of an explanation of human communication. Combining Grice's terminology with the relevance-theoretic concepts, it is fair to say that the interpretation of the "conventional" meaning of linguistic items is based on the code model, while implicatures are inferences.

---

[15] Various analysts have proposed alternative versions of this working-out schema, which can be found in, e.g., Harnish (1976:348), Gazdar (1979:41-43), Levinson (1983:135) and Horn (1989:214).

[16] A message is defined as "a representation internal to the communicating devices", and a signal as "a modification of the external environment which can be produced by one device and recognised by the other" (Sperber and Wilson 1995:4).

Nevertheless, the proliferation of alternatives to Grice's proposal makes the original framework even more indeterminate than it already was. As we have seen, Grice's model (or the model that can and has been built on the basis of Grice's suggestions) lacks a methodological basis for the determination of the "conventional" meaning of linguistic material, but it is also clear that the implicatures that can be derived on the basis of his maxims are extremely varied and numerous. The alternative versions just presented all try to be more precise by building in "constraints" with respect to the generation of implicatures. The antinomic forces that Horn and Levinson perceive in Grice's original proposal are supposed to balance and constrain each other. Sperber and Wilson's account - aptly (but unnecessarily derogatorily) described by Levinson as "the best bang for the buck" (Levinson 1989:459) - also counts as an attempt to be more explicit in the explanation of why specific implicatures are attributed to an utterance and others are not. But the fact that many researchers disagree about the actual formulation of the conversational maxims does not help to make the theory more rigid. The quarrels between people like Levinson and Carston seem to be caused by the different ways in which they have interpreted Grice's original proposals. Levinson's "heuristics" seem to involve a rather broad concept of what constitutes an implicature in the sense that they capture many more phenomena than Grice originally tried to explain. The reformulation of Grice's insights in Relevance Theory is arguably even broader, but at the same time its general principles diverge more explicitly from Grice's original ideas.

While indeterminacy is a crucial component of inferences (as Grice rightly pointed out with respect to his implicatures), it also undermines the explanatory value of Grice's principles considerably. Not unlike Levinson in his reformulation of Grice's principles, Davis (1998:35-36) provides a long list of cases in which weaker statements are not used to implicate the stronger statements (e.g., *Some died* does not implicate that it is not true that some were killed, *2 is a number* does not implicate that it is not true that 2 is an even number, even though *kill* is more informative than *die*, and *even number* is more informative than *number*). Contrary to Levinson, however, Davis feels that this is a serious problem for Gricean accounts of meaning. In his theoretical definition of conversational implicature (which can be compared to the various "working-out" schemata that have been proposed), the third aspect is considered to be of utmost importance: "(iii) The supposition that S [speaker] believes p [the conversational implicature] is required to make S's utterance consistent with the Cooperative Principle *(indeterminacy)*" (Davis 1998:13 - emphasis in the original, cf. (iii) in Levinson's "working-out schema" presented above). Davis argues that this is simply incorrect: "the theory generates erroneous predictions as readily as it generates correct ones. Indeed, it is the exception rather than the rule to find the implicatures predicted by Gricean derivations" (Davis 1998:2). Obviously, Davis' criticism is overly harsh, because Grice never stressed the fact that a certain conversational implicature is the only implicature that is triggered by his principles of conversation. As Grice made clear on a number of occasions, it is not the case that the maxims mechanistically guide the communicator to the intended implicature (even if a number of researchers have certainly tried to interpret it in this formal-deductive way, cf. section 2.2.3. on formalizations). Davis' critique may be harsh, but the fact remains that Grice's theory of conversation is by no means as precise as we would like: after all, the claims that are based on Grice's theory are important and far-reaching. Especially when the analysis of specific linguistic items or structures is concerned, Grice's maxims seem too vague to make hard-and-fast judgments concerning their meaning (cf. also Kiefer's even stronger claim that "Grice's theory and the reformulations thereof do not yield an adequate framework for research" (Kiefer 1979:71)). The separation of what is "encoded" and what is "inferred" will have to be based on more than theory-internal coherence, because the principles are consistent with too wide a range of results for the theory to be able to make such subtle distinctions. Grice's principles, as well as various reformulations of these principles, are so lax that theory-internal coherence will hardly ever be an obstacle to any meaning analysis at all. An appeal to intuition might still be acceptable when discussing a limited number of uses of a linguistic item, but it is highly problematic to base judgments concerning what is encoded and what is inferred on what the researcher assumes to be "conventional", "semantic", "encoded", "familiar" or even "wide-spread" meanings. As we have seen, this opens up the possibility of postulating highly counter-intuitive and empirically unfounded "literal" meanings, and often allows the analysis of meaning to become constrained by objectives that have nothing to do with the description of linguistic meaning at all (cf. Grice's desire to bridge the gap between logical operators and the meaning of their natural language counterparts). The fact that speakers can use a word or a sentence to mean just about anything does not mean that "conventionality" cannot be defined except by an appeal to intuition or the coherence of a theory, and certainly not when the theory in question is so construed that it can capture the fact that a sentence can be used to mean anything. Especially with respect to the meaning analysis of specific linguistic items, such a theory has the power to explain everything, which comes dangerously close to explaining nothing at all.

2.2.2. Tests of conversational implicatures

Grice seems to have been aware of the fact that the maxims by themselves are too flexible to account for the generation of extra, non-conventional meanings: they clearly explained more than they had to explain. At least, that might have been one of his motivations for devoting so much attention to the "features" of conversational implicatures, which were soon used as "tests" to distinguish these implicatures from "conventional" meanings, from "what is said" or from the dubious category of conventional implicatures. It appeared, however, that these tests were not watertight and certainly could not be used to classify meanings in terms of the categories that have been proposed by Grice in an unambiguous way. Grice maintained that conversational implicatures could be defined rigidly, and he often referred to the two most important characteristics, namely the non-detachability of implicatures and their cancelability. Especially the latter has become part of the neo-Gricean canon. Perhaps it is not exaggerated to say that, even though very good counter-arguments have been proposed, the acceptance of the cancelability of implicatures is less controversial than the Gricean maxims and the status of implicatures themselves.

Walker's (1975) and Sadock's (1978) articles are still the best introductions to the methodological problems that surround Grice's theory of conversation, especially as far as the "tests" for conversational implicatures are concerned[17]. Most of the relevant criticism is present in both articles, but I will mainly refer to Sadock's because I believe that he formulates his criticism more concisely. Walker's article is also important because it discusses Cohen's provocative (1971) article, so that Cohen's arguments can be dealt with at the same time. The basic question of both articles is: "Given some aspect of what a sentence conveys in a particular context, is that aspect part of what the sentence conveys in virtue of its meaning [...] or should it be "worked out" on the basis of Gricean principles of conversation?" (Sadock 1978:281). Sadock's analysis is rather devastating: of the six features proposed by Grice, three are immediately considered as irrelevant as candidates for a test, and the other three are also considered to be unable to distinguish the conventional from the non-conventional. Concerning the three irrelevant characteristics, the fact that conversational implicata can be characterized as being non-conventional is "completely circular" (Sadock 1978:284), because the whole idea of conversational implicatures depends on their being non-conventional; the fact that conversational implicata are not carried by what is said, but by the saying of it is considered to be a variant of this circular criterion and the fact that conversational implicata *may* be indeterminate is not only a weak criterion due to Grice's use of the modal *may*, but also due to the fact that the referential meaning of pronouns or demonstratives is also indeterminate.

The other three criteria are slightly better, but none of them is sufficient. Sadock considers the "calculability" of conversational implicatures to be a necessary condition, but not a sufficient one. First, the Cooperative Principle is also used in the disambiguation of ambiguous linguistic elements (when the ambiguity is an ambiguity of the conventional meaning of the elements in question, and not one created by a conversational implicature); second, Sadock remarks (as Grice had in fact already remarked himself) that conversational implicatures tend to become conventionalized (just like metaphors can become conventionalized). In that case, it is often possible to reconstruct the original "working-out schema" that underlies what was initially an implicature but what has now become the conventional meaning. Hence, if a meaning can be "worked out" on the basis of the Gricean maxims, it does not necessarily imply that this meaning is an implicature, i.e. a non-conventional meaning. The next candidate for a "test" is the feature that Grice calls "non-detachability", which, as we have seen, refers to the fact that implicatures are based on the meaning of linguistic elements, and not on the way in which this meaning is expressed. A possible test for implicatures could make use of this non-detachability criterion: if an utterance, which can be observed to trigger an "extra" meaning besides its "conventional" meaning, can be replaced with another utterance that has the same conventional meaning and still has the "extra" meaning, the "extra" meaning is indeed an implicature. Grice himself already noted that an important exception has to be made for the implicatures that are triggered by the maxim of Manner, because the latter are crucially dependent on the way in which a certain meaning is expressed. But Sadock notes a number of other problems: the criterion of non-detachability fails to distinguish between implicatures and logical

---

[17] I also mention Mackie's (1973:74-81) critique of Grice's analysis of conditionals, which is based on the fact that the Gricean account runs into trouble with counterfactual *if* and *even if*, because we do not seem to rely on the logical, 'material condition' meaning of *if* in those cases (but cf. Walker's 1975:144-149 counterarguments).

entailments. He argues: "It is not possible to paraphrase *Bill and Harry left* without conveying *Harry left*. Yet this is clearly not an example of conversational implicature, but of logical inference" (Sadock 1978:288). Moreover, in every language there must be expressions that trigger implicatures, but that cannot be paraphrased: everything conveyed by that expression is (trivially) non-detachable. Sadock concludes: "I am led to wonder whether anything is detachable from anything?" (Sadock 1978:290). Finally, while the cancelability test (also called "cancellation test") is probably the best test, even the cancelability feature is not sufficient to define conversational implicatures: in particular, it cannot distinguish between a linguistic element that has one conventional meaning and an implicated meaning and a homonymous word. Sadock provides the classic example of an ambiguous sentence, namely *Everyone speaks one language*, one interpretation of which can be "canceled" by adding a phrase that disambiguates the sentence: *Everyone speaks one language although no one language is spoken by everyone*[18].

Walker writes that the cancelability test cannot even differentiate implicatures from non-ambiguous sentences, because it is always possible to use these sentences loosely, so that some of their "conventional" meaning disappears[19]:

> Thus, it may be part of the sense of "It is light green now" that the thing in question really is and does not merely seem to be light green now; yet this sentence can be loosely used to make the lesser claim, when it is clear to those conversing what is intended. (Walker 1975:161)

Even more importantly, Walker already points at a problem with the cancellation test, which will become manifest in the corpus analysis of numerals: not only is the cancellation test unable to distinguish implicatures from ambiguous linguistic elements or from loose uses of univocal linguistic elements, it is often not possible to apply it in the context in which the original utterance is used. Indeed, many meanings that are claimed to be implicatures cannot be canceled in a non-artificial way:

> If the claim that a conversational implicature must be cancellable were the claim that it must be possible to find some *natural* set of circumstances in which someone could

---

[18] Cohen (1971) makes a similar remark with respect to lexical meanings: "[...] the statement *That is a flower* implies, in virtue of the meaning of the word 'flower', that the object in question forms or formed part of a plant; and this implication is canceled or deleted if the word 'plastic' is put before 'flower'. In that respect the phrases 'stone lion', 'well-painted hand', 'sub-vocal speech', etc. are all rather similar: in each case part of the normal meaning of the noun is canceled or deleted by the adjacent adjective" (Cohen 1971:56).

[19] In this context, also Burton-Roberts' (1984) critique of the cancellation argument seems relevant. According to him the cancellation test is not only unable to distinguish between a Gricean analysis and an ambiguity analysis, but is also entirely circular. He concentrates on the implicature that is allegedly triggered by using *possible p*, namely 'not necessary p': "In short, in order to demonstrate that *possible* univocally means just [the lower-bounded 'possible'] (by showing that the ['exactly'] 'possible' is conversational), we have effectively to *assume* that it means just [the lower-bounded *possible*]" (Burton-Roberts 1984:187). If we do not accept the lower-bounded 'possible' as the literal meaning of *possible*, the cancellation phrase *if not necessary* is not a cancellation of an implicature, but simply an additional specification of what is meant, containing new information. Burton-Roberts argues that this circularity is not only present in the Gricean analysis of *possible*; the argument generalizes to "the logical quantifiers and connectives" (Burton-Roberts 1984:181) as well.

produce the utterance without either conveying the implicature or violating the Co-operative Principle, then indeed it would provide us with a test which many putative conversational implicatures might fail; for example, it is not clear that there is any natural situation in which it would be conversationally pointful to say "If it had rained they would not have played cricket, though I don't mean to suggest that there is any sort of connection between the antecedent and the consequent". (Walker 1975:161)

It is clear that this is not what Grice had in mind, for he uses this kind of artificial cancellation phrases without any hesitation. As Walker makes clear, however, this abstraction from the natural context of an utterance seriously hampers the applicability of the cancellation test, and, again, makes it possible to make counter-intuitive claims with respect to the "conventionality" of certain meanings. More generally, serious doubts can be raised with respect to the acceptability of the cancellation of the "non-truth-functional grounds" reading of *if ... then*, which Grice considers to be an implicature, as the example in the citation above shows.

The six characteristics provided by Grice are not the only features that have been proposed as the basis of tests for conversational implicatures. In fact, Sadock made a suggestion to devise another test, called the "reinforceability" test, in the very same article as the one in which he demonstrated the shakiness of the original Gricean tests: "Since conversational implicatures are not part of the conventional import of utterances, it should be possible to make them explicit without being guilty of redundancy" (Sadock 1978:294). An example is provided by the utterance *some of the people went home, but not all*, in which the GCI of *some*, i.e. 'not all', is explicitly mentioned in the rest of the utterance. From then on, the reinforceability test has become part of the canonical version of Grice's theory (cf. Levinson 1983:120, 2000:15). More importantly, the reinforceability test has also survived in the guise of a "redundancy test", which actually boils down to a negative version of the reinforceability test: if an aspect of the meaning of a linguistic item is considered to be part of its conventional meaning, then it should not be possible to add an item that repeats part of this conventional meaning without causing a redundancy-effect[20]. Conversely, if it *is* considered to be a conversational implicature, it should be possible to add the extra item, without causing this redundancy-effect. Even though Horn does not often explicitly refer to this type of argument, it is one of the recurrent properties of his analyses of, e.g. quantifiers (cf. Horn 1989: Chapter Four). Crucially, however, Sadock himself indicated that this reinforceability test runs into the same type of problems as the other tests for conversational implicatures: just like the cancellation test cannot distinguish between ambiguity accounts and univocality + implicature accounts, neither can the reinforceability test. Sadock gives the same example of ambiguity, this time with a reinforcement phrase: *Everyone speaks one language and it is the same language* (Sadock 1978:294).

Nevertheless, not only Horn, but also Levinson considers that, despite the manifest problems with the tests proposed, they do give us some decisive basis for the interpretation of

---

[20] In fact, some people have claimed the opposite: Hirschberg (1991 [1985]:36) argues that "[Sadock's] notion that conversational implicatures are reinforceable builds upon Horn's diagnostic [which she calls "redundancy of conjunction"]". Hirschberg is certainly correct in claiming that Horn's notion was formulated earlier than Sadock's, but they seem to have developed the intimately related notions independently.

a certain component of the meaning of a linguistic item as being an implicature or not. Levinson (1983:120-121) supplies two more features. The first is based on the fact that conversational implicatures work with meanings, not with linguistic expressions, so that we should expect to find the same implicatures in all languages that have items that express the same meaning as the one that is expressed by the implicature-inducing element in English. In short, generalized conversational implicatures (which Levinson considers to be of linguistic importance, as opposed to the particularized conversational implicatures) should be universal. This is in fact a cross-linguistic version of the non-detachability feature, and the problems that were identified with that test are relevant here as well. The second feature concerns the Cooperative Principle: Levinson notes that when people do not adhere to this principle, the expected implicatures should disappear. He claims that this is indeed what happens in, for instance, cross-examinations in which people are expected to adhere to the truth and nothing but the truth. This implies that they will not be "as informative as is required (for the current purposes of the exchange)". But in this case it is hard to say whether people cooperate or not: it is clear that in fact they are assumed to cooperate (otherwise the cross-examination would be pointless), but Levinson argues that they only stick to the Quality-maxim. Actually, people who are being cross-examined may well be said to adhere to the Quantity-maxims as well: they are as informative as is required for the current purposes of the exchange. Of course, everything depends on who is to decide what is the point of the exchange: for the examiner it might be "getting the suspect to confess", for the suspect it might be "trying to mislead the examiner". I believe that, just like many of the other Gricean terms, also "cooperativity" is ill-defined, or, at the very least, too vague to be of use in tests[21]. In the light of the numerous and serious problems that have been identified with the tests, Levinson's claim that "[t]here is every reason for confidence, then, that the sorts of problems raised by Sadock (1978) are capable of detailed solution" (Levinson 1983:122) sounds a little unrealistic. The best he can offer is the hope that when we take all the features together, this will yield a sufficient condition for a meaning to be identified as a conversational implicature. But Levinson himself seems to realize that also this combination of tests can at best be indicative, and certainly not conclusive. The formalization of the theory of conversation, which he and others propose, is an attempt to remedy this problem (cf. section 2.2.3. on formalizations below).

One of the other researchers who have tried to formalize the theory of conversation, Hirschberg (1991 [1985]), has also stressed the flaws in the traditional tests. Most of her comments are based on earlier remarks by Sadock and Walker, but some of the others deserve to be mentioned here. First of all, Hirschberg points out that "cancellation" might be confused with "repair" (Hirschberg 1991 [1985]:26-27), even though she does consider these to be two different things. Equally interesting is Gregory Ward's remark to Hirschberg (p.c.), which Hirschberg comments on in a footnote, that cancellations seem to require some conventional

---

[21] With respect to the latter features, the standard critique of ethnocentrism by Keenan (1976), *pace* Brown and Levinson (1978), still functions as a reminder that we should be careful with postulating the universality of GCIs and the existence of a Quantity maxim. Keenan shows that the confirmation to the maxim "Be informative" depends on certain socially relevant features of the interactional setting: in Malagasy society it is sometimes considered to be morally wrong to "give as much information as is required" (or rather: what we would consider to be as informative as required), e.g., about the identity of an individual referred to. This observation is also problematic for Levinson's "non-cooperativity" test, as this once again shows that "cooperativity" is a vague notion, and culture-dependent to boot.

signaling, in the sense that a simple conjunction will generally be odd: *Some people left early and* in fact *all did* is ok; but *Some people left early and everyone did* definitely is considerably more difficult (Hirschberg 1991 [1985]:29). Nothing much has been made of this observation (by Hirschberg nor by Ward himself), but in fact it is a crucial point: there seem to be only a limited number of set phrases in the English language that indicate a specific type of correction, which are different from the type of correction phrases one might use for cases of repair.

In my opinion, the distinction between "cancellation" and "repair" is not so absolute as is sometimes believed. The fact that the normal conjunction of an utterance, which supposedly triggers an implicature, and an utterance that contradicts this implicature is not acceptable, shows that "cancellation" is more than just an indication that some relatively weak inference is "blocked". The *in fact* phrase crucially points at the fact that the utterance just used is not entirely / not exactly / not precisely what is meant. This cancellation phrase is an indication that the correction that follows is indeed a correction, but that it is not so radical a correction as corrections that would be called instances of "repair". It is absolutely crucial that we take into account the precise meaning of the cancellation phrases, because this demonstrates that the difference between repair and cancellation is very much a matter of degree. Let us take a look at some uses of *in fact*.

(18)   I live in Belgium, in fact in Antwerp.
(19)   ?I live in Antwerp, in fact in Belgium.
(20)   ?I live in Antwerp, in fact in France.
(21)   I live in Antwerp and Paris, in fact (only) in Paris.

Example (18) shows that *in fact* can signal more than simply the cancellation of implicatures. If we accept that Antwerp is in Belgium, we have to conclude that the *in fact* phrase in (18) does not cancel anything, it just signals that the utterance *I live in Belgium* will be specified. It is also demonstrated that the *in fact* phrase is generally not compatible with the reverse of (18): if it is first mentioned that I live in Antwerp, the additional comment that in fact I live in Belgium is decidedly odd (19). Example (20) demonstrates that it is hard to cancel an entailment, which is exactly what we would expect on the basis of the Gricean theory an entailment: if it is true that I live in Antwerp, it is necessarily also true that I live in Belgium, and not in France. In some contexts, however, entailments *can* be corrected by *in fact* phrases (even when excluding ambiguous linguistic items). When (21) is uttered by someone who, over the past ten years, has been living some of the time in Antwerp and some of the time in Paris, while, at the time of speaking, he or she has not been in Antwerp for months, he or she may well block the entailment 'I live in Antwerp', which is, however, considered to be an entailment of the utterance *I live in Antwerp*. Of course, neo-Griceans might rightfully claim that this is a clear instance of "loose talk", but that would open up the possibility of reinterpreting many cases of implicature cancellation as specifications of "loose talk", which would even be more harmful to the Gricean theory of conversation.

What about another cancellation phrase, e.g. the phrases containing *but*? Clearly these phrases are stronger than the *in fact* variants.

(22)   ?I live in Belgium, but not in Bruges.

The example in (22) shows that the 'specification' meaning may be present as well, although the specification is of minimal value here: because the speaker only says that he or she does not live in Bruges, all other places in Belgium are still possible. In fact, this type of use of a *but not* phrase seems most natural when it rectifies an assumption that has been made earlier, or one that could be derived from the context. Nevertheless, a correlate of (21) is possible with *but* as well (23), although it is considerably more difficult.

(23)   I live in Antwerp and Paris, but actually only in Paris.

The difficulty is signaled by the fact that *actually* needs to be inserted, which is in itself another type of 'correction' marker. In general, cancellation phrases with *but* are much harder to "correct" entailments. But that does not mean that these phrases only function as indicators of "corrections". These *but not* phrases typically indicate that an expectation that the speaker thinks the hearer might have on the basis of what the speaker just said, is actually not the case. This description is consistent with what happens when implicatures are canceled, but, again, it is not the *only* case of correction it is consistent with

(24)   My grandmother is old, but she is not slow.

In (24), the *but* phrase does not correct an implicature, but it does correct an expectation that the hearer could have on the basis of the fact that the grandmother is old. Again, this shows that cancellation is not a sufficient criterion for classifying meanings in terms of conventional and non-conventional meaning: the *but not* phrase may even apply when the relationship between two related words or expressions is simply one in which the second is an expectation on the basis of the first: *being old* does not entail *being slow*, and neither does it conversationally implicate it. Furthermore, it also shows that *in fact* and *but not* cancellation phrases are not always interchangeable (even though they are often used as such by neo-Griceans).

The only thing that the cancellation test can do, is to suggest *how strong* the expectations are that the hearer has on the basis of an utterance. This means that the results of the different cancellation tests correspond with the *degree* of certainty that the speaker demonstrates by using a certain sentence. As I will try to demonstrate in the corpus analysis of English cardinals, cancellation tests give us information about the epistemic stance of the speaker with respect to the utterance he or she produces: the easier a "meaning" of a linguistic element can be canceled, the more hesitant the speaker is with respect to the confirmation of the state of affairs, or at least with respect to that part of the state of affairs expressed by this linguistic element[22]. In (24), the expectation that the grandmother is slow is easily

---

[22] The identification of a link between "epistemic value" and "conversational implicature" is not new: especially so-called Quantity-implicatures have been said to be "epistemically modified", in the sense that, e.g., *some* does not implicate 'not all', but implicates that *the speaker knows* that 'not all' (cf. Gazdar 1979:59, Levinson 1983:135-136, Horn 1989: 233). There has been some discussion as to the correct version of this epistemic modification. Horn writes that Gazdar's (1979) proposal is too strong: "it is preferable to derive the weaker

contradicted because the speaker did not explicitly present his or her grandmother as being slow; indeed this expectation is one that the speaker attributes to a hearer, whether the hearer actually has this expectation or not. But in (25), the first part of the utterance, *It was his brother who won the semi-finals*, presents the fact that it was his brother who won the semi-finals as something the speaker is fully certain of. Therefore, the cancellation tests yield negative results, even though, again, the acceptability of the different cancellation phrases differs: *in fact* in (25) is decidedly odd, but the *but not* phrase in (26) is nearly incomprehensible.

(25)   ?It was his brother who won the semi-finals, in fact it was his sister.
(26)   ??It was his brother who won the semi-finals, but not his brother.

In my opinion, cancellation tests are rather poor criteria for the conventional / non-conventional distinction as it was conceived of by Grice, but they provide excellent means to measure the "epistemic value" of an utterance. The fact that in quite a number of cases the results of cancellation tests are compatible with the (non-)conventionality of an utterance (as predicted by the Gricean account), is an effect of an indirect rather than an immediate relationship between the fact that a meaning is a conversational implicature and the cancelability of that meaning. If a certain aspect of the meaning is a conventional part of the meaning of the item, this means that the hearer will not expect to find that component of the meaning contradicted in the rest of the utterance or the conversation. This is compatible with the view that the "conventionality" of Grice's "conventional meaning" as opposed to Grice's "conversational [and hence non-conventional] implicature" can be defined as "familiarity": we can assume that a linguistic meaning convention will be strong when it is shared by many members of the linguistic community and when that community frequently uses the linguistic item in question with that specific meaning. This implies that communicators, who reason on the basis of these conventions, will also derive expectations from those conventions: the stronger the convention, the stronger the expectation. Now, since conversational implicatures, and certainly PCIs, are typically considered to be less than strong conventions, this means that they will give rise to less than strong expectations on the part of the hearer. It is the latter phenomenon that is demonstrated by the cancellation phrases. On the basis of this definition of conventionality, we can conclude that there is indeed a connection between conversational implicatures and the passing of a cancellation test, but the connection is mediated through the "conventionality" of the linguistic item in question. This leads to a perspective in which the Gricean nomenclature should be reinterpreted in terms of degrees of "conventionality" or "familiarity": Grice's "conventional" meaning can function as the end-point of a continuum,

---

conclusion that [...] 'it is not the case that the speaker knows that ...' " (Horn 1989:233-234) instead of the stronger 'the speaker knows that it is not the case that'. Levinson (1983:136) notes that, mysteriously, some implicatures can be interpreted along the lines of the strong version, while most of the others should be interpreted according to the weaker version. I will not go into this question, but I will simply note that, even though some of the leading neo-Gricean researchers have recognized this "epistemic modification" decades ago, they have not made the connection between conventionality and this epistemic modification. More specifically, they have never given much attention to the fact that the 'conventional' meanings of linguistic items also come with a more or less explicitly indicated epistemic value.

the other end-point of which is "no meaning" at all[23], and the meanings in between can be defined as more or less conventional. It might even be possible to retain the term "PCI", as long as we redefine it as a specific part of the continuum just proposed (namely the extreme right-end stretch, going from "minimally conventional" to "not conventional at all") and, especially, get rid of a rather large number of received opinions about the "conventional" meanings of neo-Gricean darlings such as *if ... then, some, or* and the cardinals. In order to get at the facts about the conventional meaning of these items, we should concentrate on how they are used in a large number of contexts, and how frequently they are used with which meanings. These data will be much more reliable than the information acquired through the traditional "tests" for implicatures. It is no coincidence that the test that is generally considered to be the best test, namely cancelability (cf. Sadock 1978, Hirschberg 1991 [1985]), can be linked with the degree of "conventionality" as I have defined the term. But even so, the cancelability test is less reliable than a corpus analysis, because 1) the link between conventionality and non-cancelability is an indirect one, 2) as Sadock (1978) remarked and as my own examples have demonstrated, cancelability is not a sufficient condition for the status of conversational implicature, and 3) even entailments can sometimes be canceled. As Hirschberg notes in her attempt to formalize Grice's theory of conversation:

> A definition of reinforceability is made difficult for just the same reasons that cancelation and nondetachability are difficult to formalize: we are working with an inadequate representation of the conventional force of an utterance. (Hirschberg 1991 [1985]:37)

I believe that data concerning the frequency of uses of words correlated with the meanings they express in these uses can give us an "adequate representation of the conventional force of an utterance", or at least of the conventional force of the items that constitute the utterance[24].

2.2.3. Formalizations

2.2.3.1. Scales

Hirschberg's excellent survey of the qualities and problems of the Gricean theory of conversation underscores the difficulty of defining the theory in a rigid and precise way. In her discussion of "scalar implicature", she somewhat disappointedly argues that the

---

[23] It is not clear whether it is possible to give an actual example of a meaning that cannot be expressed by a specific linguistic item, or whether this end-point is an idealization. It is often argued that a single linguistic item can be recruited to mean absolutely anything at all, but it is not clear how this could be tested. In principle, it is of course trivially true that, e.g. in code language, we can agree that X means 'Y', while X and Y can be absolutely everything. In this sense, this end-point has to be understood as an idealization, and the conventionality of a certain meaning of a certain linguistic item is never zero. But, empirically speaking, it is of course impossible to check whether a certain linguistic item has ever been used to express a certain meaning.

[24] I refer here to compositionality effects, i.e. the fact that the conventional meaning of a linguistic item may be altered, influenced, or "enriched" by the surrounding linguistic material in the utterance. I will often refer to the influence of other linguistic material in the corpus analysis of English cardinals.

difficulty of formulating a satisfactory definition of conversational implicature in the abstract has led some to attempt an alternative approach: the definition of classes of conversational implicature which, as classes, can be argued to meet the hard-to-formalize criteria for conversational implicature in general. (Hirschberg 1991 [1985]:41)

Indeed, many introductions to Grice's theory of conversation repeat the same examples over and over again. Most often these are so-called "scalar implicatures", a concept originally devised by Horn (1972) to systematize the explanation of a number of apparently similar phenomena. While the concept of a "scale" is certainly very valuable, especially because it identifies how some meanings are created by - as Levinson has eloquently put it - "a Saussurean value-by-opposition" (Levinson 1987:64), it does not make Hirschberg's criticism any less poignant. Many neo-Griceans have retreated from the very wide range of applications of Grice's original suggestions to a small number of specific lexical items and linguistic constructions, the analysis of which has been repeated over and over again, until it has become some sort of dogma. The English cardinals, which I will discuss extensively by means of a corpus analysis, are a case in point.

Horn first discussed the concept of "scales" - which would later come to be known as "Horn scales" - in a section called "Scalar predicates" of his Ph.D. thesis on the "semantic properties of logical operators in English" (Horn 1972). I will only give the informal version of his definition:

> We shall assume that on quantitative scales with defined end-points the negation of this end-point (or strongest element) <u>must</u> be inferred by the listener from the stipulation of any weaker element on that scale, while the negation of non-terminal elements <u>may</u> be inferred from the stipulation of relatively weaker elements. (Horn 1972:112 - emphasis in the original)

Scales are traditionally represented as "<*S, W*>", in which the strongest element S is placed on the extreme left and the weakest on the extreme left and intermediate values are ordered according to their relative strength. Traditional examples are: <*all, most, many, some, few*>, <*and, or*>, <*n, ... 5, 4, 3, 2, 1*>, <*excellent, good*>, <*necessarily p, p, possibly p*> (cf. Levinson 1983:134). From these scales, we can derive Gricean implicatures: if we use a weaker element, the negation of the stronger is implicated. If somebody says *Some girls were having fun*, this implicates that 'not all of the girls were having fun'. Many researchers have also proposed specific "working-out" schemata, especially for these scalar implicatures, which all make use of Grice's Q1-maxim:

(i) S has said *p*

(ii) There is an expression *q*, more informative than *p* (and thus *q* entails *p*), which might be desirable as a contribution to the current purposes of the exchange (and here there is perhaps an implicit reference to the maxim of Relevance)

(iii) *q* is of roughly equal brevity to *p*; so S did not say *p* rather than *q* simply in order to be brief (i.e. to conform to the maxim of Manner)

(iv) Since if S knew that *q* holds but nevertheless uttered *p* he would be in breach of the injunction to make his contribution as informative as is required, S must mean me, the addressee, to infer that S knows that *q* is not the case [...], or at least that he does not know that *q* is the case [...]
(Levinson 1983:135, *S* stands for "speaker")

Step (i) and step (iv) are part of traditional Gricean logic, step (ii) and (iii) contain additions. In (ii), it is determined that "more informative" can be identified with "entails" and in (iii), Levinson states that the elements of the scale must be of "roughly equal brevity". Both additional features are based on Grice's original insights, but are further specified here. Concerning scalarity - the first and certainly also the most influential type of formalization - three points are worth mentioning, the first two of which are directly related to Levinson's specifications in the working-out schema: the identification of the elements of a scale, the problem of the ordering of scales (and the notion of "scale reversal"), and the problematic derivation of the semantics of an element of that scale from its position on that scale. The first two aspects have been pointed out by other critics of the neo-Gricean theory as well (Hirschberg 1991 [1985], Van Kuppevelt 1996, Davis 1998). With respect to the first problem, I will argue that Levinson's most recent ideas are still insufficient for rigid definitions of specific scales. Regarding the second problem, I will mainly draw on Hirschberg's (1991 [1985]) and Fauconnier's (1975, 1976) criticism. Finally, I believe that the third aspect has not yet been emphasized enough, even though it is evidently a crucial point (and one that is especially relevant for the analysis of English cardinals).

Levinson's statement that the elements on a scale should be of "roughly equal brevity" is intended to constrain the formation of these scales and the generation of implicatures on the basis of these scales. The most rigid account of these constraints can be found in Levinson's latest version of the theory of conversation. Levinson (2000:79-82) distinguishes between "entailment scales" and "non-entailment scales" (which relates to the problem of "ordering of scales" which will be discussed in section 2.2.3.1. immediately below) and argues that the first type is bound by the following conditions: 1) items on the same scale should be in salient opposition, 2) they should be in the same "form class", 3) they should be in the same dialect or register, and 4) they should be lexicalized to the same degree. As an example of an invalid type of Horn scale, Levinson refers to the <*iff, if*> scale (which has been used to account for the phenomenon of "conditional perfection", cf. van der Auwera 1997:267). According to Levinson *if and only if* belongs to a specialized register (presumably that of logical reasoning), while *if* is also used in everyday conversation (condition 2) and it is obvious that *if and only if* is not of "roughly equal brevity" as *if*, and, more specifically, the two elements are not lexicalized to the same degree (condition 4)[25]. Since <*iff, if*> does not meet the requirements, it cannot be a Horn scale[26]. The condition related to word class status avoids the

---

[25] Another example is provided by Atlas and Levinson (1981:44), who argue that there is no scale <*internal negation, external negation*>, because "there is no free morpheme in English that standardly means the internal negation" (Atlas and Levinson 1981:44).

[26] Nevertheless, as Matsumoto (1995:45) remarks, the scale <*kill, cause to die*> does seem to trigger implicatures, even though also the elements of this scale are not lexicalized to the same degree, and it is clear that it is not simply the manner maxim that is responsible for the implicature: *kill* is not only shorter, it is also

problems that a scale *<necessarily-p, p>* would introduce: *p* is weaker than *necessarily-p*, hence we could hypothesize that saying *p* implicates 'not necessarily p', but the utterance *two and two is four* is normally not used to mean that this is not necessarily the case. Another way of trying to limit the overgeneration of implicatures on the basis of Horn scales, is Atlas and Levinson's (1981) "aboutness" criterion, which, as they note, goes back to Gazdar's (1979:57-58) concept of "identity of selectional restrictions" or "identity of item-induced presuppositions". An example is that *<p because q, p and q>* is not a Horn scale, because *because* and *and* "introduce relations other than the kind the Horn scale is "about," the paradigm of which is logical conjunction" (Atlas and Levinson 1981:44).

While Levinson succeeds in formalizing the original Gricean insights for a limited number of phenomena, there are a number of problems with his proposals. I will limit myself to two of the more important ones. First, Gricean implicatures are explicitly defined as meanings that are inferred on the basis of the "conventional meaning" of the linguistic item or structure in question, not on the way in which these meanings are expressed. The non-detachability criterion, which Grice considered to be a fundamental characteristic of implicatures, explicitly captures this aspect of the definition. This means that we do not expect strict constraints on the form of the elements of the scale. Nevertheless, Levinson's criteria seem rather strict indeed: if we accept them, they seriously undermine Grice's claim that implicatures depend on meanings and not on forms. Furthermore, they cast doubt on the claims of universality that are attached to Grice's non-detachability feature (which, as we have seen, are stressed by Levinson in his list of features of conversational implicatures). Levinson's reference to the maxim of Manner is of course meant to legitimate this unexpected move: in some cases, there might indeed be a clash between the maxim of quantity and that of manner, in the sense that an element could be so manifestly different from another in terms of formal characteristics, that it is bound to give rise to manner implicatures that contradict or overrule the quantity implicatures which they may have given rise to as well. This is especially convincing if we accept Levinson's (iconicity-inspired) version of Grice's maxims of manner, the "M-heuristic", which states, as we have seen, that "Marked message indicates marked situation" (Levinson 2000:33), and which gives "Manner" a more central place than many other neo-Griceans have done. Levinson's additional requirement that the scalar alternatives to the linguistic item in question (which give rise to "expression alternatives" (Gazdar 1979:57), sentences in which only the scalar item is different) are equally salient can also be derived from this more general M-heuristic: in some contexts, the use of a certain item may be extremely "marked", not because of its formidable length or complexity, but because it is not generally used in those contexts, or, as Levinson puts it, because it belongs to a different register or dialect. Nevertheless, these Manner-requirements on scales will also severely (and counter-intuitively) limit the applicability of the scalar explanation: in one of the most typical domains of scalar implicatures, the quantifiers, it will counter-intuitively exclude certain "implicatures". Consider the quantifier *quite a number of*, which should be excluded from a scale *<all, quite a number of, some>* because it is clearly formally different from the other items on the scale (not unlike the formal difference between *if* and *if and only*

---

stronger than *cause to die* and the implicature that it triggers seems to be based on the difference in strength and not the difference in length.

if, at least in terms of length). If we adopt Levinson's requirements on scales *Some of the boys went to the party* will give rise to the implicature 'not all of the boys went to the party', while *Quite a number of boys went to the party* will not have the same implicature. This is highly inconsistent: if Levinson really wants to claim that *some* implicates 'not all', then there seems to be no reason why *quite a number of* should not yield the same implicature.

The second problem is that the criteria remain rather vague. As part of an attempt to formalize Grice's initially rather informally formulated ideas, this is rather disappointing. Especially the "aboutness" criterion seems rather questionable: the claim that *and* and *because* cannot belong to the same scale because they are not about the same thing, is highly imprecise. It underscores the fact that we need an independent criterion of "aboutness": of course, *and* is different from *because* in that the latter not only connects two utterances but also identifies a relationship between them ("reason"), but it is perfectly possible to say that both are "about" the same thing, because both are about connecting utterances. Especially with function words such as *and* and *because*, intuitions concerning what they are "about" are rather imprecise anyway. It might even be asked whether *and* and *because* are "about" anything at all. The concept of "aboutness" is primarily applied to sentences or utterances, and it is not clear whether it can be transposed to linguistic elements, let alone to elements such as *and* or *because*.

There are other problems with Levinson's constraints on scales. Besides being vague, the requirements seem to overlap: degree of lexicalization and "brevity", for instance, seem to be very closely related. Moreover, the different features seem to differ in terms of relative importance. If we take a closer look at Levinson's comment about the scale <*iff, if*>, we see that Levinson does not accept it, because "*iff* (*if and only if*) belongs to a specialized register and is not monolexemic like *if*" (Levinson 2000:79). While the first observation seems plausible, the second is less convincing. Suppose we are reading a text on logic, in which *if and only if* is used frequently, and also *if* is used rather often, and both are contrasted with each other on a number of occasions. In that context, it is not impossible that the use of *if* does trigger a quantity-implicature to the effect that it is interpreted as 'not if and only if'. If we accept Levinson's comments, this cannot be explained, at least not within a neo-Gricean paradigm. His general observation, that *if* in everyday conversation (i.e., non-technical, non-logical conversations) does not trigger the implicature 'not iff' is of course correct, but the fact that in such a context there is no scale <*iff, if*> is simply due to the fact that *in that context* there is no salient alternative, in other words, the implicature is not triggered because *in that context if and only if* is not normally used. This has, however, serious consequences for the theory of conversation, and Levinson's GCIs in particular, because it means that scales cannot be abstracted from the context in which the alleged elements of the scales are used. In most contexts, the scale <*iff, if*> is not relevant (in Levinson's opinion it does not even exist), but in some contexts, e.g. the one I have just sketched, it clearly does apply. This means that scales are context-dependent, and this also means that GCIs - which capture, according to Levinson, the truly linguistic effects of Gricean theory because they are "relatively invariant over changes in context and background assumptions" (Levinson 2000:5) - are also context-relative[27]. Of course, conversational implicatures have always been considered to be context-relative, but especially scalar GCIs are assumed to be less context-relative, because the scales they are derived from are assumed to be governed by context-independent entailment relationships. Actually, however, the *<iff, if>* phenomena are completely consistent with the wider consequences of Levinson's own M-heuristic: as is well known, "markedness", which is a form of "contrast", is also highly context-dependent. Just like a black circle will be "marked" on a white page, but considerably less "marked" on a brown page, linguistic items are more or less marked according to the co- and context in which they occur[28].

Besides the debate on the identification and type of elements on the scale, there has also been a rather intense discussion about the ordering principle that ranks the elements of a scale. Especially Fauconnier (1975, 1976) and Hirschberg (1991 [1985]) have made important contributions in this respect, because both have demonstrated that the "entailment" relationship, which was originally assumed to be the ordering principle (cf. Horn 1972), is too narrow a principle for the ordering of elements on scales. Fauconnier (1975:362) shows that if scalar accounts are accepted as explanations of implicatures, then the same reasoning should hold for scales the elements of which are not unilaterally entailed by the strongest element. In the utterance *The faintest noise bothers my uncle* the superlative *faintest* should be ranked on a pragmatic scale on which another superlative, namely *the loudest*, should be considered as the strongest element. But while it is obvious that if it is true that the faintest noise bothers my uncle, also the loudest noise will bother him, this is not really a consequence of the relationship between *the loudest* and *the faintest*: superlatives typically select one and only one value. This means that it is problematic to say that *the loudest noise* entails *the faintest noise*: *the loudest noise* does not "cover" the notion 'the weakest noise' (whereas *all* is typically argued to entail *some*, because *all* does "cover" the 'at least' interpretation of *some*, which is alleged to be the "coded" meaning of *some*). Fauconnier's solution is to associate scales with "proposition schemata", "for instance a loudness scale with *x bothers y*" (Fauconnier 1975:362). Fauconnier (1976:15) accepts the existence of "échelles de quantité"

---

[27] Naturally, Levinson could always claim that in the case of conversations on logic, there are special circumstances that explain the implicature of *if*. This is probably the only possibility if one wants to save the concept of "scales". But it is clear that such a solution would be very *ad hoc*. It would underscore the fact that it is almost impossible to contradict Grice's theory of conversation: whenever there is a counter-example, it is always possible to claim that it is only an apparent counter-example because there are special contextual conditions that block the GCIs. And this once again leads to the question of what is "special" and what is "ordinary" or "conventional". As has already been mentioned, I start from the assumption that frequency is the best criterion to measure conventionality. It is a criterion that is more precise than the concept of GCIs, and it might even replace that concept altogether. I hope to demonstrate with the corpus analysis of English cardinals, in which the GCI analysis is replaced by an analysis in terms of frequency, that this holds at least for the English cardinals.

[28] A similar problem concerning scales is related to what Levinson (2000:99) calls a "pseudo-scale", namely *<mountain, hill>*. This scale seems to be a valid Horn scale with respect to all of Levinson's criteria, but he argues that *John can climb hills* will not implicate 'John cannot climb mountains', because "there is no intrinsic informational asymmetry". Nevertheless, *John can climb hills* will trigger the implicature, but the existence of this implicature will depend on the context (which means, conversely, that if it is *not* triggered, it is also because of a "special" context). A context in which a group of people is classified in one smaller group of people who can climb hills, and another smaller group of people who can climb mountains, will normally trigger the implicature in question (and, considering the fact that an utterance like *John can climb hills* will be very artificial in everyday conversation, it is not unlikely that the utterance *will* "normally" be used in contexts similar to the one described).

alongside the existence of "échelles pragmatiques", and provides another example: he argues that the utterance *Les plaisanteries les plus drôles ne font pas rire Alexandre*

> peut avoir l'interprétation qu'aucune plaisanterie ne fait rire Alexandre en vertu du préjugé *pragmatique* que si une certaine plaisanterie ne fait pas rire Alexandre, une plaisanterie moins drôle ne le fera pas rire non plus. Cela dit, cette notion paraît être une extension naturelle de cette considérée par Horn. (Fauconnier 1976:14 - emphasis in the original)

Hirschberg broadens the concept of scales even further: she calls them "partially ordered sets" (posets) and classifies them in terms of their denotation: an example of e.g., "rankable entities" is *<lover, friend>*. When someone says *This is my friend John*, this usually implicates that John is not the speaker's lover. The same holds for denotations of military ranks, such as *<sergeant, corporal, private>*. Hirschberg notes that

> while *lovers* may also be *friends*, they need not be -- and *sergeants* **cannot** be *privates*; so, although some of these rankings -- which do appear to support scalar implicature -- may be described by an intuitive notion of entailment, even a very intuitive definition cannot distinguish all and only those orderings supporting quantity implicature. (Hirschberg 1991 [1985]:98)

Other examples are concerned with spatial orderings, as when a bus driver answers the question *Do you go straight up Walnut?* negatively by means of the positive assertion *To forty-fourth*, if the end of Walnut is Sixty-Third Street, or with sets, as when somebody implicates that he or she does not have apple juice when he or she answers *I have grape or tomato or bloody mary mix* to the question *Do you have apple juice?* Clearly, "informativeness" is hard to define, and certainly a reference to "entailment" will not do. The examples of Fauconnier and Hirschberg have raised important problems for the formalization of Grice's theory of conversation: either these examples are not considered to be scalar (in which case the "scope" of the scalar explanation is diminished considerably, and it is not clear how the application of the concept is constrained), or they are accepted, but then the "informativeness" requirement remains as vague as in Grice's original text, and the attempt to formalize it will be only marginally successful.

Perhaps the initial success of the concept triggered an evolution in the neo-Gricean theory of conversation that is even more important than the problems concerning the identification of the elements on the scale. Apparently, some researchers were so impressed by the concept that they started to derive the conventional meaning of linguistic items from their position in the scale. Whereas Grice tried to smuggle logical meanings into the semantic description of elements that were considered to be natural language counterparts of logical operators, Horn (1972) and many of his followers determined that weaker elements on a specific scale should be considered to have an 'at least' semantics. This was explicitly claimed for some quantifiers, e.g. *some* and the English cardinals, but it implied that all elements on all sorts of entailment scales[29] should be considered to have an 'at least' semantics. Because *all* entails *some*, both can be put on a scale. *All* is the stronger element, which means that it "covers" the meaning expressed by *some* and expresses something "more" than that. *Some*, on the other hand, is considered to have an 'at least' semantics due to the entailment relationship between *all* and *some*, which orders these elements on the scale: if someone uses an element which is part of this quantifier scale and which is stronger than *some*, e.g. *many* or *all*, to make a statement that is true, a statement that contains *some* instead of the stronger elements will also be true. Admittedly, this conception of scalar items in terms of an 'at least' semantics is, in the final analysis, based on the more fundamental truth-conditional conception of meaning that many neo-Griceans adhere to. Nevertheless, since the original concept of scales was based on an entailment relation between the hierarchically ordered elements of the scale, and since the concept of scales was accepted so widely, it certainly helped to make the case for an 'at least' semantics of the elements on the scale. In the historical survey of the neo-Gricean analysis of numerals, I will zoom in on the origins of this 'at least' conception of scalar items.

2.2.3.2. *The projection problem*
Another attempt to bring more order into the neo-Gricean theory has been captured under the name "projection problem". As we have seen, according to the theory some utterances may be said to trigger many different and often contradicting implicatures. Nevertheless, intuitively speaking, it is clear that often only one of these implicatures "makes" it to the status of inference; others are usually not accepted as part of the actual meaning of the utterance. An attempt to regulate which implicatures are preserved and which are lost (which are "projected" to surface-level, and which are not) was first presented by Gazdar (1979). Actually, "Gazdar's bucket", as Levinson (2000:49) calls the incremental model, is meant to capture other types of meanings as well (e.g., so-called "presuppositions"), but I will limit myself to a concise description of how it works for entailments and implicatures. Levinson's bucket metaphor makes clear what the principle is about:

> [W]e can capture many aspects of the defeasibility of implicatures (GCIs in particular) in the following way: a new assertion will have its content chucked in the bucket (i.e., context) strictly in the following order and *only if each incrementation is consistent with the contents of the bucket*: [...] a. entailments; b. Q GCIs i. Clausal ii. Scalar; c. M GCIs; d. I GCIs. (Levinson 2000:50)

I will not go into the distinction between clausal and scalar implicatures (cf. Gazdar 1979), but I will limit myself to an example of the relative order of entailments and the different kinds of GCIs (the latter is actually due to Levinson and not to Gazdar, but the general idea of a hierarchy of different types of meanings is Gazdar's[30]). Levinson provides an example of a GCI which is not added to the context ("the bucket"), because of an entailment it

---

[29] Non-entailment scales, like the ones identified by Hirschberg (1991 [1985]) were not taken into account, either because they had not yet been "discovered", or by stipulation.

[30] Levinson mentions Hamblin (1971) and Stalnaker (1972) as providing precursors of Gazdar's system.

is inconsistent with. In *Some Saudi Princes, and in fact all of them, are pretty wealthy*, the quantifier *some* would normally implicate 'not all', but this is inconsistent with the entailment 'All Saudi Princes are pretty wealthy', expressed by the *in fact* phrase. The entailment is added first, so the implicature is not added at all. Even though Levinson provides a hierarchy for his three types of GCIs in the "bucket" as well, he does not give many examples of how, e.g., scalar Q-implicatures might prevent M-implicatures from being added to the bucket[31]. This is not surprising because elements that trigger scalar Q-implicatures and at the same time could be said to trigger M- or I-implicatures are not easy to find, especially if we accept Levinson's additional requirements on scales (which prevents the possibility that Q- and M- implicatures ever clash with each other, because elements that trigger M-implicatures are typically not of "roughly equal brevity", or belong to different registers or word classes).

It appears, then, that the "bucket theory" is only capable of formulating correct predictions with respect to the clashes between entailments and scalar Q-implicatures, because clashes of different types of (non-clausal) GCIs simply do not seem to occur. This prediction is in fact already explicitly contained in Grice's original framework: implicatures are weaker than entailments (this is of course the basic idea behind the cancellation test). As far as the formalization of the Gricean insights is concerned, the gain is not spectacular. Moreover, as I have argued, the difference between "entailments" and "GCIs" (if any) is much better captured by a frequency-based notion of "conventionality" or "familiarity".

On the whole, the attempts at formalization have not been very successful. Approximately 20 years ago Levinson (1983:122) countered the suggestion that the notion of implicature is so broad that it allows the derivation of just about any proposition as an alleged implicature by referring to "a firm start [that] has in fact already been made in the direction of formalization", but the theory of conversation still seems to be as imprecise and overly powerful as it was when Grice first formulated it. Hirschberg's attempt to formalize scalar implicatures primarily demonstrated that no rigid definition could be given as long as notions such as "relevance", "informativeness", and, especially, "intentions" (Hirschberg 1991 [1985]:17-19) cannot be specified further. And Gazdar (1979:58) even assumed that Horn scales "are, in some sense, 'given to us'". Considering the irreducible flexibility, adaptability and negotiability of language (cf. Verschueren 1999:59-63), this is of course not surprising. In my opinion, the best way to generalize over facts concerning the meaning of linguistic structures consists in looking at a large number of examples of how these structures are used. This does not mean that Grice's insights are irrelevant, it only means that the analysis should start with linguistic data and then check to what extent these data can be explained in terms of Grice's or someone else's theoretical notions. In the neo-Gricean history of implicatures, and especially the history of GCIs, it has happened all too often that examples have been manufactured in order to prove (or disprove) Grice's claims. As I will try to demonstrate in the corpus analysis, the neo-Gricean account of English cardinals is one example of how this has led to the postulation of counter-intuitive and often factually incorrect semantic descriptions of numerals.

---

[31] Levinson (2000:155-164) tries to argue for his hierarchy of GCIs, but all of his examples involve clashes of *clausal* Q-implicatures with other types of implicatures. None of his examples trigger clashes between scalar Q-implicatures and I- or M-implicatures.

2.2.4. The architecture of meaning

This leads us into a discussion of one of the most hotly-debated topics with respect to Grice's theory of conversation and its legacy in contemporary linguistics: the differentiation of meaning. As Bach writes: "No one disputes that there are various ways in which what is communicated in an utterance can go beyond sentence meaning. The problem is to catalog the ways" (Bach 1994a:124). Many commentators of Grice have not only tried to refine his conversational principles, but have also attempted to specify the "species" and "genera" of Grice's semantico-pragmatic universe. This discussion is also important in that it underscores the truth-conditional foundations of the neo-Gricean theory of conversation. Furthermore, it will give us the framework of some of the positions in the debate on the meaning analysis of numerals, and eventually, it will lead us to the identification of one of the main reasons why the neo-Gricean description of numerals has gone wrong. I will limit myself to a determination of what is useful for that more specific discussion.

In the "prolegomena" to his William James Lectures, Grice says that with respect to the meaning vs. use question the most promising line of answer lies in

> building up a theory which will enable one to distinguish between the case in which an utterance is inappropriate because it is false or fails to be true, or more generally fails to correspond with the world in some favored way, and the case in which it is inappropriate for reasons of a different kind (Grice 1989:4)

This rigid distinction between what is true / false and what is appropriate / inappropriate has been a point of debate in the (neo-)Gricean theory of conversation from very early on. The following canonical examples, which have been collected from a variety of sources, show why. Each is related to a specific problem for the separation of truth-conditional meaning and non-truth-conditional meaning (some of them form a pair). At the very least, they show that traditional implicatures often do enter into the truth-conditional content of "what is said". Together with Grice's claim that "what is said" is the basis for the derivation of implicatures, all of the following examples are problematic for the classical Gricean theory of conversation. Much of this section will consist of a discussion how various researchers have tried to find different solutions to the problems.

(27) If the old king has died of a heart attack and a republic has been declared, then Tom will be quite content. (Cohen 1971:58)

(28) The ham sandwich is getting restless. (Nunberg 1978, qtd. in Levinson 2000:245; cf. also Nunberg 1995:115)

(29) It is not the case that Paul ate some of the eggs. (Gazdar 1979:56)

(30) It's done.
      It's done and if it's done, it's done
      (Levinson 1983:124)

(31) A square has four sides.
      Boys are boys.
      (Levinson 1983:124)

(32)   It will take some time to repair your watch. (Sperber and Wilson 1995 [1986]:189)
        The park is some distance from where I live. (Carston 1988)
(33)   Steel isn't strong enough. (Bach 1994a:127)
(34)   You're not going to die. (Bach 1994a:134)
(35)   If you ate *some* of the cookies and no one else ate any, then there must still be some left (Levinson 2000:205)

In (27), the temporal meaning of *and*, which Grice considered to be a conversational implicature that is added to the "conventional" (but actually strictly logical) meaning of *and*, is in the scope of *if ... then*, which is also considered to be a natural language counterpart of a logical operator. If the order of the conjuncts in the conditional is reversed, we get different truth values: it is quite possible that (27) is true, while *If a republic has been declared and the old king has died of a heart attack, then Tom will be quite content* is false. This demonstrates that implicatures, which are not considered to be truth-conditional aspects of meaning (let alone truth-functional aspects), influence the truth conditions of an utterance. It seems that implicatures can somehow interfere in the calculation of truth-conditional content. In (28), there is a similar phenomenon, but the problem becomes more complicated because explanations of this phenomenon usually import the notion of "literal meaning", which may or may not differ from what Grice intended by his "conventional meaning", or "what is said"[32]. Non-literal meanings, like when *the ham sandwich* does not refer to an actual ham sandwich, but to the person who ordered the ham sandwich, were also considered by Grice to be non-conventional aspects of meaning. He insisted that rhetorical tropes like metaphor, meiosis and hyperbole could be explained through his theory of conversation, and it is clear that also metonymies as in (28) were presumed to follow the general mechanism (in this case, a "flouting" of the maxim of Quality, because the speaker says something that is manifestly false: a ham sandwich cannot be restless). Nevertheless, if the hearer of (28) contests its truth, he or she will probably not allude to the fact that sandwiches cannot be restless (although this is not in theory impossible), but will argue that the man who ordered the ham sandwich is *not* getting restless. This means that the phrase *the ham sandwich* is first "worked out" and assigned a referent before the truth of (28) is evaluated. Gazdar's example in (29) is rather similar to Cohen's example, in the sense that it involves a combination of natural language

---

[32] As Lakoff has demonstrated, the difference between literal meaning and non-literal meaning can be construed in a number of different, potentially contradictory ways: "conventional literality" ("ordinary conventional language--contrasting with poetic language, exaggeration, approximation [...]"), "subject matter literality" ("language ordinarily used to talk about some domain of subject matter"), "nonmetaphorical literality" ("directly meaningful language--not language that is understood, even partly, in terms of something else") and, finally, "truth-conditional literality" ("language capable of "fitting the world"") (Lakoff 1986:292). I believe that the "extra meaning" Grice is after is distinguished from the "literal" meaning in the sense of being "non-metaphorical" and "non-truth-conditional": at least some of Grice's implicatures may very well be used in "everyday conversation" (Lakoff's "conventional literality") and they may also be part of the default register related to a certain topic of conversation (Lakoff's "subject matter literality"). Lakoff and Johnson's theory of metaphor (Lakoff and Johnson 1980) showed that the truth-conditional view of literality and the non-metaphorical view often clash with each other. More specifically, in the case of "frozen" or "dead" metaphors, there is still a metaphorical, non-literal meaning, but this meaning *is* truth-conditional (hence "literal" on another reading of "literal"). See also Powell (1992) for differences in how the concept of literality can be construed.

counterparts of logical operators as well, in this case negation and the quantifier *some*.
Gazdar's point is that, according to Grice's theory, (29) should actually mean 'Paul ate all of
the eggs', because *some* triggers the implicature 'not all'. Combined with the negation
expressed in *it is not the case that*, this yields 'it is not the case that it is not the case that Paul
ate all of the eggs', which can be simplified to 'Paul ate all of the eggs'. This is not only a
counter-intuitive interpretation, it is also a problem for neo-Gricean accounts because these
assume the combination of the 'at least' meaning of *some* with negation to yield a 'less than'
interpretation. Levinson's examples in (30) and (31) point at the fact that truth conditions
cannot be the basis (the "input") for implicatures (which they should be, according to Grice's
theory). In (30), *It's done* and *It's done and if it's done, it's done* have the same truth
conditions but not the same implicatures: the second will be usually interpreted as 'there is
nothing that can be done about it anymore', while the first will normally not trigger that
implicature. The tautologies in (31) are both necessarily true, and that is why Levinson
concludes that they must share the same truth conditions, but while *Boys are boys* typically
implicates 'boys will never change' *A square has four sides* does not trigger that implicature.
The relevance-theoretic examples in (32) are a case of what Relevance Theory calls
"enrichment" of the logical form: while it is possible to evaluate the truth of the "literal
meaning", "logical form", or "semantics" of (32), it is clear that this is not the proposition that
is expressed. The utterance *The park is some distance from where I live* is trivially true on a
literal reading, but the intended interpretation is probably something like 'the park is actually
not very close to where I live'. The latter interpretation, also called an "explicature" (Sperber
and Wilson 1995 [1986]:182-183), is clearly the truth-conditional content of the utterance; a
truth value judgment on the "literal meaning" of (32) would trivially result in the value "true"
in all circumstances. Bach makes an altogether not dissimilar remark[33] regarding (33) and
(34), even though he considers these as two distinct phenomena. The utterance in (33) clearly
needs to be completed by a "reference point" ("steel is not strong enough *for what?*") to be
truth-evaluable (this is not the case in Carston's example: truth conditions of the logical form
of (32) can be given, although these would be the wrong ones in the sense that they would not
capture the proposition expressed). On the other hand, truth conditions of the literal meaning
of (34) can be given, but they would not capture the meaning of the proposition expressed by
the speaker, e.g., when (34) is uttered by a mother commenting about her crying son who cut
his finger. Bach calls the first an instance of "completion" (the conceptually mandatory
"filling in" of a conceptual element) and the second a case of "expansion" (the "fleshing out"
of a "minimal" proposition in order to ascertain what the speaker means). Both are considered
as "implicitures", which differ from traditional implicatures in that the latter are "completely
separate from what is said and is inferred from it (more precisely, from the saying of it)"
(Bach 1994a:140), while the former "are built out of what is said" (Bach 1994a:141). Finally,
(35) is an example of what Levinson calls "pragmatic intrusion": it is generally taken to be

---

[33] Many authors on the "architecture of meaning" seem to have the tendency to exaggerate the differences
between the analysis they propose themselves and alternative accounts. In the case of relevance-theoretic
"enrichment" and Bach's "expansion"/"completion" there are indeed differences, but the general point remains
the same: Grice's original schema (in which first the truth-conditional "sentence meaning" is computed and then
this truth-conditional meaning constitutes the input for the computation of the implicatures) is a serious
simplification of what actually happens.

true because *some* implicates 'not all' and it is this meaning of *some* that is the basis of the conditional. Assuming that there are indeed cookies, the utterance in (35) will be true if the implicature triggered by *some* is computed before the whole utterance is evaluated with respect to its truth-value.

On the basis of these and other examples, a number of revisions of Grice's theory of conversation have been proposed. Some have used these examples to show that Grice's explanation does not work and should be discarded (Cohen 1971, 1977). Others have tried to rescue it by adding nuances and extra components or have even tried to redraw the entire architecture of the theory. Walker (1975:139) tries to rescue Grice's theory by redefining truth-functionality:

> [...] by calling these particles ["logical" particles such as *and* and *if*] truth-functional the conversationalist does not wish to claim that what we should normally, in everyday talk, think of as the truth-value of the complex utterance is determined truth-functionally by the truth-values we should ordinarily and naturally assign to the constituent sentences. If he were to claim this the Conversationalist Hypothesis [Grice's theory of conversation] would be so wildly implausible as not to require the lengthy treatment given to it by Cohen [1971]; for it is quite obviously *false*, in any normal acceptation, that if I stop writing this essay now the Queen will abdicate, though on a narrowly truth-functional account it would be true.

While Walker's intuitions about "everyday talk" are impeccable, what he proposes is manifestly *not* what Grice intended: Grice *did* want to claim that the strictly truth-functional meaning of logical particles is indeed the "conventional" meaning and the input for the calculation of the implicatures, and so do a large number of contemporary neo-Griceans. Gazdar (1979:57) limited the generation of scalar implicatures to "simple" sentences (i.e., sentences that contain no logical functors that have wider scope than the implicature-triggering component: *some* in (29) is in the scope of negation and therefore (29) is not simple). As we have seen, the development of the concept of a Horn scale (and the restrictions on the formulation of such scales) can also be considered as an attempt to save Grice's original insights.

More relevant for the architecture of the theory of meaning is the following question: what is the input for the computation of implicatures? Gazdar (1979:56) wonders where to "read off" implicatures from. He argues that it is impossible to read them off from the "semantic representation of the sentence" (which he considers to be synonymous with "the proposition it expresses"), because a single proposition can be expressed by many different sentences, which may have different implicatures (cf. also Levinson's examples in (30) and (31)). Gazdar and later also Levinson decide that implicatures should be read off the "sentences of semantic representation" (Gazdar 1979:57), but the problem is that neither of them really seem to have a clear picture of what these semantic representations should look like. Gazdar argues that this representation should be slightly more "surfacey" than that hypothesized by generative semanticists, but he leaves the specifics of this "semantic representation" to others to work out. Levinson (1983:125) argues that in addition to the "semantic representation" or "logical form" of the sentences, also the attendant truth conditions are important, but he excludes, once again, Manner implicatures from the general schema. The latter should be read off from the surface structure of sentences, not from the "deeper" semantic representation.

In more recent work, Levinson is more explicit with respect to the architecture of his neo-Gricean theory and he does try to give some content to the somewhat mysterious "semantic representations". Even though he still seems a bit hesitant to commit himself to the following description, he clearly does regard it as a promising line of thought, and at the very least he sees it as an answer to the problem that there appears to be a level that is semantic but not (yet) truth-conditional:

> [semantics] is not about truth-conditional content on the one hand, nor about the relations of sense that hold between sentences on the other hand. Instead, it is exclusively about a new, strange level populated by semantic wraiths -- a level of fragmentary structures, underspecification and half-information, even archi-sememes (Atlas 1989:46). The recognition of the existence of this level is one of the important sea changes in the history of semantics -- it is real enough, but it is relative *terra incognita*. (Levinson 2000:241)

At the same time, it is not clear whether Levinson really wants to establish three levels, one with "semantic wraiths", one with truth-conditional semantics, and one with (pragmatic) implicatures. Indeed, much of his *Presumptive Meanings* is devoted to a demonstration of how pragmatically derived meanings contributes to truth conditions: semantics and pragmatics interleave or interpenetrate. Levinson convincingly shows that relevance-theoretic "enrichments" and other pragmatic contributions to truth-conditional content often rely on the same Gricean mechanisms as the traditional conversational implicatures. He calls this "Grice's circle": apparently, Grice did not realize that in interpreting some aspects of what Grice considered to be part of what is said, namely the "fixing" of referents and the resolution of indexicals and ambiguity (Grice 1989:25), we sometimes have to rely on the conversational maxims. Grice thought that these maxims only become operative after the determination of "what is said". An example of reference identification is given in (36).

(36) The bridge collapsed. The wood was rotten. (Levinson 2000:182)

The identification of *the wood* as being the material out of which the bridge is made is, according to Levinson, an I-implicature (an inference to the stereotypical situation), so it is this implicature that determines the reference of *the wood*. This is an example of what Clark has called a "bridging inference" (Clark 1977). Numerous other examples are given and termed "generalized conversational implicature", even though many of these are rather different from the GCIs that Grice proposed. It appears that Levinson's reformulation of Grice's original insights (in terms of the three "heuristics") also implies a new, and much more tolerant definition of what counts as an "implicature". Again, there does not seem to be necessary and sufficient criteria, but simply a list of phenomena (cf. especially the many different things that are presumed to be I-implicatures by Levinson 2000:117-118). It is important to recognize that Levinson's concept of implicature is actually much broader than that of many of his fellow neo-Griceans (and probably broader than what Grice himself had intended).

The fact that many of what Levinson calls "implicatures" intrude on the truth-conditional content of an utterance seems to lead Levinson to the presentation of an architecture in which there are not three levels, but rather *two* "components"[34], a semantic one and a pragmatic one. This proposal lets - contrary to what he considers to be a Chomskyan uni-directional modularity - "the components talk more freely to one another" (Levinson 2000:244). He compares his proposal to routines and subroutines in a computer program: the semantic component presumably starts the process, at a certain point the pragmatic component can be called in to process certain aspects (this would be an example of a "subroutine"), and then the semantic component may take over again. Significantly, he wants to distinguish himself from authors like Bach and Carston who allegedly engage in fruitless terminological efforts, and he underscores his idea that the semantic and pragmatic component are different in terms of processes and properties. Again, however, he does not specify what these processes underlying "semantics" really are. Moreover, the "properties" he lists are not really impressive: he names "default presumption" and "defeasibility under distinct conditions" (Levinson 2000:198), but these properties are interdefinable (if they are not outright identical) and, as we have seen, even entailments are "defeasible under distinct conditions". Furthermore, I have argued that the distinction between "suspension" and "cancellation" (which are presumed to be indications of defeasibility) on the one hand, and "correction" on the other, might not be so significant after all. This means that the evidence for Levinson's conviction that there are two "components" that can be distinguished in terms of processes and properties is rather flimsy indeed[35].

---

[34] He emphasizes the fact that this "modular" construction is not a psychological claim, but rather a methodological one: "it is a method of making a simpler theory by a policy of divide and conquer, in the ultimate hope of course that a simple theory of the mind is more likely to be correct than an unmotivatedly complex one" (Levinson 2000:244).

[35] Levinson inserts a footnote to elaborate on his claim, but rather than trying to clarify it, he berates Carston for berating him. Carston (1995:239) had argued that Levinson does not provide a distinction between implicatures that contribute to "what is said" and implicatures "which function as independent assumptions communicated by the utterance", to which Levinson replies that in fact there are no differences (Levinson 2000: Chapter Four, footnote 24). The misunderstandings / misreadings seem overwhelming. At least in this respect, it seems that Relevance Theory does not seem to differ all that much from what Levinson wants to defend. Both argue that there are two different principles underlying the interpretation of meaning, one semantic (which is helpfully identified as the "code" in Relevance Theory), and one pragmatic ("default presumptions", derived through Gricean, mechanisms, what Carston et al. label "inferences"). Moreover, both allow Gricean mechanisms in the computation of a truth-evaluable proposition, and both are ready to accept that this implies that "logical forms" may be much poorer than what has traditionally been accepted. The only difference seems to be that cases of "enrichment" are not called "implicatures" by Carston, while they are by Levinson and this may imply that the mechanisms guiding these enrichments are also considered to be different from the Gricean mechanisms by Carston and not by Levinson. At that point, however, the determination of what the fundamental conversational principles are supposed to do becomes crucial, and it turns out that the Principle of Relevance and Levinson's heuristics are rather different in this respect, so that comparison becomes much more difficult. The point is not that I do not believe that Gricean inferences are different from "conventional meanings": in some cases, especially in the case of PCIs, these meanings indeed seem to be of a different kind (and they may be produced and processed by different principles). The point is that many of the meanings described by Levinson and other neo-Griceans are actually simply "conventional meanings" of the items triggering these meanings. If neo-Griceans had worked out a clear methodology to select a meaning as a "conventional" one, blatantly counter-intuitive literal meanings of, e.g., the English cardinals would not have been postulated. The question whether

It is clear that these considerations complicate the original Gricean picture considerably. Moreover, it is also evident that the differentiation of meaning, or Bach's "catalog" of the ways in which we go beyond sentence meaning, gets tied up with accounts of processing and general proposals concerning our cognitive architecture. I will not go into the advantages and disadvantages of the details of Levinson's proposals, because these are not essential for the analysis of English cardinals. Nevertheless, his account (and the various other neologism-ridden models) is important on a more general level, because it makes clear that truth conditions cannot be the sole basis of "semantics" (or, at least not of the totality of what could be called "semantics", i.e. all aspects of "logical form" or "semantic representation").

For the analysis of the English cardinals, it suffices to be aware of the fact that Gricean "conventional meanings" can be subpropositional, i.e. not yet truth-evaluable, because this will be important for one of the positions in the discussion concerning their meaning, namely the "underdeterminacy" view. In that view, certain elements have a "general" semantic meaning, which needs to be "enriched" pragmatically before the utterance becomes truth-evaluable. The traditional Gricean view adopts the weakest of two possible meanings of a linguistic item or construction: the weaker, logic-inspired, truth-functional "meaning" of *if...then* is considered to be the conventional meaning of the construction, while the non-truth-functional meaning is derived through the conversational maxims. In the underdeterminacy view, neither the weaker nor the stronger meaning is taken as the conventional meaning of the element, but instead a meaning that is general with respect to both of these meanings is assumed to be the semantic content of the linguistic form. The application of this view to Gricean phenomena dates back to at least Atlas' (1979) article on existential presupposition, but it is still very much alive. In Carston's much more recent version, the "semantic underdeterminacy thesis" is that

> [t]he linguistic form employed by a speaker inevitably underdetermines the proposition she explicitly expresses because natural language sentences do not encode full propositions but merely schemes for the construction of (truth-evaluable) proposition forms (Carston 1999:105)

Crucially, however, also the advocates of the underdeterminacy thesis do not seem to focus on how these sub-propositional, non-truth-conditional, general or underdetermined meanings can be established. Even though they contest Grice's identification of semantics with a truth-conditional notion of "what is said", they do not base their own accounts of conventional meaning on anything but theory-internal coherence and the hypothesis that truth-evaluability is indeed a crucial characteristic of the meaning of utterances, although it is not the starting-point of semantic processing.

Simplifying somewhat, the neo-Gricean methodology underlying claims of "conventional" and "non-conventional" meanings still consists of the following stages: 1) Most often a limited number of interpretations of a linguistic item or construction are assembled from earlier neo-Gricean analyses of the item in question, 2) then some

---

the 'exactly' meaning of numerals is actually an enrichment or a GCI - to name but one example - would turn out to be irrelevant.

problematic examples are added to the discussion, 3) these trigger a number of redefinitions and rearrangements of the original theoretical concepts, and 4) the choice of the "conventional" meaning of the element is then decided on the basis of the small number of examples and the concepts available. As I have argued before, this results in a profusion of pragmatic analyses of a certain linguistic item, even if nobody has ever taken the trouble to go and look at how these items are actually used, what meanings they acquire in what types of linguistic contexts, and how often certain uses correlate with certain meanings, *independent of the theoretical concepts these uses are supposed to support or contest.* A corpus analysis of the item in question is one way of giving substance to the claims with respect to the "conventional meaning" of these items, and I believe that it is this type of analysis that should constitute the basis of any semantico-pragmatic analysis. In many neo-Gricean analyses, most of the energy is devoted to a reconciliation of intuitions concerning the meaning of the item and the theoretical apparatus, but both aspects are construed so vaguely that the decisions always seem a bit *ad hoc*.

Whereas it is often acceptable for a theory to adapt its theoretical apparatus to the data at hand, the theory becomes highly questionable when the following problems are *both* present in one and the same theory: 1) the tendency to make the theoretical constructs so vague that they are capable of turning every meaning into a stronger meaning, a weaker meaning or even an opposite meaning and 2) the tendency to change the intuitions concerning "conventional" meaning, if that is required by the concepts or by ulterior motives (e.g., rescuing logic in natural language). The first problem can indeed be argued to be a correct depiction of the flexibility of language use (I do not contest that, e.g., some instances of irony might indeed have to be explained by a Gricean working-out schema), but it is the combination with the much more problematic second aspect that makes the theory so powerful that it can explain anything. In this light, the quarrels with respect to the "levels", "components" and general "cognitive architecture" of Gricean meaning analyses seem to be rather premature: how can we decide whether what we are dealing with is an "impliciture", "explicature", "implicature", "completion", or "expansion" if we do not even agree on the data that need to be covered by these concepts? If we investigate a large number of uses of a linguistic item, and we analyze instances that are selected at random and not on the basis of a theory one wants to prove or disprove, we will be ready to pick out one type of usage as the conventional meaning of the item in question. Moreover, we will also have reliable data concerning the various other uses of the item. Next, we should check whether some of the meanings of the item depend on the meaning of the linguistic item itself, or on linguistic factors that influence the interpretation of the item. Only when these influences cannot explain the "divergent" meanings that have been collected, and when these meanings do not seem to be unrelated (in which case a homonymy analysis would be in order), we can start thinking about the ways in which meanings can or cannot be derived from a "conventional" meaning. The relationship between the different meanings can then be specified in one of the various terms of the neo-Gricean apparatus: "implicatures", "semantic generality + implicatures" or "underdeterminacy + enrichment / expansion", etc. It is obvious that even then decisions will be difficult and that analyses (and especially the terminology used in the analysis) will often be partly determined by the theoretical preconceptions of the linguist, especially those concerning the importance of truth conditions, and the centrality of a notion like "proposition". Nevertheless, if we start with a corpus analysis, we will at least have information concerning the actual usage of the item in question, and our intuitions concerning what is conventional and non-conventional or implied will be able to guide us.

The latter has been stressed repeatedly by Récanati (1989, 1993), who considered the violations of semantic intuitions in neo-Gricean theory to be so blatant that he promoted faithfulness to those intuitions to the status of a new Principle, dubbed the "Availability Principle":

> In deciding whether a pragmatically determined aspect of utterance meaning is part of what is said, that is, in making a decision concerning what is said, we should always try to preserve our pre-theoretic intuitions on the matter. (Récanati 1989:310)

Récanati discusses an analysis of the utterance *Everybody went to Paris*, in which "what is said" is rendered as 'everybody in the world went to Paris', and in which "what is meant", e.g., 'every member of the Johnson and Johnson staff went to Paris', is inferred through Grice's maxims from the content of "what is said". It is against this type of analyses that the Availability Principle militates, because it "assumes a counter-intuitive identification of what is said"[36] (Récanati 1989:314). He contrasts this to a classic example of Gricean implicatures, the metaphorical interpretation of the utterance *You are the cream in my coffee*:

> everybody would agree that what the speaker says is that the hearer is the cream in his coffee: this is clearly what he says, and it is no less clear that he is speaking nonliterally. But when the speaker says 'Everybody went to Paris' [...], it is counter-intuitive to identify what he says with the [proposition] that every person in the world went to Paris [...] (Récanati 1989:314)

Now that I have argued that "semantics" cannot simply be equated with truth conditions and now that I have tried to answer the question concerning the input for the computation of implicatures by suggesting a methodology for establishing "conventional" meanings, it is time to elaborate on the consequences for the meaning analysis of linguistic elements (such as cardinals) by addressing another, closely related question: do implicatures work on entire sentences or are they allowed to work "locally" as well? This question has given rise to considerably fewer proposals, models and terminological inventions, but it is an essential one. As we have seen, Levinson seems to favor an analysis in which the semantic processing can call in the help of pragmatic "subroutines", and he relies on these subroutines

---

[36] The problem with an appeal to pre-theoretic intuition is that these intuitions can always be attacked by arguing that "the man on the street" is not educated enough to understand the niceties of distinctions between, e.g., Austin's locutionary level and the illocutionary level (Austin 1962). This is precisely what Bach does in his critique of Récanati's principle. Moreover, he argues that "untutored intuitions are educable"(Bach 1994a:137): while the man on the street may regard 'I have never eaten dinner' as a counter-intuitive reading of *I haven't eaten dinner* he will probably not say that "what is said" in *I haven't eaten dinner* and *I haven't eaten dinner tonight* are identical (while on Récanati's analysis it should be the same). Bach is right when he says that an appeal to intuitions is not the final word on neo-Gricean meaning analysis. But Récanati certainly has a point as well: many neo-Griceans seem to ignore intuitions completely. Moreover, I believe that Récanati's "return to intuitions" might actually be more relevant in the current neo-Gricean atmosphere.

to account for the computation of truth-conditional content of utterances containing elements that trigger GCIs. Relevance Theory, on the other hand, seems to be more faithful to Grice's original proposals in that they claim that implicatures are derived on the basis of explicatures, which correspond to truth-evaluable "propositions". Once again, the matter depends on what one wants to call "implicatures" and whether one accepts that "explicatures" are essentially different from implicatures or not. But it is clear that at least some researchers have shifted the application of Gricean mechanisms from the sentential level to the phrasal and even the lexical level.

This is important for the neo-Gricean history of cardinals, because it means that, while the 'at least' meaning is crucially argued to derive from the truth-conditional content of utterances containing numerals (because *four* truth-conditionally entails *three* and *three* entails *two* etc.), it is no longer the utterance in which the numeral occurs that triggers the implicature, but the scale with which the specific element is associated! This implies that there does not seem to be any motivation anymore for assuming the conventional meaning of numerals to be an 'at least' meaning: if there is such a thing as a sub-propositional semantics (and Sperber and Wilson, Carston, Gazdar, Levinson and Bach all seem to assume that there is) this means that the semantics or the "coded content" of lexical elements can and should be detached from the question concerning the truth-conditional entailments that these elements allow. Either it is accepted that pragmatically derived meanings cannot contribute to truth conditions (which seems highly counter-intuitive, and which is contested explicitly by Levinson as well as by relevance theorists), or truth conditions are given up as the determinants of "conventional" meaning or "logical form" and semantics is reduced to the specification of "semantic wraiths" (which seems the sensible thing to do). The meaning analysis of numerals will have to be a description of its sub-propositional content, and this will have to be independent of the fact that someone saying *Mary has three children* is, in some sense, speaking the "truth" when Mary actually has four kids. With an example from a domain that has not yet been colonized by neo-Gricean theory, namely the meaning of grammatical elements such as pronouns (but cf. Levinson 1987), this becomes much clearer. As Carston argues, the pronoun *he* is usually assigned a referent on the basis of contextual information, and this referent is usually taken as part of "what is said" (from Grice to Levinson). Carston argues, however, that this fixing of the referent is not a part of linguistic meaning:

> What we know when we know the meaning of the lexical item 'he', what is stored in the 'mental lexicon', is knowledge of the way it delimits the field of possible referents in any context. (Carston 1995:240)

The fact that *he* has to be linked to a referent in order to be truth-evaluable is *not* part of the linguistic content of *he*; this is not "encoded" by *he*. Likewise, I will argue that the fact that higher numerals could be said to entail lower numerals (allowing the concept of "entailment" to apply to lexical items instead of sentences or propositions) is not the basis of the linguistic description of cardinals. Paraphrasing Carston, we can say that what we know when we know the meaning of *three* is knowledge of the way it determines the cardinality of a set in any context; the fact that entailments from propositions containing *three* to propositions that contain *two* and are otherwise identical often seem to go through is *not* part of the coded content of *three*.

2.3. CONSEQUENCES FOR THE ANALYSIS OF MEANING

As I have argued, Grice's original idea to detach non-conventional inferences from the conventional meaning of a sentence and then reconnect the two via a system of principles and maxims, captures a strong intuition. Especially the phenomena that fall under the concept of "particularized conversational implicatures" seem to be explained rather well by Grice's "working-out" schema. In the evolution of the neo-Gricean paradigm, the explanation of PCIs seems to be one of the most widely accepted Gricean ideas. Even though many people have formulated new versions of the maxims, the basic idea behind the explanation of PCIs is still the same as Grice's original idea.

Nevertheless, there are many problems with the original theory, as well as with the various ways in which the original theory has been developed. One of the problems with the traditional theory of conversation is that Grice combines the explanation of non-conventional inferences with an attempt to save "logic in language". More specifically, he tries to show that the divergences between logical operators and their natural language counterparts can be explained by the same apparatus as the one he had designed to explain how people are capable of meaning more than what they say. He ignores intuitions concerning the conventional meanings of specific linguistic elements and decides that the conventional meaning of particles such as *or*, *and*, *some* etc. can be identified with the meaning of their logical counterparts. No methodological justification is given for this decision: he simply assumes that this is the case. In general, Grice never seems to concern himself with the question of how we can find the conventional meaning of a linguistic item, construction, or utterance. He does propose a number of features to distinguish specific meanings of an element or utterance in terms of "conventional meaning", "what is said", or "conversational implicature", but these do not provide necessary and sufficient properties, and Grice does not say how these meanings were found in the first place.

While quite a few neo-Griceans and critics of Grice's theory have opposed the influence of logic in the determination of linguistic meaning, very few have noted the lack of a methodological basis for the collection and differentiation of the various meanings a certain item or construction can have. I propose that the notion "conventional meaning" should be identified with "familiar meaning" and that the determination of the extent to which a certain meaning is familiar or conventional can be derived from data concerning the frequency with which a certain element is used with a specific meaning. A corpus analysis of the element of construction in question will provide the necessary data. This also implies that the distinction between "conventional meaning" and what is called "GCIs" should be seen as a continuum: what Grice considers to be the conventional or literal meaning of an element is simply a meaning that is more familiar than the meaning that Grice considers to be a GCI, typically because the former is expressed by all uses of a linguistic element (including those triggering a GCI), while the latter can only be found by deriving inferences from utterances containing that element, and in that case these inferences will not always go through. Moreover, the question of the relationship between a more conventional meaning and a less conventional meaning should first consider the possibility that this "extra", less conventional meaning is triggered by the surrounding linguistic material. If there is a correlation between the occurrence of the "extra" meaning and the occurrence of a certain linguistic element in the context - and with the typical examples of so-called "GCIs" it is very likely that there is - it is highly probable that it is the latter that triggers the extra meaning, and not the general principles of conversation. Only then the possibly "pragmatic" relationship between the more and the less conventional meaning becomes a topic for discussion.

My hypothesis would be that most of the meanings that are considered as classical scalar implicatures can be explained by an analysis of the conventional meaning of the item + the linguistic elements that influence the interpretation of the item. Pragmatic inferences only seem to be required for phenomena that are traditionally referred to as PCIs, in addition to a number of phenomena that have been focused on more recently, namely those that are captured by the notions of "enrichment", "expansion" and "completion". The latter rely directly on information that can be drawn from the context, which implies that this information is *not* part of the coded content of the item or structure that is enriched / expanded / completed. At most, the item itself signals that it needs to be enriched by contextual information and also signals what type of contextual elements can be candidates for enriching the item. The overload of new terminology and new definitions of old terminology is confusing also in this respect: some researchers have broadened the concept of implicature and especially GCI so much that many of these enrichments are labeled "implicatures". But also the "enrichment" analysis needs to distinguish between conventional meanings that can be considered to attach to the linguistic *element* itself, and the inferences that can be drawn on the basis of an utterance containing that element. While Grice's theory was rather clear with respect to the status of implicatures (they were considered to be conversational effects of uttering an *utterance*), many neo-Griceans and critics of Grice have reinterpreted his original ideas in order to apply them to the meaning analysis of *lexical items*. Especially the concept of scales seems to have stimulated the movement from the concept of implicatures as being non-conventional inferences of utterances to a concept of implicatures in which they are attached to a particular linguistic element. The quantifier *some*, e.g., was postulated to have an 'at least some' semantics, and the 'exactly some' meaning it often appeared to have, was considered to be an implicature. But this 'exactly some' meaning is not the effect of an 'at least' meaning + a 'not all' implicature: the fact that the inference that there are more than 'some' elements in a set often will not go through is not because *some* acquired an 'exactly some' meaning, but because the uttering of the utterance containing *some* allowed the inference that 'no more than some' elements are involved. The confusion between the meaning of a lexical item and the inferences that can be drawn from utterances containing that item has been detrimental to the meaning analysis of many lexical items. As I will show, also the English cardinals are a case in point.

Besides the influence of logic and the lack of a clear methodology to collect and determine the meanings of a specific item or construction, there are two additional problems with Grice's theory. First, the maxims are very vague and seem to be able to explain any inference from anything. While this seems to correspond with the intuitions concerning the phenomena referred to by the concept of PCIs, this is definitely not the case with some of the

GCIs that have been proposed. Especially neo-Griceans like Horn (1972) and Levinson (1983, 2000) have focused on these GCIs, which are considered to be somehow more "linguistic" phenomena than the PCIs. Horn tried to formalize these implicatures by his concept of "scalar" implicature, but it turns out that also this concept is hard to define. Some of the neo-Griceans have even argued that these scales are simply "given" to us. Even though the principles and maxims proposed are so flexible that they can easily capture intuitions concerning the conventional meaning of items, the fact that there is no methodology to select the conventional meaning of an item makes the analyses even more dependent on the theoretical predilections of the researcher, which may only be secondarily related to the meaning analysis of the item in question (some have perpetuated the influence of logic in the description of linguistic items, later analysts primarily used examples to show that an aspect of their theory of conversation is better than someone else's). In short, while the indeterminacy of the maxims may be intuitively plausible for PCIs, the combination of this indeterminacy with the lack of a methodological basis for selecting the conventional meaning of an item makes many versions of the theory so flexible that they do not seem to have any explanatory value anymore.

Second, the question concerning what constitutes the input for the calculation of the implicatures has brought to light that truth conditions, which are considered to be the starting point for the derivation of implicatures, typically rely on a pragmatic enrichment of the "logical form" of a sentence. This has led to a reduction of what is traditionally called "semantics": most linguistic elements will have skeletal meanings, some of which will be complemented by "cotext" (the linguistic factors that have been mentioned), others by contextual elements. Crucially, this also implies that truth-conditional relations between sentences should be detached from the description of items occurring in those sentences. Once again, the lexical level should not be confused with the level at which inferences are calculated.

3

THREE DECADES OF GRICEAN NUMERALS

In this chapter I will discuss the most important positions in the post-Gricean debate on English cardinals. The neo-Gricean story of numerals is not an easy one to reconstruct because, as mentioned before, the discussion of numerals is integrated in a larger discussion of "implicatures", "quantity-implicatures" or "scalar implicatures" in general, in which case the numerals often merely figure as one example among the many examples that have been provided. Also, the terminological incompatibility between various accounts makes it sometimes difficult to compare the different analyses and at least one neo-Gricean analyst of numerals has changed his mind during the years that have elapsed since his first contribution to the debate. I will present the analyses and the arguments for these analyses in separate sections. The selection of the authors and texts depends on the novelty of their contribution to the "cardinal debate". Many arguments are repeated time and again, and I will generally only mention those once (in the discussion of the author who first used or discussed the argument). This implies that some classic works on implicature theory in general will not be discussed in a separate section (e.g., Levinson 1983 is not discussed separately, because, with respect to the analysis of numerals, this book does not contain very many new arguments). I will, however, discuss new interpretations or evaluations of old arguments. At the end of the discussion, I will already refer to the corpus analysis of cardinals by outlining my own analysis. In this outline, I will also confront the arguments given in favor of other analyses (especially those supporting the neo-Gricean 'at least' analysis).

3.1. MINIMALISM AND IMPLICATURES: TRADITION AND EVOLUTION

3.1.1. Horn's original analysis

Symptomatically, the primal scene of the neo-Gricean treatment of English cardinals is part of a much larger discussion. The "original scene" of the 'at least' analysis of cardinals can be found in Horn's (1972:37) discussion on presupposition and his concept of "suspension". In that discussion, Horn observes that existential presuppositions as well as other types of presuppositions can be suspended by adding an *if*-phrase: whereas the utterance *The milk train doesn't stop here anymore* normally presupposes that in earlier times the train did stop here, the validity of this presupposition can be suspended by adding *if it ever did*. Horn argues that these suspension phrases are grammatical if they make the sentence true in a wider range of cases than the initial sentence (with the presupposition intact). He refers to this as the principle of "increased universality" (Horn 1972:19). Parallel to his discussion of suspension phrases, he also discusses the meanings of *only X*, which he considers to have a negative semantic part ('no one else') and a positive presupposition ('X'). This analysis is compatible with his principle of increased universality: the sentence *John has only three children, if not fewer* is possible, but *John has only three children, if not more* is not. As Horn explains, "the positive presupposition of negative-asserting *only* sentences is suspendible just in case the suspension results in admitting the possible application of an even stronger negative assertion" (Horn 1972:38). Concentrating on the numerals some more, Horn notices that the same does not hold for numerals without *only*. The situation is actually the reverse of the one with the *only* sentences: *John has three children, if not four* is possible, but *John has three children, if not less* is not. On the basis of the "increased universality" hypothesis, one would expect these sentences to contain items with a negative presupposition and a positive assertion, but this does not seem to be the case. Except, Horn suggests, perhaps for the numeral itself: "we can hypothesize that a cardinal number *n* determines the *assertion* of *at least n* and the *presupposition* of *at most n*" (Horn 1972:38). The formulation of the neo-Gricean hypothesis with regards to cardinals follows from the fact that this 'at most' meaning cannot be a presupposition of the numeral, because it fails the best test for presuppositions: it is not impervious to negation. Hence, Horn tries to account for the suspension facts by means of a principle which adds an 'at most' meaning to a cardinal, but which is susceptible to the influence of negation: a conversational implicature! The first version of the thesis, which will later be labeled "minimalism" (Anscombre and Ducrot 1978) because of the alleged "minimal" 'at least' semantics of the numeral, is already hampered by hesitations with respect to the question of whether this 'at least' and 'at most' meaning is actually a meaning of the numeral itself, or of the utterance it is part of:

> Numbers, then, or rather sentences containing them, assert lower-boundedness -- *at least n* -- and given tokens of utterances containing cardinal numbers may, depending on the context, implicate upper-boundedness -- *at most n* -- so that the number may be interpreted as denoting an exact quantity (Horn 1972:41).

The shift from the inferences that can be drawn on the basis of utterances containing numerals to the interpretation of a number is present in the neo-Gricean account from the very beginning: even though at first Horn still specifies that it is not the numerals themselves that implicate upper-boundedness, he concludes that it is *the number* that may be interpreted as denoting an exact quantity.

Interestingly, Horn very briefly considers the possibility that "upper-boundedness" is an entailment instead of a presupposition or an implicature, but he decides against it, because a cancellation clause can be added rather easily, while this is not the case with *only* sentences: *I have three children: in fact I have (even) more* versus **I have only three children: in fact I don't (even) have that many*. It is this cancellation argument that will become one of the most frequently used arguments in favor of the 'at least' analysis. He also mentions Steve Smith's (1970) ambiguity analysis of numerals (in which numerals are ambiguous between an 'at least' meaning and an 'exactly' meaning), but that analysis is discarded as well, "given the relevance of contextual information in deciding between the two possible interpretations" (Horn 1972:40) and the fact that numerals can be considered as an example of a wider phenomenon, namely scalar implicatures. Horn's argument concerning the contextual dependency of the interpretation of the numeral is the fact that the question *Does John have three children?* can be given two apparently contradictory answers: *Yes, (in fact) he has four* and *No, he has four.* Horn argues that the choice will be determined by means of contextual clues. Another important argument that Horn uses to support his 'at least' analysis is a reference to one of Jespersen's observations with respect to the combination of *not* with a numeral:

> [...] the general rule in all (or most) languages is that *not* means 'less than', or in other words 'between the term qualified and nothing'. Thus *not good* means 'inferior', but does not comprise 'excellent'; *not lukewarm* indicates a lower temperature than *lukewarm*, something between lukewarm and icy, not something between lukewarm and hot. This is especially obvious if we consider the ordinary meaning of negatived numerals: he does not read three books in a year / the hill is not two hundred feet high / his income is not £200 a year / he does not see her once in a week / the bottle is not half full - all these expressions mean less than three (Jespersen 1948 [1924]:325-326)

It is clear that this fragment has been one of the sources of inspiration for Horn's concept of scales.

In fact, Horn's (1972) account is very detailed and already contains most of the arguments that will be used in the first two decades of the short history of neo-Gricean numerals. Even the concept of scale reversal is already introduced in this early work: Horn noticed that in some contexts, the entailment relationship is reversed, and hence also the acceptability of the suspension phrases differs: *Nixon pledged to reduce the troop strength to 30,000 if not to 25,000* is ok, while the suspension phrase *if not to 35,000* is out. "Scale reversal" implies that the normal order of the elements on the scale is reversed: the asserted lower bound of these numerals is a lower bound on a negative scale. Triggers of scale reversals are considered to be of various kinds: they can be the scoring conventions in golf, but also implicit references to an upper bound in verbs like *reduce* or in modal expressions. Another recurring argument refers to the fact that the 'exactly' implicature is less strong with round numbers: the numeral *201.37* will trigger a strong implicature, while with *200* the 'exactly' implicature will be less strong[1]. This is consistent with the presumption that implicatures vary in strength, while entailments do not. Next, a forerunner of Sadock's (1984) reinforceability argument is presented as "asserting the implicature". Horn does not use numerals to exemplify the argument, but the general point is clear: the implicature can be made explicit in the utterance by adding a *but not* phrase, as in *John has three children, but not four.* A different version of the same argument could be labeled the "redundancy argument": because implicatures are not fully explicit, no redundancy effect is created if we add a phrase in which the implicature is made explicit: *some but not all of my friends are women.* With entailments, this is not possible: *exactly three, but no more than three children*

---

[1] See Sadock (1977) and Channell (1980) for more specific theories of approximations.

went to Paris. Later on in the thesis, he gives the example *Three and only three Lithuanians*: this is ok, because *only three* is supposed to make the implicature 'not more than three' explicit. But the second instance of *three* in *only three and three Lithuanians* is redundant because 'three' is entailed by *only three*. Also, because implicatures are presumed to operate on meanings and not on the way these meanings are expressed, it can be expected that there will be no separate lexicalizations for 'at least five' and 'exactly five', because the latter can be derived from the former through Gricean mechanisms:

> we can propose a universal rule that no language has cardinal numbers {n} denoting either *exactly n* or *at least n* in their general rule. In other words, it is a general fact of natural language that scalar predicates are lower-bounded by assertion and upper-bounded by implicature (if not presupposition) (Horn 1972:52)[2]

Next, the incorporation of numerals in lexical items, dubbed "lexicalization" or "morphemicization" (Horn 1972:46) is also seen to strengthen the 'exactly' implicatures: Horn provides a large number of examples, e.g., *monologue, bicycle, duo* to demonstrate this point. Finally, it is also worth mentioning that he quotes an example used by Chomsky (1972) that indicates the influence of a "superset": *2* in *2 of my 5 children go to elementary school* triggers a stronger 'at most' implicature because "the addition of the upper bound or superset of the number of the speaker's children [...] must be assumed to be relevant, and thus the implicature is safer" (Horn 1972:46), at least compared to the weaker upper bound triggered by *I have 2 children in elementary school*.

Horn's arguments are not convincing. First, just as Grice did not argue for the conventional status of logical meanings of natural language counterparts of logical operators, Horn does not argue for the conventional status of 'at least' meanings of numerals. This 'at least' semantics is simply derived from the truth-conditional properties of utterances containing numerals: Horn claims that *John has three children* is also true when John has four children. It is this observation, which concerns the truth conditions of only one type of utterance containing *three*, that leads to claims with respect to the meaning of *three* on the *lexical* level: the truth-conditional phenomenon is as it were extracted from the level of utterances and used as evidence for a counter-intuitive postulation of the lexical meaning of *three*. As I will demonstrate in the corpus analysis, this analysis is not supported by the facts of actual everyday usage.

Second, the defeasibility argument (Horn uses the cancellation as well as the suspension test) cannot be conclusive, for two reasons: 1) as we have seen in the discussion of tests for conversational implicature, the cancellation test cannot distinguish between a monosemy + implicature analysis and an ambiguity analysis, 2) the phenomena that hide behind the "cancellation / suspension test" are specific kinds of "corrections", and should not

---

[2] As pointed out to me by Johan van der Auwera (p.c.), the Indonesian language Toratán does lexicalize 'exactly n' meanings separately: Himmelmann and Wolff (1999:38) call these "limitatives" and show that in Toratán these are derived from the "atomic numbers" by "bisyllabic reduplication or, in the case of the lower digits (1-3), monosyllabic reduplication": '7' is expressed as *pitu*, while 'only 7' is *pitu-pitu*. On the whole, however, this separate lexicalization seems to be very exceptional indeed.

be taken as indications that the "cancelable" meanings are actually implicatures. As we have seen, in some contexts, even entailments can be canceled.

Third, the "contextual" dependency of the interpretation of numerals cannot be an argument for an 'at least' + implicature analysis, because the two answers to the question *Does John have three children*, namely *Yes, (in fact) four* and *No, he has four*, remain possible even if the 'at least' analysis is not accepted. With an 'exactly' meaning of *three*, the negative answer is predicted to be the more natural answer, while in the 'at least' analysis the positive one should be the more natural one. It is clear that in the "null-context" (Katz 1977, 1981) in which this example is presented[3], the 'exactly' analysis makes the right predictions. This is also demonstrated by the fact that in the positive answer the addition of a correction phrase (*in fact*) seems to be required, while this is not the case with the negative answer.

Fourth, the argument that the combination of negation + numeral usually triggers a 'less than' meaning faces the problem that it is certainly not impossible that this combination acquires a 'more than' interpretation (as Jespersen as well as Horn point out). Because both the 'at least' meaning of numerals and the negation operator are assumed to be on the same semantic level, it is not clear why the combination sometimes triggers 'less than' and sometimes triggers 'more than' meanings. In fact, Horn normally uses the variability of the interpretation of a certain item as an argument for an implicature analysis, and against an analysis in terms of conventional meaning!

Fifth, the phenomena captured under the heading "scale reversal" demonstrate clearly that the implicatures that utterances containing numerals may trigger should be detached from the analysis from the numerals as lexical items. Also, while the concept of "scale reversal" may provide a solution for the fact that the suspension test does not trigger the expected results, it is clear that this does not change anything about the fact that these examples are problematic for an 'at least' analysis of numerals. If numerals indeed have an 'at least' semantics, then it is not clear how this semantic meaning can be turned into the 'at most' meaning it is assumed to have in the examples provided by Horn: if *30,000* indeed means 'at least 30,000' it is not clear how Horn can account for the fact that in *Nixon pledged to reduce the troop strength to 30,000 if not to 25,000* this 'at least' *semantics* (i.e, a lower bound that is considered to be uncancelable) can be turned into an 'upper bound' interpretation (or a 'lower bound' interpretation on a "negative scale")[4]. Either one accepts that reversing the scale with *30,000* as an element is the same as changing the semantics of the numeral (in which case

---

[3] The concept of a null-context is in itself very problematic, as is the use of constructed examples for which no contextualization is given (cf. Searle 1981:117-136). When one uses corpora to provide data for an analysis, the problems and biases that decontextualized examples introduce disappear.

[4] Note that for Horn, the scale does not really seem to be reversed in these cases - it is just a *different* "negative" scale. This shows that in his discussion of scale reversal (Horn 1972:43), the only "semantic" content that Horn seems to attribute to numerals is a "lower bound"; the rest seems to be filled in by the scale to which the numeral belongs (and this is determined by contextual information). This leads to the conclusion that for Horn numerals are almost meaningless. They do not even seem to be capable of expressing cardinality autonomously. The meaning 'lower bound' only really means something in the light of the concept of Horn scales. This demonstrates once again how the neo-Gricean analysis derives the meaning of lexical items from the truth-functional relationships between sentences containing these numerals, rather than trying to determine their direct contribution to the meaning of the sentence in which they occur. Only the latter can provide us with plausible descriptions of their "conventional meaning", which is the basis of the meaning analysis of numerals, as (even) Grice has emphasized.

there is no hope for a unified analysis of these otherwise remarkably similar uses), or one changes the semantics of the numeral so that the phenomena of "scale reversal" can simply be explained on the basis of a combination of the semantics of numerals and whatever other non-semantic explanation can be given, without recourse to "scales" and certainly not "scale reversals".

Sixth, the redundancy argument provides an argument against the 'exactly' analysis of numerals, but it is actually also a convincing argument against the 'at least' analysis that Horn defends: if *three* means 'at least three', why is it not redundant to say *at least three*? Finally, the fact that the usual 'exact' reading of numerals seems to be less strong with round numbers such as *200* is certainly correct. But Horn ignores the fact that the 'approximative' use of a round number may also refer to a number that is slightly smaller than 200, say *199*. The numeral *200* may refer to '201' as well as '199', and neither one seems to be more difficult than the other. This is a problem for the 'at least' analysis, because if *200* really meant 'at least 200' then the meaning '201' should be expressed more naturally by *200* than the meaning '199'. It is not clear how we can get from the non-defeasible 'at least' meaning to a 'less than' meaning in utterances with round numbers. In other words, with round numbers it is not only the alleged 'exactly' implicature that is less strong, also the allegedly *semantic* lower bound seems less strong.

Seventeen years later, Horn's (1989) volume on negation contains an extensive discussion of "negation and quantity", in which he defends his 'at least' analysis of cardinals once again. Most of the arguments for this analysis are the same as the ones he used in Horn (1972), but in this new discussion he addresses some of the arguments that others have used against his original analysis, and he adds a few new arguments. In general, the new version relies even more explicitly on truth-conditional arguments and arguments from logic than the 1972 version.

He opens the chapter on "negation and quantity" with the Jespersen quote (Jespersen 1948 [1924]:325-326) on the default 'less than' meaning of the combination of numerals and negation (cf. above) and with a discussion of the sentences *a is good* and *a is not good*. Characteristically, the meaning of *good* and *not good* is not determined by means of an investigation of the meaning of the lexical item *good*, but by means of the truth judgments associated with the two sentences when they are evaluated against the background of four "contexts" (one in which *a* is "excellent", one in which it is "good but not excellent", one in which it is "mediocre", and one in which it is "bad" - as if it were possible to objectively determine the quality of an entity a^5). Since Horn writes that his "pragmatic account of the subcontrary relation generalizes to all relatively weak scalar operators, including cardinal numbers and evaluative or gradable adjectives like *good*" (Horn 1989:213), it is safe to assume that this truth-conditional reasoning remains the basis of his account of numerals as well, just like it was the fundamental argument in the 1972 analysis (note, by the way, that the analysis of numerals is once again integrated in a more general discussion, the arguments of which are simply assumed to apply to numerals as well). The notion "subcontrary relation" refers to the Square of Oppositions, an Aristotelian concept that arranges the logical

---

[5] This is of course the consequence of the rigidly truth-conditional view of meaning, in which the importance of the intersubjective nature of meaning is downplayed.

quantifiers on a square, the four corners of which are associated with one of the following quantifiers: *all, some, no (not some)* and *not all (some not)*. The subcontrary relation holds between *some* and *not all*, and Horn considers this relation as one between a quantifier and its implicature. Whereas this Square may be a useful way to portray the relationships between various logical operators, Horn's employment of it as the basis of the semantic description of natural language counterparts of these operators leads to unconvincing analyses of quantifiers and especially numerals. In some passages it even looks as if Horn does not want to accept very plausible semantic descriptions of natural language items for the sole reason that they do not seem compatible with the architecture of the Square. In his discussion of Kuroda's (1977) "every-day reading" of *some* (which is of course not considered to be 'at least some', but which is assumed to license the *entailment* 'some animals are not white' from the sentence *Some animals are white*) he argues:

> Kuroda is not dissuaded from this 'logical equivalence' by his recognition that on its everyday reading [*some animals are white*] cannot serve as the contradictory of *No animals are white*, since both these propositions would be false if all animals are white (Horn 1989:213)

Horn does not seem to realize that most (all?) people indeed do infer from the utterance *some animals are white* the fact that the statement *not all animals are white* holds as well. In describing the *linguistic* meaning of *some*, the "every-day" intuitions of language users are undoubtedly much more important than whatever concepts logicians happen to favor. Indeed, Horn's historical survey of the analyses of the *some - not all* relationship shows that not even all *logicians* agree with the overruling importance of arguments derived from the Square of Oppositions (Horn 1989:210-216). But whatever logicians may think about the correct description of 'some' as a logical operator, it is clear that a linguistic description of the English quantifier *some* cannot be refused merely because it would imply that *some* would not have contradictories. In his version of the Gricean working-out schema for the implicatures of numerals, the identification of "conventional meaning", "truth-conditional meaning" and "literal meaning" is even more explicit: "Cardinals like *3* are lower-bounded by their literal or conventional meaning; hence [*Pat has three children*] means (is true iff) Pat has at least three children" (Horn 1989:214). The citation also makes clear that the initial hesitation concerning the question whether the 'at least' meaning should be contributed to *three* itself or to the utterance containing *three* (cf. Horn 1972:41) is resolved to the advantage of the former option. The shift from "inferential" meaning to lexical meaning is thereby complete: whereas in the beginning at least some analysts were rather careful to distinguish the contribution of certain elements to the inferential properties of an utterance (which entailments does it allow and which does it prohibit?) from the lexical meaning of the element, this distinction is absent from Horn's (1989) account of cardinals.

Arguing against the 'exactly' interpretation of quantifiers, Horn again refers to his redundancy argument (if *three* meant 'exactly three', *exactly* in *exactly three* would be redundant) and adds an argument from contradiction (if *some* really meant 'some only', *at least some* would be a contradiction, which it is not). Moreover, the "generality" of the neo-Gricean account is emphasized: also the relationship between *or* and *and*, as well as that between possibility and necessity modals seems to be compatible with the relationships that hold between the corners of the Square of Oppositions. Horn assumes that this generality is an argument for the correctness of his scalar account of quantifiers, even though the "conventional" meaning of these items are derived from the same truth-conditional argument that Horn uses for his analysis of quantifiers. More specifically, the claims with respect to the "conventional" status of the alleged 'at least' meanings of *or* and modals like *may* and *can* are not based on an empirical study of all of the meanings that can be expressed by these items (let alone on data concerning the frequency with which these items express these meanings), but are simply derived from the inferences that are allowed on the basis of sentences containing these items. Crucially, the inferences considered with *or* and *can* are of the same type as the inferences that can be drawn on the basis of sentences containing numerals. It is therefore not surprising that these items appear to have similar "meanings".

Another argument that Horn uses is the so-called "monotonicity" argument, based on Barwise and Cooper's (1981) discussion of quantifiers (in their terminology, a quantifier is not the quantifying element alone, but the whole NP containing the quantifying element). In *some men entered the race early* the quantifier is "monotone increasing", which means that the predicate can be weakened *salve veritate*: *some men entered the race* is entailed by *some men entered the race early*. The same holds for *n* and *at least n*: *(at least) three men entered the race* is entailed by *(at least) three men entered the race early*. But, Horn argues, the same does not hold for *exactly three*: *exactly three men entered the race early* does not entail, nor is it entailed by *exactly three men entered the race*. The (rather implicit) argument is that *three* cannot mean 'exactly three' because it does not have the same properties as *exactly three*, while *three* should mean 'at least three' because it does have the same properties as *at least three*. Paradoxically, for Horn's theory it is crucial that even though *three* may be interpreted as 'at least three' *three* does not have exactly the same meaning as *at least three* (otherwise his redundancy argument does not seem to make sense at all, because *at least three* would have to be as redundant as *exactly three* - actually it would have to be even *more* redundant). In other words for Horn's theory it is crucial that *three* in truth-conditional tests cannot simply be replaced by *at least three* (even though Horn assumes the meaning of *three* to be 'at least three'). Also the argument from negation which Horn seems to regard as essential would not work if *three* could simply be replaced by *at least three*, because while *not three* usually has a 'less than' reading, *not at least three* does not seem to have this reading by default (it could be used to convey 'more than three', 'less than three', 'at most three' etc.). Therefore, Horn cannot rely on evidence that is adduced from the comparison of *three* with *at least three* or *exactly three*, because if *three* could be replaced with *at least three* in all kinds of inferential tests (because they express the same (semantic) meaning), a number of Horn's other arguments would be endangered (e.g., the redundancy argument and the argument from negation).

Nevertheless, already in his (1989) volume, Horn starts to doubt the validity of his scalar account of numerals. Discussing some of the rival accounts of cardinals, Horn admits that it is "undeniable that the upper-bounding implicature mechanism behaves differently with respect to cardinals than it does with other scalar values (e.g., the quantificational determiners, modals, and first-order gradable contraries)" (Horn 1989:251). He refers to Sadock's (1984) argument concerning numerals in mathematical statements, as well as to Campbell's (1981) description of the different types of processing of numerals ("phenic" or "cryptic") (cf. section 3.3. for Sadock's and section 3.2.1. for Campbell's positions). Crucially, however, he does not abandon the essentials of his scalar account, not even with respect to numerals:

> the exactness built into the cardinals as against the noncardinal determiners and the greater knowledge or information consequently presupposed in their felicitous use certainly seem to add an additional reinforcement to the scalar implicata they induce. (Horn 1989:251)

Horn merely accepts the fact that the 'exactly' "implicature" may be less incontrovertible with cardinals, but he does not change his 'at least' analysis fundamentally: in Horn (1989) *three* still means 'at least three'.

Even though Horn changed his mind later on, the original minimalist view still lives on. Levinson (2000) is a point in case. At first sight, Levinson seems to have reservations, but eventually returns to the traditional perspective. He adopts some of the arguments against the minimalist view, such as the fact that some contexts induce scale reversals. Nevertheless, as I have indicated above, the phenomenon of "scale reversal" *is* accounted for in Horn's original theory (he commented on it already in 1972), and therefore does not seem to be the best argument against the classical neo-Gricean line. Levinson discusses some of the alternatives that have been proposed (especially the indeterminacy account is mentioned, cf. section 3.2. below), but then argues that the latter often confuse the status of GCIs, pragmatic intrusion and the general nature of semantic representations before pragmatic enrichment. He does not really qualify this claim, but states that in "math-literate cultures, there will be possible confusion between English *three* and the numeral '3', with a consequent bias towards an 'exactly three' interpretation" (Levinson 2000:89). This seems to be completely beside the point, however: the 'exactly n' analysis that some authors have proposed does not seem to be linked exclusively with the mathematical use of numerals (the 'exactly' interpretation is ascribed to perfectly "ordinary" uses of numerals, as in *Mary has three children*). He also refers to the observation that the upper bound inferences with cardinals may be stronger (cf. also Horn 1989), and to the fact that the 'exactly' interpretation of numerals is less strong for round numbers. But the latter arguments do not seem to be very strong either, especially in the light of the existence of much stronger counterarguments, e.g., 'at most' interpretations of numerals (it is not obvious how these are to be derived from an 'at least' meaning). He also refers to the old "lexical incorporation" argument (cf. words like *triple* in Horn 1972), but this seems to be more of an argument *against* the 'at least' analysis. Finally, Levinson accepts that numerals may have different interpretations in different syntactic and thematic positions and concludes that "[t]hese complicating factors and confusions are sufficient to make the number words *not* the correct testbed for the whole theory of scalar implicature" (Levinson 2000:90).

In a final twist, however, he argues that the scalar account should not be given up so quickly, because there are many Australian languages that have just three number words: these have numerals for 'one', 'two' and 'three or more'. The latter is the highest value in the scale, and implicature theory would predict that this will trigger no upper bound inference. This seems to be the case in these languages, as the word for 'three' is the same as that for 'quantities with more than three elements'. Interesting as this observation may be, it is not really an argument for the 'at least' analysis: if 'three' and 'more than three' are expressed by the same word, it is natural to accept both meanings as being covered by the *conventional* meaning of the numeral in question. The asymmetry between the numerals indicating 'one' and 'two' on the one hand and the word for 'three or more' on the other might just as well be caused by the fact that the numerical is not as sophisticated / complicated as ours. Moreover, while it is true that the neo-Gricean account predicts that the highest element on a scale will not trigger Q1-implicatures, it is not always the case that these highest elements have an 'at least' meaning: *all*, e.g., just means 'all'. It is not clear what 'at least all' could mean.

Levinson's eventual defense of the classical 'at least' line does not seem very convincing. Even though he accepts some of the evidence against the scalar account, and admits that numerals do not provide the best examples of scalar implicatures, his book contains very many examples with numerals: in his discussion of indexical resolution (p.178), "ellipsis unpacking" (p.183), the conditional (p.206), metalinguistic negation (p.213), negation in general (p.255), and a general discussion of pragmatic intrusion (p.247) the numerals are called upon to demonstrate certain allegedly Gricean phenomena.

3.1.2. Existentialist minimalism

In the history of the debate, many analysts have tried to nuance Horn's original line on cardinals. One important suggestion was made by De Cornulier (1984), who argues for the "minimalist" thesis (the 'at least' analysis), but interprets the original claims in an interesting way. Surprisingly, he also mentions the ambiguity analysis of numerals, of which he assumes that it has often been argued for:

> On a souvent pensé qu'il s'agissait d'une ambiguïté irréductible de l'expression linguistique de la quantité, et que, par exemple, le mot français *dix-huit* devrait se voir assigner deux valeurs, restrictive et non-restrictive, dans le dictionnaire. (de Cornulier 1984:661)

In fact, only Smith (1970) (cf. the discussion of Horn 1972 in section 3.1.1. above) and Richardson and Richardson (1990) have argued for this position[6]. With respect to the neo-Gricean analysis, de Cornulier admits that the "restrictive" interpretation of numerals is "banal", and he gives up the modular idea of a strict distinction between semantics and pragmatics. De Cornulier assumes that numerals can be interpreted "existentially", which is,

---

[6] As mentioned, Cohen (1971) argued for a Semantical Hypothesis, in which many of the Gricean phenomena are also considered to be part of the conventional meaning. He did not apply this reasoning to numerals, however. Neither can his Semantical Hypothesis be amalgamated with an ambiguity analysis because Cohen assumes the "weaker" meaning of items such as *and* to derive from cancellation or deletion of certain aspects of the stronger version in certain contexts. In Cohen's version there is also a hierarchy between different meanings and the inference from one meaning to the other is preserved as well. Also Hirschberg (1991 [1985]:92) seems to suggest an ambiguity analysis at times. She claims that "it is generally accepted that mention of a cardinal *n* may be ambiguous between *exactly n, at most n,* and *at least n*" (Hirschberg 1991 [1985]:92), but she does not make clear how these meanings associated with the "mentioning" of a numeral are derived from the "conventional" meaning of a numeral. Moreover, in other passages, she seems to accept Horn's scalar account.

crucially, distinct from claiming that these numerals have an 'at least' semantics. An interpretation of a numeral *n* as being "existentialist" means that it is interpreted as equivalent to the statement that *there exist* n things. This means that the entailment relation between, e.g., *three* and *two* can be preserved (if three things exist, also two things exist), but it avoids the disadvantages of the neo-Gricean 'at least' analysis: "L'analyse minimaliste ne présuppose ici [...] aucune occurrence de *au moins* sous-jacente dans une 'structure sémantique profonde' et qu'il faudrait 'gommer'" (de Cornulier 1984:668).

While de Cornulier defends (his own version of) the minimalist thesis, he does qualify his defense of the scalar analysis : "une proposition contenant une expression quantitative n'est associée à une échelle implicative que si son sens s'y prête" (de Cornulier 1984:680). De Cornulier assumes that the meaning of the verb of the utterance containing the numeral can influence the eventual interpretation of the numeral. *X coûte n francs à Z*, e.g., can have the meaning 'it is necessary that there are n francs that Z gives for buying X', but it can also have the meaning 'it is necessary and sufficient that there are n francs that Z gives for buying X'. De Cornulier assumes that the scalar account is compatible with the fact that one sense of *coûter* allows the inference from *X coûte 15 F.* to *X coûte 10 F.*, while another sense of *coûter* does not.

The consequences for the meaning analysis of numerals themselves are not really clear, however. De Cornulier admits that sometimes it appears as if the scalar account does not take into account the contextual elements influencing the interpretation; but in his opinion the scalar account should not be interpreted as implying that whenever a quantifier is used this quantifier has a "non-restrictive" ('at least') value. Considering Horn's original statements with respect to cardinals ("Numbers, then, or rather sentences containing them, assert lower-boundedness -- *at least n* -- and given tokens of utterances containing cardinal numbers may, depending on the context, implicate upper-boundedness -- *at most n* -- so that the number may be interpreted as denoting an exact quantity" - Horn 1972:41) this seems a rather broad interpretation of the original scalar account[7]. De Cornulier does not seem to realize that Horn does indeed work with a "deep", semantic 'at least' meaning in the scalar account, as the citation from Horn (1972) demonstrates. He even considers the 'at least' position to be a fabrication: "Entre le 'Minimalisme' universel - défendu peut-être par personne - et un Restrictivisme universel non moins aventureux, il y a place pour un 'minimalisme' circonstancié" (de Cornulier 1984:681). But this "minimalisme circonstancié" is of course nothing other than Horn's original account; he does not seem to understand that Horn considers this "minimalisme" to be more basic, more fundamental than the "restrictive" meaning, while this seems to contradict the intuitions concerning the "conventional" meaning of numerals.

De Cornulier's version of the scalar account is in fact much more tolerant and context-dependent[8] than the original one. The minimalism that he defends does not seem to rest on the

---

[7] De Cornulier consistently refers to Fauconnier (1976), but in that article Fauconnier simply uses Horn's (1972) account to reply to some of the objections of Anscombre and Ducrot (Anscombre 1975, Anscombre and Ducrot 1976, Ducrot 1972, 1973). Because Fauconnier's (1976) account of numerals is practically identical to that of Horn (1972), I have not discussed Fauconnier's article separately.

[8] For instance, de Cornulier argues that "[o]n peut très bien penser que la signification fondamentale de *X a 3 enfants* implique la signification fondamentale de *X a 2 enfants* sans se croire obligé à priori de penser qu'il en va

claim that the minimalist features of sentences containing numerals provides the "semantic", non-defeasible meaning of numerals. He does not seem to commit himself to a characterization of their meaning; he merely wants to show that numerals may have at least two different interpretations, and that one is linked to the concept of scales, while another is not: "L'analyse 'minimaliste' [...] doit être motivée cas par cas; il n'y a pas plus de raison de la généraliser par principe à toutes les expressions de quantité, que de la refuser par principe à toutes" (de Cornulier 1984:689). But, of course, Horn's claim that the 'lower bound' asserted by utterances containing numerals is *semantic*, and the fact that this semantic meaning is used as the starting-point for a Gricean working-out schema for the 'exactly' implicature (thus promoting it to the status of "conventional" meaning), implies the generalization of minimalism that de Cornulier seeks to avoid. De Cornulier's version is actually a serious improvement of the original scalar account, but, paradoxically, he does not seem to realize this. Especially his existentialist interpretation of numerals seems to the point: numerals have an "existential" meaning, which means that the existence of a higher quantity is not included, nor excluded:

> En posant que les expressions qui expriment littéralement l' 'existence' d'une quantité *Q* n'impliquent pas la non-existence d'une quantité supérieure, l'analyse minimaliste n'implique pas que ces expressions signifient littéralement que '*Q* est un minimum', ou signifient '*Q* ou plus que *Q*'; les paraphrases du type *Q au moins*, ou *Q ou plus (que Q)*, ne sont que des traductions, commodes, mais inexactes: elles consistent évidemment à compléter la signification littérale de l'énoncé de manière à bloquer l'implicature restrictive qui pourrait se produire en leur absence, ou inversement à imposer une valeur restrictive. (de Cornulier 1984:89)

It is this characterization of the meaning of a numeral that will be the basis of my own analysis of numerals: an NP containing a numeral *n* asserts the existence of a number of elements and does not say anything about the possibility of there being more than n elements[9]. Unfortunately, de Cornulier seems to be so impressed by the apparent "power" of Horn scales that he does not realize that his version of the "minimalist" account is actually more independent of Horn's (and Fauconnier's 1976) scalar account than he is willing to admit. Crucially, he does not seem to realize that his existentialist account is rather different from the

---

de même pour les propositions *Il est 3 heures* et *Il est 2 heures* considérées globalement (de Cornulier 1984:681). De Cornulier is one of the few analysts of numerals who seem to realize that numerals can have very different functions and that this functional diversity has important consequences for the interpretation of the "value" of these numerals.

[9] In a short passage in a much more extensive discussion of two interpretations of "truth", van der Auwera suggests a similar analysis of utterances containing numerals: "[...] I would claim that the literal meaning of the assertion that B and C have three children is just the combination of the speaking-as-if-one-believes meaning [the assertive meaning] and the phrastic meaning that says that B and C have three children, *leaving it undecided whether they have exactly three children or more than three*"(van der Auwera 1985:106 - emphasis added). Leech (1983) seems to make a similar comment (although he does not directly connect it with the analysis of numerals) in his formulation of a "neutral version" of an implicature: the neutral version of the 'not all' implicature (expressed in a proposition P) of *some* is '[The speaker] does not believe that *P* is true, nor does [the speaker] believe that *P* is false' (Leech 1983:86). The latter seems to involve a non-committal attitude that is similar to what is expressed in de Cornulier's and van der Auwera's comments.

original scalar account, in that de Cornulier assumes an "existential" conventional meaning, while Horn and Fauconnier assume an 'at least' meaning. De Cornulier may well exclaim "L'existentialisme est un minimalisme!" (de Cornulier 1984:669), but in fact, it is not.

3.1.3. Salience and activation

For some researchers, the context-dependence of the interpretation of numerals turned out to be one of the most important arguments for an entirely different analysis (the underspecification or underdeterminacy analysis, cf. section 3.2. below). Others tried to incorporate minimalism into larger theoretical frameworks, emphasizing information-structural properties and effects, but holding on to (some version of) an 'at least' semantics for cardinals. Three important examples of the latter strategy are Fretheim (1992), Van Kuppevelt (1996) and Kadmon (2001).

During the last decade of the previous century, the discussions of numerals begin to emphasize the importance of factors influencing the interpretation of cardinals, rather than concentrating on the question of whether these interpretations are semantic or pragmatic (even though the latter question of course remains an important point of debate). Fretheim (1992) nuances Horn's 'at least' analysis, rather than outright attacking it: he claims that the upper bound (implicature) analysis is only possible when the cardinal is "less salient", otherwise the cardinal has an 'exactly' meaning. Fretheim supports this claim by referring to different judgments concerning the sentences *If four women were rescued by a helicopter, then four women were rescued* and *Four women were rescued, if four women were rescued by a helicopter*: Fretheim's informants said that they felt that the first was necessarily true much more often than the second. Fretheim links this with differences in the salience of *four*: in the first sentence, *four* is already present in the first part of the sentence (the antecedent of the conditional) and this makes *four* contextually more salient with respect to the occurrence in the second part. In the second this is not the case, which causes the occurrence of four women to be "new" and this newness is assumed to trigger the 'exactly' interpretation (Fretheim does not explain the link between "newness" and 'exactly' interpretations, however). Fretheim also observes that when a numeral is "rhematized" (as in *the number of women who were rescued is four*), no 'at least' reading is possible, and neither can *three* acquire an 'at least' meaning as the answer to the question *How many children do you have?* He argues that someone giving that answer "would actually be telling a lie if he happened to have more than three children" (Fretheim 1992:6), and claims that the cancellation phrase *in fact four* is much more difficult in that context - it would have to be analyzed as a case of repair. Moreover, the cancellation test seems problematic also in other contexts, because *in fact four* ought to mean 'at least four' according to Horn's account[10]. The rest of Fretheim's paper is devoted to a rather technical description of how speakers can use intonation to select 'at least' or 'exactly' uses of numerals:

---

[10] Fretheim argues that this cancellation phrase seems to generate exactly the same implicature as the one it is supposed to cancel, but this is not correct: the cancellation phrase cancels the 'not more than three' implicature and, in Horn's analysis, generates the implicature 'not more than four'. But Fretheim is right when he argues that there is a problem with the cancellation phrase, even though it is not the one he indicates. According to Horn's analysis, the hearer of *three, in fact four* has to interpret this rather simple phrase as follows: first the cardinality

My conclusion is that an addressee processing a Norwegian utterance containing a numeral must rely on context-based inference in her attempt to determine whether the speaker intended the numeral to mean 'exactly *n*' or 'at least *n*', but in this inferential process she will always be guided by the speaker's choice of intonational phrasing (Fretheim 1992:5-6)

I will not go into the details of the data on Norwegian intonation presented by Fretheim. I will only signal that in his (1995) "Postscript" (in Kasher 1998:509-511) to his (1992) paper, he replaced his nuanced critique of Horn's original position by an underdeterminacy account à la Carston (1988). He also pointed at the fact that numerals can have an 'at least' meaning even if the numeral is not presented as salient in the discourse (e.g., in sentences such as *You must be eighteen to be admitted here*).

Fretheim's article is interesting because it is the first to concentrate on the importance of intonation on the interpretation of numerals. The link he perceives between "newness" and 'exactly' interpretations of numerals seems to correspond with intuitions, and his statement that in some contexts *three* simply cannot be used to denote 'at least three' without lying (e.g., as the answer to a *how many* question) is convincing as well. His eventual adoption of the underdeterminacy account seems a bit *ad hoc*, however. In his "Postscript", no arguments are given for the correctness of this account.

Van Kuppevelt's (1996) paper sets out to tackle a number of problems related to Horn's concept of scales. He primarily tries to formulate a theory that explains the *activation* of scales (as part of a larger theory called Discourse Topic Theory): his theory is assumed to explain why some uses of scalar operators seem to trigger implicatures, while others do not. His article is especially interesting because he exemplifies his theory by means of utterances containing numerals[11]. His principal claim is that scales are activated only when the scalar element is in "comment position" (underlined in the examples), which means that it is construed as the answer to a question, as in (1):

(1) Q: How many children do you have?
  A: I have <u>three</u> children.

Numerals that are not in comment position, as in (2), do not activate the corresponding scale and receive "a monotone increasing interpretation" in the sense that "adding more referents than fourteen does not change the truth value of the sentence containing this expression" (Van Kuppevelt 1996:406).

---

is determined as being 'at least three', this is turned into 'exactly three' by an implicature, this implicature is canceled by the cancellation phrase *if not four*, then the numeral mentioned in this cancellation phrase is interpreted as 'at least four', and finally the latter is turned into 'exactly four' by yet another implicature. The complexity of this reasoning does not seem to match the intuitively rather simple interpretation of the phrase.

[11] With respect to the question whether there is a difference between numerals and other scalars, Van Kuppevelt explicitly states that there are none, and demonstrates this with a number of examples. I will not go into this discussion, however, as it does not directly contribute to the analysis of the cardinals.

(2)   Q: Who has fourteen children?
       A: <u>Nigel</u> has fourteen children.

Van Kuppevelt does not explicitly commit himself to the claim that numerals in non-comment position have an 'at least' semantics, but his statement concerning the "monotone increasing interpretation" of *fourteen* certainly suggests that he believes this to be the case. When the numeral is in comment position, as in (1), the scale is activated and a scalar inference is triggered, except when the numeral in question is the highest value on the scale (e.g. *all* does not trigger an inference), or when the answer is "unsatisfactory". The latter means that the "topic range" (which consists of all the possible answers to the question) is not reduced to one unique determination; in other words: when the answer that is provided is not considered to be conclusive. One of Horn's (1992) examples is used to illustrate this notion:

(3)   Q1   A: <How many of your friends are linguists?>
             Are <u>many</u> of your friends linguists?
       A1   B: Yes,
       <Q2> <How many?>
       A2   (In fact) <u>all</u> of them.

Van Kuppevelt argues that A1 is unsatisfactory, given the succeeding extension A2, and this explains why no scalar inference is triggered by *many*. In his theory, questions like question Q2 are only hypothetically present; they needn't be uttered (and the example is quite natural without the intervening question).
      Another famous example is explained through the concept of "topic weakening": in (4) the range of possible answers is reduced to two options: 'two or more' and 'less than two'.

(4)   F1   A: I'm a mother.
       Q1   Do I get a fixed amount of state benefit?
       A1   B: If you have at least two children, you get a fixed amount
                   state benefit.
       <Q2>   <How many children do you have?>
       A2   A: I have <u>two</u> children. (In fact I have four).

The reduction of the topic set causes *two* to be interpreted as 'at least two': the context makes clear that only 'at least two' and 'less than two' are relevant answers, and the answer *two* excludes the 'less than' option, so that the 'at least two' interpretation is selected. This does not trigger an upper bound inference, because it is the highest element of the (reduced) scale.
      Moreover, Van Kuppevelt's analysis also readily explains why numerals in comment position (5) seem to trigger inferences that are harder to contradict than numerals in non-comment position (6).

(5)   Q: How many children does Nigel have?
       A: ??Nigel has <u>fourteen </u>children. In fact he has twenty.
(6)   Q: Who has fourteen children?

> A: <u>Nigel</u> has fourteen children. In fact he has twenty.

In (6), no upper bound inference is triggered, hence there is no contradiction. This seems to be the right prediction. Van Kuppevelt makes clear that the upper bound inference, as in (5), is not defeasible: "an upper bound scalar inference [...] is an entailment and not a weaker pragmatic inference which can be canceled without causing contradiction" (Van Kuppevelt 1996:413).

Van Kuppevelt's information-structural amendments to Horn's original 'at least' analysis are certainly an improvement. The examples he provides demonstrate that a unified univocal + implicature analysis of numerals does not make the right predictions. Contextual information has to bear on the interpretation of numerals. Nevertheless, Van Kuppevelt sometimes seems to exaggerate the explanatory value of his topic-comment representations. He discusses Fretheim's (1992) judgment that cardinals only acquire an 'exactly' interpretation via an implicature when they are part of what Van Kuppevelt calls the background (which he equates with the "topic part", i.e., "non-comment part" of an utterance, even though this does not seem to correspond exactly to what Fretheim has in mind[12]). First, he argues that no evidence exists that in the latter case an implicature is triggered. This is highly questionable, however: if no cancellation phrase were present in (6A), it is very likely that an implicature 'not more than fourteen' *will* be triggered, even though the numeral is not in comment position. Second, he refers to (7) and argues that the fact that the subquestion *How many children does he have?* is possible indicates that no implicature is triggered.

(7)   Who has fourteen children?
       <u>Nigel</u> has fourteen children.
       <How many children does he have?>
       He has <u>twenty</u>.

This is a more elegant version of the cancellation test[13], but, crucially, the fact that the second question is possible in (45) does not really demonstrate that *fourteen* in (7) does not trigger the implicature, because it is easy to imagine that the conversation in (7) continues with a different question after the turn *Nigel has fourteen children*, e.g. with the question *Who else has so many children?* In that case, it is likely that the utterance *Nigel has fourteen children* does trigger an implicature, even though *fourteen* is not in comment position. This is a general problem in Van Kuppevelt's theory: since Van Kuppevelt relies on hypothetical questions and does not always consider the full range of possibilities, the evidence based on these questions

---

[12] The antecedents of conditionals that Fretheim gives as examples do not seem to establish the numeral as part of the topic (they are part of a conditional *if*-clause). Fretheim focuses on the degree of "newness" of the information, which is not exactly the same as what Van Kuppevelt means with "being part of the topic". In this discussion, Van Kuppevelt's topic-comment function (which seems to correspond more to the traditional notion of "focus", cf. Chapter 5) seems to be more relevant than the "new"-"old" distinction Fretheim refers to (though both are of course related in the sense that new information will often be focused on).

[13] Van Kuppevelt also discusses the suspension test: he assumes that the numerals in *Nigel has <u>fourteen</u> children, <u>if not fifteen</u>* (when in comment position) do not provide satisfactory answers because of the "epistemic limitation" signaled by the suspension phrase. Also, *fourteen* does not trigger the 'no more than fourteen' inference, but the whole answer *fourteen, if not fifteen* does trigger the 'not more than fifteen' inference.

cannot be conclusive. The fact that an answer can be construed as "unsatisfactory" does not mean that it actually *is* construed as inconclusive, and if it is not, an implicature will often be triggered, contrary to what Van Kuppevelt predicts.

In his discussion of Sadock's (1978) reinforceability argument, he argues that it can be used to demonstrate that numerals only trigger implicatures in comment position.

(8) How many cookies did Billy eat?
    ??Billy ate three cookies but not all.

(9) Who ate three cookies?
    Billy ate three cookies, but not all.

In (8) the *but not all* phrase is awkward and according to Van Kuppevelt this is caused by the fact that in (8) an implicature is triggered. This creates the redundancy effect. In (9) the numeral is not in comment position, no implicature is triggered, and there is no unacceptable redundancy. Again, this is an insightful refinement of the neo-Gricean canon, but it is still too simple to account for all uses of numerals. The cancellation phrases *and only three* and *and no more than three* in (10) and (11), e.g., are compatible with a construal of the numeral in comment position.

(10) How many cookies did Billy eat?
     Billy ate three and only three cookies.

(11) How many cookies did Billy eat?
     Billy ate three and no more than three cookies.

In (11), there is no unacceptable redundancy, even though there should be according to Van Kuppevelt's theory. The "reinforcement" phrase simply stresses the fact that the possibility that Billy ate more than three cookies is excluded.

Another example of how Van Kuppevelt's account is too rigid to account for the flexibility of the interpretation of numerals is given in (12).

(12) [Who bought four books?]
     Did Harry buy four books?
     No, in fact he bought five.

The acceptability of the answer *no* is hard to explain in Van Kuppevelt's theoretical framework: the numeral *four* is in non-comment position, and therefore receives an 'at least' interpretation. Nevertheless, the answer *no* seems to be acceptable, which is a problem for his theory since if one has bought five books, one has also bought at least four books (in the truth-conditional perspective on meaning that Van Kuppevelt explicitly accepts).

Finally, he also tackles 'at most' interpretations of sentences like (13).

(13) Jane can have 2000 calories a day without putting on weight.

Van Kuppevelt argues that when (13) functions as an answer to the question *How many calories can Jane have a day without putting on weight?* the numeral also triggers an upper bound scalar inference. This is certainly correct, but it misses the point: the point of 'at most' examples (cf. the discussion of Carston's 1988 examples below) is that the *lower* bound, which is considered to be indefeasible, seems to have vanished: (13) is consistent with the fact that Jane can eat less than 2000 calories without putting on weight. As mentioned, Van Kuppevelt does not really make clear what his position is with respect to the lexical meaning of numerals, but his comments suggest that he does not feel the need to change Horn's original 'at least' proposal. This implies, however, that his information-structural account, whatever its attractions, cannot serve as the basis of a unified analysis of numerals. Even though Van Kuppevelt amends Horn's theory to a considerable extent, his own analysis still relies too much on inferences, rather than on an investigation of lexical meaning. Of course, his theory explicitly focuses on the explanation of the former, and not on the latter, but the many problems for his account of numerals crucially derive from the fact that Van Kuppevelt, like many other neo-Griceans, does not start from a well-founded description of the conventional meaning of cardinals.

To wrap up the discussion of the way in which minimalism evolved during the past three decades, I will show how Kadmon's (2001) account essentially remains compatible with Horn's minimalism, however insightful her information-structural critique of his perspective may be. Kadmon already devoted an entire chapter to the analysis of numerals in her (1987) dissertation. In that chapter, she accepted the traditional neo-Gricean analysis (contra a suggestion by Hans Kamp that numerals should be analyzed as having an 'exactly' semantics). I will not discuss this (1987) discussion separately because it seems very much in line with Horn's original (1972) analysis, even if it is framed in a different theory, namely that of Discourse Representation Theory ("DRT", cf. Kamp and Reyle 1993). Kadmon insightfully restricts her attention to what she calls the N CN constructions of numerals ("numeral common noun") and argues that this construction should be treated as the DRT representation of the indefinite noun phrase. This means that the NP *three pink cats* is described as the combination of the following elements: 'cats (X)' + 'X are pink' + '$|X|=3$'. The latter notation is taken to mean that there is no indication in the NP that it is the set of *all* pink cats (in the domain of discourse). She also points out that there are differences in the interpretation of numerals with respect to their position in the clause: in predicative positions, such as in *The guests are four women and one man* numerals always receive an 'exactly n' interpretation. She accepts the neo-Gricean 'at least' analysis of numerals, mainly for the familiar truth-conditional reasons, but emphasizes that this does not mean that *three* and *at least three* have the same semantic representation: the first has two possible interpretations (with or without the 'no more than three' implicature). She also presents evidence from the interpretation of anaphora.

(14) Ten kids walked into the room. They were making an awful lot of noise.
(15) At least ten kids walked into the room. They were making an awful lot of noise.

While *they* in (15) may refer back to, e.g., twelve kids who walked into the room, this interpretation is not available in (14): in that utterance *they* must refer to ten and no more than ten kids.

Kadmon's (2001) volume on "formal pragmatics" also contains a chapter on "NPs with numeral determiners". She discusses Horn's account and also Kamp's 'exactly' account. The latter is problematic because it is not clear how we can go from an 'exactly' meaning to an 'at least' meaning by means of a pragmatic mechanism. She especially considers the possibility of "domain narrowing" (in which the utterance containing the NP is evaluated with respect to a pragmatically restricted set of referents): in that reasoning, *Leif has four chairs* is true on an 'exactly' reading of *four*, even if Leif actually has ten chairs, because the domain of the NP is narrowed to, e.g. "the number of chairs that Leif is willing to lend" (Kadmon 2001:71). Kadmon replies that this account is quite *ad hoc* and that it offers the wrong prediction that the sentence would be true if Leif has more than four chairs to lend.

This does not seem to be very convincing though. The "domain narrowing" account does not seem to make the wrong predictions when the context is taken into account. Indeed, if the concept of "domain narrowing" is construed so that it is made dependent on what is relevant in the given situation, it will not make the wrong predictions at all. If someone requests four extra chairs in order to enable four people to sit, then an 'exactly' reading of *four* in *Leif has four chairs* is compatible with what is meant, in the sense that it means that Leif has the requested set of four chairs, and this set contains four elements, no more, no less. This suggests that a combination of relevance-theoretic considerations with the concept of "domain narrowing" could solve Kadmon's problem with the 'exactly' account. But there is of course additional evidence against an 'exactly' semantics for numerals, and this evidence indeed shows that an 'exactly' semantics is not the best way to start the analysis of the different interpretations of numerals: Kadmon emphasizes the fact that *exactly* in *exactly three chairs* does not seem to be redundant.

Therefore, she repeats her (1987) claim that N CN constructions should be analyzed as simple indefinite NPs, with the extra requirement that the cardinality of the set indicated by the NP is determined as *n*. In DRT terms this means that the N CN construction *three pink cats* is true if the variable X (standing for the set) "can be matched with a set of three pink cats in the model [...] regardless of whether there are more pink cats, outside of that set" (Kadmon 2001:71). Again, she turns to the implicature account and assumes that when such an implicature is triggered the content of this implicature is added to the information[14], thus triggering an 'exactly' interpretation of the numeral. In this respect, Kadmon does not seem to make a rigid distinction between the lexical semantics of a numeral and the inferences triggered by the utterances containing the numeral either.

Nevertheless, her account is remarkably close to the "existential" analysis (de Cornulier 1984), which does try to keep the two levels separate. In fact, Kadmon's (2001) account refers to the "existential quantification" that is supposed to range over the whole discourse in DRT analyses: this is a clear qualification of Horn's 'at least' analysis. She

---

[14] As Scharten (1997) already remarked, latter-day semantic theories no longer work with a strictly truth-conditional perspective on meaning. The accounts Kadmon works with conceptualize meaning as the "updating" of information (cf. also Heim's (1983) "filing card" metaphor).

nuances traditional minimalism, which is also demonstrated by the fact that she does not consider *three* and *at least three* to be different: "*Three cats are pink* states that there is a set of exactly three cats, while *At least three cats* states that there is a set of at least three pink cats" (Kadmon 2001:72). Her statement that the former refers to a set of *exactly* three cats is confusing (given the fact that she explicitly refuses to adopt an 'exactly' semantics), but the general point is clear: NPs containing *three* assert the existence of a set containing three elements, and nothing is said with respect to the possibility of there being more than three elements. This insight makes Kadmon's analysis very valuable, even though the over-all analysis of the conventional meaning is not always crystal clear. Especially the lack of a clear definition of what the term "exactly n interpretation" means seems to cause confusion.

In a number of final remarks, she says that the 'exactly n' reading of numerals arises very often because "in most situations where one would bother to mention a number at all, exact cardinality would be relevant information" (Kadmon 2001:73). This seems to suggest relevance-theoretic considerations once again, but Kadmon never explicitly refers to Relevance Theory. Also, one may wonder why this 'exactly n' meaning that Kadmon supposes to be so prominent is not promoted to the status of "conventional meaning". She also refers to the fact that this 'exactly' reading may be caused by anaphoric use of NPs containing numerals: "such anaphora [force] an "exactly" reading of the indefinite antecedent" (Kadmon 2001:73). This is an interesting observation, but her reference to the "uniqueness" property of definite NPs as the deeper motivation behind this phenomenon seems to be a bit *ad hoc*. I will propose that it is not the anaphoricity or uniqueness of definite NPs that triggers the 'exactly' interpretation but the "definiteness" itself, which can be associated with "identifiability" (cf. Chapter 5, section 5.1.2. below).

3.2. UNDERSPECIFICATION

3.2.1. Early approaches and formulations

Around the time when Horn was finishing his dissertation, the French linguist Ducrot started to develop a theory of meaning and conversation that closely resembles Grice's earlier efforts. Later on, Anscombre joined Ducrot in refining this theory.

Their *loi d'exhaustivité*, e.g., is clearly reminiscent of Grice's Q1-maxim: "Cette loi exige que le locuteur donne, sur le thème dont il parle, les rensignements les plus forts qu'il possède, et qui sont susceptibles d'intéresser le destinataire" (Ducrot 1972:134), and also their examples sound familiar: "il nous semble peu contestable que l'énoncé *Certains chapitres sont intéressants dans ce livre* donne à entendre d'habitude: 'Certains ne le sont pas'. Cet élément [...] ne peut cependant pas être décrit comme posé [...]" (Ducrot 1972:135). Finally Ducrot's "échelles argumentatives" closely resemble Horn's concept of scales, and the claim that negation and *seulement* reverse the scale, or rather, "la valeur argumentative" is present as well (Ducrot 1973:237)[15].

The theory of argumentation developed by Ducrot and Anscombre differs from Grice's (and Horn's) in a number of respects, and the concept of "argumentative value" seems especially interesting. Other than in Horn's definition of scales, the elements on the "échelles argumentatives" are not ordered in terms of entailment but in terms of the relative strength they have as arguments for one and the same conclusion: these arguments are considered to be part of a "classe argumentative" (Ducrot 1973:227) and an argument *p* will be considered as stronger than an argument *p'* with respect to the conclusion *r* if it is accepted that if one concludes *r* on the basis of *p*, one will also accept *r* on the basis of *p'*, but not *vice versa*. The distinction with Horn's scales is that the "point" of the conversation is allowed to influence the interpretation of linguistic items and constructions much more, and, consequently, that it is not so tempting to derive conventional meanings of items from their position on the scale, or from their truth-conditional meaning:

> On voit [...] comment nous essayons d'intégrer à la description sémantique l'indication des conditions de vérité; nous refusons d'en faire le centre de la description, car nous croyons qu'elle est déterminée par d'autres caractères sémantiques, l' argumentativité par exemple (Ducrot 1973:247)[16].

Unfortunately, while Ducrot's theory seems very interesting with respect to the analysis of cardinals, and even though he does include examples containing numerals (he proposes a scale with the elements <*La place coûte 30 francs, La place coûte 20 francs, La place coûte 10 francs*), he is rather hesitant to use many of them:

> Disons tout de suite que, par prudence, nous allons exclure de notre étude les énoncés strictement numériques, ceux qui présentent une information ponctuelle repérable dans une échelle de propriétés objectivement quantifiées (nous exclurons aussi, par conséquent, *La température est de 12°, Pierre mesure 1,70m*, ou *Nous sommes à 100 km de Paris*) (Ducrot 1973:241)

Their reason for excluding numerals from their argumentative theory is that the combination with negation does not seem to reverse the scale, which, according to their theory, it should. Ducrot is bothered by the fact that *la place ne coûte pas 10 francs* and *la place coûte 10 francs* apparently can be used with the same argumentative value, e.g. when trying to argue that the ticket is cheap. Surprisingly, Ducrot does not seem to realize that the negative version is actually a better argument than the positive version, because the former says that the ticket

---

[15] Apparently, they were unaware of the resemblances with Grice's theory of conversation. Anscombre and Ducrot (1978:43) mention Grice's conversational maxims but there is no suggestion that they have borrowed their "lois de discours" from his *Logic and conversation* lectures.

[16] The deeper motivation for this theoretical move seems to be that the concept of "entailment" is "trop liée [...] à une activité particulière, le raisonnement, pour pouvoir décrire des faits généraux de langue - même si on ajoute aux implications de la logique standard des "quasi-implications pragmatiques" (Anscombre and Ducrot 1978:43).

actually costs less than 10 francs, while the positive version says that it costs 10 francs. Contrary to what Ducrot himself claims ("les énoncés numériques - source de problèmes" - Ducrot 1973:242), his theory of argumentation is capable of describing the meanings of numerals very well, precisely because (as I will demonstrate in the corpus analysis of English cardinals) the "valeur argumentative" may steer the interpretation of numerals so that they come to acquire 'at least' or 'at most' meanings.

In his analysis of *quelques* he seems to anticipate what will later be called an "underdeterminacy" analysis: he argues that on the semantic level, we do not have to decide whether *quelques* means 'quelques au moins' or 'quelques seulement'. At this level, it suffices to situate *quelques* on a scale with *beaucoup* and *tous* and the structure in which *quelques* is used will determine the eventual interpretation: as part of the antecedent of conditionals such as *Si tu as lu quelques livres de Chomsky, tu sais cela* it will acquire the 'at least' meaning (because if having read some books by Chomsky is sufficient to know something, then having read all of them is sufficient as well), but if it is part of a simple statement, it will acquire the 'exactly' meaning ('quelques seulement'), because the assertion *J'ai lu quelques livres de Chomsky* licenses the inference that the speaker has not read all of Chomsky's books[17]. Unfortunately, Ducrot's (1972) theory is rather chaotic; it is difficult to extract a clear picture of what his theory really comes down to, and his analysis of numerals is unfortunately very hesitant. On the other hand, the concept of argumentative value is an intelligent way of introducing the rhetorical structure of a conversation into the description of the meanings of utterances. Much of neo-Gricean theory on numerals does not consider the rhetorical structure of the utterances containing numerals. This is one of the important deficiencies of the 'at least' analysis of cardinals.

In a later article, Anscombre and Ducrot (1978) seem to be less hesitant to use examples with numerals. In their discussion of Fauconnier (1976) (which is a defense of the analysis proposed in Horn (1972) against the "argumentative" analysis of Ducrot and Anscombre), they refer to the utterance *Ca n'est pas cher, ça coûte 10F., peut-être même 8 F.* to show that the entailment relationship between utterances containing higher and lower numbers is reversed or even becomes irrelevant when they are used as arguments for a certain conclusion. According to Anscombre and Ducrot, it is not the truth-conditional entailment relationship that determines the interpretation of the numerals, but their "argumentative value".

Another interesting example they use does not contain numerals, but the general point is valid for the 'at least' analysis of numerals as well. In the scalar analysis of quantifiers, having drunk a quantity x means having drunk at least x. This means that the question *Quelle quantité Pierre a-t-il bue?* means 'quelle quantité Pierre a-t-il au moins bue?', which leads to the conclusion that there are an infinite number of answers to the question *Quelle quantité Pierre a-t-il bue?*, while intuition tells us that only one answer is the correct one. Of course, neo-Griceans will argue that the 'at least' meaning is actually turned into an 'exactly' meaning

---

[17] Anscombre and Ducrot (1976) also anticipate Levinson's concept of "pragmatic intrusion" (Levinson 2000): they claim that the use of *puisque* in *Je pars demain, puisque tu dois tout savoir* can only be understood if it is taken to refer to the *uttering* of the first part and not to its *meaning*. This argument is also reminiscent of the arguments used to defend the Performative Hypothesis in speech-act theory (cf. Levinson 1983:255 for discussion).

due to an implicature. Anscombre and Ducrot reply that the 'at least' analysis (which they label "le minimalisme") "impose tantôt de faire intervenir, tantôt de ne pas faire intervenir la Loi d'Exhaustivité [Grice's Q1 maxim], sans qu'il semble possible d'expliciter les mécanismes qui la déclenchent" (Anscombre and Ducrot 1978:59). Moreover, in a passage that seems to anticipate Atlas' (1979) later claims, they point out that logical relations do not tell us anything about the linguistic meaning of an element:

> [Le logicien] peut dire que tout ensemble de 15 éléments a des sous-ensembles de 10 éléments, ou, non sans une certaine audace, que toute réalité mesurable par le nombre 15 contient comme partie une réalité à laquelle on doit affecter, dans le même système de mesure, le nombre 10 - de sorte qu'une somme de 15F. contient une somme de 10 F. Mais cela ne nous apprend rien sur les prédicats linguistiques "coûter 10 F." et "coûter 15 F." (Anscombre et Ducrot 1978:61)

Out of the many analyses and principles proposed by Ducrot and Anscombre, especially the latter, more general claim seems to be important. They do not really focus on the analysis of cardinals (evidently, their analysis concentrates on items that seem to have an explicit "argumentative" value, like *même*), but their examples make clear that the "argumentative value" of an utterance containing numerals seems to influence the interpretation of these numerals. Moreover, with respect to the interpretation of numerals, the concept of "argumentative value" is not only more plausible than the 'at least' analysis (because it does not rely on counter-intuitive 'at least' meanings), it is also more precise: while in the neo-Gricean analysis the interpretations of numerals in utterances that seem to contradict the normal entailment relationships are explained away by invoking the concept of "scale-reversal", the discussion in terms of "argumentative value" grounds the interpretation of those utterances in the general rhetorical structure of the text or conversation.

Another early formulation of a version of the underspecification analysis can be found in Harnish's (1976) article. It has been widely quoted because it offers one of the first extensive and critical accounts of the consequences of Grice's theory of conversation. He was also one of the first to use the concept of "underdeterminacy" in this context. In general, Harnish seems to follow Grice's original proposals rather rigidly. He is even ready to accept rather extreme consequences of the original program, because he commits himself to a program in which the "logical form" represents "those features of a sentence that play an essential role in entailments" (Harnish 1976:313). In some cases, the neglect of a methodological foundation for the selection of the "conventional" meaning leads to rather surprising meaning postulates. Considering the fact that the utterance *Russell wrote Principia* usually is interpreted as 'Russell alone wrote *Principia*', he even suggests that "what is said" by *Russell wrote Principia* is '(at least) Russell wrote *Principia*'. The 'at least' semantics for numerals is highly counter-intuitive, but the stipulation that what is said by *Russell wrote Principia* is that *at least* Russell wrote the Principia just seems outrageous. For this study, however, it is mainly the short section in which he uses examples containing numerals that is important. And, contrary to what one would expect on the basis of the foregoing, his analysis of numerals is actually much more context-sensitive than Horn's original 'at least' analysis.

With respect to the analysis of cardinals, the most important part of Harnish's paper centers around the following example:

> suppose that you bet me that there will be 20 people at the talk tonight. We arrive and there are 25 people there. Who wins? There may be some temptation in both directions, but that seems to be because the question is *underdetermined*. It seems that the sentence *There will be 20 people there* can be used to make the following claims: (i) There will be at most 20 people there. (ii) There will be exactly 20 people there. (iii) There will be at least 20 people there. (Harnish 1976:326 - emphasis added)

The citation makes clear that 1) Harnish already took into account the possibility that an utterance containing a numeral is interpreted as containing an 'at most' use of the cardinal[18], and 2) that what later will be called the underdeterminacy analysis of numerals has actually been around since 1976 (even before Atlas' 1979 more general suggestions in that direction) (cf. also Carston 1998a for a similar observation). Moreover, Harnish makes clear that it is the context that will decide which interpretation will be selected. As his sketch of a possible context shows, Harnish's analysis comes very close to what Anscombre and Ducrot argue for in their theory of the "argumentative value":

> Suppose that in the situation imagined, I had been complaining about the poor attendance at talks and you reply with [*There will be 20 people there*] - against the mutual understanding that 20 people is a good turnout. In this context, what you said could have been paraphrased as [*There will be at least 20 people there*], and so you would win the bet. Another context could have changed the force of my utterance to either of the other two. (Harnish 1976:326)

Even though Harnish is not very explicit with respect to the conventional meaning of numerals, he does accept a logical definition of numerals that implies that numerals have 'exactly' meanings. In other words, Harnish accepts a definition of numerals that is inconsistent with the entailment relations that many neo-Griceans assume to be fundamental for their meaning analysis. Harnish even explicitly accepts the fact that the utterance *There are two events of going to Cleveland* entails *It is not the case that there is one event of going to Cleveland* and the fact that if *Two people are in the room* is true than *Therefore, one person is in the room* must be false (Harnish 1976:326-327). Apparently, the facts concerning entailment relationships between sentences containing numerals are not as evident as Horn (1972) considers them to be. Unfortunately, he does not try to explain how this 'exactly' meaning of numerals can be turned into 'at least' and 'at most' readings in the betting example.

Campbell's (1981) paper is yet another example of an article that is not specifically geared to the analysis of cardinals, while it does contain some interesting remarks concerning the neo-Gricean analysis of numerals. Again, it is not directly critical of the minimalist thesis, but it does cast some doubt over the 'at least' analysis. Campbell's main intention is to

---

[18] Contrary to Carston (1998a), Harnish does not really exemplify this 'at most' reading. Furthermore, the contexts in which such an 'at most' reading might be likely to occur are not specified.

demonstrate that the old distinction between conscious and unconscious psychological structures and processes is still relevant: the first refers to "effortful, reportable cognition" and is called "phenic", while the second is identified with effortless, unreportable cognition and labeled "cryptic" (Campbell 1981:95). Interestingly, Campbell uses Horn's (1972) analysis to illustrate this difference. He points at the fact that the 'exactly' interpretation of *two* in (16) does not seem to involve conscious effort: "it is hard to imagine A in this situation deliberating *does B mean exactly 2 or at least 2?* and resolving the equivocality of the scalar [by a Gricean working-out schema]" (Campbell 1981:99).

(16)   A: How many children do you have?
         B: Two.

On the other hand, the interpretation of *two* in (17) does seem to involve conscious effort.

(17)   A: Do you have two children?

This use of *two* may be taken as 'at least two' or 'exactly two', depending on the context. Campbell argues that in the context of (17) it is probable that the hearer will try to determine the speaker's exact intentions by initiating a repair (*Do you mean exactly 2 or at least 2?*) or by treating the question as an indirect request for information and answering *I have four*, rather than merely answering by *yes* or *no*. He concludes: "So my claim here is that under different circumstances a listener may be aware or unaware of the equivocality of a scalar and may resolve the equivocality by effortless or by effortful inference" (Campbell 1981:99).

Even though Campbell accepts Horn's analysis, the 'at least' analysis of cardinals is used more as an example of his psychological notions than as an actual endorsement. Campbell even inserts hedges with respect to the validity of Horn's analysis (Campbell 1981:99). The intuitively plausible phenomena he presents are interesting in that they seem to constitute a problem for the 'at least' analysis: if it is indeed true that *two* in (16) is "cryptically", i.e. "automatically", interpreted as 'exactly two', might it not be more plausible to accept this 'exactly' analysis as the conventional analysis of *two*? If intuition and introspection tell us that the 'exactly' interpretation of *two* in (16) is not "worked out" as other Gricean implicatures seem to be worked out, but rather immediately arrived at, this might be because the conventional meaning of *two* is not 'at least two' at all. And might the "equivocality" (a term which, by the way, seems to suit an ambiguity analysis better than a univocality + implicature analysis) of *two* in (17) not be explained by the less direct or "phenic" nature of the realization that (17) can be answered positively even if the number of children you have is not two but four? In other words, it is rather probable that in (17) it is not the 'exactly' interpretation that requires conscious effort, but the 'at least' interpretation. Campbell's data might be more naturally interpreted as evidence for the fact that Horn's claim that numerals have an 'at least' semantics is wrong than as evidence for the existence of rather mysterious "cryptic" processes, especially considering the fact that Grice himself, as well as many of his followers (including Horn), have stressed the importance of the working-out schema for the status of implicature[19].

As a final example of the forerunners of the underspecification analysis, Kempson's (1986)[20] account may be mentioned. Her story is still rather similar to Horn's original analysis – the "ambiguity" she identifies is of the "pragmatic" sort – but relevance-theoretic arguments are starting to impinge on minimalism.

She emphasizes the fact that the linguistic meaning of sentences has to rely on contextual information to be truth-evaluable. Her proto-relevance-theoretic account presumes that numerals have two interpretations ('at least n' and 'exactly n') and that these interpretations can be explained as a case of ambiguity or as an instance of a univocal item triggering an implicature in certain circumstances. Kempson considers the numerals to be a typical example of how scalar implicatures work. Even though she eventually disagrees with Horn's analysis, she even calls them "one of the core cases of scalar implicatures" (Kempson 1986:80). The largest part of her discussion of numerals concerns the combination of numerals with negation.

As mentioned in the discussion of Horn (1972), the default 'less than' meaning that is triggered by this combination was used by Horn as an argument for the 'less than' semantics of numerals. Kempson now considers the fact that this combination may sometimes trigger a 'more than' reading: *Mark didn't eat three biscuits, he ate four.* Horn (1985) had argued that this reading is triggered by the fact that in this utterance there is a different type of negation, called "metalinguistic negation"[21]. This metalinguistic negation is supposed to be non-truth-conditional: its basic meaning is rendered as 'I object to U' or 'I refuse to say U', where U is an utterance and not a proposition, so that it can also explain apparently divergent cases of negation as in *I'm not a TrotskyITE, I'm a TrotskyIST* (where capitals indicate heavy stress). Hence, in the example with the numeral, the speaker does not commit himself to the claim that it is wrong that Mark has eaten three biscuits; he or she merely rejects the (non-truth-conditional) upper bound implicature. Kempson doubts that all combinations of numerals +

---

[19] In fact, soon after Campbell's paper, Horn borrowed Morgan's (1978) concept of "short-circuited implicature" (Horn and Bayer 1984), for cases in which the implicature is in principle *calculable* "but is not in practice actually *calculated* by speakers operating with the relevant usage conventions" (Hòrn and Bayer 1984:404). The remarks with respect to Campbell's "cryptic" processing hold for "short-circuited implicatures" as well: if a certain meaning does not seem to be worked out, why not accept it as a *conventional* meaning rather than as an implicature? In fact, in some passages Horn himself seems to go in that direction, when he argues that the development from metaphor (typically explained as an implicature) to idiom can be compared with the development from "usage convention" to "meaning convention" (Horn and Bayer 1984:405). But if some implicatures have become conventionalized and if implicatures are, by definition, non-conventional, why still call them "implicatures"?

[20] Part of the discussion in Kempson (1986) can already be found in Kempson and Cormack (1981), but the latter article focuses on the problems of "scope" that arise when more than one quantifier is used in one and the same utterance. See also Bach (1982:601-602) for an attack of Kempson and Cormack's analysis of *Justin didn't eat three carrots: he ate four* and Kempson and Cormack (1982:609-610) for their reply. The latter discussion does not address the analysis of cardinals directly either; it is primarily concerned with the question whether negation acts on the numeral before the "strengthening" of the numeral (i.e., before the hypothesized 'at least' semantics is turned into an 'exactly' meaning by means of an implicature) or after.

[21] I do not discuss Horn's (1985) paper separately, because it mainly deals with the explanation of metalinguistic negation and does not contain new arguments with respect to the analysis of numerals apart from his discussion of the combination of numerals and metalinguistic negation, which is summarized in this section.

negation that trigger a 'more than' reading can be explained by the concept of metalinguistic negation: typically, in cases of metalinguistic negation such as *He's got more students, not 'four' students*, the second part does not provide evidence for or against the fact expressed in the first part. In the utterance *Mark didn't eat three biscuits, he ate four*, the second part does seem to provide evidence for the fact that the proposition expressed in the first part is incorrect, so this cannot be a case of metalinguistic negation. Also, utterances containing metalinguistic negation are normally not paraphrasable by means of *it is not true that* phrases: *?It's not true that I'm a TrostkyITE, I'm a TrostkyIST*, while *It's not true that Mark ate three biscuits, he ate four of them* seems more acceptable[22].

At that point in the article, Kempson seems to argue for an ambiguity analysis, solely on the basis of the claim that, e.g., 'more than' interpretations of numerals cannot always be explained by the concept of metalinguistic negation. But this "ambiguity" is considered to be a pragmatic ambiguity, i.e. the various interpretations of numerals should not be taken as different semantic meanings: "The conclusion that there is a lot more truth-conditional ambiguity than is contributed by the language in question is unavoidable" (Kempson 1986:88). This means that Kempson does not defend a semantic ambiguity analysis, but it also implies that the neo-Gricean analysis of numerals is not accepted.

Kempson's eventual solution is that the contextual information will decide which interpretation a numeral will acquire. In the context of an application for a state benefit (in which one gets the benefit if one has two children) *two* in the answer *I have two children* to the question *How many children do you have?* will acquire an 'at least' meaning, because this interpretation is the "optimally relevant" one (cf. Chapter 2, section 2.2.1. for the general principles underlying Relevance Theory). If the context is changed to a conversation between two mothers, the numeral will be interpreted as having an 'exactly' value, because in this case that interpretation will be the most relevant one. In her (second) discussion of the combination of a numeral and metalinguistic negation, she appears to hold on to Horn's 'at least' proposal all the same (at least with respect to the determination of the conventional meaning of numerals), because she says that in this combination one has to ignore the "lexically stipulated meaning" (and the context makes clear that an 'at least' meaning is being referred to) in favor of the "relevance-restricted one" (Kempson 1986:97). In cases with normal, truth-conditional negation, the interpretation of the numeral will be 'less than n' unless an 'exactly' interpretation is more relevant.

On the whole, Kempson's analysis seems attractive because it demonstrates how important the influence of context may be in the interpretation of numerals. Nevertheless, the acceptance of the 'at least' hypothesis with respect to the conventional meaning of numerals is disappointing. Just like Horn and many other neo-Griceans, Kempson does not provide an empirical basis for this hypothesis. This explains why her conclusions with respect to the analysis of numerals do not seem to be very different from Horn's. The only genuine difference is to be found in the explanation of the combination of numerals with so-called metalinguistic negation: whereas Horn seeks to explain away these phenomena by claiming

---

[22] Kempson uses an example with *some* and *all* (which indeed seems slightly more acceptable), but it is clear that the general point holds for numerals as well.

that negation is ambiguous between a truth-conditional use and a metalinguistic use, Kempson lets the context decide.

3.2.2. Underspecification, underdeterminacy and enrichment

The first explicit defenses of an underspecification account of English cardinals can be found in the work of Robyn Carston. Carston's (1988) paper primarily concentrates on a general discussion of the advantages of relevance-theoretic accounts over more traditional neo-Gricean ones. The "enrichment" thesis (cf. Chapter 2, section 2.2.4.) is also exemplified with numerals, however. In this paper, the underdeterminacy thesis can already be found, which will be discussed more extensively in Carston 1998a: she assumes the numerals to have a single sense, "neither an 'at least', an 'at most' nor an 'exactly' sense, these being determined pragmatically at the level of explicit content" (Carston 1988:174). In this paper, her main argument in favor of this analysis is that sentences containing numerals fall within the scope of logical operators: *If there are three books by Chomsky in the shop I'll buy all of them.* In this utterance, it is clear that *three* must have an 'exactly three' meaning *before* the conditional is processed, because the speaker evidently does not mean that he or she will buy 87 books by Chomsky, if the shop should happen to have that many. Also the interpretation of the sentences *Mrs Smith doesn't have three children; she has four* and *Mrs Smith does have three children; in fact she has four* (the first of which is obviously problematic for the 'at least' analysis) can be explained in an enrichment account. In the relevance-theoretic analysis, the two sentences acquire different enrichments of the logical form, as determined by the principle of relevance.

Carston's (1998a) paper contains an extended version of her brief (1988) remarks regarding cardinals. The basic analysis remains the same, however. Carston identifies two main problems with the 'at least' analysis: 1) it cannot deal with 'at most' readings and 2) the eventual meaning of the enriched numeral is truth-conditional, and not "merely" an implicature. In her own analysis, the "logical form" or "literal meaning" of numerals is underdetermined and has to be enriched by pragmatic inferences. The numeral *three* means [X [THREE]]:

> This representation overtly requires that material be supplied pragmatically to instantiate the variable X; that is, the necessity of a process of pragmatic enrichment is signalled in the logical form (semantic) representation of the utterance (Carston 1998a:208)

She also criticizes the accounts by Van Kuppevelt (cf. section 3.1.3. above) and Scharten (cf. section 3.2.2. below): she remarks that the latter do not give any deeper explanation for the strong influence of topic-comment structure on conversation, she wonders why the 'exactly' meaning which Scharten accepts as the *semantic* meaning of numerals is defeasible, and she gives a counterexample to the theory.

(18)   Q: How many months have 28 days?
        A1: <u>One - February</u>.
        A2: <u>They all</u> do.

According to Carston, Van Kuppevelt's account predicts that the default answer should be A2, while it is in fact A1.

While Carston's request for a deeper motivation of the information-structural influences is certainly legitimate, her claim that Scharten accepts the 'exactly' meaning of numerals as the "logical form" of numerals should be qualified. As will be discussed immediately, it is not really clear what semantic description Scharten selects as the conventional meaning of numerals, and it is possible that she intends them to have an "existential" meaning (de Cornulier 1984). Also, since Van Kuppevelt is not clear with respect to the interpretation of numerals in questions, it cannot be taken for granted that he would analyze them as having an 'at least' meaning. Therefore, it is not clear whether (18) constitutes a real counter-example to his theory.

Interestingly, Carston also provides a survey of the possible positions with respect to the conventional meaning of numerals. She identifies five possibilities: 1) a polysemy account, 2) the traditional 'at least' analysis, 3) an 'at most' analysis 4) an 'exactly' analysis and 5) an underdeterminacy analysis. Option 1 and 3 are quickly set aside (the first is unattractive due to Modified Occam's Razor, the third might be theoretically possible but seems highly counter-intuitive and is not defended by anybody); the second option seems unacceptable for the two reasons that have already been mentioned, so only option 4 and 5 remain. The problem with the adoption of an 'exactly n' semantics of numerals is that the other readings must be derived via a pragmatic weakening process, presumably something like Sadock's (1984) principle of "loose-speaking". Carston points out that this principle might be the explanation for the "approximation" effect of round numbers, but does not seem to apply to the interpretations of numerals under discussion.

The underdeterminacy analysis is considered to have an additional advantage over the 'exactly n' analysis in that it seems to have an intuitively more plausible explanation of the well-known data in (19).

(19)   Q: Does she have three children?
        A1: No, she has two.
        A2: ?Yes, (in fact) she has four.
        A3: No, she has four.

Carston argues that the markedness of A2 is an argument for the sense-generality account, because in that analysis it is possible to go back and reprocess the numeral. This seems to be a correct description of what happens in A2: first *three* is interpreted as 'at least three', and then it is reinterpreted as 'exactly three'. It is this reprocessing that is supposed to account for the slightly divergent grammaticality judgment. An 'exactly' semantics (with pragmatic loosening) is capable of explaining the same phenomenon, "but it is much less clear how the process of repair or reanalysis is to be explained" (Carston 1998a:209). Another argument is that if numerals had an 'exactly' semantics, the combination *exactly n* should create a redundancy effect, which it does not. Carston does not really consider these arguments to be conclusive however: "[i]t seems to me that both the sense-general and the two-sided punctual semantics remain live options, though each has its problems and neither is fully worked out" (Carston 1998a:210).

Scharten's (1997) dissertation is similar to Van Kuppevelt's (1996) article (cf. section 3.1.3. above) in that it also makes use of the notions of "topic" and "comment" and also assumes that numerals acquire an 'exactly' interpretation when they are in comment position (she doesn't refer to the concept of "scale activation" but assumes that numerals in this position are interpreted "exhaustively"). I will discuss her views on cardinals in the section on underspecification because that is the position she seems to take, even though her analysis is not always clear as to the semantic description of numerals. She emphasizes that many of the problems in the neo-Gricean account are caused by a confusion of the lexical and the information-structural level:

> I will argue that the fundamental assumption that the problem of one- and two-sided ['at least' and 'exactly'] readings is a problem of lexical semantics and pragmatics is misguided. The difference between the one- and the two-sided interpretations is the result of processes at the level of discourse. (Scharten 1997:9)

She also nicely points out that there may be different conceptions of "what is true": there is a judiciary notion of "speaking the whole truth" (which seems to correspond with the way in which truth-conditional semantics uses the notion), but there is also an everyday notion of "truth", which differs from the first, but which is also important (if not more important) in communication. And her truth-value judgments differ from those of Horn: "when [a] numeral is used as an answer to a *how many*-question [...] the "exactly"-interpretation is truth conditional" (Scharten 1997:40). When it turns out that there are actually more elements than indicated by the numeral mentioned by the speaker, the speaker will have lied. Moreover, she refers to the fact that the truth-conditional perspective on semantics is on the wane in present-day semantic research, in the sense that it is now widely accepted that contextual elements can influence truth conditions (cf. also section 2.2.4. on the "architecture of meaning" in Chapter 2 above). "Semantics" can no longer simply be equated with "truth-conditional meaning", nor can "pragmatics" be identified with "non-truth-conditional meaning".

Scharten mentions a large number of familiar arguments against the 'at least' analysis: the redundancy argument (if *three* meant 'at least three' then *at least three* would be redundant), problems with the definition of scales (if the scale <*exactly n, n*> were accepted, it would trigger the wrong results; and there does not seem to be a compelling reason to refuse the scale), the existence of 'at most' readings of numerals, and a number of other arguments I will not repeat here. With respect to the 'at most' readings, she notes that these are not caused by the numeral itself, but by the presence of "main sentence predicates" (Scharten 1997:54), such as *can* and *enough* in Carston's 'at most' examples.

(20)   She can have 2000 calories a day without putting on weight.
(21)   The council houses are big enough for families with three kids.

She notes that necessity modals trigger the opposite effect in Carston's 'at least' examples.

(22)   In Britain you have to be 17 to drive a motorbike.
(23)   Mary needs three A's to get into Oxford.

And also the 'at least' reading of the "state benefit" example is explained with reference to contextual elements. If (24A) is uttered by a mother with four children applying for a state benefit for mothers with at least two children, this "requirement" context may create the same 'at least' effect as the necessity modals just discussed.

(24)   Q: Do you have two children?
       A: I have two children.

Scharten uses a graded concept of "correction / cancellation". While, as we have seen, many neo-Griceans tend to exaggerate the difference between "repair" and "cancellation", Scharten speaks of extra (intonational or lexical) marking of "correction" (25), while a "modification" of an item not in comment position needs much less emphasis (26).

(25)   Q: How many pupils are there in your class?
       A: <u>33</u>. NO wait, <u>31</u>.
(26)   Q: How many sheep do John and Jane own?
       A: <u>Four</u>. Besides, / In fact, / But her name is Jean.

As she points out with respect to the neo-Gricean analysis:

> According to implicature theory, when the continuation involves a stronger value (e.g., a higher number) it is an instance of implicature cancellation, but when it involves a stronger value (a lower number) it is an instance of correction. This asymmetry is not supported by any empirical differences. (Scharten 1997:68)

Unfortunately, her account is rather unclear with respect to the conventional meaning of numerals. She rightly argues that numerals indicate the cardinality of a set and she assumes that *three* means |3| (Scharten 1997:73). This notation is used to indicate that the set under discussion has three elements. She does not tackle the question of how this definition of *three* differs from the positions proposed in the literature: is it an "existential" meaning à la de Cornulier (1984), is it an 'exactly' meaning à la Sadock (1984) (cf. section 3.3. below), does it have an underdetermined meaning (Carston 1988), or is *three* ambiguous between 'at least', 'exactly' and 'at most' meanings?

Also her discussion of the pragmatic "overlay" of this '|n|' meaning is not very clear: in comment position the numeral is said to acquire an 'exactly n' meaning through a process of exhaustive interpretation, but in non-comment position she argues that "we generally find the interpretation pattern described by Radical Pragmatics: the preferred reading of a numeral is 'exactly n'", only to add immediately that "this is easily overruled in favour of an 'at least' reading" (Scharten 1997:76). For numerals in non-comment position, she seems to use the same distinction as Fretheim (1992) does: "old" numerals (numerals that have been introduced earlier in the discourse) are interpreted exhaustively (receive an 'exactly n' reading) by default, with "new" numerals the 'exactly n' interpretation is only the "preferred interpretation" (Scharten does not make clear whether there is a difference between "default strategy" and "preferred interpretation", though). Further on she makes clear that this 'exactly n' interpretation (in non-comment position) is due to a default rule in Discourse Semantics (the framework in which her analysis is situated) and the 'at least' interpretation is triggered due to the presence of an existential quantifier. The first is the default interpretation because it is associated with "specific reference" (when there is no doubt with respect to which individuals are denoted) and this type of reference is assumed to be preferred over non-specific reference (when the identification of individuals is unclear).

On the whole, Scharten's analysis is a useful variant of the theory proposed by Van Kuppevelt. Whereas Van Kuppevelt still seems to work with an 'at least' semantics for numerals, this is not the case with Scharten. Unfortunately, Scharten's account of the semantics of numerals is not very clear: the '|n|' meaning is not specified with respect to the alternatives offered by other analysts of numerals. Moreover, also the explanation of the eventual interpretation of utterances containing numerals seems a bit muddled.

Three years after his defense of the neo-Gricean analysis of quantifiers, the various arguments for an underspecification analysis urged Horn to reconsider his 'at least' analysis of cardinals. His (1992) paper does not contain any new arguments, but the paper is remarkable because Horn gives in to his critics, at least with respect to his analysis of the cardinals: he argues that "while a strong case can be made for an enrichment analysis of the meaning contribution of the cardinals, it does not extend in any linear fashion to other scalar values" (Horn 1992:172-173). To support this claim, he refers to a number of characteristics that numerals have, but other scalars do not seem to have: he mentions Sadock's argument from mathematical statements (cf. next section), scale reversals (with reference to Sadock's (1984) claim that it is possible to use numerals with an 'at most' meaning, while it seems impossible to use *some* with an 'at most' meaning), the weakening effect of round numbers on 'exactly' implicatures, the strengthening of these implicatures with numerals under incorporation, Koenig's (1991) observations with respect to the "distributed" and the "set" readings of numerals (cf. next section), Campbell's (1981) observations with respect to the "phenic" and "cryptic" interpretations of numerals, as well as Fretheim's (1992) intonation arguments. For the purposes of this study, Horn's claim that these arguments do not hold for non-cardinal scalars is not immediately relevant, but it is remarkable that he chooses an underdeterminacy analysis of numerals (while, e.g., Koenig opts for an 'exactly' analysis). Unfortunately, Horn does not provide any arguments for his preference for the enrichment analysis over other non-'at least' analyses of cardinals.

3.3. MARGINAL POSITIONS: PUNCTUAL SEMANTICS AND AMBIGUITY

Besides the two main accounts, i.e. the minimalist and the underspecification account, a number of other analyses have been suggested, starting either from an 'exactly' semantics (punctual semantics) or an ambiguity analysis.

Sadock's (1984) article contains a nuanced defense of the "radical pragmatics" program, of which the 'at least' analysis of numerals is one example. At the same time, Sadock warns that "radical Griceanism" will lead to a meaning analysis that will not be able to explain how language functions. He describes a radical interpretation of Horn's analysis (in which *three* does not mean 'three', but an expression containing *three* would merely imply the truth of the same expression with *two* instead of *three*, but not with *four* instead of *three*) and argues that in such an analysis the English cardinals would mean hardly anything anymore: "There is simply not enough conventional content left in the number words for any pragmatic theory to use as input" (Sadock 1984:143). He also refers to the mathematical use of numerals in utterances like *Three is the square root of nine*: this type of statement is incompatible with the statement that the truth-conditional content of *three* or *nine* is 'at least three' and 'at least nine'. It is not clear how damaging this argument is for the 'at least' analysis: the latter is so extremely flexible that Horn may argue that the 'at least' meanings of numerals in mathematical contexts are always turned into an 'exactly' meaning, by way of an implicature.

Sadock's article is also important because he argues that numerals are different from other scalar elements like *some*. It does not seem to be possible to use *some* in such a way as to implicate 'at most some'[23]. Sadock makes clear that the radical interpretation of Horn's analysis should not be attributed to Horn himself, but

> [i]n order both to capture the correct range of contextual understandings of the various quantifiers and to account for the asymmetry between the exact and inexact ones, it seems to me that a less radical pragmatic theory than even Horn's might be required. (Sadock 1984:143)

Sadock proposes an 'exactly' analysis of numerals; the other interpretations of numerals should be derived via a pragmatic principle of "loose-speaking", so that a speaker "using *three* to indicate 'three or more' would then be conveying less than his words imply, rather than more" (Sadock 1984:143). It is not clear whether Sadock means by this that a numeral *n* means 'exactly n' or rather something akin to de Cornulier's "existential" meaning of *n*, but his statement that "exact quantifiers have exact meanings" (Sadock 1984:143) seems to suggest the former.

A similar stance can be found in Löbner (1985). As the title of his paper ("*Drei ist drei*") already indicates, Löbner assumes the semantics of a numeral *n* not to be 'at least n', but simply 'n'. This reminds us of Harnish's (1976) position, but Löbner's claims are much more outspoken. He is surprised that the counter-intuitive 'at least' analysis of numerals has come to be the traditional analysis and he claims that the opposite analysis is much more plausible: "Es ist vielmehr umgekehrt: die Zahlwörter bedeuten 'n', und in gewissen Kontexten ergibt sich als *logische Folgerung* die Bedeutung 'n oder mehr'" (Löbner 1985:314 - emphasis in the original). Löbner stresses the distinction between the meaning of *n* and the inferences that are

---

[23] This seems to be incorrect, however: if a child asks her father *Can I have all the cookies?*, *some* in the answer *You can have some* will have an 'at most' interpretation.

allowed by asserting utterances containing *n*. Just like with Sadock (1984), it is not clear whether an 'exactly' semantics for numerals is endorsed or an "existentialist" analysis[24].

Löbner lists five arguments for his relatively unspecified 'n' meaning of numerals: 1) He argues that it is not possible to refer back to a set of entities by using a numeral that is higher than the numeral that was originally used to indicate the cardinality of the set: *Hier sind zwei Briefe. Sie sind beide / *alle drei für dich.* The cardinality expressed by the anaphorically used numeral must correspond with the exact quantity expressed by the first numeral. This argument does not seem to be very strong, however: Horn would probably not claim that *zwei* and *drei* have the same meaning; he would merely claim that the latter entails the former. Therefore, it is not obvious that Horn's analysis requires *three* to be an anaphor for *two letters*. 2) Löbner, apparently unaware of Sadock's (1984) paper, also argues that it is impossible to calculate with numerals having 'at least' meanings. 3) He perceives a distinction between numerals and other scalars (a position that Sadock had also argued for), because whereas *sehr viel* is a "more specific" expression than *viel*, *drei* does not seem to be more specific than *zwei*: *Ich brauche viel Geld, und zwar sehr viel* is possible, but *Ich brauche zwei Bier, und zwar drei* is not. This suggests that numerals have some sort of built-in "exactness", which other scalars seem to lack. Nevertheless, in English it is of course unproblematic to say *I need two beers, in fact even three* just like it is possible to say *I need a lot of money, in fact even an enormous amount of money* 4) He also refers to the behavior of numerals with particles such as *schon* and *nur*: *Anna hat nur neun mal "Gesundheit!" gesagt* is ok, while *?Anna hat nur mindestens neun mal "Gesundheit!" gesagt* seems unacceptable. This argument is not very damaging to Horn's account, because it is not clear whether he would accept that the meaning of *n* is the same as that of *at least n* (in the neo-Gricean line of reasoning, it might be argued that the latter is different from the former in that it cannot trigger an 'exactly' implicature because of the presence of *at least*). 5) The fifth argument is actually based on the same idea as the previous one, and fails for the same reasons: *dreißig* can co-occur with *mindestens*, but *mindestens dreißig* (which is taken to be equivalent with *dreißig*) cannot: **mindestens mindestens dreißig*. Löbner's arguments are not very convincing. However, as they intend to support an opinion on the semantics of numerals that had not yet been voiced so clearly, his article seems worth mentioning.

The most explicit defense of a "punctual" analysis of cardinals can be found in Koenig (1991). Koenig's article directly addresses the question of the interpretation of numerals and categorically rejects Horn's 'at least' analysis. Many of the arguments he uses against the neo-Gricean account are by now familiar, but I will mention his most important arguments nonetheless, because most of them are formulated slightly differently. Koenig refers to the fact that if the 'at least' analysis were correct there would be no words naming specific numbers in any language, because in the neo-Gricean analysis they "logically refer to the ascending half-line beginning at the mathematical number" (Koenig 1991:141). This is a rhetorically enhanced version of the claim that the neo-Gricean analysis reduces the semantics of numerals so much that there is hardly anything left for the hearer to go on.

---

[24] In fact, Löbner confusingly calls the 'at least' meaning "die existentielle, schwache Deutung" (Löbner 1985:311).

Next, Koenig reiterates the redundancy argument, in two versions. The first version, attributed to Paul Kay, consists of the observation that if the neo-Gricean analysis were correct *at most* and *at least* would have rather different functions: the latter would be merely blocking an 'exactly' implicature, while the former would change the meaning of the numeral much more radically. But there does not seem to be a reason to accept such an asymmetrical account of *at most* and *at least*. The second version refers to the addition of *more than*: if *three* meant 'at least three', *More than three people came* ('more than at least three'?) does not seem to make any sense.

Moreover, Koenig also points at the problematic nature of deriving semantic descriptions of lexical items from the truth-conditional behavior of the utterances containing them: from the utterance *DOGS are not cute, ALL ANIMALS are cute* (capitals for heavy stress) it is not possible to determine the semantics of *dogs* to be 'dogs or other animals'. Also, Koenig is the first to remark that there is a difference between "distributed" and "set" readings of numerals[25]: the first is the familiar one that can be found in interpretations of *Mary saw three men*. The second points at a much less discussed reading, the one that is elicited when *three boys carried a sofa up the stairs* is interpreted as a single event involving three boys (and not three events involving one boy each). Koenig now argues that only distributed readings give rise to what he calls "scalar entailments": *Mary saw three men* entails *Mary saw two men*, but *Three boys together brought a sofa up the stairs* does not entail *Two boys together brought a sofa up the stairs*. Hence, even if it is accepted that meanings of lexical elements may be derived from the entailments that can be inferred from sentences containing them, the 'at least' analysis would still be problematic.

Interestingly, Koenig also refers to the influence of the "conversational goal", in the line of the concept of "valeur argumentative" proposed by Anscombre and Ducrot (cf. section 3.2.). If the point of the utterance is to provide an argument for the cheapness of a book, the cancellation phrase seems grammatical even if it contradicts the "indefeasible" 'at least' semantics of the numeral: *It's pretty cheap: it costs $10, in fact $5*. He also refers to what I will call the "epistemological principle" in the corpus analysis (cf. section 5.3.3. in Chapter 5): with reference to Anscombre and Ducrot (1983), Koenig argues that the entailment from *having drunk three glasses of cognac* to *having drunk two glasses of cognac* is based on "world-knowledge of consumption". This inference is generally a correct one, but this is no reason to integrate it in a description of the linguistic meaning of *three* or *two*.

Koenig does not stop after having denounced the 'at least' analysis, but offers a solution of his own. His account is based on the fact that lexically, cardinal numbers "denote their ordinary mathematical value" (Koenig 1991:146), which is later specified as an 'exactly' meaning, at least for numerals in "count phrases". He distinguishes this lexical meaning explicitly from the effects that numerals may appear to have on the sentential level, where they may trigger a 'not all' implicature. Also, Koenig's analysis is sensitive to the fact that the various uses of numerals cannot simply be amalgamated. He assumes that numerals in "measure phrases" should be associated with the "set readings" of numerals in count phrases, because *three inches of rope* denotes "an amount of rope equal to three inches", and

---

[25] Horn (1992:174) attributes a similar argument to Atlas (in a lecture given at the Katholieke Universiteit Leuven in 1990).

utterances containing such a measurement phrase do not seem to entail utterances containing the same phrase with a lower number replacing *three*.

Even though Koenig's arguments against Horn's 'at least' analysis are very convincing, there are problems with his own analysis as well. First, if one accepts the questionable practice of treating the semantic description 'at least three' to be exactly equivalent to the meaning expressed by *at least three* (which Koenig clearly does), and if *three* really meant 'exactly three', it is strange that *at least three* ('at least exactly three') is a possible combination: part of the function of *exactly* seems to be the explicit exclusion of the possibility that there are more than three elements involved. Second, even though Koenig certainly is justified in differentiating between different usage types of cardinals, his judgments concerning the entailments of utterances containing measure phrases seem at least questionable: I suspect that at least some people would accept the reasoning that if a book costs $20, it also costs (at least) $15. As far as their entailments are concerned, utterances containing measure phrases do not seem to be very different from utterances containing count phrases: just like some people would accept the entailment just mentioned, some people will accept that if Mary has three children, she also has (at least) two children. And the people who refuse the entailment with the measure phrase might actually be refusing the entailment of the "children" utterance as well. Finally, another of Koenig's arguments to support the same differentiation within the uses of numerals does not seem to be very convincing either. He claims that numerals in count phrases differ from those in measure phrases because *This book DOESN'T cost $20, it costs $30* is acceptable, but *Mary DOESN'T have three children she has FOUR* allegedly is not. This does not seem to square with intuitions, however, at least not with ours.

Finally, at least one paper offers an account of cardinals that seems to favor an analysis in terms of the ambiguity of numerals. The tone of Richardson and Richardson's article on the neo-Gricean *status quo*, on the other hand, is remarkably sharp:

> [...] a (meta)theoretical movement informally known as radical pragmatics has been remarkably successful in convincing many that it is desirable to reduce all of pragmatic theory to a few grand principles and that even such a highly simplified pragmatic theory can radically extend its domain of explanation at the expense of other domains (Richardson and Richardson 1990:498)

They argue that Radical Pragmatics has gone too far in reducing the semantic content of linguistic elements. With respect to their attack of the 'at least' analysis of numerals, they reiterate Sadock's (1984) evidence from mathematical statements, but convincingly add that the phenomena are by no means restricted to mathematical discourse: if numerals have 'at least' meanings, it is not clear how the utterance *I took six cigarettes with me, gave one to Fred and two to Ed, so I still have three* can be understood[26]. With respect to Horn's claim

---

[26] It is strange that many researchers (such as Levinson 2000:88) keep referring to Sadock's (1984) mathematical argument, while the example *I took six cigarettes with me, gave one to Fred and two to Ed, so I still have three* by Richardson and Richardson (1990) is based on the same idea, but shows that the argument is *not* restricted to the mathematical register.

that an ambiguity analysis would introduce an infinitude of ambiguous terms, they argue that this does not seem to be very problematic[27]:

> Horn has confused the unimportant question of how many items are "in the domain" of an ambiguity with the important question of how much apparatus is required to handle the ambiguity. There is no reason to believe that an "at least n" - "exactly n" ambiguity would require much machinery at all. (Richardson and Richardson 1990:501)

Unfortunately, their contribution is mainly a negative one: they do not present a well-construed argument for the analysis of numerals. From their comments, it is clear that they favor an ambiguity analysis, but the specifics of such an analysis are not discussed. Therefore, their contribution is mainly important for their "everyday" version of Sadock's mathematical argument, and their more theoretical attack of the alleged all-importance of Modified Occam's Razor. They emphasize the damage this principle has caused to the semantic description of natural language counterparts of logical operators.

3.4. SUMMARY AND 'ABSOLUTE VALUE'

By way of conclusion, let us list the various analyses that have been proposed during the last thirty years, together with their pros and cons. The bulk of the summary will of course concern the 'at least' analysis, because this is the analysis that has been defended and attacked most often in the literature. I will also introduce the 'absolute value' analysis and indicate the connections with similar analyses that have been proposed.

1) 'At least' analysis = univocal 'at least' meaning + 'exactly n' implicature

<u>Pros</u>

1) The truth conditions of sentences containing numerals show that a sentence containing a higher numeral entails the same sentence with a lower numeral.
2) Numerals are often interpreted as having 'exactly' meanings. This is not the "conventional" meaning of numerals, because this 'exactly' meaning is defeasible, while conventional meanings are not. The implicature can be lifted either via cancellation or suspension: *John*

---

[27] Eight years later, Davis (1998) will express much the same sentiment, although his version seems to be motivated better. He argues that he does not see why Modified Occam's Razor should be so important and he mentions William Lycan arguing in defense of the Razor that "[i]t is not just that positing extra senses complicates the semantics [...] It is that every single extra sense would have to be *learned* separately" (Lycan qtd. in Davis 1998:20). Indeed, it seems that this is the argument on which much of the persuasive force of the Radical Pragmatics program rests, even though it is hardly ever made explicit. Davis rightfully remarks that this argument is not very convincing: "Although the ambiguist does impose extra demands on the learning process, the Gricean appears to place extra demands on the interpretation process. Instead of the familiar process of selecting the most likely sense from the list of previously learned senses on the basis of contextual clues, the Gricean asks the interpreter to engage in the sophisticated reasoning presented by the Working-out Schema" (Davis 1998:20).

has three children, in fact four / if not four vs. **John has three children, in fact two / if not two.*

3) The combination of a numeral with negation usually triggers a 'less than' meaning, which can easily be explained if one adopts an 'at least' semantics for numerals: if *three* means 'at least three', the negation of *three* will be 'less than three'.

4) Questions with numerals often can be answered in two different ways: *Does John have three children?* can be answered by either *Yes, (in fact) he 'has four* or *No, he has four*, depending on whether the question is or is not assumed to have implicated an upper bound.

5) The so-called "redundancy argument" states that if *three* meant 'exactly three' then *exactly* in *John has exactly three children* would be redundant, which it is not. A corollary of this argument refers to the fact that if *three* meant 'exactly three', *at least three* would be a contradiction.

6) Implicatures seem to be "reinforceable": it is possible to make the 'no more than n' implicature explicit: *John has three children, but not four* vs. **John has three children, but not two.*

7) As the 'exactly' meaning is triggered by an implicature, the degree of defeasibility of this 'exact' meaning differs: under incorporation the 'exact' reading is practically conventionalized (*tripod, bicycle*); also the "roundness" of numerals plays a role.

8) The scalar account is generalizable to many other phenomena: other lexical items fit perfectly in the neo-Gricean account of numerals. It also squares with Horn's (1972) analysis of *only*.

9) There is also cross-linguistic evidence for the neo-Gricean analysis: languages usually do not have separate lexicalizations of 'exactly n' meanings and 'at least' meanings, because the former can be derived from the latter. Even though there is at least one language (Toratán, cf. above) that has separate lexicalizations for 'exactly n', this cross-linguistic observation seems to hold for the majority of the world's languages.

10) The 'at least' analysis allows links between logic and linguistics logical relations: not only are the entailment relations preserved, also the monotonicity of NPs containing *n* seems to be in line with the monotonicity of NPs containing *at least n*.

Cons

1) The determination of the conventional meaning of numerals as 'at least n' is not based on the most frequent meaning of numerals. Moreover, it is highly counter-intuitive. The analysis does not take into account the crucial distinction between the lexical semantics of a numeral and the entailments that can be derived on the basis of utterances containing that numeral.

2) "Defeasibility" is a matter of degree: the distinction between *in fact* phrases (called "cancellation phrases") and correction phrases (*I mean, actually,...*) is not qualitative but quantitative. Moreover, the cancellation test cannot distinguish between an implicature account and an ambiguity account and some elements of uncontroversially "conventional" meanings are defeasible as well: *plastic flower* "cancels" the meaning that the plant is biological. The fact that *John has three children, in fact four* is easier than **John has three children, in fact two* is not an effect of the meaning of *three*, but is related to what I call the

"epistemological principle": knowledge of the world tells us that if one has four children, one also has three children, but not vice versa.

3) The default 'less than' interpretation that is triggered by the combination of a numeral and negation is an argument for the 'at least' analysis that has not really been refuted. Researchers have referred to the fact that this combination may also trigger a 'more than' reading, which indeed makes the argument less strong. But Horn and others have referred to the "metalinguistic" nature of negation in those cases. I will propose a solution to this problem in the corpus analysis, again with reference to the epistemological principle.

4) The fact that a question containing a numeral can be answered positively and negatively is actually an argument against the 'at least' analysis: in a situation in which the hearer knows that John has four children, the answer *No, he has four* to the question *Does John have three children?* seems to be the default answer. The positive answer - *Yes, (in fact) he has four* - seems to rely on special contextual conditions and requires there to be a correction phrase (*in fact*).

5) Also the redundancy argument provides a good argument *against* the 'at least' analysis: if *three* meant 'at least three', why is *at least* in *at least three* not redundant?

6) The "reinforceability" argument is also not fully refuted by the arguments in the literature. In the analysis, I will propose that the reinforcement phrase simply *adds* a meaning to the lexical meaning of the numeral, which was not there before (not as part of the conventional meaning, nor as an implicature).

7) "Lexical incorporation" and "roundness" effects are arguments against the 'at least' analysis: in the first type of phenomena, no 'at least' meanings can be found; in the second, sometimes 'less than n' is also a possible interpretation, which must be mysterious in an 'at least' analysis, in which this lower bound is not defeasible.

8) With the respect to the generalizability of the scalar account, many people have argued that numerals are in fact atypical, and Horn (1992) has accepted this distinction. It seems more likely, however, that *three* and *some* do not differ that much. More specifically, it seems unlikely that *some* has 'at least some' as its conventional meaning.

9) The fact that there are no separate lexicalizations for 'at least n' and 'exactly n' is not an argument for the 'at least' analysis: in principle, it is possible (and it is in fact intuitively more plausible) that *n* means 'exactly n' and that the 'at least n' meaning is triggered by other means. Nevertheless, I will propose that *n* means neither 'at least n', nor 'exactly n', but what I will call "absolute value n".

10) Logical arguments are relevant in logical descriptions, but cannot be used in an analysis of numerals that explicitly starts from the *conventional* meaning of a numeral, as Grice's theory of conversation does. Furthermore, while some logical arguments might be rescued by an 'at least' analysis of numerals, mathematical calculations are endangered by it: if *two* meant 'at least two' it is not clear why $2+2$ necessarily equals *4* and not 'at least four'. The latter argument can also be transposed to everyday communication: *I took six cigarettes with me, gave one to Fred and two to Ed, so I still have three* would be strange in an 'at least' analysis of numerals.

2) ambiguity analysis

Pros

This account covers the various meanings that can be expressed by numerals and avoids the problems of the 'at least' analysis.

Con

This analysis is not attractive at all, because the various meanings of the numerals seem very much related to each other. Simply accepting these meanings as conventional meanings of numerals seems to provoke an unnecessary proliferation of the senses of numerals.

3) 'exactly' analysis + pragmatic mechanism

Pros

This account captures the intuition that when people say *three* they do not mean 'at least three'. It also solves the problems with the mathematical statements and their "everyday" counterparts.

Cons

The 'exactly' analysis cannot explain why *exactly* in *exactly three* is not redundant. Moreover, *three* does not intuitively mean 'exactly three' but simply 'three'. Finally, it is not clear which pragmatic process should be used to explain the shift from the 'exactly: the principle of "loose-speaking" does not seem to apply, and the concept of "domain narrowing" might depend too much on contextual input to allow the type of rigid account that is required by the formal framework in which the principle is used.

4) underdeterminacy + enrichment

Pros

This account also captures the various uses of numerals and avoids all the problems of the 'at least' analysis. Moreover, many other phenomena show that the "logical form" of linguistic elements is very often underdetermined. Also, it explicitly allows the possibility that a numeral receives an 'approximately n' interpretation, while these readings are problematic for 'at least' and 'exactly' accounts.

Cons

Intuitively, numerals do not seem to be in need of "enrichment" to an 'at least', 'at most' or 'exactly' value. Whereas typical examples of enrichment (such as the enrichment involved in the interpretation of *I haven't eaten breakfast*) indeed signal the fact that the proposition expressed is not complete, and needs to be "enriched", this does not seem to be the case for numerals. Moreover, the 'at least', 'exactly' and 'at most' values of numerals in certain utterances and contexts can be related to the presence of linguistic or contextual material inducing that specific interpretation.

5) 'absolute value' analysis

As I will try to demonstrate in the corpus analysis of numerals, numerals in N CN constructions should be regarded as having an 'absolute value' meaning as their conventional meaning. This 'absolute value' position is derived from the observation that a numeral *n* indicates that the cardinality of the set indicated by the NP containing *n* is |n|, and, crucially, that nothing is made explicit with respect to the possibility of there being more than n elements in that set. This implies that the conventional meaning of numerals is unambiguous, not identical to 'exactly n' or 'at least n', and does not need to be enriched pragmatically. In the corpus analysis, I will demonstrate how the other interpretations of *n* ('at least n', 'at most n', 'exactly n', 'approximately n', 'more than n' etc.) can be arrived at.

This analysis shows partial resemblances with de Cornulier's (1984) "existential" analysis of numerals in that I will also assume a link between the meaning of a numeral (in fact the meaning of an NP containing a numeral) and the concept of "existence". It also resembles Carston's (1988, 1998a) underdeterminacy analysis in that I will also adopt a maximally general meaning of a numeral as the conventional meaning. It is similar to the analyses by Van Kuppevelt (1996) and Scharten (1997) in that I will try to find linguistic manifestations of the information-structural influences on the interpretation of numerals. And it resembles Kadmon's DRT-analysis, to the extent that she also presumes a link between the interpretation of a numeral and the assertion of existence of an NP containing a numeral. Nevertheless, the 'absolute value' analysis proposed here differs from all of these accounts in one or more respects. Moreover, the discussion about the different "values" of numerals will only be part of the corpus analysis. Unlike many neo-Griceans, I will try to differentiate between the various uses of numerals, and I will also devote attention to those uses that are not fully "cardinal", but function (pro)nominally or even as proper names.

4

GENERAL CORPUS ANALYSIS OF THE FORMS AND FUNCTIONS OF ENGLISH CARDINALS

4.1. PROLEGOMENON: THE ENGLISH LEXICAL CATEGORY "NUMERAL"

Going through the more general literature on parts of speech as well as through the English-oriented descriptions of word classes (mainly grammars), one cannot help noticing the inconsistency and/or hesitation with which the cardinal numerals (*zero* + *one, two, three* etc. ad infinitum) are assigned a place in a particular word class system. Nevertheless, Sasse (1993:646) points out that numerals have been part of the traditional ten-member system ever since medieval grammarians added this category to Dionysius Thrax' system, which was based largely on the morphology of the Classical Languages. As is well known, also a whole number of modern grammars still tend to work within that system, or at least position themselves vis-à-vis that tradition.

Is that the only reason why numerals are so often allowed to form a part of speech on their own? The following English grammars all treat the numerals in a separate section: Scott et al. 1973 [1968], Van Roey (1982), Thomson and Martinet (1980), Greenbaum (1996) and Poutsma (1916). This does not necessarily mean that they explicitly regard numerals as a separate word class, but in so far as they do not address the issue head-on, at least the suggestion is there.

Other grammarians are much less consistent. Jespersen (1972 [1933]:68) treats numerals together with pronouns, but as a separate class. Elsewhere, however, Jespersen allows them a separate subsection under the rubric of "quantifiers" (Jespersen 1970 [1949]:580ff). Quirk et al. (1985) somewhat ambiguously discuss numerals in a section on "pronouns and determiners" (Quirk et al.1985: 333-398), thereby indicating that numerals are in some way linked to pronouns ("Both cardinal and ordinal numerals can function like pronouns [...] or like postdeterminers" - Quirk et al.1985:394), while setting them apart at the same time. Christophersen and Sandved (1970 [1969]:69-72) deal with numerals when discussing determiners (part of a section on "function words") and also Giering et al. (1987 [1986]) treat them under the "determiners" subheading, as does Huddleston (1984) (opting for the term "determinatives"). Baker (1995) classifies numerals as a part of quantifiers or "quantity words". Givón (1993) deals with numerals under the heading of "minor word classes", but defines them as "a sub-class of more *exact* quantifiers. They are noun-modifiers that connote number [...]" (Givón 1993:81 - emphasis in the original). Finally, to round off this non-exhaustive survey, two cross-linguistic assessments: Schachter, in his cross-linguistic survey of parts of speech, classifies numerals as "noun adjuncts" (Schachter 1985:35), and more precisely as an example of "quantifiers", while Sasse (1993) treats numerals under a separate subheading. Nevertheless, Sasse nuances his classification: "Numerals [...] rarely constitute a word class distinct from those of nouns or adjectives" (Sasse 1993:682).

Nobody will be surprised at these apparent inconsistencies: the classification of linguistic material into parts of speech is famous for problems that accompany any attempt at definition or categorization. Still, even if the English numerals make up one of the smaller categories (and might be more likely to be absorbed by bigger classes), it is not too difficult to define them vis-à-vis other linguistic items, semantically and in terms of morphology (e.g., the open – closed class dichotomy), as well as on distributional and syntactic grounds.

4.1.1. Semantics

First, the English numerals can be separated from other parts of speech on semantic grounds: they are the only linguistic elements that allow a one-to-one mapping between a counting practice and a categorized reality. As fine-grained indications of quantity, they allow the language user to add up, subtract, multiply etc. units of a particular kind. Furthermore, all numerals have very similar functions, so that the meaning of each member can be fully defined in terms of other members. The specific way in which this word class is organized seems to be a unique characteristic of numerals. Also, numerals are semantically different from adjectives because they do not denote properties of objects (Reinhardt 1991, Frege 1990 [1884]), as well as from determiners, because they do not seem to locate the head-noun relative to the realm of discourse in the way that articles do (Reinhardt 1991). While Reinhardt certainly is correct in distinguishing the function of cardinals from what she calls the "central determiners", her claim that "indefiniteness is no inherent feature of cardinals and that phrases such as *three days* contain a phonetically empty indefinite plural determiner" (Reinhardt 1991:199) unfortunately relies on a chimerical plural determiner. Langacker more accurately argues that cardinals, like other "absolute quantifiers" (such as *many, several, few*) are "true quantifiers" (offering "a direct description of magnitude"), while "relative quantifiers" (such as *some, no, all*), just like Reinhardt's "central determiners" ("central" because of their central position with respect to the other determiners), are best considered as grounding predications (locating their head in the ground, i.e., the speech event, its participants, and its setting) (Langacker 1987:489, 1991:82).

Finally, the specificity of the function of numerals also lies in the fact that they are part of a very sophisticated subsystem of natural language (mathematics) and in the fact that they can be represented orthographically in two different ways.

4.1.2. Open - closed class

Second, cardinal numerals constitute a specific category due to their intermediate position between open class and closed class items: as Quirk et al. remark, they have characteristics of closed classes in that it is not possible to simply introduce "new" numerals, while it is possible to create new nouns. Furthermore, "numerals constitute a miniature syntax of their own" (Quirk et al.1985:74, cf. also Sasse 1993:682 and Brandt Corstius 1968). Indeed, there is a clear tendency to view numerals as one separate group, for the simple reason that they can be listed. A typical description of the English numerals enumerates the "irregular" ones and then lists a recursive set of rules to create the higher cardinals (Jespersen 1948 [1924]:37). Again, this is specific for the class of numerals: even though the members of certain other word classes can also be exhaustively enumerated (articles, demonstrative pronouns, etc.), none of these have as many members and none of these rely on a relatively simple recursive set of "construction rules".

4.1.3. Syntax

As far as their syntactic behavior is concerned, a first way to characterize numerals is by pointing out their occurrence both as heads of nominal phrases (as nouns or pronouns[1]) and as adnominals. They share this characteristic with some quantifiers[2], some interrogative pronouns and the demonstratives. As the latter co-occur in a fixed order with cardinals, the distributional specificity of the cardinals is easy to pinpoint: they follow members of the other three classes.

(1)   These/all three books are special.
(2)   Which three books are special?
(3)   I would like these/all three.
(4)   Which three would you like?

---

[1] Here, as elsewhere, I will adopt Quirk et al.'s rather broad conception of pronouns (Quirk et al. 1985:335-398): "Semantically, a pronoun may be a 'pro-form' in any of the [following] three senses: [...] (A) It may substitute for some word or phrase (as *one* may substitute for a noun, and therefore be a 'pronoun' in a quite literal sense. (B) It may signal, as personal pronouns like *her* do, that reference is being made to something which is given or known within the linguistic or situational context [...] (C) It may stand for a very general concept, so that its reference includes the reference of untold more specific noun phrases: *somebody*, for example, indicates a broad class of people including *a girl, a man, a secretary*, etc." (Quirk et al. 1985:335). And while Quirk et al. indicate that "syntactically, most pronouns function like noun phrases rather than nouns", they clearly do not regard this as a *conditio sine qua non*. In their discussion of numerals they indicate that numerals "can function either as determinatives or as heads in the noun phrase" (Quirk et al. 1985:393), and their examples of pronominal numerals do not only include what I have called the "nominal" use of *two* (as in *Two is an even number*), but also include examples such as *nine* in *There are nine*. I admit that my use of "pronominal" is often very close to the meaning of "anaphorical", but I use "pronominal" because the uses of *two* that I call pronominal generally function as the head of the anaphorical noun phrase.
[2] Because of semantic incompatibilities, "intermediate" quantifiers (Horn 1989: 236) like *many, (a) few* and *a lot of* do not combine with cardinals, which makes it impossible to distinguish them from cardinals on the basis of their relative positions in the noun phrase. But these mid-range quantifiers cannot be preceded by *all*, while cardinals can.

This distributional behavior has been referred to by a number of grammarians. Christophersen and Sandved (1970 [1969]:70-71), for instance, point out that determiners are most often mutually exclusive, but numerals may be preceded by *the, these, those* or a genitive: *the three friends,* but **the my sisters.* This separates the numerals from most other determiners, even though quantifiers like *many* and *few* can occur in that position as well. Unlike *few*, however, adnominal numerals cannot be preceded by the indefinite article: *a few houses,* but **a three sisters.* Unlike *many,* the numerals can be preceded by *all* without the aid of a definite article: *all three cars,* but **all many cars.* Also, Christophersen and Sandved repeat the observation that determiners (and hence, in their classification, also adnominal cardinals) can be distinguished from adjectives because determiners cannot be preceded by intensifiers like *very,* while adjectives can.

Quirk et al. (1985) make a similar distinction, assigning cardinal numerals to the subclass of "postdeterminers", as opposed to the class of "central determiners" (the articles) and "predeterminers" (*half, all, double*). These classes are defined by their relative position in the noun phrase. The postdeterminers are further subdivided into four groups: cardinals, ordinals, closed-class (*few*) and open-class (*a number of*) quantifiers.

Moreover, the cardinals are special in their limited capacity to function as heads of subject-NPs, either pronominally (they share this capacity with other quantifiers, cf. (5)) or "abstractly, i.e. without any association with any particular persons, animals or things" (Poutsma 1916) (6), but also as object-NPs (7) and preposition-initiated adverbial phrases (8).

(5)   There were ten hunters. Seven were good-looking, a few were sick and none was bright.
(6)   Twelve is to four as three is to one. (Poutsma 1916:1231)
(7)   You have two books. We have three.
(8)   We will meet at eight.[3]

Even though this is syntactically invisible, the abstract use in (6) is clearly different from the metalinguistic use that allows each word to be used as the head of an NP (as is also orthographically indicated through the absence of quotation marks).

(9)   "Oink" is a pig-like interjection.

Also, cardinal numerals can function as predicates.

(10)   She is sixty.

---

[3] There is a question of ellipsis here: clearly, the sentence can be complemented with *o 'clock,* or even, in some contexts, with *hundred hours (eight hundred hours).* Nevertheless, even the possible ellipsis of *o 'clock* does not turn *eight* into an adnominal; it remains, arguably, the head of the adverbial phrase. The reliance on deleted elements when determining the part of speech status of a certain item is only legitimate when the version with ellipsis is somehow marked in relation to the full version: if the version with ellipsis is not considered odd (anymore), it should be safe to consider it as it stands. This is the case with *at eight hundred hours*: the latter is clearly marked when compared to *at eight,* and not *vice versa.*

(11)   We are five.

In Table 1, some relevant aspects of the syntactic behavior of numerals are compared to that of adjectives, "intermediate" quantifiers, demonstratives, other quantifiers and interrogatives, which all have the capacity to function as heads of an NP as well as adnominally. The table makes clear that numerals can be defined as a separate category on syntactic grounds and also shows that they are very similar to adjectives, but also resemble intermediate quantifiers and demonstratives.

TABLE 1

SYNTAX OF NUMERALS COMPARED TO OTHER WORD CLASSES

	Head / Adnominal	Co-occurrence with definite article	Co-occurrence with *all*	Gradability (co-occurrence with *very*)
Numerals (*two*)	H + A	+	+	-
Adjectives (*blue*)	H + A[4]	+	+	+
"Intermediate" quantifiers (*many*)	H + A	+	-	+
Demonstratives (*these*)	H + A	-	+	-
Other quantifiers (*all*)	H + A	-	-	-
Interrogatives (*which*)	H + A	-	-	-

Finally, the cardinal numerals can feature in a whole number of highly idiosyncratic constructions, most of which are not compatible with members of the other word classes in the table. The constructions I have gathered were either found in Poutsma (1916) or in the corpus. I will list only a few.

(12)   He picked the flowers *one by one*.
(13)   One car *in / out of* ten breaks down after ten years of use.
(14)   *Two or three* girls were dancing.
(15)   Out of the *thirty or so* theatres, [...] one has a choice between eight average musical comedies. (Poutsma 1916:1233).
(16)   There are *four of us*.

---

[4] Adjectives occur as heads of a NP (e.g., *the innocent*), be it only marginally.

4.1.4. Conclusion

These observations corroborate Reinhardt's finding, in one of the very few articles on the part of speech status of English numerals, that the English cardinal numerals indeed fall between determiners, adjectives and nouns (Reinhardt 1991:201). The specificity of this intermediate position is legitimately expressed by their being categorized as a class, the cardinals. Nevertheless, the determination of the part of speech status of a number of related linguistic elements can never be fully conclusive. As Croft has recently pointed out (Croft 2000), many of the English grammars as well as the more recent cross-linguistic typologies of parts of speech (e.g. Hengeveld 1992) show methodological insecurities: they either go for a "lumping" approach, or for a "splitting" approach, often without any rigid argumentation. Hence, the question is not so much whether there are grounds to identify an English word class called numerals. That question would not seem to be very interesting because the answer will ultimately always hinge on the categorizations of the specific language-researcher that can never be fully conclusive or definitive (cf. Bloomfield 1970 [1933] and Crystal 1967 for early versions of this claim). As Stassen notes, in the context of a discussion of different Sundanese grammars, "different grammarians may propose different practical solutions, but all of these solutions will inevitably suffer from a certain degree of arbitrariness" (Stassen 1997 qtd. in Croft 2000:67). What is important, however, is the observation that there are good grounds to view the English cardinal numerals as a group of linguistic items with very similar characteristics. They constitute a relatively well-defined object of investigation.

4.2. FORMS OF *TWO*

I will present my corpus-based analysis of English numerals in separate case studies, each drawing attention to different aspects of the meanings of numerals. First, I will deal with *two*, which I will take as a model for the way in which numerals denoting small numbers function in English. "Small numbers" refer to the series from one to nineteen, which are formally characterized by independent lexicalizations[5]. The corpus analysis of *two* constitutes the major part of the analysis of numerals. It is divided into two important parts, one devoted to the expression of "cardinality" (which is related to the parts of speech discussion and the philosophical account of the concept of number, and which will concentrate on the *degree* to which numerals express "cardinality" - Chapter I), and the other, larger part devoted to an analysis of the various *values* ('exactly', 'at least' etc.) of numerals (which relates to the general theoretical discussion of neo-Gricean accounts of numerals - Chapter II). In other, much smaller case studies I will analyze the behavior of numerals denoting round numbers (*ten* and *one thousand*), and the behavior of larger non-round numerals (*twenty-two*). Finally,

---

[5] Strictly speaking, only the numerals *one* through *twelve* have forms that do not use other numerals as constituent parts, but the *-teen* in *thirteen* through *nineteen*, as well as a specific word order, sets them apart from all higher non-round numerals.

I will also discuss the various ways in which speakers and writers of English modify their numerals by means of so-called "restrictors".

Taking *two* as a representative case for the English way of indicating small numbers is defendable on at least three grounds. First, and most importantly, in the BNC-corpus I have used for this analysis, it is the second most frequent numeral, after *one*, which was not chosen because it has a specific conceptual status and a number of different functions. Second, *two* is not a so-called "round number" (Pollmann and Jansen 1996), and as such the analysis below avoids the special characteristics of these round numbers (including "approximation" - Horn 1992:173), which have been pointed out repeatedly (Horn 1972, 1989, 1992, Sadock 1977). Third, there seems to be no reason why the behavior of *two* would be significantly different from that of *seven* or *thirteen*.

One thousand instances of *two* were compiled from the British National Corpus[6]. These were analyzed in terms of form and function, and the relevant correlations between the two. As for the formal properties, the place of the numeral in the noun phrase and the general constitution of the NP containing the numeral were felt to be important. Pronominal and adnominal uses were distinguished. The position and syntactic function of the NP in the clause in which it occurred was indicated, and also the "restrictors" modifying *two* were listed, just as the idiomatic constructions with *two*. With respect to the functions of the numeral, each "solution"[7] to the BNC-query was evaluated as to its "cardinality meaning". It quickly became apparent that not all uses of numerals correspond equally well to this supposed core meaning (Frege 1990 [1884], Hurford 1987). Also, the nouns quantified by *two* were classified semantically and a general characterization of the meaning of the whole NP was given for each solution, in terms of 'exactly', 'at least', 'at most' or 'absolute value' readings, and the trigger for the relevant interpretation was indicated. The presence of a definiteness-marker in the NP turned out to be very important for the interpretation of the numeral. Besides the formal and functional properties of the numerals, I tried to implement two of the traditional tests for implicature in the corpus analysis: the cancellation and the suspension test. As some theorists have also relied on redundancy-tests when determining the meaning of numerals (Horn 1972 and many of his followers, cf. Chapter 3), these too were implemented. In this way, the most important empirical tests that have been used in the past thirty years constitute an essential part of the corpus analysis. Confronting these tests with corpus data provided two kinds of results: in most cases, the meaning analysis of *two* could be refined, but in some cases it was the tests themselves that needed to be qualified. As became clear, the classical cancellation- and suspension tests are incompatible with most of the corpus data. Also the effect of negation on the interpretation of numerals was investigated separately.

---

[6] I refer to Burnard (1995) for details on the composition of the BNC. As will become clear in the examples we use, the BNC collects data on written as well as on spoken English. I do not distinguish between these two types in the analysis. Also, I simply copy the material from the BNC, which means that we do not add or remove punctuation, nor do I correct spelling mistakes or other typos.

[7] I will adopt the BNC term to refer to contextualized tokens of *two* from the BNC.

4.2.1. Adnominal and pronominal uses of *two*

The corpus analysis showed that *two* is primarily used as an adnominal: out of 1000 solutions, *two* was used adnominally 766 times.

> (1) <FRG 81> If we take the neighbourhood studies and the telephone survey together, we can see that **two** different sets of goals are pursued by means of two entirely different methods.

Pronominal uses are much less frequent: in 11.6% of the solutions *two* functioned as a pronoun[8].

> (2) <KDE 1646> Those twins. They was nice. They were beautiful and she had two others didn't she? No one. No she had **two**.
>
> (3) <KB0 3852> Mm. It's also a question isn't it, of whether you appoint a man because he's a good preacher or secondly because he's a good pastor. That's really the question isn't it? Mm. You never get the **two**?

An example of a partitive construction, which is also considered to be a pronominal use, is given in (4).

> (4) <ARK 830> `Makes sense!" Howard's pompous manner changed, his voice went up several decibels. `If it was Paula that means I have **two** of my staff as fugitives from justice"

Specific idiomatic constructions in which *two* does not directly modify a noun were also assigned to this pronominal group. In these idiomatic phrases, the numeral typically does not occur to the immediate left of the noun it modifies. Note also that in this type of construction, the noun (*day*) is not marked for plural.

> (5) <K63 240> She got injured in her back somewhere, but er it was national news, I mean it was in The Mirror and all the papers and it became a, for a day or **two** it was er it was in everywhere, and the theory is that er it was this erm very very dry summer and a very very wet autumn and a bit of dry rot in the timbers somewhere, but it was it was another How long did it actually take you to get out of there?

In 3.8 % of the cases, *two* did not occur adnominally or pronominally, but seemed to function as a noun, e.g., in a game (6), where a specific token that is used in a game (a card?) is called by its name, or in a mathematical exercise (7), where *two* is used to refer to the mathematical number 2. In this somewhat heterogeneous category, I also included very context-specific

---

[8] Once again, I refer to the fact that I adopt a broad notion of what is pronominal (cf. the Prolegomenon of Chapter 4): uses of *two* which function as the head of a noun phrase and which are anaphorical in function will be called pronominal. These include also elliptical uses of *two* (cf. Chapter 4, section 4.3.4.2.).

uses of *two,* e.g., as names of lots in an auction (8) or results of soccer games (9). Formally speaking, these uses of *two* belong together in that they do not integrate easily into the syntactic pattern of the clause. Often, there is not even a clause which they could be said to constitute a part of. This category of uses will be called "nominal", because that seems to be a label that captures the forms of *two* enumerated here. However, I will not attach any semantic claims to that label. Also, the label will not be used in the meaning analysis. Here, it is just meant as a shorthand term for a class of syntactically rather idiosyncratic constructions in which *two* appears. In the mathematical uses of nominal *two,* the numeral does seem to participate in a larger syntactic construction, but, typically, this construction is derived from the structure of mathematical calculations, and as such it is rather idiosyncratic with respect to the constructions in the English language (cf. section 4.3.6. below).

> (6) <KCP 8862> Er, six. I wanted a bloody six or Seventeen. a seven. Seventeen. Ah shit! Seventeen . No, six pair's eight. Ay? Ooh we still haven't bodged up! **Two**. Seven, thank you. Three. Tuppence. Fifteen two three, four, five And Take the lot, go on two , three, four, five, that's a good one! No good staring at it Joy, get it
>
> (7) <KRH 114> Now it may for the game that if he can cover the square number twelve, he will score more points than if he covers the square with the nine. So it will matter then to the child that if he types in four times **two** plus one, it's got to be the right version of that sum.
>
> (8) <HUS 205> Forty five forty five offered and selling forty five to my left, all done at forty five, in all at forty five. Forty five pounds and that's for five **two** two. Five two two sir.
>
> (9) <KS7 15> Carlisle United nil, Hereford United one; Chesterfield one, Torquay United one; Halifax Town nil, Darlington nil; Northampton Town two, Aldershot one; Scunthorpe United **two**, Maidstone United two; Walsall nil, Peterborough United one

Also, *two* sometimes occurs in a highly specific construction, in which the syntactic function of the numeral resembles both a predicatively used adjective and a pronoun: in (10), *two* denotes age and can be compared to adjectives like *old* or *young,* but can also be interpreted as a pro-form for *two years (old).* In (11), there is another type of *two,* which refers to the indication of time. It can be associated with adverbs such as *tomorrow* or *yesterday,* but it can also be seen as an abbreviated form of *two o'clock* (which is itself more an adverbial construction than an NP) or even of the somewhat odd *two hours after noon* (which leads back to an adnominal use of *two*). Because of their close relationship with the nominal uses (both show a considerable degree of abstraction, are non-adnominal and cannot easily be reduced to pronouns), I decided to put them in the same category. In the meaning analysis below (section 4.3.), I will differentiate between these meanings.

> (10) <ASN 835> `Naples, let me see. It would have been 1935 or `36. Henry was only **two**, I remember. 1935. Yes, it must have been.
>
> (11) <EF1 539> `Get hold of Sabrina and C.W. Tell them I want them here by **two** this afternoon."

In 1.4 % of the solutions, *two* figured explicitly in a counting sequence (12). I also collected the numerals that primarily seem to help orienting or coordinating an activity (13). The former example reminds us of how people use numerals to indicate rhythm in order to coordinate certain activities.

> (12) <KCU 10613> One, **two**, three, four, five, six, seven, eight, nine. You counted two instead of one then, I mean one instead of two
> (13) <FUL 1747> Yeah. It is. Next time any other business Right. So. Hello Den. I've I've just come back on that D **two** stop three. No. Sorry. Yes. Please do Den. Right. The, the D two stop three the work of an Ah. urgent nature Yeah.

In 65 cases the solutions of the corpus analysis were not relevant, either because *two* formed part of a larger numeral or a name, or because the function was unclear. One solution featured *two* as a full noun, which is demonstrated by the presence of the article *the*.

> (14) <FM5 303> Right right. you got the the O H is the bit you want twice so write it down put the brackets round it and then the **two**.

TABLE 2

FORMS OF *TWO*

766/1000 adnominal uses of *two* (76.6%)	116/1000 pronominal uses of *two* + ellipsis (11.6%)	38/1000 nominal uses of *two* (3.8%)	14/1000 uses of *two* in a counting sequence (1.4%)	66/1000 other uses of *two* (6.6%)

4.2.2. Analysis of the NP containing *two*

As far as the construction of these NPs is concerned, the most important question is whether the noun phrase containing *two* also contains a determiner, and, more specifically, whether it contains a marker of definiteness (be it a definite article, a demonstrative or a genitival construction). This influences the meaning of the numeral considerably (cf. Chapter 5). In general, 25.1 % of the solutions contained an NP in which *two* is preceded by a determiner. For obvious reasons, numerals almost never occur with indefinite articles (*one* and *a* have similar functions and are mutually exclusive; the higher numerals indicate plurality, while the indefinite article *a* can only be used with singular nouns). In 0.5% of the cases, however, the NP was introduced by an indefinite article all the same (15).

(15) <EA0 637> We conducted a **two** year study to assess the effectiveness of the family smoking education and smoking and me projects in influencing smoking behaviour.

In this construction a so-called "attributive noun" (Quirk et al. 1985:1333) is itself quantified. The numeral forms a single unit with the first noun (*year*) to form, together with the second noun (*study*), the core of the NP. Hence, the noun itself may very well be singular, even if it is modified with a numeral like *two*. This corresponds with the general observation that attributive nouns are usually number-neutral and that premodification is normally less explicit than postmodification (compare *an absence of ten years* with *a ten year absence*) (Quirk et al. 1985:1333).

Other elements that may be part of the phrase containing *two* are prepositions: in 31.8% of the solutions, the NP is introduced by a preposition (16). In the discussion of the functions of numerals, it will appear that some prepositions will also influence the meaning of the numeral, be it indirectly, as part of the way in which a certain state or activity is expressed[9].

(16) <K3A 66> After **two** weeks, drain off the liquor from the fruit pulp and store the purpley liquid in a screwtop bottle just like the one it came out of in fact.

Also, in 3.3% of the cases, the numeral itself is modified by an "ordering modifier" (17), like *latter* or *previous*, or *first*:

(17) <A6J 404> she'd been enthusiastically interested at college and during the first **two** years after she had qualified;

---

[9] In a "test-drive" of this corpus analysis, I classified all NPs containing the numerals in question (*two* and *zero*) according to the word class of the first element of the NP (determiner, preposition, adjective, participle etc.) (Bultinck 2001). I refrained from doing that here, as the results of the research in this specific subarea were not immediately relevant to the description of *two* as such (i.e., when it is described in isolation and not in comparison with *zero*). Only the occurrence of determiners, and, to some extent, the presence of prepositions in the NP are directly relevant to a meaning analysis of numerals.

TABLE 3

ELEMENTS IN NP CONTAINING *TWO*

In 25.1% of the NPs, *two* is preceded by a determiner. In 0.5% of the total number of NPs, this determiner is indefinite.	31.8% of the NPs contain a preposition	12.2% of the NPs contain a restrictor (cf. section 4.2.3. below)	3.3% of the NPs contain an "ordering modifier"

Next, also the syntactic function of the NP and its position in the clause were determined (frontal (23.2%), central (34.5%) or final (31.7%)[10]). In itself, these parameters were not expected to be of direct relevance for the interpretation of numerals, even though e.g. topicalization may influence the interpretation of numerals. Also, by looking at the way in which the NP functions in the whole clause, some interesting constructions were found, e.g., the adjectival construction in (18).

> (18) <B3C 950> However, of primary importance is the portfolio of work presented at interview, which should display evidence of high potential creative ability and accomplishment in drawing as well as **two** and three-dimensional work.

Within the adjective *two-dimensional* the numeral fulfils the canonical adnominal function, but this construction is noteworthy because *two* freely combines with a denominal adjective (*dimensional*) here. This structure is comparable to other adjectival constructions such as *blue-colored* or *sad-looking*, but in the latter expressions, the second part is typically a participle instead of a denominal adjective or adverb[11].

The three largest groups as far as syntactic function is concerned are the adverbially used NPs (26%) (19), the subject-NPs (22.5%) (20), the direct object-NPs (16.4%) (21), and *two* as (part of an) adjunct to a head of an NP (13.4%) (22)[12].

---

[10] "Frontal" refers to the phrase-initial position, "final" to the final position in the phrase and "central" to intermediate positions. 10.6% are irrelevant (e.g., because the NP is the only constituent in the "sentence", or the numeral is part of a counting sequence).

[11] In the BNC, a word-query on "two-" elicited all compounds with *two* as the first constituent. The search yielded *two-hourly* and *two-divisional* as similar constructions. Adjectives do not seem to combine with denominal adjectives to form a single compound adjective, even though they can combine with non-denominal adjectives (*a dark-grey coat*).

[12] The other groups are prepositional objects (3%), appositions (0.4%), predicates (4.7%) and a miscellaneous group (13.6%) with undecidable and borderline cases.

(19) <HU4 2285> Saliva and esophageal fluid were taken from **two** subjects and pooled.

(20) <HXY 1506> In one major respect it is different, though: her **two** pauses of 0.6 seconds (lines 11 and 13) are interpreted as signals that other speakers may now have the floor.

(21) <JY2 1210> With a lean finger he indicated an unusual mask-like carving on the centre panel, showing **two** identical faces looking in opposite directions.

(22) <AR2 112> He imagined small, cheaply staged pictures of sexual tortures involving ropes and wires - the kind of things which Boy had not yet done. He imagined a full-page, black and white photo of **two** barechested men (their chests shaved), photographed in daylight, walking down the street, gazing squarely at the camera, holding hands, one of them holding an alsatian straining at a leather leash.

TABLE 4

SYNTACTIC FUNCTION OF NP CONTAINING *TWO*

Adverbial	Subject	Direct Object	Adjunct	Other (21.7%)
(26%)	(22.5%)	(16.4%)	(13.4%)	

Finally, some NPs containing *two* showed specific constructions in which the numeral is placed after the nominal head it modifies (23), or constructions in which *two* and the noun it modifies together form a unit that is itself modifiable (cf. (15) above). The latter structure is rather flexible in its combinations so that this construction may result in highly complicated NPs like (24), in which the preposed nouns serve to name the head noun (*concept*), rather than indicate its size, length or duration (as in (15) above) and (25), in which the attributive nominal *two tone* is postposed vis-à-vis its head noun and coordinated with the adjective *monochrome*, foregrounding its own adjectival nature.

(23) <KGL 618> Alistair yes, there's always the That, those, yes, that goes into your section **two** of your log.

(24) <HKV 3079> The "one country, **two** systems" concept agreed by China was based on Hong Kong's colonial administration system rather than on parliamentary democracy, he warned.

(25) <GU9 259> Not surprisingly, the `Laura Ashley" palette was always highly distinctive; from the moment the shop opened it was clear that their prints, either monochrome or **two** tone, were being produced in colours nowhere else available.

The distribution of *two* with respect to its occurrence with singular/plural nouns is shown in Table 5:

TABLE 5

ADNOMINAL *TWO* WITH SINGULAR AND PLURAL NOUNS

BEFORE SINGULAR NOUN (9/766=1.2%)	AFTER SINGULAR NOUN (24/766=3.1%)	BEFORE PLURAL NOUN (733/766=95.7%)

There is not a single instance of *two* in the sample corpus that is placed immediately after a plural noun.

4.2.3. Restrictors

Of all occurrences of *two* in the sample corpus 12.2% were accompanied by a restrictor. In my terminology, a "restrictor" is any linguistic element that directly modifies the cardinality meaning of a numeral[13]. The restrictors found in the corpus were classified according to their meaning: the largest group (46 solutions) is the one in which an 'approximately' meaning combines with an 'at most' meaning (26). The majority of instances in this group do not feature one-word restrictors, but multiple-word idiomatic constructions in which the modification expresses an "interval", i.e. a range in between two numbers (27).

> (26) <ANF 979> For almost **two** weeks Modigliani worked on the painting, an unusually long time for him and perhaps the only time when he agreed to `continue" a painting.
> (27) <HD3 164> One or **two** ageing members of the team have encouraged younger men to join to ensure continuity, and so some of any funds donated may be allocated to training.

Other groups contain solutions with 'at least' (28), 'at most' (29), 'exactly' (30), 'approximately' (31) modifiers or a combination of 'at least' and 'approximately' restrictors (32).

> (28) <KE2 6426> I don't know ho certainly I know there had been at least **two** peo different lots of people living in ours before we moved in, and I would think there were probably more than that.
> (29) <J6V 651> Unless the reports are agreed, the parties are at liberty to call experts whose reports have been disclosed, limited to **two** medical experts and one non-medical expert of any kind.
> (30) <HR3 1206> Without the absolute power of an Egyptian Pharaoh one could scarcely test the consequences of an experiment involving the manipulation of people's

---

[13] In Chapter II, I will look at a number of linguistic elements that *indirectly* modify the cardinal meaning of numerals (e.g., definiteness markers). These elements will not be called "restrictors" because their principal function is not the modification of the cardinality meaning. They may, however, have an indirect influence on the expression of cardinality.

lives, for example forcing a percentage of the population to emigrate or insisting that each fertile married couple produce exactly **two** offspring.

(31) <G09 1238> `They were made by the village cobbler and cost fourteen shillings: they'd last about **two** years if you got them clumped at the end of the first year."

(32) <FRT 1319> This brought together in a simplified form a number of remedies obtainable from a Divisional Court of the Queen's Bench Division consisting of **two** or three judges.

The precise functions of the different restrictors will not be discussed here, as they will be the subject of a separate analysis (cf. Chapter 5, section 5.5. below).

4.2.4. Complex constructions

The English numerals form part of specific complex constructions remarkably often. No less than 10.4% of all uses of *two* constitute part of a combination of a numeral + a number of other elements. In this discussion of the formal features of numerals, I will simply mention some of these complex constructions.

The construction in (33) is remarkable because two adnominal numerals are conjoined by the conjunction *or*. In (34), *two* is also used adnominally, but it is *one* that determines the cardinality in this partitive construction. The construction in (35) is but one example of how numerals combine with prepositions to indicate intervals.

(33) <ADH 314> But it should be clear that while one or **two** methods may be the most important for attributing coins to a mint or dating them, almost any other consideration can be important, depending on its relevance or on the accidents of survival.

(34) <B7G 77> The group of researchers that has seen the first indications of a Z particle is code named UA1, and is one of the **two** teams that reported the evidence for the W particle earlier this year.

(35) <B7K 1329> The southern oscillation reverses irregularly, but typically at intervals of from **two** to five years.

4.3. FUNCTIONS OF *TWO*: CORPUS ANALYSIS

In order to make a first classification of the meanings of *two*, the solutions were categorized in groups, according to the extent to which they indicate "cardinality". As argued above (cf. the prolegomenon in section 4.1.), numerals indicate cardinality when they signify the number of elements a certain set of objects contains. In other words, numerals that express cardinality specify the numerosity of a group of entities. The discussion of the Gricean theories on numerals showed that this is perceived to be the most important use of numerals. This is confirmed by the corpus analysis. But the extent to which specific uses of numerals demonstrate this cardinality function is a matter of degree, and this fact has not been given its proper place in the traditional grammatical analyses, let alone in the neo-Gricean treatment of numerals. In general, the wide range of uses of numerals is not fully acknowledged. Some perfectly acceptable uses are nearly always excluded from the discussion.

In the following sections, the main uses of numerals will be discussed in terms of the extent to which they express "cardinality". First, the fully cardinal uses will be presented. In the following three cases (*two* as label, as indication of time and as a pronoun), there remains a link with the cardinality function. In the latter four (*two* as a symbol, *two* in mathematical language games, discourse-structural *two*, and other uses of *two*), the connection with the cardinality meaning has become very tenuous. Each section starts with a short discussion of a typical member of the group, followed up by a longer discussion of interesting deviations from that standard example. In this way, the ensuing discussion on degrees of "cardinality" will also feature detailed discussions of a number of uses of numerals that would otherwise remain unnoticed. The frequencies of the various uses of *two* are given in Table 6.

TABLE 6

DEGREES OF CARDINALITY

Pure cardinal	74.1%
Label	2.5%
Temporal	1%
Pronominal + elliptical	11.6%
Symbol	0.1%
Mathematical	1%
Discourse-structural	less than 0.1% (not in corpus sample)
Others	3%
Irrelevant	6.7%[14]

The last two sections of this part on cardinality will address the relationship between adnominal form and cardinal meaning (1.2.2.9.) and suggest some general parameters that influence the expression of cardinality of numerals (1.2.2.10.).

4.3.1. Cardinal *two*

In (36) and (37), the most frequent situation (74.1%) is exemplified. In (36) *two* modifies a concrete noun, in (37) an abstract noun, but in both cases the conceptualization is the same: a certain part of reality is presented as a group of entities, and the number of elements of this group is explicitly indicated by the numeral.

(36) <FRK 1343> Nothing more was seen or heard of the **two** men, and after a few days, the event was forgotten.
(37) <CMN 447> He lays particular stress on **two** consequences of this analysis, both of which are presented as advantages of Marx's theory.

---

[14] Solutions in which *two* is part of a larger numeral or part of a name.

In both sentences, the numeral modifies a noun that indicates a set of objects (a set of men and a set of consequences). This is typically indicated by the plural marking on the noun.

4.3.2. *Two* as a label

4.3.2.1. Standard examples
In the appositive use of numerals (Quirk et al. 1985:1316-1317) *two* functions as a label, or part of a label, and the cardinality function recedes into the background. Formally, these uses are characterized by the position of the numeral (to the right of the head noun) and the number of the noun (always singular). The numeral is primarily used to distinguish other instantiations of the head noun, not so much to indicate the number of elements of the group of objects indicated by the noun. In (38), e.g., it is presumed that in the domain of discourse there is also a *part one* or possibly even a *part three*; *two* is used to distinguish this particular part from the others. To put it bluntly: *part three* does not mean that there is a group of three parts, but that there is a (one) part that is called *part three*[15]. This use of *two* can be called "name-like" because it singles out one specific referent, just like proper names do. In (39) *two* is even more name-like: (39) does not say that there are two Fs and that *F two* is the second F. There is no such thing F, the existence of which is allegedly affirmed (of course the existence of a key *F two* is understood, and there may be something like a series of "F-keys"). Clearly, *F two* refers unambiguously to one specific key on the keyboard (probably of a computer). Consequently, *two* in (39) ranks low as far as the expression of cardinality is concerned. The utterances in (40) and (41) contain similar examples of the "singular noun + numeral" construction. They show that in these "label" uses the link with counting practices is still present (*two* in *World War Two* indicates that there have been at least two world wars, while *two* in *division two* suggests that there are at least two divisions), but the prominence of the cardinality meaning is clearly reduced. These numerals identify a specific instance of the entity their nominal head denotes and, at the same time, give an (inconclusive) indication of the cardinality of the complete set of these entities. As mentioned, they are similar to proper nouns in that they help to pick out one and only one referent.

>(38) <K22 517> Video-Taped report follows BLACKPOOL LINDA
>. TOWNLEY/Stroud Labour Party CLIVE SOLEY MP/Lab Hammersmith Voice over
>In part **two**: Putting the boot in.
>(39) <HDV 654> What did you say then. If you press F two F two, that's what I was after, yes. If you press F **two**, and then do what? It loses the chopped, the end of it.

---

[15] Incidentally, the numeral in *part three* does give us some information about the cardinality of the group consisting of 'all parts'. In a "label" construction N NUM (noun numeral) this number will generally indicate that the number of Ns is NUM or more than NUM. This information can be inferred from the "label" construction in question, but this is not part of its "coded content". This is illustrated by the fact that an inference from the N NUM construction to a cardinality judgment can easily be rectified:
A: This is part three of the "Test your intelligence" series.
B: Oh, I see. Where are the other two parts, then?
A: Actually, there is no second part. It was never released. But part one is on the shelf.

(40) <J1M 203> He then won at Wembley with Birmingham, before repeating the cup winning feat with Stoke AND leading the club out of division **two**.
(41) <K94 1038> In a `sellers market", similar to that which pertained in the United Kingdom after World War **Two**, there was little need for promotional activity because demand exceeded supply and whatever was produced was taken up immediately by the market.

Nevertheless, the cardinal dimension is not entirely absent: the labeling could have been done through other means just as well (e.g., with letters (*part A, part B* etc.) or with full names (*the part called "Putting the boot in"*)). By using numerals, there usually remains a link to the act of counting, which is fundamental for the concept of cardinality. Syntactically, this "label" use can be called "appositive": appositive constructions often feature names, e.g., in the combination of titles and proper names (as in *general Powell* or *Mary, the leader of our team*) (Quirk et al. 1985:1300-1321)[16].

4.3.2.2. Marginal labels: Counting the seconds one two three

In order to show the complexity of these uses of numerals, some "label" uses that diverge from the picture that has just been sketched will be discussed in more detail. In the category of "labeling" uses there are intricate constructions that do not fully match the appositive uses described in the previous section. By way of an example, let us concentrate on (42), which I will discuss in detail and at length because it combines diverse functions of numerals in an interesting way. The numerals in (42) differ manifestly from the uncontroversially appositive uses: formally, they are marked compared to the singular noun + numeral constructions described in the previous section, and this formal distinction corresponds to a different meaning. More specifically, (42) presents *two* as an element in a counting sequence, but at the same time it conceptualizes *two* as a label. In this sentence, *two* certainly does not exemplify a usage that demonstrates a high degree of cardinality, but it does not exactly fit the "labeling" use either.

(42) <A6T 2317> He counted the seconds, one, **two**, three, four, and then it hit the tent with a fury that he had never known, he inside in his sleeping bag with his feet braced against the dome pole facing the onslaught.

In this construction, the counting is done explicitly, but the cardinality reading is, paradoxically, less prominent. The construction strikes us as atypical, or at least as belonging predominantly to spoken language, even if it can be used in written language, as in this case. Obviously, this is no reason to refrain from analyzing it. If *two* is only minimally cardinal in (42), what is it then?

The difference between (42) and its truly adnominal counterpart *He counted two seconds* is subtle, but nonetheless essential: the first portrays a state-of-affairs that is conceptualized as one in which different instantiations of the same category (seconds, in this

---

[16] Significantly, Quirk et al. rank these "naming relations" or "appellations" (Quirk et al. 1985:1309) as the highest on their scale of apposition.

case) are being named, one by one. In the sentence *he counted two seconds*, the conceptualization is such that attention is drawn to the group of objects affected by the activity of the agent ("seconds"), and in a second step the number of elements of this group is indicated. In (42) the objects that are counted are not even explicitly indicated; the noun *seconds* is not repeated. This demonstrates that *two* in (42) is less prominent as far as the expression of cardinality is concerned. It also shows that if *two* in (42) functions as a label, it does so in a special way.

The numerals *one, two, three, four* are positioned immediately to the right of the noun and the numerals certainly function as labels. Maybe it is an appositive construction? Contrary to standard appositive constructions, however, not every numeral is accompanied by a noun. The numerals in (42) might be compared to an enumeration of the names of, e.g., someone's children (43), rather than to a series of appositive constructions as in (44).

> (43) He recited their names: Johnny, Mary, Lucy, Christopher.
> (44) And here we have the number one, followed by the number two and the number three.

Furthermore, when (42) is compared to Quirk's classification of appositive constructions, it transpires that there is not a single type that exactly matches the characteristics of the sequence of numerals in (42). The category that best resembles it as far as the form is concerned, is "reformulation based on factual knowledge", exemplified in (45):

> [From Quirk et al. 1985:1311]
> (45) *The Nordic countries*, or *Denmark, Finland, Iceland, Norway, Sweden, ...*

Note that in spoken English the conjunction *or* can easily be omitted. In this example, there is a definite plural NP, juxtaposed to an enumeration of different lexical items, which all exemplify the type indicated by the NP. It is the association with this type of construction that gives (42) its appositive flavor.

Nevertheless, as already mentioned, the construction in (42) is not really an example of apposition. The context of this kind of expression is crucial: the counting of the seconds is probably a way to measure time, but it could just as well have been a way to help the speaker fall asleep. These contexts are so unique to expressions with numerals that a comparison with (43) can only be part of the story. Perhaps the best way to characterize this use of *two* is to call it "epenthetic": it can be compared to the onomatopoeic exclamations in *He hit Johnny in the face, Bang!, Bang!, Ouch!* But the numerals in (42) are still slightly different in that they give information as to how many seconds it took before "it hit the tent", while the epenthetic exclamations do not necessarily correspond one-to-one with the number of hits Johnny received (they seem to illustrate the intensity of the slaps, rather than the number of hits).

In (42), the agent is first represented as counting seconds, and then this action is exemplified by a series of numerals. Benacerraf's distinction between "transitive" and "intransitive" counting may prove helpful in this context: in "transitive counting", one counts entities that are independent of the counting act. This corresponds to the transitive use of the verb *to count*. In intransitive counting, nothing is counted, but the speaker simply recites the number sequence (Benacerraf 1965:49-50). Benacerraf gives the example of a preoperative patient who puts on an ether mask and is asked to count as far as he or she can. This situation is similar to the one in (42) or the one of the child who is counting sheep in order to fall asleep. A corresponding linguistic expression was found in the BNC.

> (46) <JYC 622> She sighed. `All right. Can I have a book to read, then?" `I'm afraid it's no to that, too. Give your head a chance — count sheep if you can't get to sleep."

"Counting sheep" is certainly not a typical instance of transitive counting (the child is not confronted with a set of sheep the cardinality of which has to be determined), but it does not fit the paradigmatic examples of "intransitive counting" either. "Counting seconds" as well as "counting sheep" both seem to belong to a middle class in between transitive and intransitive counting: the practice corresponding to the linguistic expression is very similar to the one of the preoperative patient, but its linguistic structure (*count* + direct object) is the same as that of expressions of transitive counting.

In (42), the number sequence itself leads the progression of the counting. It is not "governed" by a group of visible objects, in the sense that the end-point of the counting does not coincide with the counting of the last uncounted entity. No one-to-one relationship between one specific numeral and a pre-existent entity is established. The expression presents the state-of-affairs as if there were indeed entities that are being counted one by one, but in reality the counting of the seconds does not involve any one-to-one relationship. The counting stops when an event external to the act of counting signals the end of the temporal stretch to be measured (in this case something that hits the tent the speaker is sitting in). Every numeral functions as a label for a new second. Other than in the appositive uses of numerals, however, the label itself is not really important: the numerals will normally not be used to refer to separate sheep or seconds. The label of the last unit is important in the case of counting seconds, but not *qua* label: it indicates the cardinality of the group of seconds that have passed. This is an example of how some specific uses of numerals fit the traditional semantic categories rather badly: *two* in (42) is reminiscent of how names function (because names have unique denotation, just like these numerals each refer to one and only one count), and the conceptualization of this sort of counting is certainly one of "putting labels on things", but it is certainly not reducible to that image, because it has special characteristics of its own.

A comparison with other divergent uses emphasizes the specificity of (42) still more. Looking for similar uses of numerals in the BNC, I came across the following example.

> (47) <A0N 1229> When everyone expected him to break into a nimble tune, he played a slow air that sounded Irish in the long luxuriant unfolding of each phrase. People listened entranced, laced together by the tendrils of the melody. It finished, he tapped his foot, one **two** three four, and then he did launch into a jig, springy and violent.

This sentence is very similar to the one in (42), although there is no explicit mentioning of what the numerals are supposed to refer to. Obviously, the sequence of numerals is meant to illustrate the way in which the musician is tapping his foot, but this is suggested by implication. Because there is no noun present, the numerals cannot be said to be in an appositive relation with the noun phrase. At the most, *one, two, three, four* could be considered as appositive to the predication *counting the seconds*. Be that as it may, in (42) there is an explicit link between the sequence *one, two three, four* and the seconds that are being counted. This causes the name-like character of the numerals in (42) - the numerals are mapped one-to-one to a single point in the counting of the seconds - a quality that is absent in (47).

Another example shows that I have left out one fundamental fact in the analysis of (42): the analysis is further complicated by the depictive nature of the sentence. The speaker is clearly *describing* someone who is counting and the enumeration *one, two, three, four* is designed as some sort of "copy" of what the speaker is doing (mentally or linguistically). It is clearly a representation of a counting act, rather than the enumeration of numerals that accompanies a real counting sequence, as in (48).

> (48) <ADA 2241> Start counting. Sheep in the shelter, count them. One **two** three four five six not yet seven eight nine no no ten eleven twelve wait thirteen fourteen no ! fifteen not yet ! sixteen wait, wait, wait seventeen wait !

In (48), the well-known sequence of numerals is exemplified. The example is also from a novel, but it is part of a dialogue, and can therefore be considered as a registration of spoken language. Other than in (42), the linguistic autonomy of the sequence of numerals is complete: it does not resemble any other linguistic structure at all. The sequence in (48) illustrates the "pure" counting act. It is clear that any description of (48) must make reference to the accompanying pointing act, which is the standard procedure for 3- to 5-year-olds, but which can be "internalized" later (Fuson and Hall 1983:55-56). It is this context that can explain the function of *two* in (48). Essentially, in this sort of transitive counting act, each counting word is assigned to a single referent.

The counting sequence in (42) is clearly different: it is introduced in a larger syntactic construction, and its function becomes much more difficult to describe. It is as if the speaker wants to remind the addressee of how people count; as if the numerals in (42) are "quoted" in direct speech. It is the representation of this counting act that makes it possible to view *two* as a label for the specific (the second) second. Because the seconds are conceptualized as entities (as direct object of the verb "to count"), it is possible to construe the counting act as labeling each second by means of a numeral, just like in the "pure" counting act. Therefore, the highly complicated function of *two* in (42) can be considered as the result of a superposition of the typical representation of a "transitive" counting act onto a description of someone who counts in order to measure time. The first component is expressed in the transitive construction *count seconds*, the second in an enumeration of the numerals *one, two, three, four*, which exemplifies the counting act. Both are superimposed because the enumeration of the numerals is a representation of the passing of the seconds.

In comparison, (49) is relatively simple.

> (49) <BMS 2339> At the bottom: my purse. I opened it. Counted it. Fifty pounds in notes — one **two** three four pound coins — two 20ps and three 2-pences.

In this sentence, the counting sequence is described (the example is from a novel, just like (42)), but the sequence is part of an enumeration, which identifies the contents of the purse. The sequence *one, two, three, four* is a representation of the counting act, which is also comparable to the use of numerals in (42), but the numerals do not fulfil an appositive function here. Nevertheless, also in (49) there is a superposition of two separate functions: on the one hand the numerals function as the representation of the number sequence, on the other hand the numeral *four* is reinterpreted as a simple adnominal. This is clear from the construction *four pound coins*, which is an example of the typical adnominal use of numerals. Moreover, because of this reinterpretation of *four*, all previous numerals in the counting sequence acquire an adnominal interpretation as well. The adnominal function of numerals is superimposed on their function as representation of the counting sequence.

4.3.2.3. *Number two*

To round off the analysis of "label" uses of *two*, I will take a look at another specific construction, one in which *two* is part of the phrase *number two*. It will appear that this entire construction can function as a label of a noun, but it will be shown that *number two* fulfils a range of other functions as well. The appositive construction in (50), e.g., is a mixture of two specific usages of numerals: on the one hand the internal structure of the phrase *number two* is clearly appositive, but in (50) it is also anaphorical in that the *whole* phrase *number two* stands for "one of the things" mentioned before (it replaces the larger construction *thing number two*) and it refers back to one of the three "things" mentioned before.

> (50) <JK1 566> But, you could, you could just imagine, you've got three things, one, each one is interdependent on the other, change one and the others will change. So if you change number one and number **two**, it is possible to keep number three the same.

In that respect, it is different from appositive constructions like *part three* discussed above (section 4.3.1.2.): in (50) *number two* does not refer to a certain number (its meaning cannot be paraphrased as 'the second number', while *part three* can be paraphrased as 'the third part'), but the phrase as a whole refers to a thing. In other words, while the typical appositive uses of numerals specify the name of the entity denoted by the noun in the appositive noun-numeral construction, in (50) the numeral first ties up with *number* to differentiate itself from the other numbers (*number one* and *number three*), and only then, in a second step, the whole construction becomes anaphorical: *number two* replaces the noun *thing*. It refers back to an entity that was mentioned before or that is present in the context of conversation (either as part of the background or through accommodation (Thomason 1990)[17]). It must be emphasized, however, that this anaphorical feature is not always present in *number two*-constructions. *Number two* can be used in a range of other appositive constructions as well as in discourse-structural constructions. An additional corpus search

---

[17] Thomason (1990) describes "accommodation" as a "special case of obstacle elimination" (Thomason 1990:343). In this study, I will mainly use the term "accommodation" to refer to the pragmatic construal of contextual assumptions that are necessary to interpret an utterance.

yielding 200 instances of *number two* revealed a number of interesting uses. I will discuss the most significant ones below.

Example (51) contains a use of *number two* that comes very close to that of the standard appositive noun-numeral constructions. Remarkably, only two out of two hundred instances of *number two* (1%) featured this type.

> (51) <AYK 1647> Since I also all know how to halve things (and are usually pretty familiar with the two times table), try this instead. Division : You can use a similar method for dividing by 50 because it is always easier to work with the number **two**.

In this sentence, *two* is indeed an instance of the category "number": the phrase *number two* specifies the name of the number, just like *three* in *chapter three* specifies the name of the chapter.

However, there is a subtle distinction between the two uses, which is formally expressed: the presence of the definite article in (51) emphasizes the appositive character of the construction (without it, *number two* would be anaphorical and would license the hearer to go and look for an antecedent, which simply is not there), whereas the elements of phrases like *chapter three* seem to form a unit with more internal cohesion. While *chapter three* picks out a referent by virtue of the combination of elements the meanings of which can be paraphrased as 'chapter' and 'the third in the series of chapters', *the number two* in (51) is interpreted as identifying a definite number, namely the number two. The position of *two* as part of the series of natural numbers is not brought to the fore. This is further demonstrated by the fact that *part three, chapter five*, or even *scene two* can be paraphrased by making use of an ordinal as 'the third part', 'the fifth chapter' or 'the second scene'. In (51), *the number two* cannot be paraphrased as 'the second number'. This shows that the latter construction is much closer to the standard appositive one in that the two components are semantically more autonomous. The definite article in *the number two*, together with the fact that *the number* can be left out in (51), indicates that this construction is more similar to appositive constructions like *the Belgian author Hugo Claus* than it is similar to constructions like *chapter three*. The internal cohesion of *chapter two* or *division two* is borne out by the fact that the noun cannot be left out.

> (52) ?? He then won at Wembley with Birmingham, before repeating the cup winning feat with Stoke AND leading the club out of two. [instead of: *division two*]

In general, the construction *division two* is more similar to proper names than *number two* in statements like *number two is my favorite number*, where the numeral in itself already refers to an entity and the addition *number* is strictly appositive. This appositive use is linked to the platonic conception of numbers as real, existing entities. The difference in meaning remains very subtle, though.

Other uses of the phrase *number two* include constructions in which it is placed immediately to the right of a noun, and which I will call the pure "label" use of *number two*.

(53) <A1C 596> While his mother was watching Look North he crept downstairs and phoned the poly, but they told him Dr Barraclough wasn't available till next week. That was blow number one. Blow number **two** was Eunice Snell's complete failure as a mother.

Crucially, in this construction (25.5% of the total number of instances of *number two*), not *two*, but the entire phrase *number two* functions as a label that specifies the name of the entity. It is comparable to the *chapter three* construction and other standard examples of *two* as a label, but the presence of *number* makes the 'series' reading of the numeral more prominent. Occasionally, *number two* occurs pre-nominally with the same meaning.

(54) <HGF 1269> Finally, Gran was ready. `Ready as I can be," she said loudly and poked her with her stick. `This is my number one leg, girl, and you're my number **two** leg, so get up. Come on." When she walked with Gran, she could feel the trembling through every limb and felt glad to be young and strong as a tree.

In another type of construction, *number two* does not modify a noun.

(55) <HGF 467> No new music until the next cheque. Rae rifled through the jumble of cassettes and hauled out seven unmarked possibilities. Number one was Bob Dylan and she cut it off after the first sneering words of despair. Number **two** was static and reggae, pirated from the pirate station DBC years before in Paddington. Marianne Faithfull, Marlene Dietrich, tragedy and camp. Then the third and last cassette yielded Mozart and she smiled.

I will call these uses the 'enumeration' use of *number two*. They constitute 25.5% of the sample corpus (cf. also (50)). In these constructions, the phrase can function anaphorically (55-56) or not (57). In (57), the use of *number two* is clearly parasitical on the practice of schematizing entities or events in written language. *Number one, number two* etc. can be understood as a vocalization of enumeration symbols such as *1), 2)* etc.

(56) <KS7 172> However, Brighton were not overawed and they came back with a penalty through Small after seventy three minutes. Burne netted number **two** for .Brighton and these two sides go to the south coast in the week.
(57) <J92 86> Right er plenty of minutes so I'll, I'll quickly read them out, and then if anyone's got any matters arising they know what Er number one Wentworth are booking both not Goodricke. Number **two**, I sent off a letter saying about people not coming and er Wentworth haven't sent a I dunno.

In (56), *number two* refers to 'goal number two' or 'the second goal'. Because the context is clearly that of a game of soccer, the antecedent of *number two* can be easily construed.

In (57), however, the context is that of someone reading out a list of items. In the latter example the hearer can also come up with an antecedent (e.g., *issue* or *item* as in *issue/item number two*), but that will be much more vague. The principal function of *number two* in (57) is structural: it orders the subjects to be dealt with. In (56), it primarily represents an entity that was mentioned before or that is to be recovered from the context. This corresponds with its syntactic behavior: in (56) *number two* fulfils a clear purpose in the sentence (as direct object of *netted*), but in (57) it stands apart from the rest of the sentence, which functions independently.

In (58) and (59), yet another use of *number two* is exemplified. In this construction, *number two* has a 'ranking' function, which not only imposes an order on things (as in the 'enumeration' uses), but also a hierarchy. With 41% of the corpus solutions, this 'ranking' use is definitely the major function of *number two*. One obvious context for these uses is all sorts of rankings, such as the pop charts.

> (58) <A17 422> Shortly afterwards, Sinitta and David split up and she signed a major recording deal which culminated in her single So Macho reaching number **two** in the charts, only missing the top spot because of Chris De Burgh's Lady in Red.
> (59) <CHB 2504> Little wonder, then, that the top of the US Hot 100 currently reflects a nationwide interest in babies. For, at the time of writing, at Number **Two** is TLC 's `Baby, Baby, Baby", co-produced by Kenny `Babyface" Edmonds, the same producer sharing the credits of Boyz II Men 's chart-topping `End Of The Road".

In this ranking use, *number two* can also function as a nominal modifier that is placed in front of the noun (as opposed to the postnominal "pure label" use of *number two*, which is similar to the 'label' uses of *two* in general, cf. section 4.3.2.). In the following example *number two* qualifies the noun in such a way that it defines its quality in terms of some ranking (in this case, the ranking of the best batsmen in the world)[18].

> (60) <CH3 1131> Brian Close, Ray Illingworth and Fred Trueman wanted a tearaway fast bowler but were overruled when paymasters Yorkshire TV insisted on the world's number **two** batsman.

The sample corpus also revealed 'ranking' instances of *number two* as head noun of an NP: as the predicate of a copula construction (61), in an appositive construction (62), or with an anaphoric load (63). In these examples, *number two* stands for 'number two company' and 'Britain's number two tennis player', and this antecedent has to be reconstructed from the context[19].

---

[18] This group consists mainly of 'ranking' uses that feature as head noun (64/82 solutions), but there are also 'ranking' uses that appear prenominally:
<CSH 426> Hewlett-Packard Co is likely to steal DEC's thunder and whisk away its number **two** position as the second largest computer vendor in the US by 1994, Hembricht & Quist analyst Robert Herwick says.
These prenominal uses constitute a small subgroup (18/82).

[19] Which comes very close to saying that the *number two* construction is elliptic here. Whether this construction is to be called elliptic or anaphoric is largely a terminological question: it is clear that the phrase *number two* is in itself semantically underdetermined and that the identification of the referent depends on extra contextual information (in example (63), e.g., the caption *TENNIS* will be sufficient). It is of course not an anaphor in the sense that it must be "bound" by linguistic material in the same clause or even the linguistic cotext. The latter is a syntax-driven, theory-specific definition of "anaphor", which is not adopted here. *Number two* in (63) seems to be an instance of a "bridging cross-reference anaphor" (Huang 2000:7). The anaphor is "one that is used to

(61) <CP8 284> Todd said the company is now number one and number **two** in the Finnish and Scandinavian markets respectively.

(62) <CP1 246> ALCATEL INCREASE OPTICAL FIBRE PRODUCTION Alcatel Cable SA, Douvrin, France is increasing its optical fibre production to meet demand - when two new plants come on full stream in the middle of next year, annual output will grow to 930,000 miles from the 590,000 miles it did last year, bringing it close to the current number **two**, AT&T Co, but still way behind the 1.25m miles produced annually by Corning Inc.

(63) <HJ4 5590> TENNIS British number one Jeremy Bates, playing for Raynes Park, lost to British number **two** Chris Wilkinson 7-6 6-4 in the Everest National Club League Premier Division match at the Royal Berkshire Club. Bates, 5-4 up in the first set tie-break broke a racket string in the middle of the next point and eventually lost the tie-break 7-5.

Some of the instances of *number two* in the sample corpus featured uses in which *two* not only refers to a second place in some ranking, but in which it specifies a particular kind of entity denoted by the whole phrase. In (64) the prenominal *number two* determines a kind of jib (a kind of sail), in (65) to a kind of dog (presumably an artificial *ad hoc* category).

(64) <AMU 664> `One of your men who is quick on his feet and who understands ropes." While Louis ducked into the saloon, Trent made his way forward. He selected the number **two** jib, clipping the spring shackles to the forestay. Even in the light breeze a bigger sail would have made towing the Zodiac dangerously uncontrollable.

(65) <A6T 1896> In fact, the dogs could not wait to get in. Each time we went for another animal all those left howled and fought their chains to get close to us so as not to be left behind. As we collected a dog it would lurch towards the car, the rest falling silent in their disappointment. Our only problem was with the doubling up. Get the wrong number **two** dog in with a number one and the cuddly koala in your arms turned into megatooth. We filled the spare holes with harnesses.

The phrase *number two* can be used in very different ways. The meanings expressed by *number two* can be classified into four groups: (1) the pure "label" use in which the phrase occurs immediately to the right of the head noun (*emergency motion number two*) (25%), (2) the "enumerative" use, in which *number two* is itself the head noun of the NP, and which

---

establish a link of association with some preceding expression in the same sentence or discourse via the addition of background assumptions" (Huang 2000:249). Huang names three characteristic properties: first of all, the anaphor must occur in the context of its "antecedent" (usually the anaphor is definite and the "antecedent" indefinite); second, there is a semantic or pragmatic relation between the anaphor and its "antecedent"; third, "antecedent" and anaphor are not strictly co-referential. These three conditions seem to be met in (63), even though the anaphor is strictly speaking not a definite NP (but the near-synonymous expression *Britain's number one* would have turned it into a definite NP). Even so, the "anaphor" (*British number two*) is clearly much more "definite" than the "antecedent" *tennis*, in the sense that the former explicitly refers to a single individual (there can only be one British number two), while the latter merely specifies the discourse topic. The other two requirements are met in a more straightforward way.

functions as an anaphoric element (*he scored [goal] number two*) or as an item structuring the discourse (*number two: the financial situation*) (26%), (3) the "ranking" use, in which *number two* not only denotes the position of the element in question in a series or sequence, but also implies some hierarchical relationship (*he's the bank's number two*) (42%), 1% of which consists of the instances of *number two* that denote a specific "kind of" entity, and (4) the instances in which *number two* refers to the mathematical object 'two' (1%). Of the 200 solutions, 12 were considered to be irrelevant (they formed part of a larger numeral or a name) (6%). The analysis of the sample corpus shows that not all uses can be classified under the "label" category of *two*, even though the entire construction *number two* often does function as a label. Moreover, it is clear that even with respect to this single construction, the degree of cardinality of *two* varies considerably from one use to another.

TABLE 7

USES OF *NUMBER TWO*

Pure label (25%)	Enumerative (26%)	Ranking (42%)	Mathematical Object (1%)	Irrelevant (6%)

4.3.3. Clockwise: *two* in indications of temporal location

Other uses of *two* that are clearly incompatible with a full-fledged cardinality reading can be found in indications of time.

(66) <JYF 1463> Around **two** in the morning she was just nodding off when suddenly her telephone rang again.

In (66), *two* locates an activity on a temporal line by lexical means[20]; the temporal position is expressed in an adverbial phrase. Example (66) exhibits one of the traditional conceptualizations of time, in which the time of one day is divided into two sets of twelve hours, one a.m. and one p.m., and the elements of this set are all named by different numerals. In this construction, a numeral like *two* is as it were liberated from its cardinal function in order to express a point of orientation. Evidently, the link with the counting sequence on which the temporal grid is based is still felt. *Two in the morning* can be paraphrased as *two hours after midnight*. This brings out the cardinality reading, which itself derives from counting the hours of the first set of twelve hours, the hours after midnight. The paraphrase, however, sounds a bit *recherché*: (66) is clearly an example of how some uses of numerals have become relatively independent of the counting practice that still informs most of their uses.

---

[20] The localist metaphor (Brisard 1999) is meant to indicate that in this construction the numeral is connected to a conceptualization of time in terms of space. The "time line" indicates the progression of time and is mapped onto the temporal domain, and as such forms one of the sources of localism.

Numerals only constitute part of the machinery used to locate events in time by means of what could be described as a "clock system". This linguistic domain is determined by the technological innovation of the clock as an instrument to keep time and the more or less arbitrary decisions that were made to turn this into a metric system (such as the division of one day into two sets of twelve hours). In (67) to (69) combinations of *two* and lexical items from the vocabulary typical of this type of "time telling" are illustrated. These expressions are yet another example of how numerals participate in specific subfields of the English language - linguistic domains that are governed by rigid rules which are specialized for that domain. Witness, e.g., the limited number of prepositions that can be used when telling time in this clock system: it is possible to say *ten to two* but not **ten before/in front of/on two*, or the idiomatic expressions *half past two* or *a quarter to two*. I will not dwell on the lexical and grammatical intricacies of this subfield, as I am not concerned with the expression of time, but I do want to stress the specific role played by numerals in this field.

> (67) <H5E 452> This is going to be an interesting meeting, Alan says it will be over by **two** thirty because he's organized for some training to happen then on er disciplinary issues.
> (68) <KNY 1923> Right and anyway, wants to see us about a quarter past **two** I wanna look at Howard's willy.
> (69) <B24 409> Occasionally, after refreshments - two would go in at two o'clock, two more at half past **two**, and so on - the only time you could have a natter with your colleague was when you left the station and you saw the sergeant going in for his refreshments.

It is important to point out that *two* may retain some or all of its cardinal qualities in some temporal adverbials. Numerals function very often as part of the expression of all sorts of measurements, and this is also the case for time.

> (70) <BNV 818> Being a close friend of Legrand and Couvelaire, I was not surprised when I first flew the prototype **two** years ago: soft and light as a feather, brilliant as a refined piece of thinking on how an ideal aircraft should fly, powerful as a civilianised fighter

In (70), *two* marks the cardinality of a specific group of temporal units. Note that in the latter example the temporal adverbial marks the temporal location of an event through the expression of duration (the duration of the time that has elapsed counting from the moment of speaking), while in the adverbials above *two* is part of a construction indicating a temporal location of an event. More generally, the "cardinal" use of numerals in temporal expressions allows the expression of duration (71) as well as the location of events in time (72). The non-adnominal temporal uses of numerals focused on in this section only have locational temporal meanings, not durational meanings.

> (71) <G09 1238> `They were made by the village cobbler and cost fourteen shillings: they'd last about **two** years if you got them clumped at the end of the first year."

(72) <A6J 404> There, she had been happy in Pakistan; she had been happy in the Peckham house at least for the first year; she had been happy working for Graham; she'd been enthusiastically interested at college and during the first **two** years after she had qualified; she had been completely delighted when she had got the job she now had: a tenants' association garden in a dreadful estate in Hackney, but where she, with a community group, had planned the garden from scratch and had made a small desert blossom like a rose.

4.3.4. Pronominal *two* and ellipsis

4.3.4.1. Standard examples

As argued above (section 4.2.1.), pronominal uses of *two* make up 11.6% of the occurrences of *two*. As mentioned (cf. section 4.1.3. of the Prolegomenon), I make use of a broad notion of what is "pronominal" (cf. Quirk et al. 1985:335ff)[21]. The question concerning the status of these uses - nominal or pronominal - rests on two basic types of distinctions. The first is a formal criterion and is an argument against the pronominal status: while pronouns usually cannot co-occur with determiners, numerals can: **the you* versus *the two*. This is an argument in favor of the "nominal" status of *two* in these constructions. But the functional distinctions favor the "pronominal" label: nouns usually conceptualize entities, while *two* in these constructions first of all encodes the *cardinality* of a group of entities. Just like other pronouns such as demonstratives or possessives, *two* refers to entities only indirectly, i.e. through a number of characteristics of those entities (where these entities are located (demonstratives), who the entities belong to (possessives), or how many entities the group contains (numerals)). Nouns present entities directly. Second, these uses of *two* are manifestly anaphorical. Even though nouns can refer back to an antecedent noun, this is not the prototypical function of nouns. Because the functional aspects seem to overrule the importance of the formal argument, I have decided to call these uses of *two* pronominal.

In this section, I will zoom in on the pronominal character of a number of uses of *two*. It is clear that these pronominal uses combine their pronominal function with a cardinality meaning. The pronominal uses do not form a monolithic group, but show a great diversity. In this section, a number of these uses will be looked at in detail, because the degree of "pronominality" has an effect on the extent to which numerals express "cardinality". If *two* is used pronominally, it can no longer be a "pure" cardinality marker.

A simple example of pronominal *two* is given in (73).

(73) <A04 1537> As a sound is a mantra, so an image is a yantra, the **two** used together making a powerful combination for spiritual exercises.

In this construction, the function of *two* is first and foremost to refer back to the antecedent (in this case *mantra* and *yantra*), but the pronoun clearly keeps its cardinality function as well, in

---

[21] Also contained in this group are elliptical uses of *two*, in which *two* functions as the head of the NP because the (semantically understood) head has been ellipted. I will give examples of this phenomenon in this section.

the sense that the pronoun gives information about this antecedent. It construes the antecedent as a group (abstracting from the differences between *mantra* and *yantra*)[22] and indicates the number of members of that group, much like English personal pronouns refer back to the antecedent and indicate its gender. Pronominal numerals can be used unambiguously when there are two potential antecedents that can be distinguished on the basis of their cardinality.

(74) I will divide them into two groups: these two girls all have to wear a black hat, while those three girls have to wear a blue hat. The **two** will then attack the three.

4.3.4.2. Elliptical two as the predicate of a copula
A more complicated construction containing *two* can be found in (75)[23].

(75) \<AL3 20\> Mr John Watson, 41, of March, Cambs, has been fined £30, with £20 costs, by magistrates for simultaneously fishing with three rods where the limit is **two**.

In this sentence, *two* does not directly refer back to an antecedent, as there is no antecedent that matches the cardinality of the pronoun exactly. On the basis of the anaphorical flavor one could presume this use of *two* to be pronominal, because the reference is clearly to two rods, and not just to two "entities". But this is better described as a case of ellipsis; it meets all five of Quirk's criteria for ellipsis (Quirk et al. 1985:884-888): (1) the ellipted words are precisely recoverable: the missing word in (75) is of course *rods*. (2) the elliptical construction is grammatically "defective": it is true that some normally obligatory element of the grammatical sentence is lacking. In this case, the head of the noun phrase is lacking. (3) the insertion of the missing words results in a grammatical sentence (with the same meaning as the original sentence) (76).

(76) Mr John Watson, 41, of March, Cambs, has been fined £30, with £20 costs, by magistrates for simultaneously fishing with three rods where the limit is **two** rods.

(4) and (5): the missing word(s) are textually recoverable and are present in the text in exactly the same form. This is the case in (75).

Typical of the elliptical construction is that the presence of the numeral establishes a link back to a given group of entities through a numeral, precisely when it indicates a different cardinality. Pronominal uses of *two* replace the nouns they refer back to by virtue of the same cardinality.

---

[22] This abstraction does not boil down to an *effacement* of all differences. The differences are simply not focused on: the distinctions between *mantra* and *yantra* are still present. Also, it is not clear under what hyperonym the two concepts can be categorized (except for a vague term such as 'things'), and there is no real need to accommodate for this lack. Intuitively, this is not a case of ellipsis (cf. the discussion of (84) in section 4.3.4.3.). This shows that the pronominal usage of *two* indeed reduces its "cardinality" function: it is not primarily meant to indicate the numerosity of a certain set, but the numeral functions first and foremost as a pointer to an antecedent (or, more precisely: two antecedents together).

[23] This sentence did not appear in the sample corpus, but was taken from the entire BNC-corpus by means of a special extra query.

(77) <BM1 526> The truth is probably more complex than that. Careful investigation often shows that these people have a dual problem: they are sensitive to foods and chemicals on the one hand, and they are hyperventilating on the other. Which came first is anybody's guess, but the **two** are now working together to make the patient even more ill.

In (77) the numeral indicates to the hearer / reader that he or she has to look for two things that have been mentioned before. The cardinality is crucial in this case: if the co- or context had introduced a clearly delineated set of two elements and an equally clearly delineated set of three elements, the cardinality of *the two* would have been sufficient to establish the correct reference. In the elliptical example (75), *two* does not refer back to a specific set of rods, it simply serves as the head noun of the NP, and in this way marks the absence of the "real" head noun (the head noun that is understood). The difference with, e.g., personal pronouns is notable: while personal pronouns refer back to their antecedent via one or two characteristics of that antecedent (e.g., gender and number), numerals in elliptical constructions can be used to refer back to an antecedent (and in this way allow the hearer/reader to construe it) even if they do not indicate any of the characteristics of the antecedent.

Quirk et al. (1985:901) write, however, that noun phrase ellipsis "involves some degree of parallelism between the elliptical construction and the antecedent". It is this parallelism that enables the elliptical construction to "change" some characteristics of the noun it refers to: "By virtue of this, some item(s) in the elliptical construction can be said to repudiate, or semantically cancel out, some item(s) in the antecedent. Thus, *the tallest* in [78] may be said to repudiate *the oldest*" (Quirk et al. 1985:901), while of course the reference to "girls" is preserved.

(78) Although Helen is *the oldest girl in the class,* Julie is the tallest [X].

They also note that the term "repudiate" "is especially appropriate where the two constructions are in a contrastive relationship" (Quirk et al. 1985:901). This is exactly what happens in the example of elliptical *two: two* is in contrast with the three rods that Mr John Watson used.

In fact the distinction between "ellipsis" and Quirk's "substitute forms" is not so strict as it might seem. Clear instances of such substitute pro-forms are uses of *one* as in (79).

(79) The girl was distributing brochures. I had to have one too.

Quirk et al. (1985:869) note that "[u]nlike *he, it,* etc which stand for noun phrases, *one/ones* is more literally a 'pro-noun' ", in that it replaces only the noun, and not the whole phrase. Crucially, Quirk et al. list also "the indefinite or quantifier pronouns *some, none, any, few/fewer/fewest* [...]" as such substitute forms. They do not explicitly include the numerals in their list, but their examples show that they belong to the same category. As an example of the substitute forms *a* few, *several,* and even *enough,* they provide a sentence (80) in which *two* could be used just as well (81).

(80) John and I went looking for *mushrooms*. He found *a few* [= a few mushrooms], I found *several* [=several mushrooms] and we soon had *enough* [= enough mushrooms] for breakfast.

(81) John and I went looking for *mushrooms*. He found *two* [= two mushrooms], I found *several* [=several mushrooms] and we soon had *enough* [= enough mushrooms] for breakfast.

Quirk et al. note that

[i]t is difficult to tell, in these cases, whether the pronoun is to be considered an example of substitution or ellipsis. [...I]t seems reasonable to treat the construction as one of ellipsis rather than of substitution. [...] However, we shall propose to deal with cases like this as 'virtual ellipsis' [...], *ie* as cases of a substitution of *X* for *Y*, where *Y* contains a homomorph of *X*. (Quirk et al. 1985:871)

Because of this similarity with "substitute forms", I decided to group these elliptical uses of *two* together with the clear cases of pronominal *two*.

More generally, the phenomenon in (75) can be related to Langacker's decision to view plurals as derived from a noun stem that labels a type (Langacker 1991:75). In his discussion of nominal structure, he distinguishes this noun stem from a formally identical stem that is specifically singular: while the latter picks out one specific instantiation of a type, the former only identifies the type. The analysis presented here fits very well in that picture. In (75), the numeral *two* refers back to the type introduced by *three rods*, not to the instantiations of this type. That is why the cardinality of the set of rods can be changed (or "repudiated") by a pronominal element: the phrase *three rods* picks out three separate entities or instantiations of the type *rod*. *Two* in (75) does not refer back to the three instances of rods, because the number denoted is not *three* but *two*, but to the type. Given the Langackerian interpretation of the plural noun, it is easy to see how the *two* can be linked to its antecedent. In his view, every nominal indicates a single instance of one of three classes of common nouns: singular count noun (*a rod*), plural nouns (*rods*) and non-plural mass nouns (e.g., *gravel*). A singular noun and its corresponding plural represent distinct categories. The cardinal that functions alongside a plural noun can be seen as somehow conceptually external, or secondary, to the identification of the class the entity itself belongs to. In the line of Langacker's views, (75) could be said to feature two "portions" of one mass noun[24]: *three rods* as well as *two (rods)* indicate an instance of *rods*, but each assigns it a different cardinality. Evidently, *three* and *two* do share a specific characteristic, namely the indication of the

---

[24] For Langacker, plurals are a kind of mass noun. The only difference between plurals and what is traditionally called a "mass noun" (e.g., *milk*) is that the first is a "replicate mass" while the second noun is a non-replicate mass noun: "[...] a plural is special because it profiles a mass that we can think of as being formed by replicating indefinitely many times a discrete entity that we are accustomed to dealing with individually - I thus refer to it as a replicate mass" (Langacker 1991:78).

cardinality of a group of objects[25]. As such, *two* in (75) does two things: first, it refers back to a "portion" of rods through the identification of the "type"; second, it redefines its cardinality.

As already mentioned, there are also so-called "relative quantifiers" (quantifiers that specify a quantity in relation to a reference mass, as opposed to the class of "absolute quantifiers", which the numerals belong to) that illustrate the same phenomenon.

(82)   - Did you catch all of the thieves?
       - No, I only caught some.

As in (75), in (82) a quantifier refers back to a group of entities that has been mentioned before, while at the same time changing the relative quantity of the group that is singled out. Significantly, *some*, just like the cardinals, can be used adnominally as well as pronominally. Just like *two* in (75), *some* in (82) is pronominal because it refers back to an antecedent, by relating to a single group of objects of one type (*rods* or *thieves*) that was mentioned before (or is somehow contextually accessible). And both quantifiers express a quantitative meaning on top of that pronominal function, by indicating the size of that group, either in absolute and precise terms (*three rods*) or in relative and rather vague terms (*some thieves*). This double function explains why the cardinality function of pronominal *two* is less outspoken.

One more remark is in order here, which is not related to the elliptical/pronominal character of *two* in the original *rods*-example (75), but to the indefiniteness of *two*. In that utterance indefiniteness plays an important role: **for simultaneously fishing with the three rods where the limit is the two* is twice ungrammatical. But while the ungrammaticality of *the three* rods is merely an effect of the fact that the rods had not been introduced earlier in the discourse, the definite article is incompatible with the second mentioning of the rods, not because it lacks an anaphor, but because of the discursive context. Indeed, the specific nature of the rods is totally irrelevant in this construction: the jurisdictional context explains why the specificity of the rods is abstracted from. The regulation only considers the numbers of rods, not the rods themselves. If *two* were combined with a definite article, a set of two rods should have been mentioned before (or should have been retrievable from the context). In that case, the numeral would not be able to refer to a set of entities while at the same time changing its cardinality. That is why the indefiniteness in (75) is crucial.

4.3.4.3. Divide into two
Other interesting cases of elliptical/pronominal[26] *two* can be found in (83) and (84).

(83) <H7X 241> When one cell divides into **two**, the two daughter cells aren't necessarily the same as each other.

---

[25] It is tempting to say that antecedent and pronoun share the feature "plurality". But this conflicts with the possibility of using *one* in exactly the same constructions. Sentence (75) remains perfectly grammatical when *one* is substituted for *three*: *[...] for simultaneously fishing with three rods where the limit is one*. Langacker claims that "[o]ne can be thought of as a limiting case in this regard, as it specifies the size of a degenerate replicate mass comprising only a single component entity" (Langacker 1991:82).

[26] Also in this example the question whether these are examples of elliptical *two* or pronominal *two* is not so clear (cf. previous section for discussion).

(84) <HDB 562> Inside of Little Stonham was one room, which was split in **two**.

In (83) the numeral *two* stands for 'two cells' and as such the construction is similar to the elliptical one in (75). Nevertheless, other than in (75), *two* is not a predicate of the copula *be*, but part of an adverbial phrase, closely linked up with the verb *divide*. Verbs like *divide* and *split* (84) typically occur with *in(to)*-phrases that indicate the parts into which a certain object (often expressed in the subject of the clause) is divided. As such they are perfectly compatible with an adverbial phrase indicating *how many* parts the object divides/splits into as well. In (83) this object (*one cell*) is divided in two parts, but the understanding is that these parts themselves form two full, separate cells, not just parts of cells: this is a typical anaphor(*two*)-antecedent(*cell*) construction. In (84), however, the referent of *two* is much less clear. Obviously, the pronominal *two*-construction cannot be paraphrased as 'two rooms'. Since no other referent seems to be available in the immediate cotext, the hearer will have to construct one contextually. This is where the typical *divide in(to)*-construction becomes important, as that will be the basis for supplying some nominal head of the adverbial: *two* in (84) will be interpreted as 'two parts', 'two segments', or 'two sections' etc[27]. The question is whether this can still be called an elliptical/pronominal use: strictly speaking there is no antecedent present, and the "antecedent" that the speaker or hearer may construct is only present in the general background information of the speech participants. This phenomenon certainly does not correspond to the standard definition of an antecedent. Neither does it meet all of the criteria for ellipsis in Quirk et al. (1985:884-888): the "elliptted" word is not precisely recoverable, the construction is not really grammatically "defective" (as when *sing* is ellipted in, e.g., *She can't sing tonight, so she won't [sing]*), the missing words are not textually recoverable and are not present in the text in the same form.

4.3.4.4. Degrees of pronominality: what about you two?
Finally, (85) is even more complicated: it shows how intricately a numeral can be linked up with a pronoun.

---

[27] This is not merely a question of the argument structure of *divide*, because the argument structure in itself cannot predict the semantic nature of the adverbial complement of *divide*. The argument structure of *divide* allows an adverbial complement of the form *into N*, but it cannot predict that *two* in (84) can be paraphrased as *two parts* (as opposed to e.g., *two flowers*). To describe this kind of anaphor/ellipsis (cases in which the anaphor/ellipsed word can be easily reconstructed from general background information), we seem to need a notion that is similar to Pustejovsky's concept of "co-specification" (Pustejovsky 1991, 1995, Pustejovsky and Bouillon 1996, cf. also Jackendoff 1997:47-82 on different kinds of "enriched composition"). The term "co-specification" is meant to indicate that not only predicates can choose arguments, but that arguments can choose their predicates as well: *potato* chooses the simple 'change-of-state' meaning of *bake*, while *cake* adds a 'creation' meaning to the meaning of *bake*. In traditional generative terms, I would say that *divide into* is subcategorized for the nouns *parts* or *segments*. But neither of these nouns is present in (84). Stretching Pustejovsky's concept a little, we could say that the interpretation of *two* as meaning 'two parts' is a consequence of co-specification: *divide into* is specified for a limited group of lexemes that express the concept 'division', pronominal *two* points to an antecedent that is not present in the immediate cotext, nor can it be retrieved immediately from the speech situation; hence the antecedent of *two* is construed as 'parts', or 'segments'. The differences with Pustejovsky's argument are clear: the typical examples of co-specification concern the combination of a verb and a noun, each of which have full lexical content. Nevertheless I think that the term can throw light on this particular verb/anaphorical numeral construction as well.

(85) <B3J 2772> With an irritated raise of the eyebrows, he called to Renee who was observing the group from the other end of the bar, and made the request. Renee shot a disapproving glance at Knocker and began preparing her drink. Nigger turned his attention to Yanto and Billy. `What about you **two**."

Here, *two* postmodifies the pronominal *you*. *Two* seems to be a pure indication of cardinality, since the pronominal function is already taken up by the personal pronoun. Syntactically speaking, *you* seems to be the head and not *two*, because *two* can be left out, while *you* cannot[28]. On the other hand, the position of *two*, together with the very explicit deictic function that *you* appears to carry out (comparable to an accompanying "pointing" act (real or imagined)), allows a pronominal interpretation of *two* as well. The function of *two* in (85) comes very close to the way it functions in the paradigmatic examples of pronominal *two* such as in (86).

(86) <K1L 556> Two brothers have been arrested in the Irish Republic in connection with the murder of a woman in a boarding house. Christine Campbell's body was found five months ago in a suitcase hidden in the loft. The **two** have already appeared in court, and are expected to be extradited to Britain.

And alongside *you two* there is also a construction with a demonstrative (87).

(87) <FSW 1090> I've been in two minds about whether to bother with the ABA this year, but the news that Baroness Thatcher and Margaret Atwood are to share a platform at a Book and Author Breakfast has made my mind up for me. With the possible exception of Jeanette Winterson and Jackie Collins, I can think of no two women less likely to benefit from each other's company than these **two**, and I foresee fireworks.

With the demonstrative instead of the personal pronoun *you*, the numeral seems to take on a more pronominal function. Demonstratives can function as full pronouns as well.

(88) What about these?

Also in the construction in (87), *two* is not the head of the NP, but, semantically speaking, when demonstratives are combined with a numeral in this type of construction, the latter seems to carry most of the pronominal load. For the phrase *you two* the situation is much less clear: the "pronominality" of *you* and *two* seems more balanced.

Why should this be so? It appears that there are two relatively independent factors at work: 1) the relative position of the elements in the NP; 2) the meaning of the elements.

---

[28] This is only one of the traditional criteria for "headship" (cf. Fraser, Corbett and McGlashan 1993), but it is the most important one for our purposes here. There is no distinction between *you* and *two* in this example with respect to most of the other criteria: both can be considered to be the "determinants of concord" (both are plural), both can be considered as the "semantic argument", etc.

First, as for the position of the elements, English determiners usually occur before the noun (Quirk et al. 1985:253). When a full noun is absent, the rightmost element in the NP automatically seems to replace the full noun, simply by taking its position. Both the construction with the demonstrative and the construction with the personal pronoun have *two* as rightmost element; hence the numeral is felt to be more pronoun-like.

Second, the function of the element placed to the left of *two* is also important. It is this function that distinguishes *these two* from *you two*. The difference between *you two* and *these two* is subtle: while the combination with *these* seems to leave the pronominal character of *two* more or less intact, the combination with *you* makes it more ambiguous, in the sense that *you* normally does not function as a determiner, while *two* does.[29] *Two* can function as a pronoun, just like *these* can act as a determiner, so it seems that in the phrase *these two* the numeral as well as the demonstrative could be the pronominal element, but because *two* is placed to the right of *these*, it seems natural to take *two* as head. In that analysis, *these* is simply an adnominally used demonstrative, contrasting with *those* in the combination *those two*. But in (85) the form *you* (which is the form of the independent pronoun *you* as opposed to the possessive form *your*) suggests that *you* is pronominal as well - what else would *you* be? Only *two* can function as a determiner and a pronoun; *you*, in this form, only occurs as a pronoun. Consequently, the numeral in (85) may indeed only be indicating the cardinality of the group of addressees. Nevertheless, due to the similarity of *you two* to *these two* and due to its rightmost position in the NP, *two* retains a pronominal character.

Furthermore, *you two* not only resembles *these two*. It is important to bear in mind that *two* can also occur with a simple article. This shows once again that the syntactic criterion for "pronominality" is not sufficient: in (89), it is uncontroversial that *two* functions as the head of the NP - it cannot be left out. Nevertheless, this construction comes very close to the one in (85).

> (89) <HLC 228> It had nevertheless become increasingly clear that Ashrawi and Husseini, negotiating the final version of the Palestinians' "letter of assurances", were acting in close liaison with PLO headquarters in Tunis. The **two** reportedly denied reports that they had left their London hotel to attend the Palestine National Council (PNC) meeting in Algiers in September [see pp. 38453-54], and the PLO news agency Wafa on Sept.

On the whole, in the construction *you two* the numeral is less pronominal than in the paradigmatic pronominal uses of *two*, but it definitely retains some of its pronominal character. And because it is still to some extent pronominal, *two* is not exclusively a cardinality marker in this construction.

Finally, it is also remarkable that this "personal pronoun + numeral" construction is rather limited. In the sample corpus *two* was only found in combination with the second person pronoun. In the BNC, there were some constructions with *we* (90) and even a few with

---

[29] Of course, the possessive form *your* is a variant of *you* that is used as a determiner, but in (85) it is *you* that creates the pronominal effect.

us (91), although in the latter example neither *us* nor *two* are head of an NP, because neither can occur independently.

> (90) <AC7 1458>`A fire always reminds me of my brother Charlie. We **two** were the youngest in the family and had lovely times together.
> (91) <CHX 218> The Tortoise said, `I'm betting you I'd win a race between us **two**."

Furthermore, this sort of construction is clearly limited to the lower numerals.

> (92)   ?What about you five?[30]
> (93)   ??What about you six hundred and two?

The construction in (92) might be possible in a context in which ten people are divided into two teams of five people each. In such a context the speaker would presumably use *you five* contrastively. Evidently, (93) is difficult due to pragmatic reasons: it is unlikely that someone addresses a group of people in terms of the number of people the group consists of, when a simple *you* would usually suffice to address them properly. Indeed, it could even been suggested that constructions like *you two* are similar to the substandard American English *you all*, usually abbreviated to *y'all* or *yall*. The latter might be described as a suppletive plural marker. Because the distinction between second person singular and second person plural is not marked in English, the form *y'all* would answer to the need to make that distinction. In this vein, it might even be suggested that the vague status of the elements of *you two* is a sign of grammaticalization: *two* would then be a suffix indicating dual number. But it is questionable whether *two* will ever be fully grammaticalized.

The extent to which *two* functions pronominally varies significantly from construction to construction. There are straightforward examples of pronominal *two*, but there are also constructions in which *two* functions as a predicate of an elliptical copula construction, or in combination with a personal pronoun or a demonstrative. All these uses differ in degree of pronominality, and hence also differ in the extent to which their expression of cardinality is prominent or not. If *two* is used anaphorically, the anaphorical function is at least equally important as the indication of the cardinality of the group of entities it refers back to. It is clear that the concept of "cardinality" that is often presupposed in neo-Gricean as well as anti-neo-Gricean analyses of numerals is not so clear-cut as one would have hoped.

---

[30] Remarkably, the construction *the five of you* is fully acceptable, even though it fulfils the same function. This shows that the *you two* construction is less conventionalized than the partitive *the n of you* construction.

4.3.5. *Two* as the name of a symbol

In (94), there is another divergent usage of *two*.

> (94) <FM5 303> O H now how many of those do you want? In brackets. Great. And there are two. Right right. you got the the O H is the bit you want twice so write it down put the brackets round it and then the **two**. Right.

Here, *two* indicates the written symbol *two*, probably as part of a chemical notation. It is not the adnominal use of *two,* but neither can it be assimilated to the "mathematical" uses (cf. section 4.3.6.). This *two* is much more similar to a prototypical noun, denoting a concrete object with definite boundaries, than it is comparable to a modifier of a noun. In fact, in some contexts, this *two* could indeed refer to, e.g., a plastic sign TWO that can be placed on a blackboard, in which case it would simply be such a prototypical object. In this case, however, it is much more likely that *the two* refers to a written symbol: this symbol shares some of the characteristics with the plastic object, but also lacks some of them (e.g., the fact that it can be manipulated manually). On the whole these uses of *two* are more noun-like than the mathematical uses described above, because in this case, the language game they are part of resembles the canonical, folk-theoretical conceptualization of interaction with objects, rather than that of mathematical calculations[31]. In the linguistic expression of interaction with objects, this object is expressed by a common noun. This noun interprets the object and puts it in a category, which, in turn, captures some of its characteristics. This is what happens in (94): *two* is reinterpreted as a common noun, namely the noun that categorizes all signs or notations of two that resemble the shape of the Arabic symbol *2* (and/or the shape of the English word *two*, but this use is rather marginal).

4.3.6. Mathematical uses of *two*

A different usage domain in which numerals also seem to be emancipated from their cardinality function is the field of mathematics. In (95) and (96), *two* denotes a mathematical object, as (part of) a solution to a calculation.

> (95) <FYA 1638> You've done drawing graphs of er Y equals Done vectors Y equals **two** X minus three.

---

[31] The notion of a language game resembling another language game may seem to stretch the concept of language games itself. Indeed, when Wittgenstein introduced the notion, he did this, among other reasons, to emphasize the singularity of specific uses of linguistic elements, as they are embedded in specific forms of life. The diversity of language games is exemplified in a list in which "solving a problem in practical arithmetic" explicitly figures (Wittgenstein 1972 [1953]:12) as a separate game. Nevertheless, it seems intuitively clear that the notion of "resemblance" can also be applied to language games: the concept of "resemblance" is not incompatible with the singularity or autonomy of language games. Indeed, in one passage, Wittgenstein explicitly referred to the possibility of comparing language games (Wittgenstein 1972 [1953]:50) In fact, the resemblance between how words are used in one language game and how they are used in another may very well help people to learn different meanings of polysemous words.

(96) <K6J 340> What would the fourth root of sixteen be? Eesh erm Oh hell's bells. It's about two isn't or something ? It's very very close to **two**, yes.

In (95), the cardinal function is still prominent: it is used adnominally with X as head noun, and *two X* quite unproblematically reduces to *one X + one X*, even if the noun X is not marked for plurality (which shows that this adnominal use of *two* is nonetheless divergent from other adnominal usages as in (36) or (37)). In (96), however, *two* clearly isn't used adnominally, much less pronominally. It is one of the mathematical uses of *two* in the corpus that are very difficult to reduce to other uses of numerals, or, for that matter, canonical patterns of other word classes like proper names or adjectives. The main reason for the irreducibility of the mathematical language game is that it is governed by its own set of conventions: numbers, and hence also numerals, can be operated on in mathematics, but only in a limited number of ways. The two instances of *two* in (96) both result from canonical mathematical calculations: the fact that this is spoken language[32], complete with hesitations and interjections, does not influence the basic pattern that is dictated by the usual mathematical conventions. Note that this usage of *two* is not the same as in answers to *how many*-questions in less specialized domains of linguistic intercourse.

(97) How many children do you have? Two.

In (97) *two* can be described as an adnominal with an elliptical noun, a noun which can easily be retrieved from the immediate cotext. The link with an existing set of children is prominent. This is not the case in (96), in which all reference to the existence or non-existence of things is abstracted from. Indeed, the presupposition of a language-independent world (in this case a world independent of the mathematical language game) is totally absent. In the parallel universe of mathematics, numerals can indicate quantities of mathematical objects, but they can also name numbers. The question is how these uses of *two* relate to the usage of English proper nouns and common nouns.

Returning to the use of *two* in (96), it transpires that with some mathematical uses, specifically those uses in which numerals are not used to quantify variables, any reference to a concrete object is absent. To take another example, in (98), *two* does not signify a written symbol, much less a full-fledged object, but it denotes a quantifier that has become so abstract that it functions almost like a noun. Indeed, it is no longer a quantifier, because there is nothing left for it to quantify.

(98) <GYP 731> One, one is an operation add or subtract. What does add mean? Adding the two values to together. What does it mean, you're still using adding, what does add mean? Put them together you know? Okay, what does it mean in terms of the number line? the number line there, and we want to do something like **two** add three, what does that mean?

---

[32] Burnard 1995:393 identifies this fragment as an extract from a tutorial lesson.

Still, this use of *two* does not fit easily in one of the traditional classes of common nouns (Quirk et al.1985:246). In this construction (cf. also sentences such as *two plus two equals four* or *seven times two equals fourteen*), *two* does not belong to one of the three classes of common nouns. It cannot be used with an article, which means that it cannot be a count noun. It is hard to use in the plural form,

(99)　?*Twelve twos minus three threes equals three fives.*

nor is the singular form compatible with *some*, which would identify it as a noncount noun.

(100)　**Some two plus five equals seven.*

Indeed, the absurdity of the latter example is indicative of one of the fundamental characteristics of this use of numerals: there is no room for vagueness; any imprecision is banned from this kind of basic mathematical language, not only on a conceptual level, but also grammatically. If some examples leave room for uncertainty, it is typically the uncertainty of the speaker who is trying to solve a problem. In (96), the imprecision or "approximative nature" of the answer, marked through lexical means with the use of *about* and *or something* is typically a vagueness external to the mathematical problem itself.

It is the imperfection of the human mind that introduces the vagueness, not the mathematical system itself. The fact that lexical means of making numerical statements more imprecise are perfectly grammatical in some mathematical contexts, while more grammatical means (e.g. expressing a numerical as a "mass" via a non-count construction) are impossible in itself already suggests that the imprecision that is present in some mathematical uses of numerals is external rather than internal to the mathematical language game[33]. Typically the lexical material used for this purpose consists of adverbs like *about*, or *approximately*. Evidently, this observation primarily shows that a numeral is not conceptualized as an unbounded "mass", not in the mathematical name-like uses, and certainly not in cardinality uses. This is also borne out by the fact that in these mathematical contexts, expressions of vagueness are impossible when they occur as part of the problem, instead of as part of (an attempt at) an answer (101).

(101)　*What would the fourth root of about sixteen be?

---

[33] This raises a potentially interesting question concerning the relationship between grammaticalization on the one hand and the expression of vagueness on the other: if it is accepted that lexical means (e.g. *approximately, about, more or* less etc.) are the most basic means of expressing vagueness (in the sense that if vagueness can be expressed at all, it will always be expressible via lexical means), then it could be hypothesized that constructions and contexts that also allow more grammatical means (e.g. the count/non-count distinction) to express imprecision demonstrate that these constructions and contexts are conceptualized as inherently vague, or, at least, as having vague boundaries. If we look at, e.g., the suffix *-ish* as it is used with color terms as in *this dress is brown or brownish rather than purple*, we may perhaps see this phenomenon as an extra indication that colors are conceptualized as a continuum, rather than as mutually exclusive categories. Checking this hypothesis would of course require an extensive analysis of the various expressions of vagueness on the one hand and conceptual domains on the other, and this lies beyond the scope of this study. In each case, it is clear that numerals in mathematical uses are inherently "exact".

It could be argued that these basic mathematical operations are not defined for numerals that are modified by approximativizing elements. This is reflected in grammar. But it is clear that in these specific contexts, lower numerals like *two* are definitely not to be associated with common nouns, be they count or non-count[34].

Maybe, then, *two* functions as a proper noun in these mathematical examples? Proper nouns, just like the numerals in the mathematical context under discussion, indeed do not ordinarily collocate with definite or indefinite articles or *some*, nor do they occur in the plural form[35]. These formal characteristics may lead one to think that *two* in these contexts is comparable to proper nouns like *Washington* or *Hans*. Nevertheless, the denotation of the proper nouns is typically restricted to uniquely identifiable parts of reality, while we usually do not think of numbers in that way. Also, these uses of *two* (here defined by the formal characteristics they share with proper nouns) occur only in a very restricted number of constructions. The test sentence Quirk et al. (1985:245) use to distinguish their classes of nouns is "I saw ...", in which various realizations of proper and common nouns (with or without article, singular or plural etc.) can be filled in. Obviously, *I saw two* does not make any sense in a non-pronominal reading of that sentence. Indeed, the few constructions in which this type of *two* does occur are all derived from the mathematical code: expressions like *two minus three equals minus one* or *seven subtract three* all appear as English realizations of a non-natural language. They strike us as imperfect, somehow makeshift representations of an originary mathematical language - English "translations" of a universal scientific language. *Vice versa*, proper nouns like *Brussels* cannot occur in these mathematical constructions.

Therefore, even though these uses of *two* seem to resemble the class of proper nouns the most, it seems safe to say that the mathematical uses of *two* exemplified in (96) and (98) cannot be assimilated to a traditional class of nouns and must be seen as a separate category.

4.3.7. Discourse-structural *two*

As already mentioned in the context of the analysis of certain *number two* constructions, numerals can have discourse-structural uses. These uses are - relative to other uses of numerals - very rare. I did not find a single instance of this use in the sample corpus, but I extracted two from the BNC.

> (102) <A6E 357> I remember having some really interesting discussions with him when we'd go and see a band somewhere. All of us were checking new bands out the whole time. For two reasons. One, like any new band we were checking out the opposition. **Two**, it was a strange time. There was a rock `n" roll vacuum. We were looking for anybody who could help fill it.

---

[34] The third category of common nouns identified by Quirk et al.(1985:246) is a mixed category of nouns that can function as count or as non-count nouns, e.g., *brick*. Evidently, this is completely incompatible with the use of numerals in the mathematical contexts under discussion.

[35] Exceptions are certain geographical names, e.g., *the Alps, the Balkans*, etc.

(103) <A6T 1264> Our chief problem is where to go from here. We have three basic alternatives. One, to bike up Kungsleden to Abisko and get wet; **two**, to cycle 600 kilometres around the road via Kiruna and Abisko to Narvik for our journey home; or three, hire a plane to take us somewhere else.

Its meaning is quite clear: it orders the elements of an utterance in a sequence, and the relationship between the elements is usually one that can be compared to co-hyponymy in lexical semantics: they are supposed to be on the same level of generality. Most often, the elements of the utterance that are structured by numerals in this way are items on a list: in (102) it is a list of "reasons", in (103) it is a list of "alternatives". In these uses, the numerals certainly do not belong to the core of the predication, but operate on a more general, discourse-structural level. The cardinality of this use is reduced due to its main discourse-structural function, but remains present: the last discourse-structural numeral in the series will usually also indicate the cardinality of the group of elements the list consists of. Also, each numeral identifies the sequential position of the element in the list, separates it from the others and thus makes it available for further cross-reference.

4.3.8. Other uses of *two*

A not insignificant group of solutions in the sample corpus featured a variety of uses that do not fit easily in one of the above categories. They include counting acts (104), (105), as well as counting acts with orientation / synchronization / schematization uses (106), (107), number spellings (108) and even soccer scores (109). These uses differ considerably in terms of cardinality: the counting act in (104) seems to feature an almost pure example of cardinal *two*, but this is mainly because the utterance ends with an adnominally used *five* so that the numerals mentioned earlier (including *two*) can be interpreted retroactively as adnominal numerals as well (compare *counting the seconds one, two, three* in section 2.1.2.2.). In (105), however, there is a counting act in which *two* does not seem to be fully cardinal: it is simply a recitation of the number sequence. The synchronization and schematization uses, in (106) and (107), feature extremely low cardinality: it might be possible to conceive of *two* as indicating a label for a certain "submovement" in a larger coordinated movement (e.g. in a dance routine), but even that rather farfetched interpretation includes a "label" use of *two* (which already features reduced cardinality). In (108) a number (a "shares index") is spelled one digit at a time. This use is of course linked to some sort of measurement, but that link is highly complicated. Also, value-measurements that are spelled out digit by digit cannot be said to feature a prominent cardinality meaning. It is only in very abstract terms that *two* in (108) refers to a (part of a) number of members of a set, if at all. Finally, *two* in the soccer scores in (109) could be taken as pronominal: in that reading, *two* would stand for 'two goals', and would then be cardinal to a certain extent. But also in this case, the construction is too idiosyncratic to assess the cardinality of *two* in that construction in a rigid and unambiguous manner.

(104) <KPV 4642> If you've got a kitchen upstairs, it defeats the object of you're having a fridge Unless you bring up and down the stairs. wouldn't you. The thing is though, we've got erm, got one, **two**, three, four, we've got five fridges.

(105) <FUH 1017> You've got a lot of really useful money here haven't you so you can you can work these out. **Two** three four five six seven Four five six seven. Right seven five Ps how much will that come to? Erm ten twenty thirty five.

(106) <KBW 14591> and then one, two, three, four with that hand That's it Oh it's just the same as that one Well it is except you've got to go one, two, three, four, clonk, clonk, clonk, clonk one, **two**, three, four That's it, and then swap hands but you go like that, go on then, Yes, , one, two, one, two, one, two, three, four, one, two, three, four, one, two, three, four

(107) <KBW 14678> OK and then it goes right, OK ready? One, two, three, four one, two, three, four, one, two, three, four, one, two, three, four, one, two, three, four, one, two, three, four, one, two, three, four one, **two**, three, four one, two, three, four, one, two, three, four, one, two, three, four, one, two, three, four, one, two, three, four, one, two, three, four, one, two, three, four That was good, started out just getting going.

(108) <K21 3893> The hundred shares index closed down twelve point five at **two** five five three -12.5 at 2553.0 The pound is up at one dollar, seventy seven and down at two marks, fifty.

(109) <KS7 11> The Beezer Homes League Southern division: Witney one, Canterbury one. The Vauxhall League, division two south; Bracknell one, Abingdon Town two. The South Midland League premier division; Pyrton one, Thame four. The South Midland League Trophy; Shenley and Lowton five, Oxford City two. The Hellenic League; Abingdon United nil, Rayners Lane three; Banbury nil, Almondsbury nil; Carterton **two**, Swindon Athletic two;

4.3.9. Relationship between adnominal form and cardinal function

While the corpus analysis reflects an overwhelming correspondence between adnominal uses and the expression of cardinality, the reverse is not the case. If an English numeral is used adnominally it will always express cardinality to some extent, but cardinality needn't be expressed with adnominally used numerals: numerals expressing cardinals can also fill the predicate slot of copula constructions. Constructions like (110) can be found in the BNC, but were not found in the sample corpus, which demonstrates that they are rather marginal.

(110) <HR3 1696> A deficiency of some manually-digitized data is due to the inclusion of more points than are needed to define the position of a line to a given level of accuracy. For example, the number of points needed to define a straight line is **two**.

TABLE 8

FUNCTION OF *TWO*	FORM OF *TWO*	EXAMPLE
Pure cardinality	Preposed adnominal	*I saw two children.*
Label	Postposed adnominal	*We saw part two yesterday.*
Temporal[36]	Nominal	*At two, she went out.*
Anaphorical	Pronominal / Elliptical[37]	*The two were chasing a cow.*
Symbol	Nominal	*Put the two here.*
Mathematical	(Adnominal)[38] / Name ("proper noun")	*Two plus two equals four*
Discourse-structural	Name	*One, it is majestic. Two, it is expensive.*

In general the relationship between the forms and functions of *two* can be schematized in the table above. Note that only the meanings that have been highlighted in the cardinality discussion above are presented in this table. Other aspects of the meaning of numerals (e.g., the interaction of adnominal *two* with their nominal heads or the ensuing discussion on 'exact', 'at least', 'at most' and 'absolute values' readings of cardinals) are not mapped here. The table indicates tendencies (be it very strong tendencies), not water-tight correspondences.

4.3.10. Degrees of prominence of cardinality

It should by now be clear that any attempt to reduce the meaning of English cardinal numerals to a monolithic concept of cardinality is misguided. The English cardinal numerals occur in very different constructions and these constructions all influence the extent to which the numeral in question expresses cardinality. Setting up a hierarchy of numeral constructions in terms of degree of cardinality remains a highly intuition-driven undertaking. Nevertheless, a number of criteria - indicating tendencies rather than hard-and-fast rules - can be listed. The first option of each dichotomy indicates a higher degree of prominence of the cardinality meaning.

---

[36] As pointed out before, this is limited to the non-adnominal uses of *two* in temporal expressions.

[37] As mentioned before, I use a broad conception of the term "pronominal". Syntactically, the term indicates the characteristic of constructions with *two* in which the numeral is the head of the NP and in which it can occur with a determiner (unlike pro-nouns such as *these* or *ours*). Semantically, these uses are pronominal because *two* must refer back to an antecedent and refers to an entity only indirectly (through the indication of the cardinality of the group of entities it represents). Of course, the category "pronoun", like any category, can only be defined by referring to both its syntactic and semantic characteristics (cf. Schachter 1985, Croft 2000). For an elaborate discussion of pronominal / elliptical / nominal *two*, cf. section 4.3.4. on pronominal and elliptical uses of *two*.

[38] In fact, uses of *two* such as *two x minus three* reduce to simple cardinal uses of *two*. But the constructions in which this type of adnominal *two* occurs are specific for mathematical language.

1) does the numeral exclusively indicate cardinality or does it also fulfil other semantic duties?

2) does the numeral form a unit with a noun or is it independent?

3) if the numeral forms a unit with a noun, is it in an adnominal or an appositive relation to that noun?

4) if it does not combine with a noun, is the numeral used pronominally or not?

5) if it does not combine with a noun, and if it is not pronominal, is the numeral independent, or does it combine with a determiner?

6) if the non-pronominal numeral is not combined with a noun nor a determiner, is it discourse-structural, or does it belong to the kernel predication?

The first criterion is relatively independent; the other five are all interconnected. It seems self-evident: pure cardinality markers (*two* in *Mary has two children*) restrict themselves to expressing the numerosity of a group of entities, while other uses combine this function with other functions. However, this does not necessarily mean that the latter are "less cardinal": it could very well be that, e.g., pronominal uses of *two* express cardinality as such and combine this function with their pronominal function. In other words, there does not seem to be a straightforward method to decide between two positions: does the pronominal function somehow make the cardinal meaning less prominent, or does the pronominal function simply come "on top of" the cardinality meaning?

In my opinion, the solution lies in between both options, and the confusion arises from mixing semantics (the "coded" meaning of *two*) with pragmatics (the meaning of *two* as it is used). Evidently, the expression of cardinality in using *two* pronominally does not qualitatively differ from the cardinality expressed by "fully" cardinal uses. To the extent that pronominal *two* expresses cardinality (and it certainly does, to some extent), it expresses it fully. It is not less explicit in the determination of cardinality than its N CN counterpart. As far as the coding of cardinality is concerned, both provide information that is equally precise (in fact, pronominal uses can even be said to be slightly more precise, cf. the discussion on cardinality readings in Chapter 5 below). But, of course, there is a marked difference in *prominence* of both meanings: with the pronominal uses, the expression of cardinality inherent in pronominal *two* is in fact redundant, because the cardinality in itself is already known to the participants. In fact, it is precisely because the cardinality ('two') is already known, that *two* can refer back to an antecedent. In the following (constructed) stretch of discourse, the cardinality component of the meaning disambiguates the anaphor.

(111) Mary and Sandy were playing in the meadow. More than twenty cows were watching them in amazement. But the **two** didn't seem to care.

In (111) the anaphorical *two* refers back to a group of entities. It cannot be the group of cows, because the cardinalities of the anaphor and the antecedent do not match. It must be the girls, then, because the cotext is such that the girls can be construed as a group consisting of two elements. If *the two* were replaced by *they*, the anaphor would be ambiguous. It is the cardinality of the anaphor that secures an unambiguous interpretation. In addition, it is clear that the phrase *the two* does not contain new information by itself (it is the topic of the sentence), which explains why the expression of cardinality is not foregrounded. It is important to emphasize, however, that this is a matter of how *two* is used. The question is not directly related to the coded meaning of *two*: this explains the paradoxical statement that both "N CN" uses of *two* and pronominal uses of *two* express cardinality to the same extent, while the expression of cardinality is more prominent in the first than it is in the second. It should be clear that whenever the phrase "degrees of cardinality" is used, it refers to degrees in prominence. But of course, "coded meaning" and "prominent meaning" are interrelated: the existence of the first is a condition for the second. In case a specific use of *two* does not express any cardinality at all (e.g, in uses of *two* as the name of a symbol), it follows that the prominence is zero.

The second criterion is more straightforward, because it formulates the form-meaning correlation that seems to hold quite generally among uses of *two*: N CN constructions correlate with high prominence of cardinality, non-adnominal uses rank lower as far as cardinality is concerned. A notable exception, an exception that will recur, is the copula construction described in the previous section: utterances like *Two is the number of people present; twenty-eight is the number of people invited* function as "singular terms". The numeral functions independently, but still expresses pure cardinality. This seems to be the only exception to the rule. Within the group of uses in which *two* is combined with a noun, prenominal *two* is more prominently cardinal than postnominal *two*. In utterances that do not fit easily in the traditional syntactic descriptions of sentences and clauses and which feature more or less "autonomous" uses of *two* (such as *two* in counting sequences, or discourse-structural *two*), the cardinality of *two* is less manifest. It is hard to judge whether non-autonomous post-nominal *two* is "more cardinal" than these autonomous uses, or even than pronominal uses. It certainly features a higher degree of cardinality compared to other autonomous uses, e.g. mathematical *two* or *two* as the name of a symbol. While also this "autonomy criterion" is not unproblematic, it can serve as a reasonably reliable indication of prominence of cardinality.

The third criterion is clear: if *two* is used appositively, the prominence of its cardinality is considerably less than when it is used adnominally.

The fourth question distinguishes pronominal and non-pronominal uses. Pronominal uses combine a cardinality meaning with another function (the pronominal function). While it is certainly true that some non-adnominal but pronominal uses are in general more "cardinal" than non-adnominal, non-pronominal uses (e.g. temporal uses or symbol uses), this is, again, more of a tendency than a rule: not only the cardinal "copula" uses of numerals (*the number of points is two*), but also the discourse-structural uses constitute exceptions. The latter are both non-adnominal and non-pronominal, but cannot be said to be less "cardinal" than the pronominal uses. These constructions are, however, very rare, as both did not even occur once in the sample corpus.

The fifth criterion distinguishes non-adnominal, non-pronominal uses with a determiner from those without and as such it singles out the least cardinal of all uses of *two*, namely the "symbol" use of *two*, which is the only non-adnominal non-pronominal use that allows a determiner.

The last criterion links syntactic cohesion with cardinality, but again the question is not unambiguous, mainly due to the existence of the cardinal "copula" uses. These clearly express cardinality (be it via the detour of a "number" as a platonic object) and are closely tied to the predication as they are the subject of the clause. Other non-adnominal, non-pronominal uses of *two* that belong to the kernel predication (e.g., temporal uses, symbol uses) are less "cardinal" than discourse-structural *two*.

It is clear that these criteria can only hint at the complicated nature of the expression of cardinality. In fact, the "cardinality-hood" of uses of numerals must be assessed one expression at a time, with an account of the context in which the expression occurs. In the analysis above, I have tried to exemplify this type of utterance-specific analyses, but I have also tried to come up with a classification. The list of criteria based on this classification is not meant as an instrument for the "measurement" of cardinality, but serves as an indication of general tendencies.

With respect to the neo-Gricean discussion in Chapter 2, the gradual nature of "cardinality" does not seem to influence the interpretation of the so-called "N CN"-constructions (Kadmon 1987, 2001), the uses of numerals as "pure" cardinality markers. Indeed, it is possible to delimit the object of investigation to such an extent that only constructions of the type *Mary has two children* are considered. The "pure" cardinal uses of numerals can be separated from the diverse impure uses, and this is possible on pure formal grounds: whenever you find the sequence "numeral + plural common noun", pure cardinality is expressed. In other words: the N CN construction is monosemous, at least as far as cardinality is concerned. But it is also clear that this construction does not exhaust all expressions of cardinality, nor all uses of English numerals. The lexical semantic analysis of an item like *two* should at least yield the data on the basis of which semanticists can choose between a polysemous or monosemous (or maybe even homonymous) account. It is also clear that an assessment of the prominence of the cardinality meaning, as a component of the meaning expressed by *two*, is crucial in any meaning analysis of numerals. Finally, the formal restrictions of the neo-Gricean account of numerals (in which only N CN constructions are discussed) obscure the fact that their analysis should in principle generalize to all expressions of cardinality, how impure or complicated these may be. At the very least, it should test whether the scalar account is also applicable to these impure uses, and if it is not, it should be able to come up with non-*ad hoc* reasons why this should be so. I will address this problem in section 1.3.9. of Chapter II.

4.3.11. Domains of use

Part of the description of the functions of *two* should aim at an inventory of the "domains of use" of *two*. The numeral is involved in the expression of all sorts of meanings, but while the previous discussion focused on the cardinality meanings expressed by *two*, the following will describe succinctly in what types of usage contexts the cardinal numerals occur. This inventory can be compared to the Lakovian inventories of metaphorical structures, in which a certain source domain is mapped onto a target domain (Lakoff and Johnson 1980, Lakoff 1987, Lakoff and Johnson 1999), although in this case the source domain is reduced to the linguistic form *two* (thereby avoiding the usual vagueness of the definition of a source domain). The various "target domains" listed below, will receive a much more vague definition. The analogy with Lakovian metaphors is only partial, however. The list below tries to capture cognitive domains in which *two* is used and sometimes "use" is indeed the only verb that is general enough to describe what the numerals do, in the sense that a denotational account would miss the point completely. But also uses of *two* in more frequent usage contexts such as measurements reduce to a referential account only with great difficulty.

The most important domains of use are:
1) number of entities
2) measurements (spatial, temporal, "portions")
3) time indications
4) mathematical calculations
5) values (number spellings)
6) counting sequences
7) age
8) labels of entities and persons
9) symbol
10) arguments, reasons (discourse-structural)

Below, I present some examples of each category.

1) *number of entities*

This is by far the largest group. Arguably, this group should also contain the next category (because measurements can be conceived of as a number of entities on a certain measuring instrument, e.g., a ruler or a thermometer), but because expressions of measurement typically do not construe the measured entity as a number of entities, and because the counting act implied by measurements is qualitatively different from the counting acts described in the examples below, I decided to put them in a separate category. The entities in question may be concrete (112), abstract (113), or sets of entities (114).

> (112) <EA2 260> In two cases the screening programme identified **two** affected boys in a sibship before the elder boy had been diagnosed (table II).
> (113) <CTY 663>The **two** forms of reason do not exist independently of each other, as different forms of reality, but exist in relation to each other in an economy comparable to Derrida's differential `stricture".
> (114) <ASL 441> But if at the eight-cell stage the embryo was separated along the plane of the third cleavage into **two** groups of four cells, then each of these two fragments developed quite differently.

2) measurements: a large group consisting of uses of *two* in all sorts of measurements, which can be subdivided in a number of subgroups:

*Spatial measurement: length (115) and distance (116)

(115) <B0A 1931> The tunnel was built by the Leeds and Thirsk Railway, and is a little over **two** miles in length.

(116) <GW3 551> Well, when I was about **two** miles from Penzance the engine stopped and wouldn't start again.

* Temporal measurement: location (via an expression of measurement, relative to a temporal index) (117) and duration (118)

(117) <FNT 2090> **Two** days later, a Comrade Tulayeva came to fetch him. From above her vast chest, she looked at him disapprovingly.

(118) <G09 1238> `They were made by the village cobbler and cost fourteen shillings: they'd last about **two** years if you got them clumped at the end of the first year."

* Portions: abstract (fractions (119)) and type-specific (120)

(119) <CM5 1600> On the other hand, against the backdrop of recession, rising unemployment and Government policies on welfare and the family, women have lost important employment protection and maternity rights, unemployment amongst women has almost tripled and any new jobs are mainly part-time and low-paid; women still earn only **two** thirds of average male pay.

(120) <CBC 3043> ALCOHOL: One pint of beer (240), **two** glasses of mulled wine (144), two spirits and mixers (210), two glasses sweet white wine (220)

3) time indications (with the clock as guideline (121))

(121) <B24 409> Occasionally, after refreshments - two would go in at two o'clock, two more at half past **two**, and so on - the only time you could have a natter with your colleague was when you left the station and you saw the sergeant going in for his refreshments.

Also in this domain *two* can be used adnominally, with the same caveat: *it is two minutes past eleven* is certainly possible, and also functions as a temporal indication, but only via an expression of measurement.

4) mathematical calculations

(122) <KPB 186> Go on you do that one. You've got a dotted four, dotted semigrave. Right. Half of four is **two**. Mhm. Add another two Mm. is four.

5) values, such as stock market ratings are spelled (123), all types of codes (124, 125) or soccer scores (126)

(123) <K21 3893> In it's place a memorial to their lost lives. Major meets French and Danes to discuss Europe Nepal aircrash victims' families fly to Kathmandu Channel Four researcher on bail charged with perjury FTSE down 12 The hundred shares index closed down twelve point five at **two** five five three -12.5 at 2553.0.

(124) <JP1 256> Hopefully he's halfway through it with erm erm so that should come up. Okay? Okay. . No end date. it's two four O two four five O five or **two** seven. remove Yeah oh it's quite a big value. .

(125) <KDA 5213> Oh no I hate it when than ha when that happens, you fucking pull off the corner and the top don't come off. It's a real bitch to try and get into. Here are Mark put **two** five one O O seven one, about five seven or eight. Yeah if you could.

(126) <KS7 15> Chesterfield one, Torquay United one; Halifax Town nil, Darlington nil; Northampton Town two, Aldershot one; Scunthorpe United **two**, Maidstone United two; Walsall nil, Peterborough United one;

6) counting sequences (127) and other recitations of number sequences for all kinds of purposes (e.g., synchronizing actions, codes, orientation (128) etc.)

(127) <KBW 14591> Well it is except you've got to go one, two, three, four, clonk, clonk, clonk, clonk one, **two**, three, four That's it, and then swap hands but you go like that, go on then, Yes, , one, two, one, two, one, two, three, four, one, two, three, four, one, two, three, four

(128) <KBW 15077> Oh come on Christopher come and sometimes it in the right panel, that's the right panel there and then it goes in the left hand and then it goes to the right hand and then it goes to the left then right, the left, the right, left, right, left, confusing, but it's that hand to start with and go like this one, **two**, three, four it goes one, two, three, four they go one, two, three, four hang about, you see what it says here oh you don't play that one, just the something for you to write underneath, I thought it was complicated Did, did,

7) age

(129) <ASN 835> `Naples, let me see. It would have been 1935 or `36. Henry was only **two**, I remember. 1935. Yes, it must have been. Early summer.

Of course, also adnominal uses are possible in this domain, even though in constructions such as *he's two years old*, the numeral denotes age only via the detour of measurement, more specifically, temporal measurement.

8) labels of entities or people (numerals as ordering devices (130), or as indices (131))

(130) <KDR 141> Robin Oh we've got Robin he's er W five Oh sorry Steven Steven Mm, mm yes, got him er Kevin S **two** yes Lou S three yes David S two yes Neville S one A, what's the difference between the one As?

(131) <C87 210> If you reach the later levels, you'll find 'em on Side **Two** of the cassette.

9) symbol

(132) <FM5 303> Right right. you got the the O H is the bit you want twice so write it down put the brackets round it and then the **two**.

10) arguments, reasons (discourse-structural)

(133) <A6E 357> I remember having some really interesting discussions with him when we'd go and see a band somewhere. All of us were checking new bands out the whole time. For two reasons. One, like any new band we were checking out the opposition. **Two**, it was a strange time. There was a rock `n" roll vacuum. We were looking for anybody who could help fill it.

Within these domains, six basic uses of *two* can be distinguished. The categorization that derives from the corpus analysis is very similar to the categories that Fuson and Hall used for their psycholinguistic research of the acquisition of number words (Fuson and Hall 1983).

(1) The expression of cardinality is clearly the most important function of *two*.

(2) The expression of measurement is the second most important function. I follow Fuson and Hall in their description of this use as a derived kind of cardinality use: "In a measure context, the number word describes the numerousness of the units into which some continuous dimension of an entity has been divided; that is, it tells "how many units" there are in some entity" (Fuson and Hall 1983:79). This category includes the spatial, temporal (locational and durational) and "portion" measurements, but also includes indications of time (*two o' clock*), age, values of stocks etc.

(3) Numbers are also used as part of the number sequence, either as a counting practice or just for recitative purposes (cf. Benacerraf's distinction between transitive and intransitive counting (Benacerraf 1965)). Fuson and Hall call the latter "sequence number words" and argue that these may be used "for various purposes - for sheer practice, for timekeeping (e.g., saying the words to 20 in Hide-and-Go-See), for showing-off (*I can count higher than you can*) [...] (Fuson and Hall 1983:53). It goes without saying that these "sequence number words" are typical for children. The discourse-structural uses of numerals can be regarded as a somewhat atypical instantiation of this "sequential" use of numerals.

(4) When a numeral is used as the name of the written symbol 2, it functions as a count noun.

(5) A numeral can also be used in codes, often for identification of location or for coordinating activities. Fuson and Hall give a number of examples of this use in "nonnumerical number word contexts": "Telephone numbers, driver's license numbers, football jersey numbers, and dorm food ticket numbers are a few of the many such applications" (Fuson and Hall 1983:93).

(6) The use of numerals in a strictly mathematical context is so specific that it deserves a special category. It is to some extent derivative of the cardinality use (in the sense that mathematical statements are abstracted from empirical phenomena with sets of entities).

4.4. A SPECIAL CASE: *ZERO*

To round off this general survey of the forms and functions of numerals, I will take a look at probably the most special numeral in the English language, *zero*[39]. Considering the extraordinary status of the *concept* 'zero', it is altogether not surprising that *zero* is rather extraordinary: in the general history of numbers, 'zero' was invented rather late compared to other numbers (Menninger 1970 [1958], Ifrah 1998 [1994], Kaplan 1999). 'Zero' also sticks out conceptually because of its close relation to negation, by virtue of its semantics of 'absence' or 'nothingness'. There is no other number concept that can be associated with any of the "Aristotelian" quantifiers (the quantifiers that are part of the Aristotelian square of oppositions: 'all', 'some', 'no'). The A, I and O corners of that square cannot be linked to a number, but 'zero' can be connected to the E corner[40]. Also, the concept 'zero' occupies a specific place in the philosophy of mathematics. Gottlob Frege defined 'zero' separately from all other numerals: "0 ist die Anzahl, welche dem Begriffe 'sich selbst ungleich zukommt'" (Frege 1990 [1884]:87). Also cross-linguistic information confirms the specificity of *zero*, at least as far as frequency is concerned: Dehaene and Mehler (1992) note that in the seven languages they have looked at, "[t]he frequency of zero is much lower than that of the other numerals" (Dehaene and Mehler 1992:5).

Besides the conceptual peculiarities of the concept 'zero', the English word *zero* is special in that it has many competitors as far as the expression of the concept of 'zero' ('absence of members' in cardinality readings, 'nothingness' in more (pro)nominal readings) is concerned, as opposed to other numerals (there is only one word to express the concept 'twenty-three', namely *twenty-three*). Near synonyms of *zero* are *naught* or *nought*, *nil*, *zip*, *zilch*, various collocations ending in *all* (*sod all, bugger all, Sweet Fanny All*), sports terms like *love* and *duck* and of course the quantifier *no* in various forms and combinations (*nobody, no-one, nothing, none* etc.).

While this is in itself not unimportant, the oddity of *zero* manifests itself in a number of other ways. More specifically, *zero* differs from the other numerals with respect to the extent to which they correspond to the general characteristics of the word class numerals. The question of parts of speech proves an excellent way to demonstrate the specificity of *zero*. I would suggest that the categorization of linguistic material into classes of parts of speech can be an important heuristic tool for semantic research. Conversely, the sort of usage-based syntacto-semantic analysis I will exemplify below should be read as an argument for the consideration of fine-grained intralinguistic analyses even when addressing the largest cross-linguistic questions concerning parts of speech. Obviously, such analyses can point at the

---

[39] This section is based on the research reported on in Bultinck (2001).

[40] For the claim that this Aristotelian square has linguistic and possibly also conceptual relevance, cf. Horn (1989: 252-267), van der Auwera (1996) and van der Auwera and Bultinck (2001)).

difficulties that go together with every categorizing or generalizing activity (the *topos* of "the borderline case" in papers on parts of speech, e.g. Croft 2000, Anward 2000, but also in traditional grammars), as well as showing how lexical items can change categories under semantico-pragmatic pressure (Croft 2000, Anward 2000). Moreover, the analysis also demonstrates how intricate and complicated the relationship between the semantic functions of an item and the word class it belongs to can be.

In this section, I will try to determine the relationship between *zero* and the word class that is traditionally referred to as the class of cardinal numerals, by comparing *zero* with *two*. It will become clear that *zero* is definitely not a prototypical numeral. I will compare the distributional and syntactic behavior of *zero* with that of *two*, which can be regarded as a far less problematic member of the class of cardinal numerals. I compared one thousand instances of each from the British National Corpus. I will deal with *zero* separately and then compare the results with those of *two* in a separate section.

Like any cardinal numeral, *zero* is used adnominally (362/1000) as well as (pro)nominally (628/1000). The ten instances in which *zero* functioned as a verb were considered irrelevant.

4.4.1. *Zero* as adnominal

I will first discuss *zero*'s behavior as an adnominal, ordering its uses according to the way the head it quantifies is marked for number. The general distribution can be found in Table 9:

TABLE 9

ADNOMINAL *ZERO*

Singular noun	Plural noun	Adjective or participle
(295/362=81.5%)	(62/362=17.1%)	(5/362=1.4%)

One of the most surprising results of the corpus analysis is the fact that in most cases *zero* co-occurs with nouns that are marked for singular number (268/362=74.0% instances in which *zero* precedes the singular numeral; 27/362=7.4% in which it is postposed).

(134) <B12 1100> Per capita GDP fell, on average, 3.8 per cent annually from 1981 to 1984 and scarcely reached **zero** growth in the latter part of the 1980s.

The semantics of *zero* in this construction is very close to that of *no*. Nevertheless, it differs from *no* in that *zero* is neutral rather than negative. The difference between *no growth* and *zero growth* is that in the first the existence of a growth is denied, while in the second the "size" of the growth is determined and given a value[41]. The difference, hence, is one of perspective; in the first the situation is construed negatively, in the second the absence is indicated more neutrally, via the detour of a numeral. Also, the version with *zero* suggests a finer measurement and relies on the concept of a scale; the one with *no* relies on the notion of presence/absence or existence/non-existence. Intuitively, I would say that this use of *zero* is slowly encroaching upon the domain of *no*, but diachronic research should confirm that intuition.

If *zero* does co-occur with plural nouns (which it does in 62 instances), it usually (47/62=75.8%) does not quantify the noun, but forms part of that noun, which is itself quantified by means of plural-marking.

> (135) <C95 2289> Clearly butterfly and angelfish require space, **zero** levels of toxins, high oxygen content, as natural and varied a diet as possible - and no external shocks.

Obviously, (135) does not mean that butterfly and angelfish require 'no levels of toxins'. It means that they require an environment in which the level of toxin is zero ("value-reading" of *zero*). Still, *zero* does take plural nouns with a regular quantifying meaning, be it only marginally (15/62=24.1% of the group in which *zero* quantifies plural nouns, but only 15/362=4.1% of the total of adnominal uses of *zero*). In these cases *zero* indicates the cardinality of a set of elements; it indicates the number of members of a group.

> (136) <B16 889> One reason for the upward straggle is the existence of a floor of **zero** dollars below which no country can fall (in theory), whereas there is no ceiling.

A fourth type of adnominal use has to be mentioned, in which *zero* is placed after the singular noun (as mentioned at the beginning of this section, only 27 instances of this were recorded). Here, *zero* functions as part of a name (cf. the "label" uses of *two* described in section 4.3.2.) and thus becomes a referential device.

> (137) <ARW 1487> After a three day trek across the desert, the group reached ground **zero**, the point directly above the buried bomb, stopping the countdown with only seven minutes to go.

Another 5 instances of adnominal uses of *zero* were recorded, in which *zero* modifies an adjective (*zero valent*) or an adjectival participle (*zero rated*).

Also, I looked at the element introducing the NP in which *zero* occurred: determiner (139/362=38.4%), preposition (90/362=24.9%), or *zero* itself (90/362=24.9%)[42], because this sheds light on the meaning of *zero*, especially when it co-occurs with singular nouns.

---

[41] Naturally, the term "value" as it is used here does not refer to the values of numerals I will discuss in the corpus analysis of *two* (e.g. 'absolute value', 'exactly n' value etc.) (cf. Chapter 5). In the discussion of *zero*, I refer to the everyday usage of *value*.

[42] The instances in which *zero* functions as a postposed modifier (*ground zero*) were not analysed as far as the initial elements are concerned.

(138) <FSA 1487> 2. For a given number of information arrivals, there is **zero** correlation between volatility and volume.

(139) <FEF 1439> At t = 0 the ring is released with **zero** initial velocity [...]

(140) <FRG 405> However, each social group in Bradford uses the **zero** variant more than the corresponding group in Norwich.

With *zero* (138) or a preposition (139) as first element of the NP, *zero* often receives an interpretation that is closer to 'no' than when the NP is introduced by a determiner (140). In the latter case, *zero* functions much more often as part of a naming device (hence it is used mainly for referential purposes, rather than for quantifying / modifying goals).

For similar hermeneutic reasons, adverbs and adjectives qualifying *zero* were indicated in the corpus analysis.

(141) <C97 149> Part of the job of your filtration system (commonly referred to as `biological filtration") is to ensure that ammonia levels are kept at or near **zero** levels.

(142) <ALG 27> In the central hilly region 70% of the annual herbage production is obtained in the spring with near **zero** summer production.

4.4.2. *Zero* as head

For the 628 usages of *zero* as head, the findings were ordered according to syntactic function of the phrase. The results can be found in Table 10. The 65 (10.4%) uses of *zero* as part of a name or an orientation phrase were not included in the table.

TABLE 10

SYNTACTIC FUNCTION OF *ZERO* AS HEAD: RELATIVE FREQUENCIES

Adjunct	Adverbial	Apposite	Direct object	Predicate	Subject
116/628	188/628	9/628	56/628	182/628	12/628
(18.5%)	(29.9%)	(1.4%)	(8.9%)	(29.0%)	(1.9%)

I will give an example and the relative frequency of each of the main types:

- *Zero* as head of subject

> (143) <FEU 1052> Each of these classes is then divided into nine divisions, and these in turn can be divided into nine sub-divisions or sections; **zero** is reserved for books of a general nature.

In this function, *zero* is most often used as the name of a conventional symbol whose meaning has to be explained. Usually, *zero* is followed by verbal forms like *signifying, symbolizes, represents, refers to*. The context is often technical and/or mathematical.

- *Zero* as head of object

> (144) <FEF 1040> Substituting it into eqn (4.10) would always yield **zero**, and that is obviously incorrect because the right-hand side may be finite.

Zero as head of an object can have different meanings. The corpus analysis, however, showed that in more than one fourth of the cases (16/56), *zero* co-occurs with *reach, exceed,* and *approach*, implying a very frequent value reading of the numeral. Another significant sub-group is related to the expression of the outcome or output of a (mathematical or other) operation (with *yield, produce,* and *give*) (10/56).

- *Zero* as head of predicate

> (145) <FSA 367> If all the transactions costs are **zero**, this condition collapses back to the previous no-arbitrage equality.

Together with the "head of adverbial"-group, this group contains most instances of *zero* used as a head. I also included the 18 instances of pseudo-predicates: those in parentheses, e.g., in which *zero* can be seen as the predicate of an elliptical copula-construction with a phrase of the surrounding sentence.

> (146) <EUS 1176> On other computers an operation code value (perhaps **zero**) is allocated to a special no-operation instruction.[43]

On the whole, *zero* as head of a predicate overwhelmingly calls for value-interpretations.

- *Zero* as head of an adverbial phrase

> (147) <B78 629> Once poison has temporarily reduced rat populations to almost **zero**, predation by barn owls can slow the recovery.

---

[43] Actually, in this instance *zero* could be interpreted as part of a subject NP as well.

Whenever *zero* is the head of an adverbial phrase, the phrase is introduced by a preposition. In nearly all cases, *zero* functions as the value of the starting-point or end-point of a dynamic state of affairs, be it evolution, variation, growth or change. The few exceptions are hard to group under one denominator; they include *zero* as a mathematical object (as in *divided by zero*), as a static value (*is at zero*) and as an indication of position (*set to zero*).

- *Zero* as head of an apposite phrase

This is a very small miscellaneous class, consisting of apposite constructions that often have causative-like meanings.

(148) <CAN 159)> Rewriting inequalities such as (10.3) in this form shows that by allowing a constant term in the objective we can effectively make the goal **zero** for all objectives.

- *Zero* as head of adjunct (part of subject/object/predicate/adverbial/apposite phrases)

This last subclass consists of sentences with *zero* in which the syntactic function of the numeral is not clearly delineated and/or relies on the intraphrasal syntax. In the following examples, *zero* is a head, but not the head of a phrase at sentence-level, but a head of part of a subject phrase (149), object phrase (150), predicate (151), adverbial (152) and apposite phrase (153) at the intraphrasal level.

(149) <FRN 1356> A value of **zero** means no V&agr;J&agr; rearrangement.
(150) <FEF 905> For one thing, a photon at rest (if you could get one to rest!) has a mass of **zero**.
(151) <FNR 1233> As the conversion rate is significantly different from **zero**, we must reject the possibility that both populations decay exponentially, and conclude that CD45Ro phenotype cells do revert to CD45RA phenotype in vivo.
(152) <FAV 899> The team at Stanford achieved its record resolution by using liquid helium gas as a coupling medium at a temperature just above absolute **zero**, 0.1 K.
(153) <CAD 2607> The first S in SSC comes from the fact that its magnets rely on coils of superconducting wire, which work only when chilled to about -269C, 4C above absolute **zero**.

Functional generalizations concerning this mixed class are hard to make, because *zero* functions in a myriad of ways, which is of course related to the variety of phrases in which it functions as a "subordinate" head. Since I intend to focus on the sentential level, I will not pursue the issue of the intraphrasal functional capacities of *zero* here.

Also the initial element of the phrase in which *zero* occurs will be looked at, just like with the adnominal uses of *zero*: a determiner (154), preposition (155), or *zero* itself (156)[44].

---

[44] One phrase in which *zero* occurred started with the participle *approaching*.

(154) <CM2 1254> Conventionally, those patterns whose left-hand or most significant bit position contains a **zero** represent positive values, and those where it contains a one represent negative values.

(155) <A6C 1569> Although the intention was that the allowable dolphin kill be gradually reduced each year to **zero**, since the introduction of the Act 800,000 dolphins have been killed by US purse seiners alone.

(156) <EV9 1115> Sections 3.6-3.16 are concerned with magnetostatics, where electric fields are assumed to be **zero** and the interrelationship of J, H, and B are studied.

Remarkably, from the 628 cases of *zero* as head, only 24 of the phrases containing *zero* started with a determiner (3 of them started with a preposition but contained a determiner in front of *zero* as well), while 240 started with *zero* itself and 298 with a preposition.[45] This is markedly different from the situation with the adnominal uses of *zero*, where the determiner-initiated phrases formed the largest group. Why does *zero*, when it functions as the head of a phrase, almost never take a determiner?

The most obvious reason is the fact that *zero* almost exclusively co-occurs with nouns that are marked for singular number, in which the meaning of *zero* is not quantificational *sensu stricto*, but seems to be linked more closely to the noun it precedes. Hence, this "integrated" *zero* is no longer incompatible with the occurrence of a determiner (cf. the discussion of the distributional features of numerals in section 4.1.3. of the Prolegomenon to this corpus analysis). When *zero* functions as a head, the only way the phrase that contains *zero* can be introduced by a determiner is when *zero* functions as a full-fledged noun, since *zero* does not function pronominally. This, however, does not happen very often. Indeed, the 24 cases of determiner + *zero* all seem to *refer* to the number zero, i.e. the mathematical object, or the Arabic, orthographically distinct and in that sense also perceptible sign. In each case, *zero* is construed as a thing, which it is not in the determiner + adnominal uses of *zero*. Even though *zero* functions relatively speaking more often nominally than e.g. *two* (cf. the "degrees of cardinality" discussion of *two*), its use as a full noun is still marginal.

The modifiers of *zero* as head are best divided according to their word class status. Note that this two-way distinction is different from the distinction made for the modifiers of adnominal uses of *zero* (namely, a distinction according to whether the adjective or adverb modified *zero* itself or a *zero* + noun construction).

Example (157) is an example of an *adverbial* modifying the phrase in which *zero* occurs; in (158) *zero* is modified by an adjective. Not surprisingly, the function of the adjectives contrasts with that of the adverbials in that the first denotes a property of *zero* and the second denotes a property of the relation between *zero* and the entity that *zero* is predicated of. The fact that *zero* can take adjectival as well as adverbial modifiers once again demonstrates the in-between nature of *zero*: adjectival modifiers suggest a more nominal use, adverbial ones a more adjectival use.

---

[45] The cases in which *zero* arguably functions as a head, but semantically functions as a name or a device of orientation or an element in a counting sequence were not analyzed as far as the initial elements of the phrase is concerned, because this did not seem to make sense. They are discussed separately.

(157) <EA9 961> When TR2 is conducting its collector voltage will be approximately **zero** and the l.e.d., D3, will become illuminated as a consequence.

(158) <A19 1126> American scientist working for the Astrophysics Institute at the University of Colorado in Boulder have created the lowest temperature ever recorded - one millionth of a degree above absolute **zero**.

Also, *zero* as head is modified much more often (67/628) than adnominal *zero* (6/362). This is not surprising: heads are always more likely to be modified; in the case of adnominals being modified, they could be described as modifiers being modified. This second-level modification is cognitively less basic.

Finally, there is also a miscellaneous class of uses, with *zero* as part of a proper name (159)[46] (sometimes without any clear link to the numeral-meaning, (160)), but also, and more importantly, with *zero* as part of an orientation (161, 162) or the spelling of a number (163, 164). The instances with *zero* as part of a proper name meant here are different from "label" uses such as *ground zero*, because in (159) or (160) *zero* does not indicate the "n-th" instance of a series of Ns (as *part two* is the second instance in a series of parts). These uses are often ignored in discussions of numerals, most probably because they do not fit into "normal" syntactic units too easily. There are 65/628 instances of these various uses of *zero* in the corpus sample. No instances were found in which *zero* was a part of a counting sequence (whereas *two* occurs in counting sequences quite naturally).

(159) <AAK, 113> The cult of precision reaches its apotheosis in the presidential code name: **Zero** One.

(160) <CGL 1571> The aircraft was not so manoeuvrable as the Japanese **Zero**, but its strength far exceeded the Zero in a dive.

(161) <ECX 1006> The pilot was informed: 'India Hotel landing runway two six left hand, QFE one **zero** zero one".

(162) <FME 382> Where is he? Well usually usually not always but just about always he's at home he hasn't gone anywhere so how far away is he zero as well so you get zero **zero** goes through the origin.

(163) <F8E 108> The substance that's most frequently measured is actual the chl is actually the chlorine content and the salinity is one point eight **zero** six five five times the chlorine concentration.

(164) <FM4 1134> One point eight. One point Well what would you Oh ze oh **zero** eight, yeah sorry zero eight . Yeah, okay.

Within this category, the group in which *zero* functions as part of a name is by far the most important (44/65). The question is whether this use of *zero* is still connected to the numeral *zero*. In most cases, it seems to be only very remotely linked. As the name of a

---

[46] In (159) a link between the name *Zero One* and the importance of someone like the president is easily established. The number *zero one* is probably the very first number used in the code system referred to in the example.

character in a novel, it vaguely refers to related meanings of nothingness and absence. As a name of a fighter plane, it might carry hints of physical/mechanical properties of the plane, or it may connote precision, or even death. In each case, this relatively frequent use of *zero* as part of names suggests a special interest in *zero* among certain speakers of English, which is much less present in the case of *two*. This special interest is not incompatible with the fact that *zero* is so often used as an adnominal modifier of singular nouns: in the latter case, as already mentioned, *zero* takes on name-like qualities.

4.4.3. Comparison of *two* and *zero*

The results of the comparison of the behavior of *zero* to that of *two* can be summarized in Table 11. For the sake of clarity; I have provided an example of *zero* or *two* below each observation.

TABLE 11

ZERO AND *TWO* COMPARED

ZERO	TWO

GENERAL

ZERO	TWO
Primarily used as (nominal) head (62.8%)	*Primarily used as adnominal (76.6%)*
<EW6 413> Black (1976) took the view that, since the initial margin is not an investment and there is no payment (receipt) of S t , the sum invested is **zero**. In consequence, it is not possible to define a rate of return on a futures contract, and some other type of analysis must be used which does not require the use of the sum invested.	<HU0 2222> I was there the night she exhumed her father's body and had his rotting remains tossed into the Thames. God rest them both, **two** good women viciously treated by a cruel man!
Not in partitive, interval, classifier and other idiosyncratic "numeral structures"	*Often used in idiosyncratic "numeral structures"*
*****Zero** of the children came back.	<FP2 1104> A useful starting point is to note that **two** of the three factors just mentioned as having influenced the law's development have little application in modern conditions. <G0P 2490> It had few ornaments: a

	vase or **two**, an ashtray and a couple of ceramic figures.
Used for a range of non-prototypical purposes (as part of a proper name, in orientation sequences or in number spellings; not in counting) (6.5 %)	*Hardly ever used as part of a proper name and less often for non-prototypical purposes (spelling and counting sequences) (1.4%)*
<FAN 580> He categorised the politicians who would deceive the people under the label `Mr **Zero**".	<KBW 14707> Right, you ready? Right, one, **two**, oh, hold on one, two, three, four one, two, three, four , one, two, three, hold on, hold on
Infrequently used numeral (cf. Dehaene and Mehler 1992); 2,287 solutions in BNC	*Most frequently used numeral (cf. Dehaene and Mehler 1992); 156,114 solutions in BNC*

ADNOMINAL USE

Most often in front of singular nouns (74.0%)	*Very rarely in front of singular nouns (1.2%)*
<B12 1100> Per capita GDP fell, on average, 3.8 per cent annually from 1981 to 1984 and scarcely reached **zero** growth in the latter part of the 1980s.	<FR0 3372> `There is the Doctor's ship." `Sorry, but it's a **two** seater," said a familiar voice.
Rarely in front of plural nouns (17.1 %)	*Almost always in front of plural nouns (95.7%)*
<B16 889> One reason for the upward straggle is the existence of a floor of **zero** dollars below which no country can fall (in theory), whereas there is no ceiling.	<G3D 15> It may stop after one or **two** drinks or it may go on into a spree.
If in front of PN, then often combined with PN to form an (in itself quantifiable) noun (75.9%); value-reading	*Hardly any integration with PN to form a quantifiable noun; cardinality-reading*
<C95 2289> Clearly butterfly and angelfish require space, **zero** levels of toxins, high oxygen content, as natural and varied a diet as possible - and no external shocks.	<APD 1360> There was considerable ambivalence, too, about a final **two** state solution implicit in the Arafat-Husayn initiative and the 1983 Fez plan.
Postposed uses with singular nouns (7.4%)	*Postposed uses (3.1%)*
<EUS 156> When this routine has completed its operation, it returns to the interrupted program by using the	<KDM 2527> What game's this one Em? Terminator two. That's . What is it? Terminator two. Terminator **two**.

| old program counter contents stored in location **zero**. | Terminator number two. |

USE AS HEAD

No anaphorical use (referring to an antecedent)	*Almost always anaphorical use (referring to an antecedent in the co- or context)*
* I didn't get any farmhouse chairs. The **zero** I did not get were in beech.	<KD5 4816> Yeah, I know but I did get those two nice farmhouse chairs Yeah. in beech so you can't Yeah, worked out alright. Is that those **two** ?
Meaning of the head can be related to the function of the phrase in which it occurs (S: name of symbol, O: value-readings (point of orientation or output), P: value-readings, ADV: starting-point or end-point)	*Meaning of the head depends on the meaning of the antecedent it refers to, most often pronominal two just refers to persons or "things"*
S - name of symbol: <FEU 1052> **zero** is reserved for books of a general nature. *O - value-readings (point of orientation or output):* <FEF 1040> Substituting it into eqn (4.10) would always yield **zero**, and that is obviously incorrect because the right-hand side may be finite. *P - value-readings:* <FSA 367> If all the transactions costs are **zero**, this condition collapses back to the previous no-arbitrage equality. *ADV - starting-point or end-point:* <B78 629> Once poison has temporarily reduced rat populations to almost **zero**, predation by barn owls can slow the recovery.	<CG6 649> As ordinary, non-handicapped children develop, the three aspects of language are co-ordinated, to a considerable degree, so that changes in one are associated with changes in the other **two**. <FSC 386> There were very few people who were allowed to tease her, but these **two** could just get away with it.

MODIFICATION / QUANTIFICATION

If modified, then only marginally by restrictors (8%)	*If modified, then most often by restrictors*
<FME 226> Each is different in mild degrees and minor sensations from its neighbours. But because each refuses to acknowledge its neighbours, the net effect in terms of the streetscape is less than **zero**.	<HR3 1206> Without the absolute power of an Egyptian Pharaoh one could scarcely test the consequences of an experiment involving the manipulation of people's lives, for example forcing a percentage of the population to emigrate or insisting that each fertile married couple produce exactly **two** offspring.
Used with property-indicating modifiers (adjectives)	*If not modified by 'at least', 'at most' or 'exactly' restrictors, then by approximative restrictors*
<FAV 154> The catch is that it operates only at temperatures just above absolute **zero**.	<KCX 5139> I worked for about **two** month and I were four hundred pound in rent arrears.
Not used with quantifiers	*Can combine with quantifiers like every*
* Every zero minutes, I woke up.	<EE5 712> While we were outside, the duty Corporal was doing the rounds of the barrack rooms, checking for cleanliness and tidiness; every **two** or three minutes a pair of boots would sail out of the window, or there would be the sound of a locker crashing to the floor.

4.4.4. Conclusion

Zero can be assigned to the class of cardinal numerals, but it diverges from other cardinals like *two*. Primarily used as a head, it behaves much more nominally, less pronominally (not for reference to antecedents, like *two*), and often even as (part of a) name (postposed uses in adnominal position, "abstract" uses as head (with or without property-indicating modifiers), and as part of proper names). When it is used adnominally, it expresses values of different types of measurement (*zero growth*), while at the same time restricting the reference of its head rather than indicating cardinalities of sets. This is another demonstration of its predominant name-like function. Furthermore, this explains why *zero* is excluded from idiomatic constructions with numerals, which are typically used for expressing cardinalities. As a head, its different meanings can be related to the syntactic function of the phrase in which it occurs, while the meaning of *two* is dependent on the meaning of its antecedent. *Zero* does not occur in counting sequences, but it is used for a range of other functions. Finally, *zero* is only marginally modified by restrictors, but it is compatible with property-indicating adjectives. *Two*, on the other hand, is predominantly modified by restrictors.

This shows that the analysis of *zero* not only yields yet another example of a "borderline case" in part of speech theory, but it also demonstrates how word class categorizations are useful on the meta-linguistic level. A fine-grained analysis of syntacto-distributional differences between a certain item and other members of the category the item belongs to helps to map the semantics of the item in question. In addition, *zero* is interesting for part of speech theory in that it diverges in its behavior from other numerals under semantico-pragmatic pressure. Because of the competition with negation and its lexicalizations, and because of the extraordinary conceptual nature of 'zero' itself, *zero* leaves the classical domain of application of numerals, and acquires a number of specific functions: predominantly nominal and even name-like functions, as well as points of orientation, indications of value, starting points or end-points of evolutions. One claim of part of speech theory holds that core members of parts of speech can be characterized by their semantico-pragmatic functions (Croft 2000, Anward 2000). Hence, if it transpires that *zero* (arguably a member of the class of cardinal numerals) diverges from the core semantico-pragmatic functions of cardinals, non-prototypical syntactic and distributional behavior are expected. This is exactly what the corpus analysis reveals. As such, this analysis corroborates a much more general argument in contemporary part of speech theory.

5

'AT LEAST N', 'EXACTLY N', 'AT MOST N' AND 'ABSOLUTE VALUE' READINGS

5.0. METHODOLOGY

Now that it has been shown that "cardinality" cannot be taken as a monolithic concept, it is time to focus on the central question in the neo-Gricean analysis of English cardinal numerals. Despite the over-all gradual nature of the cardinality concept, the uses of numerals that have been called "pure cardinal" uses can be separated from the other, more complex uses. The so-called N CN uses of numerals generally correspond to the perspective on cardinals that is taken for granted in the neo-Gricean tradition: they express the numerosity of a set; they identify the number of elements of a group. This does not mean that the "hybrid" uses can simply be ignored (a general account of numerals should aim to explain all uses of numerals)[1], but it does mean that the traditional debate on cardinals is a valid one, one that still needs a definitive answer. With the following corpus analysis I hope to contribute to this answer.

As argued in Chapter 2 and 3, the traditional Grice-Horn-Levinson-line on cardinals involves two layers: the semantics of N CN uses of numerals is taken to be 'at least n', while the dominant 'exactly n' reading is assumed to be the effect of a conversational Quantity 1-implicature. For the sake of convenience, I will repeat the principal arguments in favor of such an analysis. As I have indicated in Chapter 3, Larry Horn first proposed this analysis in his (1972) thesis. He withdrew his Gricean account in 1992, but it is still accepted by many leading researchers, with variable degrees of caution and various amendments (Van Kuppevelt 1996, Krifka 1999, Levinson 2000, Allan 2000, 2001). The prime arguments in favor of the neo-Gricean analysis are:

---

[1] In this respect, Kamp and Reyle (1993:452-463) and especially Kadmon (1987:59-109, 2001:68-76) are more careful in restricting their statements about numerals to specific uses than Horn or Levinson. Before his conversion to the underdeterminacy-analysis (Horn 1992), Horn wrote quite indistinctly: "My pragmatic account of the subcontrary relation generalizes to all relatively weak scalar operators, including cardinal numbers and evaluative or gradable adjectives like *good*" (Horn 1989:213). Levinson (2000: 87-90) also speaks of "the number words", although he does admit that "there are perhaps genuine differences in interpretive freedom between number words in different syntactic and thematic positions" (Levinson 2000:90).

1) truth conditions: 'three' entails 'two', hence *three* entails *two*, but not *vice versa*

2) defeasibility of the 'exact' meaning; either via cancellation or suspension (*John has three children, in fact four / if not four* vs. **John has three children, in fact two / if not two*)

3) behavior under negation (*John does not have three children* usually means 'less than three')

4) behavior in questions (*Does John have three children?* can be answered by either *Yes, (in fact) he has four* or *No, he has four*, depending on whether the question is or is not assumed to have implicated an upper bound)

5) redundancy (if *three* meant 'exactly three' then *exactly* in *John has exactly three children* would be redundant) and contradiction (if *some* meant 'exactly some', *at least some* would be a contradiction)

6) reinforceability (*John has three children, but not four* vs. **John has three children, but not two*)

7) variable degree of defeasibility of 'exact' meaning (under incorporation the 'exact' reading is practically conventionalized, in other contexts it does not even arise; also "roundness" plays a role)

8) generality of the scalar account (other lexical items fit perfectly in the neo-Gricean account of numerals and in the so-called Square of Oppositions); it also squares with Horn's (1972) analysis of *only*

9) typological generalizations (lexicalization of 'exactly n' is unheard of)

10) logical relations (entailment relations, monotonicity)

Despite the wealth of arguments in favor of the neo-Gricean account, it will by now be clear that this is not the analysis that I will adopt. In Chapter 2, the more theoretical arguments (generality of the scalar account, the argument concerning logical relations, the defeasibility concept etc.) have been discussed. In this section, I will look at actual uses of numerals, and try to test the neo-Gricean hypotheses.

The decision to analyze the meaning of English numerals by means of an elaborate corpus analysis may be surprising for those acquainted with the "cardinal debate" sketched above. While corpus analyses have become standard heuristic procedures for determining the meaning of a wide variety of grammatical or lexical material, a corpus analysis of English numerals has never been presented before. Undoubtedly, the historical context of the discussion on English numerals, viz. Laurence Horn's logic-inspired texts on semantics and pragmatics and his influence on practitioners of (some kind of) formal semantics, constitutes one of the reasons why nobody in the neo-Gricean debate on numerals has studied usage-based data.

Nevertheless, the discussion of the writings of the progenitor of the theoretical framework inspiring the 'at least' analysis in Chapter 2 showed that such an empirical, frequency-based analysis is very much in the line of his thinking. Even though Grice never refers explicitly to the possibility of a corpus analysis, his somewhat laborious attempt to arrive at a definition of "conventional meaning" suggests that the "corpus method" can be seen as the methodological outcome of his theoretical insights. Let us repeat that Grice defined the meaning of a word or a sentence as what speakers *standardly mean by them*:

> It seems to me, then, at least reasonable and possibly even mandatory, to treat the meaning of words, or of other communication vehicles, as analyzable in terms of features of word users or other communicators; nonrelativized uses of "meaning$_{NN}$" are posterior to and explicable through relativized uses involving reference to word users or communicators. More specifically, what sentences mean is what (standardly) users of such sentences mean by them; that is to say, what psychological attitudes toward what propositional objects such users standardly intend [...] to produce by their utterance. (Grice 1989:350)

The passage just quoted is from Grice's "Retrospective Epilogue" to the collection entitled *Studies in the way of words* (Grice 1989). In the original William James lectures similar comments can be found with respect to the nature of "conventional meaning", especially in his discussion of the distinction between statements of "timeless meaning" - "statements of the type "X means '. . .'", in which the specification of meaning involves quotation marks" (Grice 1989:119) - and "occasion-meaning" (e.g. the ironic usage of *genius* in the sentence *John is a genius*, when the opposite is meant). The first is a close approximation of what is called "conventional meaning": it is what we are after when we are trying to determine the meaning of a word or a sentence (Grice uses the term "utterance-type") in a specific language. The second is intricately connected to the concrete use of a specific word or utterance-type by a speaker. In the first case we try to describe what a *linguistic element* means, in the second we look at what a *speaker* means in using that linguistic element:

> I argue in support of the thesis that timeless meaning and applied timeless meaning [roughly the timeless meaning of an utterance-type as it is uttered, which, for instance, makes it possible to choose the relevant meaning of an ambiguous word] can be explicated in terms of the notion of utterer's occasion-meaning (together with other notions), and so ultimately in terms of the notion of intention. (Grice 1989:91)

The determination of what is meant by a certain speaker using a certain linguistic structure is in Grice's (repeatedly voiced) opinion always to be derived from the speaker's intentions, regardless whether the speaker uses "literal" meanings or implicatures to make his intentions clear.

In the context of the analysis of the meaning of English numerals, we are not so much interested in the occasion-meaning of numerals, but in arriving at a general picture of the meaning of those numerals in the English language. As we have seen, the neo-Gricean analysis starts with an 'at least' meaning for numerals and derives the other interpretations by means of implicatures, according to (some version of) Grice's original working-out schema:

> To work out that a particular conversational implicature is present, the hearer will rely on the following data: (1) the conventional meaning of the words used, together with the identity of any references that may be involved; (2) the Cooperative Principle and its maxims; (3) the context, linguistic or otherwise, of the utterance; (4) other items of background knowledge; and (5) the fact (or supposed fact) that all relevant items

falling under the previous headings are available to both participants and both participants know or assume this to be the case. (Grice 1989:31).

Usually, much attention is paid to phase (2)-(4) in this schema. I contend that the neo-Gricean analysis is wrong because it has neglected phase (1). If Grice is right about the intentional foundation of meaning, the "conventional meaning of the words used" should be derived from the utterer's occasion-meaning of the words used. Therefore, if we want to establish the conventional meaning of numerals, we have to get a clear picture of what users of numerals standardly mean by them. Now, it is obvious that it is not possible to get a *direct* look at large numbers of speaker intentions: not only would it involve countless requests for introspective study of the many individual speakers' intentions when using numerals, it is doubtful whether speakers would spontaneously relate these intentions to the linguists' fine-grained categorizations ('at least', 'at most', 'exactly'). As a fairly reliable approximation of this ideal, I propose to investigate large samples of how numerals are used in actual, real-life situations. A rigid and detailed corpus analysis of the various ways in which the linguistic element is used is an empirically verifiable method to assess the conventional meaning of a linguistic element, in Grice's sense of that term. By means of a corpus analysis, the timeless meaning of a linguistic structure can be evaluated by generalizing over large numbers of occasion-meanings of that linguistic structure.

Before exemplifying this insight by means of a large corpus analysis of English numerals, it is perhaps useful to look at a potential theoretical objection to this methodology, related to the link between conventionality and frequency. One of the main merits of this approach is that it forces the linguist to look at a large number of contextualized uses of the linguistic element under investigation. Especially in the logic-inspired neo-Gricean tradition, the data (consisting mostly of example sentences) were often constructed by the linguist himself, so that there was always the danger that these examples had been (consciously or unconsciously) selected to fit the linguist's hypothesis. A corpus analysis, on the other hand, always starts from the data and will have to account for every single usage type. Not only will this result in a much more complete picture of the behavior of the linguistic element, it will also allow the linguist to quantify over the behavior of the linguistic element. The radical consequence of this view is that the most frequent meaning of a linguistic item is also the best candidate for the status of "conventional meaning" of that item. I argue that this is correct, even if that meaning is not the meaning that is standardly used as the basis for implicature-driven derivation of other meanings. At first sight, this seems to go against the spirit and the practice of Grice's own analyses, which always start from the "logical" meaning as the conventional one, while deriving other meanings by strengthening them pragmatically.

Let us first look, once again, at one of Grice's own examples to clarify my position. As has been discussed in Chapter 2, Grice refers to two meanings of the word *or* in his *Further Notes on Logic and Conversation*: the first meaning is described as the meaning of the logical connector in $A \lor B$ and is called the "weak" meaning; the second meaning has the same meaning, complemented by the condition that there is some non-truth-functional reason for accepting that $A \lor B$, "i.e. that there is some reasonable (though) not necessarily conclusive argument with $A \lor B$ as conclusion which does not contain one of the disjuncts as a step (does not proceed via A or via B)" (Grice 1989:44). The latter is called the "strong meaning". Grice argues that the weak meaning should be adopted as the conventional meaning, because the extra meaning component of the strong meaning can be canceled, as in *The prize is either in the garden or in the attic. I know that because I know where I put it, but I'm not going to tell you.* The second reason Grice offers is in fact another implicit argument for the use of corpus analyses: "We might argue that if *or* is supposed to possess a strong sense, then it should be possible to suppose it (*or*) to bear this sense *in a reasonably wide range of linguistic settings*" (Grice 1989:45; my emphasis). Since it is not possible to say *Suppose that A or B* with *or* having the strong meaning, the latter cannot be the conventional meaning.

This fully conforms to my claim that the most frequent meaning is the conventional one, but it does call for an important specification of that claim. Naturally, the different meanings that can be assigned to a certain linguistic element can be related to each other. In fact, when the meanings that are found for one and the same word are totally unrelated to each other in a synchronic setting (thereby excluding relations between words which are reflexes of diachronic evolutions and which are no longer transparent to language users), the word would be considered ambiguous, and there would be good grounds to argue that the word in question has two (or more) "conventional meanings", which exist side by side and which can be teased apart at Grice's level of "applied timeless meaning". It is obvious that when trying to decide which of a number of different related meanings should be selected as the conventional meaning, the most frequent meaning will often be the most abstract or vague meaning. In the case of *or*, e.g., the logical meaning is rightly considered by Grice as the conventional meaning, not because it is easier to use it as a basis for deriving the strong sense, but because all uses of *or* exhibiting the strong meaning also, inherently, have as part of their meaning the weak sense of *or*. That is what it means to say that the most frequent meaning is the conventional meaning.

An objection that calls for a similar elucidation was made by Robyn Carston (pers. comm.). She sketched a hypothetical situation in which an extensive corpus analysis of a word shows two meanings to be more frequent than any others, with each of them as frequent as the other, and neither apparently induced by the linguistic context in which they appear. She offered the example of *hit* with and without an intentional component of meaning as in *She tripped and hit the wall* and *She took a stick and hit him* and wondered whether *hit* should be considered ambiguous. Again, this is a case in which two meanings of the same word are clearly interrelated: since the meaning without the intentional component ('come into contact with a lot of force') will be part of the meaning of any "intentional" use of *hit*, the meaning without the intentional component should be considered as the conventional meaning of *hit*, simply because it is more frequent. This also shows that the question of the conventionality of a certain meaning is a question of degree: just like meanings can be more or less frequent, they can be more or less conventional. The second example given by Carston concerns the word *bachelor*: this can occur with the meaning component 'eligible for marriage' as well as with the meaning 'irresponsible, fun-loving, not interested in a committed relationship'. A corpus analysis would have to show whether these two meanings are indeed equally frequent (which I doubt), but the theoretical point remains the same: if it turns out that both meanings are equally frequent, they will be equally conventional. My guess is, however, that the meaning component "unmarried" will be even more frequent and therefore more conventional. The relationship between the two senses, and the potentially ambiguous status of the word *bachelor* would have to be investigated before the quantitative data can come into play.

Also in the context of numerals, it is important to realize what kind of data the corpus analysis can yield. It is absolutely crucial that there is a distinction between the "coded" meaning (i.e., the meaning that is expressed by the linguistic elements themselves, cf. Grice 1989 [1967], Carston 1988, 1998a, 1998b, 1999, Récanati 1989, Bach 1994a, Sperber and Wilson 1995 [1986], Levinson 2000)[2], which should be tested by means of a corpus analysis, and everything that can somehow be attributed to an utterance but that is not "encoded" in the linguistic elements of that utterance ("implicature", "explicature", "enrichment", "completion", "expansion"). On the level of the coded meaning, questions of truth and falsity are not relevant; what counts is what is expressed by the linguistic element as linguistic element. This means that the corpus analysis presented below is only part of the story (be it undoubtedly the most essential part).

In 85,7% of the sentences with *two*, the "value"[3] of cardinal *two* could easily be determined on the basis of a grid of four possible cardinality readings: the whole sentence in which *two* occurred, either as an adnominal (74.1%) or as a pronominal (11.6%)[4], was interpreted as denoting a cardinality corresponding to either 'at least / more than two', 'at most / less than two'[5], 'exactly two' or 'two - absolute value'. The procedure was as follows: first, the meaning of the whole sentence was assessed in terms of the cardinality it expressed, and in a second phase, the meaning contribution of the linguistic elements relevant for the expression of cardinality was determined. These elements obviously include the numeral itself, but are not limited to them: also restrictors, modal expressions and determiners are clearly capable of transforming the cardinality expressed. In 14.3% of the cases, a classification of the cardinality expressed in terms of the four categories was considerably more difficult, either because *two* appeared in one of the idiomatic constructions described in Chapter I (e.g., it is much harder to specify the already reduced cardinality-meaning of *two* in *part two* in terms of the four possibilities just listed, because it is not even clear whether these values apply to "impure" cardinality uses), or because *two* formed part of a larger numeral (in

---

[2] Other terms that are used to indicate the "coded content" are "logical form", "semantics", "conventional meaning", "standard meaning", "semantic representation", or "literal meaning". These terms may differ slightly in their respective meanings, cf. Levinson (2000:195) and Chapter 2 for a more extensive discussion.

[3] In this section, I will speak of the "value" of a certain use of *two* as opposed to the "meaning" of *two*: the latter term refers to the uses of *two* I discussed in the analysis of cardinality (e.g., "temporal meaning" of *two*), while the term "value" will be reserved for specific distinctions within one particular "meaning" of *two*, namely cardinal *two*. A value of *n* can be either 'at least n', 'at most n', 'exactly n' or 'n - absolute value'. I will explain these terms in the next section.

[4] The pronominal uses of *two* were analyzed together with the pure cardinal uses because, as pointed out in section 2.1.4. of Chapter I, the pronominal nature of *two* generally does not influence the expression of cardinality as such. The hybrid nature of pronominal uses of *two* derives from the fact that *besides* their cardinality function, these pronominal uses fulfil other semantic duties as well. As I will see, however, this pronominal nature does influence the specific value of the cardinality expressed.

[5] The categories 'at least two' and 'more than two' on the one hand and the categories 'at most two' and 'less than two' on the other hand were taken together, because both explicitly indicate that a number higher than / lower than two (also) obtains. This makes them different from 'absolute value' and 'exactly n' uses. There are of course important differences between 'at least n' and 'more than n' and 'at most n' and 'less than n'. I will come back to this distinction in the separate discussion of 'at least n / more than n' and 'at most n / less than n'.

which case it was considered irrelevant). As we have seen in Chapter I, *two* often occurs in constructions that deviate from the canonical numeral-common noun construction; in those cases, it is not easy to decide whether the cardinality expressed is 'at least two' or rather 'exactly two'. For instance, it is clear that in (1) or (2), *two* cannot be characterized in these terms.

(1) <K22 517> Video-Taped report follows BLACKPOOL LINDA TOWNLEY/Stroud Labour Party CLIVE SOLEY MP/Lab Hammersmith Voice over In part **two**: Putting the boot in.
(2) <FM5 303> O H now how many of those do you want? In brackets. Great. And there are two. Right right. you got the the O H is the bit you want twice so write it down put the brackets round it and then the **two**. Right.

This shows, once again, that the traditional analyses of numerals have been very limited in their scope: when the meaning of English numerals was discussed, it was nearly always in terms of the four categories listed above (actually, in the beginning only two categories were recognized, 'at least two' and 'exactly two', cf. the discussion of Horn 1972 in Chapter 3). Before addressing the specific problems of the "less cardinal" uses of *two*, I will discuss the presumably less problematic N CN uses in terms of 'at least n / more than n', 'exactly', 'at most n / less than n' and 'absolute value' readings. Afterwards I will check to what extent the analysis can be transposed to other uses of numerals and whether these uses raise further problems for the neo-Gricean approach.

Table 1 shows the distribution of the various interpretations of *two* in N CN and pronominal uses in the sample corpus. Table 2 and Table 3 specify the distribution for N CN uses and pronominal uses separately.

TABLE 1

VALUES OF CARDINAL *TWO* IN N CN **AND** PRONOMINAL USES

Absolute Value (390/857=45.5%)	At least / more than two (33/857=3.9%)	At most two / less than two (69/857=8%)	Exactly two (365/857=42.6%)

TABLE 2

VALUES OF CARDINAL *TWO* IN N CN USES

Absolute Value (349/741=47.0%)	At least / more than two (30/741=4.0%)	At most / less than two (43/741=6.0%)	Exactly two (319/741=43.0%)

TABLE 3

VALUES OF CARDINAL *TWO* IN PRONOMINAL USES

Absolute Value (41/116=35.3%)	At least / more than two (3/116=2.6%)	At most / less than two (26/116=22.4%)	Exactly two (46/116=39.7%)

It is perhaps necessary to emphasize once more that these tables reflect the values of *two* as they are triggered by the *whole* utterance. They show the distribution of the various interpretations of *two* + the linguistic elements that influence the interpretation of *two*: if modifiers such as *exactly* occurred, if definiteness-markers were part of the NP in which *two* functioned, or if the co- or context provided modal meanings, this obviously influenced the over-all value of the cardinality expressed. I deliberately opted for such a "comprehensive" account, because only in this way the meaning contribution of *two* could be established. I decided not to follow the traditional method, which consists of first adopting a presupposed meaning of cardinals and then checking how this meaning is subsequently altered in actual uses, because the essential question concerns precisely the semantic status of the numeral in question. Hence, I first tried to establish an over-all picture of the specific value of *two* that is expressed in the utterance, with due attention to the cotext in which the utterance occurred, and with hypotheses as to the speaker intentions behind the utterance[6]. In a second stage, I tried to disentangle the "meaning complex" that is caused by a combination of the numeral and whatever other linguistic elements that happen to influence the cardinality value.

In its general methodology, this corresponds to what I would like to call the "hermeneutical approach", suggested in, among others, Geeraerts (1988:652). Geeraerts defends semantics as a human science, in the Diltheyan sense of the word:

---

[6] It goes without saying that these hypotheses remain speculative. Nevertheless, if Grice is at least partly right in his intentionalist account of meaning, a reconstruction of the context in which a certain utterance was expressed AND a reconstruction of the intentions of the speaker are essential to any comprehensive meaning analysis. The corpus methodology that is adopted here does not enable us to retrieve the speaker intentions behind each utterance from the speaker him- or herself. But even if that were feasible, I highly doubt whether the results would be significantly different from the ones I will present here. I even doubt whether such inquiries into speaker intentions would yield definitive answers (e.g., it is not evident that speakers have a clear picture of what their intentions were when they produced a certain utterance, neither is it clear whether different speakers would reproduce these intentions in comparable and quantifiable ways, etc.). In the analysis of the corpus materials, I often had to rely on intuitions. I believe that my estimations will correspond to the real intentions of the speaker and to those of the reader.

Also, while this corpus method only yields an analysis of the "coded content" of numerals (and not of the "implicatures" that can be triggered while using an utterance containing a numeral), this does not mean that reference to the intentions of the speaker has to be excluded from the analysis. As Grice made perfectly clear, in the final analysis, also the conventional meaning of linguistic elements has to be derived from speaker intentions. The first clear statement to this effect runs as follows: " "*x* means$_{NN}$ (timeless) that so-and-so" might be equated with some statement or disjunction of statements about what "people" (vague) intend [...] to effect by *x*." (Grice 1989 [1957]:220).

Next to being historically and culturally orientated, the human sciences in the Diltheyan sense are hermeneutical par excellence: they try to reconstruct the original experience that has lain at the basis of particular forms of human expression that have been transmitted from earlier times to the present day; they look for the expressive intention behind historical forms of expression.

Geeraerts argues that historical-philological semantics - a period in semantic research that he locates in between 1870 and 1930 - is the intellectual forefather of present-day cognitive semantics. The similarities between the two paradigms are striking, and the approach is equivalent, even though the historical-philological semanticist had a tendency to focus on older stages of the language, on "texts from dead languages or from previous stages in the development of a living language" (Geeraerts 1988:656): "Its basic methodological act is therefore the *interpretation* of those texts". In other words:

> The primary methodological step of the historical semantician is that of the historical lexicographer and the philological scholar: to interpret historical texts against the background of their original context by trying to recover the communicative intention of the author. (Geeraerts 1988:652)

I do not wish to align myself fully nor exclusively with Cognitive Semantics, but I fully subscribe to this "hermeneutical" approach of semantic research. I contend that this is also the right approach for the investigation of elements that are traditionally not part of the corpus of the lexical semanticist, such as connectives, quantifiers, and, specifically, also numerals.

5.1. ABSOLUTE VALUES AND 'EXACTLY N' VALUES OF *TWO* IN N CN AND PRONOMINAL USES

In 45.5% of the cases under discussion, the cardinality expressed in the utterance containing *two* is more specifically to be described as 'two - absolute value'. I will first specify what I mean by this term and then I will describe the various ways in which 'absolute value' readings of *two* manifest themselves in the sample corpus.

5.1.1. Increasing the number of positions - the concept 'absolute value'

(3) <AR2 112> He imagined small, cheaply staged pictures of sexual tortures involving ropes and wires - the kind of things which Boy had not yet done. He imagined a full-page, black and white photo of **two** barechested men (their chests shaved), photographed in daylight, walking down the street, gazing squarely at the camera, holding hands, one of them holding an alsatian straining at a leather leash.

In (3), someone is described as imagining a photograph of two bare-chested men. The classical positions in the cardinal debate leave open two, at most three options as far as the interpretation of *two* is concerned. The prime mover of the cardinal debate, Horn (1972), concentrated on two options: 'at least two' and 'exactly two'. Fourteen years later, this was still the received opinion: "Numerals have two interpretations, 'at least *n*' and 'exactly *n*', and the question is whether this is a phenomenon of linguistic ambiguity or a case of a unitary core meaning plus implicature imposed by pragmatic principles" (Kempson 1986:80). Even in 1998, Carston could write about the 'at most' reading that "this third reading for number terms has been largely ignored by the neo-Griceans, who have been concerned only to show how a bilateral ("exactly n") understanding is derived" (Carston 1998a:203-204). Later, especially through the efforts of Carston (1985, 1988, 1998a), this extra option was acknowledged: some utterances containing numerals clearly should be interpreted as expressing 'at most' values[7]. Utterance (4) illustrates such a use.

    (4)   You can eat **two** apples a day.

As described in Chapter 3, this observation, together with more general (relevance-) theoretic reasons, led Carston to present her underdeterminacy-thesis. This hypothesis left room for three options: 'at least', 'at most' and 'exactly' interpretations.

    These positions have come into existence through decades of arguments about the right meaning analysis of numerals and the definition of these positions is now often taken for granted. But actually, these positions imply much more than what has been taken for granted. Much of what has gone wrong in the cardinal debate derives from the lack of accurate definitions of these positions.

    The 'at least n', 'at most n' and 'exactly n' interpretations can be analyzed as follows:

'At least n'   = necessarily n + possibly more than n
'At most n'   = possibly n + not possible more than n
'Exactly n'   = necessarily n + not possible more than n + not possible less than n

In other words, assigning an 'at least' value to a certain use of *two* means that this use of *two* is taken as expressing the fact that the group of entities denoted by the NP contains necessarily n members AND the fact that the group in question may contain more members than n. Likewise, in the case of 'at most n' the utterance is interpreted as indicating that the group may contain n members, but certainly does not contain more than n members. With 'exactly n' readings, the meaning of the numeral consists not of two, but of three meaning components:

---

[7] In fact, at first sight it might seem that Horn (1972:43) does refer to uses of numerals that can be compared to these 'at most' examples. Utterances such as *Mary can live on £15 a month – and in fact she can live on (even) less / *more* and *Kipchoge can run a mile in 4 minutes, if not 3:58 / *4:02* resemble, at least to a certain extent, Carston's 'at most' examples, but have traditionally been analyzed in terms of "scale-reversal". It is clear that the meaning of these numerals cannot be incorporated in a traditional 'at least' analysis (because the normal entailment relations do not hold), but neither can they be interpreted as 'at most n': 'Mary can live on at most £15 a month' is obviously not a good paraphrase of the utterance mentioned by Horn. I will come back to these examples in section 2 and section 3.3.

1) the group contains necessarily n members, 2) it necessarily does not contain more than n members and 3) it necessarily does not contain less than n members.

Three facts are notable about these analyses: first, the 'at least', 'at most' and 'exactly' labels are not atomic primitives; they can be analyzed further and reformulated and the new formulation is more transparent. The reformulation also shows more accurately how the three meanings are interrelated. Second, they emphasize the fact that numerals very often express modal meanings, or, more precisely, that numerals contain modal elements, or - in still other words - that uses of numerals are intricately linked with a general assessment of the likelihood of a situation, as envisaged by the speaker. It is remarkable that the heavily logic-inspired neo-Gricean tradition never really acknowledged this, especially in view of the similarities between quantifiers, connectives and modals that are generally recognized (Horn 1972, 1989, van der Auwera 1996, 2001, van der Auwera and Bultinck 2001)[8]. Of course, the reformulations given above are by no means revolutionary; they are probably the most straightforward definitions of the concepts at hand, and certainly Larry Horn must have been aware of them. But the fact is that this modal aspect of numerals has never been emphasized, while it is demonstrably part of more than half of the cardinality uses of numerals like *two*. Crucially, since modal meanings can vary in strength, the various positions cannot be seen as binary values: as I will demonstrate below, these positions are idealizations and actual language use shows that there are many positions in between these extreme points. The third observation that can be made on the basis of the definitions given above is certainly the most important one: the three traditional classes, 'at least', 'at most', and 'exactly' do not exhaust all possible uses of numerals in English. Indeed, it is fair to say that the three classes do not cover the most important use, the type of usage I have labeled 'absolute value' use. The 'absolute value' use of numerals is at first sight rather similar to the 'exactly n' use of numerals, but differs from it on at least three crucial points.

First, in both uses, the group of elements denoted by the NP is determined as having n elements, but in 'absolute value' uses, nothing more than that is expressed. While 'exactly n' uses of numerals explicitly indicate that the possibility of there being more than n members in that group AND the possibility of there being fewer than n members is ruled out by the speaker, 'absolute value' uses of numerals do nothing of the sort. The latter are much simpler, cognitively and semantically speaking: they carry less semantic load. Naturally, while 'absolute value' uses of *n* do not involve an explicit commitment of the speaker to the possibility that the set of entities in question may contain more or fewer than n elements, the presentation of the set of entities as being in existence allows the inference that *there are n entities*, and consequently that the cardinality of the set in question is not less than n. It is, however, important to realize that this inference is not explicitly encoded; it is not of the same order as the possibility that is expressed in 'at least' uses of *two*. In the latter, the possibility

---

[8] It is certainly true that Horn came close to mentioning this fact on at least two occasions in his PhD-thesis. He describes the meaning of the numeral constructions such as in *That bowler is capable of at least a 250 game* as 'possibly 251' (Horn 1972:44). And in his paragraph on correlations between logic and language he associates quantifiers with a specific "degree of knowledge about the world" (Horn 1972:133). *At least some* is described as having a value bigger than 0 ("indicating total negative certainty") and smaller or equal than 1 ("indicating total positive certainty"). Also his descriptions of numerals in terms of a "lower bound" and implicatures that trigger an "upper bound" is of course compatible with this modal definition of the various positions.

that there are more than n entities is explicitly marked - the function of *at least* is precisely to make explicit that this possibility is included. And whereas a normal NP containing *two* is not explicit in its commitment that not fewer than two entities are involved, the phrase *no less than n* is a way to indicate precisely that. But because the fact that the cardinality is 'not less than two' is already inferable from the simple 'absolute value' use of *two*, the phrase *no less than two* is primarily associated with an additional rhetorical meaning: it primarily expresses the speaker's surprise at the fact that the cardinality of the set in question is so high.

Second, the 'absolute value' uses can be characterized by their relatively low degree of prominence. The other three uses of *two* potentially[9] promote the expression of cardinality to (one of the) "prominent points" of the utterance. This "prominence"[10] can be compared to the concept of "focus" in at least one its definitions, namely the one in terms of an "answer to a WH-question"[11]: if an element can be construed as answering a WH-question, it is "focal" or maximally "prominent" in the utterance (i.e., it is construed so that it will attract the attention of the speaker). The higher degree of prominence that is inherent in non-'absolute value' uses is crucial in that it signals to the hearer / reader that the speaker "made an effort to be precise", instead of just using *two* in its unmarked, 'absolute value' sense. Quoting one of Levinson's basic insights into the operations of human communication (the so-called "M-principle"): "What's said in an abnormal way isn't normal" (Levinson 2000:38). The speaker should indicate a non-stereotypical situation by means of linguistic material that is marked and the hearer should interpret marked material as "non-stereotypical" in some way. This is precisely what happens in the case of uses of numerals that diverge from the 'absolute value' uses. As already mentioned, 'absolute value' uses of numerals are cognitively the most simple, most basic uses. All sorts of strategies are used to diverge from this basic use: other uses present a numeral as excluding or explicitly including the possibility of there being more or the possibility of there being less, in variable degrees. These degrees correspond with degrees of markedness. And markedness is one way of making a linguistic element "prominent" in an utterance.

As already mentioned, focus by means of intonation is a much stronger strategy to make it "prominent", i.e. to attract the attention of the hearer. Levinson (2000:39) contrasts *Bill stopped the car* with *Bill caused the car to stop*: not only will this induce a different interpretation of what has really happened (the second utterance strongly suggests that Bill didn't stop the car in the usual way), the marked expression *caused the car to stop* is also prominent. But also this relative prominence can be overruled by stress.

---

[9] "Potentially", in the sense that the linguistically codified meaning of the three non-'absolute value' uses by default carries a sense of "precision" (not in the more technical sense of 'exactly n', but in the sense that the speaker has concentrated on his expression of cardinality), but the focalizing effect of this "precision" can always be overruled by stronger focus markers such as stress on other constituents than the numeral or the NP containing the numeral. Obviously, if other constituents are stressed heavily the markedness of, e.g. the focus on an 'exactly n' use of *two* will be relatively weak because the focus on the stressed constituent will be much stronger, cf. the next section (section 5.1.3.).

[10] Note that (the acoustic marking of) focus is also informally described in terms of (prosodic) prominence by Kadmon (2001:250).

[11] Sgall et al. (1986:207-216) trace this definition back to Hatcher (1956).

(5)   Q: Who caused the car to stop?
        A: Bill caused the car to stop.

In this exchange, *Bill* is clearly most prominent, because it is in focus position. I definitely do not claim that the marked uses of *two* always cause them to be the focus of the utterance (although markedness is certainly compatible with focalization), I simply claim that the non-'absolute value' uses of *two* differ from 'absolute value' uses in that the extra meaning components (the modal meanings) of the first generally "prepare" them to be more prominent than the latter.

Third, the absolute value uses, like the one in (3), do not explicitly encode the speaker's epistemic stance towards his expression of cardinality. Unlike the three classical positions in the cardinal debate, an assignment of a particular use of *two* to the 'absolute value' class does not imply that this use of *two* denotes a lack of confidence, or, alternatively, a feeling of absolute certainty of the speaker concerning the statement he has uttered.

In principle, two positions are possible with respect to the epistemic load of 'absolute value' uses of *two*. Theoretically speaking, it is possible to claim that 'absolute value' uses do imply an explicit expression of the epistemic relationship of the speaker towards the utterance that he produced, namely the fact that the speaker is certain ("more or less certain", "more certain than uncertain") that the statement he produced corresponds with reality. But another option presents itself as more natural, namely the possibility that 'absolute' value uses of numerals are relatively unspecified as far as the epistemic attitude of the speaker is concerned. Of course, when a numeral occurs as part of a statement, which contains no explicit modality markers, the expression of cardinality will always inherit some of the "assertive" force that is part of the illocutionary force of a statement. In (6), e.g., *two* indicates the cardinality of the set of hands that are denoted by the NP, and it is indeed understood that the speaker feels no reason to doubt this expression of cardinality.

(6) <EFW 1069> Once again there was silence. People looked at each other in astonishment. Then a man at the back of the hall began to clap, and someone else joined in. Soon the clapping became fierce applause. Such was the enthusiasm that you might have thought that the Collector had just sung an aria. But hardly had the applause for the Collector died down when **two** hands reached up and dragged him down the stairs by his braces and into the crowd. "I expect they're anxious to chair me around the hall," thought the Collector triumphantly. His success had come as a complete surprise to him. However, nobody seemed anxious to chair him round the hall, or anywhere.

This is, crucially, different from saying that the speaker presents his statement with respect to the cardinality of the set of hands (that reached up to drag the Collector down the stairs) as something that he is certain of. Intuitively, it is clear that in such uses of *two* nothing is specified as to the epistemic state of the speaker, at least not with respect to the expression of cardinality. In this case it is not even clear whether the number of hands is really very relevant or important. In this case, the context suggests that it is not.

It must be emphasized that this description of 'absolute value' uses is also an idealization, just like the other three positions. As will be seen in the discussion of the corpus material, there are many gradations in the class of 'absolute value' interpretations: some uses imply slightly more certainty (in the sense, e.g., that when a cardinality statement is disconfirmed later in the rest of the context, this change is less expected than with other uses, not in the sense that this use makes the speaker's epistemic stance explicit) than others. Especially the difference between 'exactly n' interpretations and 'absolute value' interpretations can be subtle because it is subject to a number of variables influencing their meaning (e.g., the syntactic construction of the clause in which it occurs). When 'absolute value' uses are said to be neutral as far as the speaker's epistemic stance is concerned, this neutrality is considered to be an end-point of a continuum that ranges from absolute neutrality to (at least some) epistemic suggestion. But when this epistemic component reaches a relatively high level of explicitness (e.g., when *two* is combined with a definiteness marker), the particular use of *two* is described as an 'exactly n' use.

These considerations and especially the one concerning "prominence"/"focus", will reoccur in the analysis, because they will be one of the crucial factors in the determination of the meaning of cardinal uses of *two*. In that sense, the "dynamic semantics" analyses by Van Kuppevelt (1995, 1996) and Scharten (1997), in the Discourse Representation Framework, which operates with question-answer structures (cf. Chapter 3, sections 3.1.3 and 3.2.2. above) are certainly an improvement compared to the relatively context-insensitive interpretations of Horn's early analyses. At that point, I will also discuss how Van Kuppevelt's and Scharten's accounts differ from my own analysis.

Beside the "prominence" factor, there is one other essential element in the analysis of the values of *two*: the link between 'absolute value' meanings and the notion of "existence". Whereas the 'absolute value' uses of *two* lack any explicit indication concerning the epistemic attitude of the speaker towards what s/he utters, at least some of them seem to harbor an expression of existence. Naturally, this is not a feature of *two* itself, but indirectly contributes to the meaning of *two* through the NP that contains *two*. In interpreting (6), e.g., there is the distinct intuition that the existence of a group of hands (with cardinality two) is asserted, or, at the very least, added to the set of presuppositions of the speech participants, possibly without drawing their attention to these hands explicitly (in the non-technical sense of the term "presupposition", i.e. relegated to the "common ground", cf. Stalnaker 1978[12]).

Of course, these existential statements are made relative to a specific context. That means that in (6) the existential component of the meaning of *two hands* is not adequately described as 'there are two hands in the universe'. Via the mechanism of domain narrowing (cf. Chapter 3, section 3.1.2.), which restricts the application of the quantifier, it becomes clear that the existential commitment of (6) holds "for the domain of individuals relevant to

---

[12] The precise nature of the existential load of numerals in non-focal NPs will be dealt with later. Strictly speaking, even Stalnaker's definition of the "common ground" is not sufficiently adequate to describe these uses. The DRT concept of adding individuals to the "universe" (of discourse) (Kamp and Reyle 1993, Kadmon 2001) may actually be a more precise term, although in DRT there is no room for differences in prominence of different elements. Stalnaker's "common ground" is linked to the notion of "presupposition", which captures this prominence aspect better.

the conversation", as Kadmon (2001:70) puts it. Nonetheless, the intuition that the existence of two hands is somehow contained in (6) remains unscathed.

5.1.2. 'Absolute value' and 'exactly n' readings of *two* in the corpus: a continuum

First, I will focus on the distinction between 'absolute value' uses and 'exactly n' uses. I will discuss the other values of *two* in section 2. Since much of what will follow depends on the distinction between 'absolute value' and 'exactly n' interpretations of numerals, I will start with one extra example of an 'absolute value' use of *two*, to which the concepts and insights from the previous section (the 'absolute value' position, its epistemic load in comparison with other values, and its relation to the notions "focus" and "existence") can be applied.

> (7) <AM7 1270> Whichever outcome, the credibility of the team and the motivation of its members will inevitably be compromised. By contrast, an effectively constituted team will move through each of the stages, spending a maximum amount of time in the performing" stage (see Figure 5.4b). The determinants of effective and ineffective teams include a wide range of variables, but **two** which are particularly relevant in this context are the basis cn which the team is constituted in terms of the definition of roles and the way in which the relationship between those roles is determined.

Just like in (3), it should be clear that an 'at least', an 'at most' or even an 'exactly' paraphrase cannot capture the meaning of the cardinality expressed in these utterances. In (7) the speaker asserts that the determinants of effective and ineffective teams include two particularly relevant ones, which is different from asserting that the determinants include *exactly* two particularly relevant variables on the three points mentioned above: first, 'exactly n' uses *explicitly* exclude the possibility of the determinants including less than two particularly relevant variables and the possibility of it including more than two particularly relevant ones. This is related to the second difference: the point of this utterance is not so much the determination of the cardinality of the group of variables, but the presentation of the variables themselves. In this context, *two* is primarily used as discourse-structural information to the hearer. The correct paraphrase is not: "the number of particularly relevant variables is exactly two", but: "hearer, I will now name two particularly relevant variables, namely X and Y". The identification of this X and this Y are the prominent points of the utterance: in this context, *two* can hardly be construed as the answer to a question, if at all.

> (8) ??Q: How many variables are particularly relevant in this context?
> A: [...] two which are particularly relevant in this context are the basis on which the team is constituted in terms of the definition of roles and the way in which the relationship between those roles is determined.

A much better question would be the following:

> (9) Q: What are particularly relevant variables in this context?

A: [...] two which are particularly relevant in this context are the basis on which the team is constituted in terms of the definition of roles and the way in which the relationship between those roles is determined.

The 'exactly n' use, on the contrary, presents the cardinality expression as being more important or noteworthy and is therefore more likely to appear in focus position (i.e. with a high degree of prominence). Once again, this is not a question of binary values: there is a difference in degree of prominence. Third, in (7) the epistemic stance of the speaker towards his or her expression of cardinality is indicated only very slightly (or perhaps even not at all), whereas 'exactly n' uses of *two* explicitly focus on this epistemic load.

The remainder of this section will be devoted to a list of factors that influence the 'absolute value' uses of *two*. These cause a change of meaning so that the interpretation of *two* progressively approaches the 'exactly n' meaning. I will describe a continuum from pure 'absolute value' uses to pure 'exactly n' uses. Obviously, at this level of semantic analysis the distinctions that can be made will be very subtle. Furthermore, these distinctions rely to a very large extent on intuition, and the relevance of some distinctions may sometimes not be immediately clear. I do believe, however, that these distinctions have real impact on meaning interpretations of numerals, although also these factors will not imply a choice between two binary opposites, but rather refer to a property or feature that these uses can be said to have to a certain degree.

The most important factors are the following:
- presence of 'exactly n'-restrictors (such as *exactly, only*)
- presence of definiteness-markers (such as definite articles, possessives, genitives...)
- focalization of *two* by lexico-syntactic means (as opposed to through intonation, which I exclude because of the limitations of a corpus analysis); when addressing this factor, I will in general refer to the question how naturally the phrase containing *two* can be construed as the answer to a "topic-constituting" question (cf. Van Kuppevelt 1996)
- syntactic function of the NP in which *two* occurs: in temporal adverbials (and some other types of adverbials) the meaning of *two* is generally more towards the 'exactly n' end of the scale than in subject phrases. Furthermore, *two* in subject NPs is generally more 'exactly'-like than *two* in direct object NPs

These factors influence the meaning of cardinality uses of *two* to the extent that they present *two* as having an 'exactly n' value rather than an 'absolute value'. I will concentrate on the latter three factors, as the first one is self-evident: the addition of *exactly* to a numeral will result in that numeral acquiring an 'exactly n' meaning. In the discussion, I will start from the empirical data concerning the relation between syntactic function of the NP containing *two* and the interpretation of *two*. This relation is the factor with the weakest influence on 'absolute value' uses, but it allows me to present important distinctions that cross-cut the syntactic distinction as we go along. The section on the 'absolute value'-'exactly n' continuum will conclude with a discussion of some minor[13] factors that influence the interpretation of numerals.

Before starting the rather extensive discussion of the influence of the syntactic structure of the NP on the interpretation of numerals, I will focus on the most important of the factors listed above: the influence of definiteness on the interpretation of numerals.

The definite article changes the function of the NP (or the PP) radically: as is well known, the primary function of the definiteness-marker is to refer the hearer back to an antecedent NP, either one that was already present in the speech context, or one that has to be "accommodated" (Lewis 1979, Thomason 1990 - cf. section 4.3.2.3. above). The primary function of indefiniteness (which can optionally be indicated by an indefinite article, but often the mere absence of a definiteness marker will do[14], as in this case (Lyons 1999:33-34)) is to introduce a new referent or a new group of referents into the universe of discourse. Introducing a new referent is crucially different from referring to an already familiar one with respect to the interpretation of numerals: when a group of objects is introduced the attention is drawn to the presentation of the group, the conceptualization of a collection of entities as being in existence. This is what makes them "known" or identifiable[15]. Referents originally introduced by means of indefinite NPs allow the speaker to refer back to them (obligatorily by means of definite NPs!). Lambrecht calls the grammatical category of definiteness "an important grammatical correlate of the cognitive distinction between identifiable and unidentifiable referents" (Lambrecht 1994:79)[16]. That is why groups of objects represented by an NP or PP that is marked as indefinite are compatible with the interpretation of the *two* contained in that NP as having an 'absolute value'. The PP in (10) introduces two groups (and consequently conceptualizes them as being in existence), and as far as the cardinality of the group of groups is concerned it does nothing more than that: it doesn't focus on the expression of cardinality, let alone on its "exactness".

(10) <HU2 4415> Thus, in the present study we evaluated gastric clearance of indigestible markers, orocaecal transit time, colonic transit time, and gall bladder contraction in **two** groups of diabetic patients who differed as to whether they had or did not have signs of autonomic neuropathy affecting the cardiovascular system.

---

[13] They are minor in the sense that they occur relatively seldom in the corpus, not in the sense that their effect on the meaning of *two* is unimportant.

[14] Lyons uses the example *I bought three books this morning* to demonstrate that indefinite noun phrases do not need the indefinite article (Lyons 1999:33).

[15] The concept "known" is expressed by many different terms in the literature. Lambrecht (1994) offers a very careful description of relevant distinctions, including "topic" (which he defines in terms of "aboutness") - "focus" and "identifiable"-"unidentifiable" (Lambrecht 1994:109). It is the latter distinction that corresponds with the use of the term "known". "Identifiable referents" can be in one of three "activation states" (Chafe 1987): active referents are "currently lit up", accessible or semi-active referents are in a person's "peripheral consciousness", inactive referents are "currently in a person's long-term memory". Important for our purposes is that all three kinds are correlated with the use of definiteness markers (although this co-occurrence is certainly not obligatory - Lambrecht 1994:108), while "the tendency is strong for unidentifiable referents to be coded as indefinite noun phrases" (Lambrecht 1995:108).

[16] Lambrecht (1994:80-81) notes some exceptions to this general tendency: "specific indefinite NPs", e.g., such as *a book* in *I am looking for a book* can be interpreted as referring to a specific book. In that case the referent is identifiable to the speaker (but not to the addressee).

It seems that is this "identifiability" feature, which is strongly correlated with definiteness, that explains the relatively strong exclusion of the possibility that there are more referents than two in definite NPs that contain *two*. In other words, *two* in definite NPs receives an 'exactly n' reading, because the identifiability that is usually marked by definiteness-markers implies that the group denoted by the NP has clear and well-defined boundaries. When NPs refer back to a group of entities, their existence is taken for granted and, by default, not focused on. Because the prominent feature is no longer the *existence* of a group of objects, but the reference to such a group, it becomes crucial that this group is delineated clearly. The more prominent the boundaries of a certain object are, the easier it becomes to identify it and, a fortiori, to refer back to it. Clearly, the 'absolute value' use of a numeral offers boundaries that are considerably more vague than those offered by 'exactly' uses. If, as we have seen in the previous section, 'exactly n' can be defined as the combination of three meaning components: "necessarily n + not possible more than n + not possible less than n", then *two* in definite NPs is certainly much more similar to the idealized 'exactly n' use (which can be found in NPs such as *exactly two children*) than to the 'absolute value' uses. 'Absolute value' uses are, by definition, considerably laxer in the exclusion of other possibilities, and the two extra components in 'exactly n' uses present the "boundaries" of the cardinality of a certain group in a much more prominent way. A numeral that is used as part of an NP that is marked as being indefinite is, metaphorically speaking, exclusively "productive": the primary function of the introduction of a new referent is *adding* something to the universe of discourse. The difference between (10) and the constructed example (11), in which *two* is replaced by *three*, boils down to the fact that in (11) yet another referent of the same type (namely, a group of diabetic patients) is added to the universe of discourse.

> (11)   Thus, in the present study we evaluated gastric clearance of indigestible markers, orocaecal transit time, colonic transit time, and gall bladder contraction in **three** groups of diabetic patients who differed as to whether they had or did not have signs of autonomic neuropathy affecting the cardiovascular system.

This is different from what happens when *two* is replaced by *three* in examples with definiteness markers.

> (12) <HD8 270> Satan does not realise that real freedom is found in obeying the voice of reason. He cannot obey God and subsequently finds himself trapped in his own cocoon. The self pride he showed in the first **two** books is shown to be the very cause of his gradual destruction and inner hell.
> (13)   Satan does not realise that real freedom is found in obeying the voice of reason. He cannot obey God and subsequently finds himself trapped in his own cocoon. The self pride he showed in the first **three** books is shown to be the very cause of his gradual destruction and inner hell.

In (13) nothing is added to the universe of discourse at all. The substitution of *two* by *three* only changes the cardinality of the referent that has to be accommodated: by virtue of the meaning of *the*, the PP *in the first three books* refers back to an antecedent that has to be found in the context or that has to be accommodated.

Another way to make clear the difference is what could be called the "*actually*-test": when comparing the same NPs with and without definiteness-markers, it transpires that a revision of the cardinality statement is much more unexpected with the definite NP than with the indefinite NP.

> (14)   The self pride he showed in **two** books - actually in three books – is
> shown to be the very cause of his gradual destruction and inner hell.
> (15)   !The self pride he showed in the **two** books - actually in the three books
> is shown to be the very cause of his gradual destruction and inner hell.

It is also remarkable that the same holds when changing to a lower numeral, although the effect is stronger for both options.

> (16)   !The self pride he showed in **two** books - actually only in one book – is
> shown to be the very cause of his gradual destruction and inner hell.
> (17)   !!The self pride he showed in the **two** books - actually only in the/that
> one book - is shown to be the very cause of his gradual destruction and inner
> hell.

Also here the distinctions are subtle. These *actually*-phrases can be compared to the cancellation and suspension tests (cf. Chapter 2). The *actually*-test may look like a variant of Grice's cancellation test (often exemplified by means of numerals as in *two, in fact three*), but the way in which it is used is very different. Whereas Horn's suspension and cancellation tests depend on the grammaticality of an indication of a higher or lower cardinality (*John has three children, if not four* vs. **John has three children, if not two*), the "actually" test does not rely on grammaticality judgments. Since many speakers consider the insertion of *actually* to be an expression of "repair" of the speaker, anything can follow *actually* without making the sentence ungrammatical. The "*actually*"-test only serves as an illustration of the intuition with respect to the degree to which a certain NP containing a numeral *n* excludes the possibility of there being more than *n*. The speaker changes the content of the utterance in mid-sentence in all four utterances, but the naturalness with which this may happen varies. The "*actually*-test" is a measure of this degree of unexpectedness: how easy is it to imagine that the speaker would insert such a mid-sentence *actually*-phrase? In (14), e.g., the "mistake" is less severe than in (15). When the numeral is combined with a definite article (*the self pride he showed in the two books*), the NP refers back to entities that were already part of the universe of discourse. If the speaker inserts an "*actually*-phrase" as in (15), it can only be interpreted as a performance error: the speaker meant to say *three* but it came out as *two*. In (14), however, the situation is different: the *actually* phrase can very well be interpreted as simply a "stronger version" of the earlier statement ("correction"), as opposed to an entirely new statement ("repair"). Of course, a stronger version of a statement is less unexpected than an entirely new statement. In general, the linguistic context of the definite NPs will have already introduced the set of two entities (in this case, books), i.e. the cardinality of this set has already been established. A sudden change with respect to this cardinality will be rather unexpected - if imaginable at all. It will usually be considered as a performance error, because it is not in line with what had been said earlier.

The same holds for (16) when compared to (17). The fact that the *actually*-test will show the repair of 'absolute value' uses to be unexpected as well (even though they are still better than 'exactly n' uses) can be predicted on the basis of the definition of 'absolute value' given in the previous section: an 'absolute value' use of *two* conceptualizes two entities as being identifiable in existence. If it appears that in reality there are more than two entities (of the kind indicated by the NP) in existence, this does not contradict the existence of the two entities mentioned earlier. But because the NP containing the numeral not only expresses existence (through identifiability), but also cardinality, a change to *three* retroactively means that *two* must have been a mistake. However, if the cardinality of the group of entities is reduced to one, it is not just the cardinality that has to be changed. It also means that the existence of one of the entities denoted by the NP is contradicted. This accounts for the difficulty with which the correction can be expressed. Note that that a phrase of "repair" such as *X, er, I mean Y* would also be a good test-phrase to measure the degree of "surprise" or "unexpectedness" caused by the change of cardinality.

> (18) The self pride he showed in **two** books - er, I mean in three books - is shown to be the very cause of his gradual destruction and inner hell.
> (19) !The self pride he showed in the **two** books - er, I mean in the three books - is shown to be the very cause of his gradual destruction and inner hell.

But the differences between definite NPs containing *two* and indefinite NPs becomes clearer when relatively weak correction phrases are used. The phrase *X, er, I mean Y* exclusively signals and repairs performance errors, whereas the *actually* phrase is more ambiguous -- it can also introduce a "stronger version" of the statement. For very crude performance errors, *actually* seems to be much less adequate:

> (20) The self pride he showed in **two** crooks - er, I mean books - is shown to be the very cause of his gradual destruction and inner hell.
> (21) !!The self pride he showed in **two** crooks - actually, books - is shown to be the very cause of his gradual destruction and inner hell.

Another type of weak correction phrase is of course Horn's well-known "suspender" phrase.

> (22) The self pride he showed in **two**, if not three books is shown to be the very cause of his gradual destruction and inner hell.
> (23) !The self pride he showed in the **two,** if not three books - er, I mean in the three books - is shown to be the very cause of his gradual destruction and inner hell.

This is clearly the "weakest" correction phrase of the three: (22) does not even necessarily mean that the speaker changed his or her mind mid-sentence, he or she could have intended to mark the extra possibility (namely, of there being more books in which he or she showed his self-pride) as valid from the very moment he or she started uttering the sentence. Also, the transition from *two* to *three* in (23) is considerably smoother than the one in (15). But (23), with the definiteness marker, is undoubtedly more difficult than (22), without the definiteness marker.

I will refer rather often to the *actually*-test in the following discussion. I have noticed that the grammaticality/acceptability judgments concerning these *actually*-phrases may differ, because some people find any type of correction or repair possible as long as it is marked by *actually*. Nevertheless, the *actually*-test is useful to corroborate intuitions concerning the interpretation of numerals because at least to some speakers not all types of correction phrases are equally plausible or surprising. Furthermore, it is important to stress that with this *actually*-test, it is not the traditional grammaticality judgment that is elicited, but rather a measurement of the degree of surprise with the hearer. Speakers who find *any* statement following *actually* acceptable should interpret the exclamation marks (instead of question marks) in front of sentences (indicating unexpectedness) as an evaluation of the *likelihood* of a speaker using the specific *actually*-phrase in the sentence under discussion. Grammatically speaking, all of these phrases are "correct", but I am interested in the extent to which the hearer of this *actually*-phrase can be assumed to be surprised.

Further evidence for the status of definiteness markers as 'exactly n' triggers can be found by looking at other values. In this respect, the difference between 'absolute value' and 'exactly n' is the same as the difference between 'at least n' and 'exactly n', although the second difference is greater than the first. In 'at least' uses, the possibility of there being more elements than n is explicitly indicated; 'absolute value' uses are neutral with regards to this possibility; 'exactly n' uses explicitly exclude the possibility of there being more elements. When the meaning of *two* in (12) or *three* in (13) is compared to the 'at least' value of the same numerals, the importance of the "delineation" argument becomes clearer. It is extremely hard, if not impossible to imagine that the numeral in the construction "definite article + numeral + noun" should be interpreted as 'at least n'. The possibility that there are more than n elements is excluded by this combination.

But also the 'at most' value offers more evidence. As Carston (1985, 1998a) showed, numerals can obtain 'at most' interpretations in modal contexts:

[Imagine a context in which John is too fat. Together with his mother, he has gone to the doctor. The doctor told them that he should eat less for dinner. He suggested that John eat no more than two apples or two eggs. Now John wants to eat three apples. His mother replies:]

    (24)   John, you can eat two apples or you can eat two eggs, but that's all you will get.

Clearly, in this context, *two* has an 'at most' value. This 'at most' value crucially depends on the presence of modal *can*: the imperative version in (25) and the simple indicative one in (26), both without the modal, do not feature 'at most' values.

    (25)   John, eat two apples!
    (26)   John eats two apples.

Yet, when the numeral is combined with a definite article, the 'at most' value is lost immediately, even if it occurs in the same modal context.

(27)   John, you can eat the two apples or you can eat two eggs, but that's all you will get.

Of course, the context would have to be adapted slightly, i.e., presumably the apples must have been mentioned before (or must have been present in the context) in order to allow the presence of a definite article. But this doesn't change the essence of my point: the combination of a definite article with a numeral causes this numeral to function as an 'exactly n' numeral. The only possible reading of *two* in (27) is an 'exactly n' value.

It is worth pointing out that this feature is not an inherent feature of definiteness markers, however, because it is obvious that an anaphoric definite NP can refer back to a vaguely defined group of objects (i.e., vague with respect to its cardinality).

(28) Yesterday I saw some soldiers walking down the street. There was also a little girl. The soldiers were laughing loud, but the girl didn't seem to notice.

This shows that the "clear delineation" feature of NPs that was suggested as an explanation for the 'exactly n' interpretation of *two* in definite NPs is only a matter of preference, rather than an absolute condition. Groups, the cardinality of which is kept vague, can be referred to by means of a definite NP. But that does not mean that the idea that identifiability of a group becomes higher when its cardinality is given is not correct: it simply means that definite NPs can also capture groups the cardinality of which is not given. This suggests that the impossibility of an 'absolute value' interpretation of *two* in NPs or PPs in which the noun is marked as definite is due not solely to the definiteness of the definite article, nor to the nature of adnominally used numerals, but to a combination of both. The meaning of the construction "definiteness marker + numeral + noun" involves the combination of identifiability (definiteness) + cardinality (numeral). This combination triggers the 'exactly n' meaning because each element of the group is presented as identifiable, not necessarily in its individual characteristics, but at least as a member of that group. Presenting each element as identifiable as a member of a group means that each individual element is conceptualized as *separately* identifiable. That implies that the speaker who utters a "definiteness marker + numeral + noun" construction gives the hearer thereby the guarantee that he has "checked" each element with respect to its identifiability. This means that the speaker gives the hearer the guarantee that his cardinality statement is correct and precise and that the possibility that there are more members in the group is excluded. The latter is the definition of the 'exactly n' meaning of numerals. While it is generally so that numerals can have 'absolute value', 'exactly n', or even 'at least n' uses, when they co-occur with a definite article their range of values seems to be restricted to 'exactly n'.

Furthermore, Kadmon (2001:72) observes that the 'at least' interpretation of numerals and the 'exactly n' interpretation differ from each other in anaphora possibilities. She uses the following pair of examples.

(29)   Eleven kids walked into the room. They were making an awful lot of noise.

(30)   At least eleven kids walked into the room. They were making an awful lot of noise.

She does not make the distinction between 'absolute value' and 'exactly n' uses (but cf. the discussion of her position in Chapter 3), but her remarks on the difference between 'exactly n' and 'at least n' uses of *two* in the examples above differ from the analyses above only qua force[17], not qua argument:

> For many speakers, including myself, the following judgments are unshakable: In [29], *they* must refer to a set of eleven kids, while in [30], *they* can refer to the set of all the kids who walked into the room, even if there were more than eleven. Suppose, for example, that twenty kids walked into the room (in which case the first sentence in [29] is true). *They* in [29] can't possibly refer to all twenty kids, but *they* in [30] can. (Kadmon 2001:73)

The combination of the definite article and a numeral indicates that the referent of the NP was already present in the given context, but also allows the inference that the cardinality of the group indicated by the NP was known, or becomes known now, and is determinate, because the elements of the group are identifiable.

In this context, the distinction between the 'exactly n' use of *two* we find in *exactly two* and the one we find in the definite NPs has to be emphasized. It is intuitively clear that the possibilities that are normally excluded by 'exactly n' uses (namely, the possibility that the cardinality of the group denoted by the NP or PP is higher or lower than n) are also excluded by "definite article + numeral + noun" constructions, but not with the same force. In other words, whereas in clear examples of 'exactly n' uses of *two*, such as in (31), the exclusion of the possibilities 'more than n' and 'less than n' is manifest, the construction with the definite article does not make this exclusion equally prominent. It is only through the identifiability function of the definite article that the more or less "neutral" 'absolute value' interpretation is disabled, and not directly as with an *exactly*-restrictor.

> (31) <HR3 1206> A system that presents ethical problems to the experimenter is the demographic system. Without the absolute power of an Egyptian Pharaoh one could scarcely test the consequences of an experiment involving the manipulation of people's lives, for example forcing a percentage of the population to emigrate or insisting that each fertile married couple produce exactly **two** offspring.

The various phenomena that have been described so far allow an evaluation of the 'absolute value' interpretation as the most simple, or most basic use of a numeral like *two*. It is the default "starting-point" of any interpretation of *two* in the sense that as soon as other factors

---

[17] Which is not surprising, since the difference between 'at least n' uses and 'exactly n' uses is, in this respect, of the same quality as the difference between 'absolute value' uses and 'exactly n' uses. As mentioned, the difference between the two differences is a quantitative one, in the sense that the first difference is greater than the second.

come into play (modality, restrictors, definiteness markers etc.) the meaning is modified in the direction of one of the three non-basic interpretations.

After having discussed the most important factor among the factors that influence the value-interpretation of numerals, we are ready to look at the data concerning the relationship between value-interpretation and the syntactic construction that contains the numeral in question.

5.1.3. Syntactic function of the NP containing *two*

The general distribution of the four values for cardinality uses of *two* (i.e., the purely cardinal uses + pronominal uses)[18] according to the syntactic function of the NP they are part of is given in Table 4.

TABLE 4

VALUES OF ADNOMINAL AND PRONOMINAL *TWO*

Syntactic function of NP containing *two*	Absolute Value	Exactly two	At least /more than two	At most / less than two	TOTAL
Adverbial	75/249 (30.1%)	128/249 (51.4%)	14/249 (5.6%)	32/249 (12.9%)	249 (29.1%)
Direct object	112/166 (67.5%)	36/166 (21.7%)	3/166 (1.8%)	15/166 (9.0%)	166 (19.4%)
Subject	123/244 (50.4%)	103/244 (42.2%)	7/244 (2.9%)	11/244 (4.5%)	244 (28.4%)
Other[19]	80/198 (40.4%)	98/198 (49.5%)	9/198 (4.5%)	11/198 (5.6%)	198 (23.1%)
TOTAL	390/857 (45.5%)	365/857 (42.6%)	33/857 (3.9%)	69/857 (8.0%)	857 (100%)

---

[18] As already mentioned, pronominal uses were also included, even though their pronominality introduces effects on the meaning of numerals that adnominal *two* does not feature. The reason why I decided to include pronominals and not other "divergent" (in terms of their cardinality) uses of *two* is that the cardinality expressed by pronominal uses is still relatively pure (as explained in the section on pronominal *two*, the cardinality feature is less prominent, but not less precise). I will come back to the extra meaning effects of pronominal *two* in a separate section.

[19] The other groups are prepositional objects (which fall in between the class of direct objects and the class of adverbial phrases, such as *on two people* in *I called on two people*; cf. Quirk et al. 1985:1155-1161), appositions, predicates and a large group of adjuncts (117/857=13.7%). The adjuncts were not represented separately, because the syntactic function of the NP in which *two* occurs is not even partially determined by the noun that is modified by *two*, but by a head-noun that is different from this noun.

5.1.3.1. Two *in adverbial phrases*

The differences in distribution are striking. Let us start with the uses of *two* in which *two* is part of an adverbial NP: there are considerably fewer 'absolute value' uses of *two* (30.1%) in adverbial NPs than in general (45.5%). Why should this be so?

In (32), the example of an 'absolute value' use of *two* we used in the discussion of definiteness is repeated, while (33) exemplifies an 'exactly n' use.

> (32) <HU2 4415> Thus, in the present study we evaluated gastric clearance of indigestible markers, orocaecal transit time, colonic transit time, and gall bladder contraction in **two** groups of diabetic patients who differed as to whether they had or did not have signs of autonomic neuropathy affecting the cardiovascular system.
> (33) <HWB 1220> The quadrangular bays of the ceiling have formal floral designs in colour on gilt backgrounds. From the ground floor of the church the viewer absorbs the impact of the immense church. Dominating the interior is the vast, shallow cupola supported on its tremendous pendentives and flanked by the half domes on the **two** long sides. The marbles are still rich and some of the mosaics are visible, but in general the colour is disappointingly dark and dull, showing little of the brilliance it once had.

In (32) two groups of diabetic patients are conceptualized as "being in existence", and nothing is said as to the possibility of there being more groups of patients. In (33), however, the group of sides is presented as given, known or identifiable, which is emphasized by the presence of the definiteness-marker (in this case the definite article *the*). As has been shown in the general discussion of the influence of definiteness markers on the interpretation of numerals, *the two* in (33) must be interpreted as referring to 'exactly' two sides, rather than as an instance of an 'absolute value' use of *two*.

The presence of definiteness markers in adverbial phrases is the first piece of the puzzle concerning the 'absolute value'/'exactly n' distribution in adverbial NPs or PPs. Let us take two more examples.

> (34) <HB3 541> the chance would be substantially reduced if the marriage had already lasted some time and there were children. in this case the plaintiff had committed adultery with **two** different men in the space of four or five years.
> (35) <EWA 1466> Or a similar division might have been made by a comma in [12]: [13] With a click, the discreet door shut. This punctuation would have made some difference to the reader's processing of the sentence; [14] in particular would have made the "click" seem a matter of importance and surprise in its own right, dividing the reader's attention between the **two** events, instead of making him see them as integral parts of a whole.

Again, the first context induces an 'absolute value' interpretation (or, more precisely, leaves the default 'absolute value' meaning intact), while the second causes the 'exactly n' interpretation. As in more than a third of the 'exactly n' cases, the 'exact' value is triggered by the presence of a definiteness marker.

TABLE 5

DEFINITENESS MARKERS IN 'EXACTLY TWO' USES IN ADVERBIAL PHRASES

80/128 (62.5%) 'exactly n' uses of *two* in adverbial NPs that do not contain definiteness markers	48/128 (37.5%) 'exactly n' uses of *two* in adverbial NPs that do contain definiteness markers

It is clear that the divergent distribution is not so much caused by the syntactic nature of the PPs in which the numerals occur, but that it depends on the functions and markers that these PPs allow, or better, prefer. In other words, this means that there does not seem to be an inherent factor in the adverbial phrase - as a syntactic construction - that engenders this distribution. The fact that there are significantly fewer instances of 'absolute value' uses of *two* as part of adverbial phrases than on average is at least partially due to the fact that these adverbial phrases are less often used to introduce new referents. Typically, adverbials are marginal syntactic elements in the sense that they do not belong to the core of the predication. The introduction of a new referent is preferably marked explicitly - it usually is the focus of attention[20] - and hence the NP through which this is achieved is most likely part of the core of the predication. If new referents are introduced through adverbials after all, these referents will usually not be very relevant in the discursive context, in the sense that they will usually not be "taken up". They will generally not make it to topic status[21], as in the following examples.

> (36) <EDM 737> She became an independent student and financed herself through two scholarships, an equal opportunities grant and a state loan. Pauline decided much later in life that she wanted a degree. Of all our mature students she was the only one who began to study engineering after a career break to bring up a family. By the time she returned to study she was a widow in her mid thirties with **two** daughters to support. Her high school, like Julia's, had never suggested that she go to college, and it was the financial pressure of being the family breadwinner that made her consider it.

---

[20] "Focus" is a term with a long history and very different, very technical meanings, dependent on the particular theory one happens to favor. Indeed, the connection between "focus" and "new (information)" has been made at least since the early days of the Prague school (cf. Sgall et al. 1986), but other researchers are hesitant to frame focus phenomena in that binary scheme. Some of them even argue for more than one type of focus (Erteschik-Shir 1986, Kiss 1998). The hypothesis concerning the effect of syntactic constructions on value-interpretations of numerals will, however, be based on the simple "new"-"focus" connection, and, crucially, the markedness of the type of construction with respect to the introduction of new referents (direct object phrases are the default option, subject phrases present the introduction of new referents as more marked).

[21] As has been mentioned before, these remarks are only valid as long as no other focus-triggers come into play. It is perfectly possible to find referents that are introduced in adverbial phrases that make it to topics if these adverbials are focused on, especially by prosodic means (capitals):

A: WHERE did you say you found the diamonds?

B: I found them IN A SMALL BLACK BOX.

A: Was it heavy?

B: No, it was rather light.

(37) <HJ4 7721> BELLEEKS Bomb fears after fertiliser theft POLICE were today on full alert amid fears the IRA could use four tonnes of stolen fertiliser to make another huge bomb. The fertiliser, Richardson's Nitro Pack 2644, was packed onto **two** pallets on a lorry which was stolen from Belleeks, in south Armagh. The robbery happened last Friday but police have not been able to trace the whereabouts of the blue-coloured Ford truck, registration, B31 BBD.

(38) <J12 1036> There is a striking analogy here with crystal growth, except that it happens in **two** dimensions, not three. When a crystal is formed, for example by cooling of a melt, crystal grains of different lattice orientation are formed in different places; as the whole material solidifies these meet on grain boundaries - the counterpart of the line from A to B in Fig. 22.2.

In (36), (37) and (38), new referents are introduced, namely two daughters, two pallets and two dimensions, but none of these are taken up as the topic of the following utterances. But of course, there are exceptions to this rule. One of the notable exceptions is the construction in which *two* is used in an adverbial phrase to signal to the hearer / reader the number of entities (reasons / arguments / places etc.) that will be enumerated in the following clause. When they are referred to in the following stretch of discourse, it is usually merely to specify their nature in a concise way, and not to entertain them as topics of conversation, at least not for very long.

(39) <CDD 888> Thus in February 1977 the opposition to Raybestos developed on **two** fronts: in Ovens against the factory, in Ringaskiddy against the dump. The opposition to Raybestos was unusual in that it involved the formation of an autonomous women's group, in which up to 30 women became involved. This women's group was set up because of dissatisfaction with the lack of action by the male-dominated Ovens committee.

(40) <B7K 231> The curriculum was tested in 20 states. Two school authorities rejected the section on nuclear disasters. Sister Eillen Regan, from the board of education of the Roman Catholic archdiocese of San Francisco, says the board shunned it for **two** reasons: `It treats nuclear war as survivable and implies nuclear war is a political option". The archdiocese took its lead from the schools in neighbouring Oakland, which also rejected FEMA's plan, Regan says.[22]

---

[22] It is relatively hard to find uses of *two* in indefinite adverbial phrases that carry an existential load, mostly because these adverbials use temporal nouns (cf. the discussion of this phenomenon in this section). Even when they do not use temporal nouns - as in *for two reasons* - the existence of the entities referred to by the NP is not so prominent as in the typical case of referents introduced by indefinite direct object NPs. In (39) or (40), e.g., one could argue that the two fronts and the two reasons are conceptualized as "existing", but this is clearly a weaker form of "existing" than the one we find in, e.g., *There are two fronts in this war*, or *He gave two reasons for his behavior.* Obviously, the type of referent that the NP corresponds with (and also the action conceptualized by the verb) is of considerable importance in this respect. But even if that factor is taken into account, it transpires that adverbial NPs typically introduce referents that are less compatible with the type of existential presuppositions we are discussing here than direct object NPs do (as is evident from the overwhelming amount of temporal nouns such as *weeks*, which certainly do not correspond with the prototypical notion of an entity).

If these examples are framed in a question-answer scheme, this means that *on two fronts* and *for two reasons* can indeed be taken as the foci of both sentences. But it is also clear that the real answers to the questions *Where did the opposition to Raybestos develop?* and *Why did the board of education shun the section on nuclear disasters?* are not the PPs containing *two* but precisely the identification of the "two fronts" and the "two reasons", namely *in Ovens against the factory, in Ringaskiddy against the dump* and *It treats nuclear war as survivable and implies nuclear war is a political option.*

On the contrary, in many 'exactly n' uses of *two* in adverbials, the NP / PP refers back to referents that have been explicitly introduced in the previous stretch of discourse.

(41) <FAB 2379> He shook his head and sat on the bottom of the bunk beds. `No, actually, I ain't." Charlie frowned and stopped in the middle of taking off his shirt. Terry did look bad. He sat beside him. `What's the matter, bruv? You got aggravation?" His voice was low. Even though there was only a year between the **two** boys, Charlie looked on Terry as his little brother.

(42) <HPM 1268> Although the previous scale had the advantage of corresponding to actual measured accident statistics it proved relatively awkward for subjects to use and is clearly subject to what Poulton (1989) terms logarithmic response bias. The main dependent variables in this study (i.e. those of memory performance) are nonetheless identical to those used in the previous study, thus direct comparisons can still be made between the **two** studies.

And when *two* is used as part of a definite NP that nonetheless contains new information, this new information is actually often accommodated information: information that is presented as given, but which is actually new information that has to be "accepted", or inferred from the context[23]. In those cases, these referents may function as the topic of the following utterances, but this does not change anything about the value-interpretation of the numeral[24]. As will be repeated later, in this context (as in many others), semantics overrules pragmatics[25].

---

[23] This corresponds to Lambrecht's notion of "inferentially accessible" referents (Lambrecht 1994:100): "the case of accessibility via inference from some other active or accessible element in the universe". In Lambrecht's terminology, "accessibility" is a subspecies of "identifiability".

[24] Example (43) is an example of *two* as part of an adjunct: arguably, *in the **two** years of an A level History course* is an adjunct to the direct object phrase *the place of an essay*, rather than an adverbial phrase. But this does not influence the essence of the general remark.

[25] Naturally, here as elsewhere, "semantics" and "pragmatics" are meant as graded terms, not as binary opposites. What is meant here is that with respect to the interpretation of *two* the influence of the definiteness-marker *the* overrules the fact that the NP containing the numeral introduces a new topic. This new topic can be considered as the focus of the sentence and NPs in foci often refer to entities of which the existence is assumed. As we have seen, the affirmation "existence" is the dominant trait of 'absolute value' uses. Kadmon (2001:254-255) notes that the meaning of "the focal presupposition" is more adequately described by means of Jackendoff's (1972) notion "under discussion" (cf. also Rooth 1996), but her account nonetheless suggests that elements in focal position often do trigger an existential presupposition. Her counterarguments against this claim all involve examples in which there is no existential presupposition because it is denied by the semantics of the cotext. She claims, e.g., that the utterance *NOBODY* [focus] *likes Bill* does not have an existential presupposition: "this example is perfectly felicitous even though it explicitly denies the claim that someone likes Bill" (Kadmon 2001:154). I believe that this example should rather be analyzed as a case of semantics (the "coded" meaning of *nobody*)

(43) <FU3 1797> But many of those people who spend time making a good copy need not do so if they thought about the essay properly beforehand. What is more, there are hidden dangers in following the "in rough then neat" approach. In order to appreciate those hidden dangers we should understand the place of an essay in the **two** years of an A level History course. Two years have been set aside to allow time to study a period of History in sufficient depth. It is also time to perfect the skills of the historian.

The presence of definiteness markers can only be part of the story, because only 37.5% of the 'exactly n' uses of numerals in adverbials co-occur with definiteness markers. The second important influence on the interpretation of numerals in adverbial phrases is the conceptualization of time (and to some extent also space[26]) in adverbial phrases. Let us take a look at a typical temporal adverbial from the sample corpus.

(44) <ACN 390> As house becomes a serious commercial proposition (in a recent poll of 13- to 17-year-olds, nearly 40 per cent made `acid house" their musical preference), many are going underground, viewing dance music as an art form rather than a way to generate karma with bank managers. `**Two** years ago, the media conspired to kill off acid," say Ubik. `Now we're entering an era of home-grown technological exploration that will defy categorisation. The prospects are infinite."

Intuitively, this use of *two* excludes the possibility of it being more than two years ago more forcefully than the use of *two* in (45) excludes the possibility of Sara having stepped past more than two bodies.

(45) <A0R 2136> Apart from that I leave you to make your own sleeping arrangements. Nick, the dog isn't allowed in here." `It was only because of the glass. I'll put a mat in the kitchen for him later. Would anyone prefer whisky?" Next morning Sara woke to find Rodney asleep and early sunshine seeping between the curtains. Downstairs she stepped past **two** sleeping bodies in the living room and closed the front door quietly behind her. One of the cows mooed as she passed their field.

The rationale behind this is that temporal adverbials contain "temporal nouns" (such as *years*) that do not carry any existential meaning, at least not in this construction. In this construction, the NPs are expressions of measurement, not of existence. The greater extent to which *two* in

---

overruling the influence of focal meanings (whether one decides to call it a presupposition or not, it is clear that it is "weaker" than the encoded meaning of *nobody*).

[26] The bulk of the adverbials that received an 'exactly n' readings were temporal adverbials, not spatial adverbials. That is why I will speak primarily of temporal adverbials, even though the argument remains the same for spatial adverbials such as *from two yards*:

<CBG 3152> But after brilliantly turning away Simon Barker's 23rd-minute header, Kearton had no chance as Sinton followed up. After Rideout's dismissal, Everton were under siege as Gary Penrice and Sinton appeared to have opened the floodgates - which Les Ferdinand promptly shut again by blasting over from **two** yards. Ludicrously, Rangers believed they had the game already well won.

The non-existence argument, which I will explain immediately, holds also for this kind of spatial adverbials.

temporal adverbials excludes the possibility of there being more than *two* (when compared to *two* in other adverbials such as in (45)) has nothing to do with any inherent property of these temporal nouns. I have drawn an example from the corpus in which the "temporal noun" is part of an object NP.

> (46) <C88 1501> Pond sediment a danger THE future of the pond at the Newman Collard Recreation Ground in Liss looks brighter thanks to a working party who have set about restoring and repairing it. Led by parish councillor Jan Dyer who has spent **two** `very successful days" working with fellow councillors and other people from the village at the pond site, the working party are now waiting until the pond is dredged before carrying out further work.

In this example, there is a perfectly normal 'absolute value' use of *two*: no extra "certainty" is marked, in any way. The possibility that parish councillor Jan Dyer has spent more than two days is not explicitly mentioned, but it is not explicitly excluded either. The *actually*-test (47) yields a result that is compatible with the interpretation of *two* in (46)[27] - the degree of unexpectedness of this new version is relatively low (compared to, e.g., the same statement with a definiteness marker, as in *Jan Dyer who has spent the two, actually the three 'very successful' days*, which would qualify as an 'exactly n' use).

> (47) Pond sediment a danger THE future of the pond at the Newman Collard Recreation Ground in Liss looks brighter thanks to a working party who have set about restoring and repairing it. Led by parish councillor Jan Dyer who has spent **two**, actually three `very successful days" working with fellow councillors and other people from the village at the pond site, the working party are now waiting until the pond is dredged before carrying out further work.

The fact that days, weeks, months etc. can be conceptualized as either in existence or not (in which case they will often be expressions of measurement, as they are here), points at the importance of the function of adverbial phrases in the interpretation of *two*.

As we have seen (cf. section 4.3.3. of Chapter 4), temporal adverbials come in two forms in the sample corpus, the "durational" adverbials (48) and the "locational" adverbials (49).

> (48) <KBH 6719> Cheeky cheeky. Cheeky cheeky. What do you need to buy for your bunny? Something to put for put inside. Oh stuffing. Yes What's the matter sweetheart? Your eyes hurt? You going to have a sleep after lunch today? No. You

---

[27] In both cases, the *actually*-test becomes slightly more difficult because the utterances are clearly from prose texts, the first from a novel, the second from a newspaper article. In expository prose, "correction" and "repair" phrases are always more unexpected than in spoken communication, for obvious reasons. I will come back to this when I deal with the suspension and cancellation test (section 3.1.1. and 3.1.2.). For now, it is important to stress the relative differences of "unexpectedness" of the *actually* phrases between *two* in temporal NPs in adverbial phrases and non-adverbial phrases.

have been good for **two** minutes. Oh no. Yes you have Not a choice no. Not a choice Adam's going fishing? I don't think so no he'll probably going tomorrow.

(49) <CBC 9595> James Gilbey was quoted as saying: `They were messages of complete desperation. Please, please help." Further shocks were to come: the reason behind Diana's sometimes gaunt appearance was her battle with the binge-and-vomit eating disorder bulimia, from which she had suffered since the first year of her marriage. **Two** days after the serialisation began, Gilbey confirmed that interviews with him were presented `fairly and accurately". In the following weeks, readers were told that Diana was reconciled to the fact she would remain married to Charles, but that they would lead separate lives.

In both types there are 'exactly n' uses of *two* and in both types the temporal entities are not conceptualized as being in existence: the temporal adverbial does not introduce new referents in the sense that some other adverbials or object phrases introduce new referents (cf. section 5.1.3.2.). That is not its primary syntactic function. This does not mean that the temporal entities that are used to locate a certain state of affairs (or give the duration of a certain state of affairs) cannot be referred back to in the following utterances.

(50) <K1D 2665> It's part of our heritage in a way Male speaker It's just madness. I'd come back tomorrow given the chance Voice over In a statement the W.Midlands Regional Health Authority said they needed vacant possession for the property to be handed over to a private housebuilder for development. **Two** years on nothing's begun. The authority spent twenty thousand pounds on the eviction, half what the squatters say they'd have paid in rent over the two years.

Crucially, however, these two years are not picked up as the topic of the new utterance. In the first use of *two*, the numeral functions as part of a locational temporal adverbial, while in the second it is part of a durational adverbial (*over the two years*). The definiteness marker in the second occurrence identifies the two years as being the same as the two years of the previous utterance. The function of the definiteness marker remains the same as in the previous uses of *two* in definite NPs: it presents the time span that is mentioned as something that is identifiable in the context. As we have seen, this adds an extra "exclusive" force to this use of *two*: not only can temporal entities that are part of a locational / durational adverbial hardly be conceptualized as being in existence, the temporal entities are also presented as identifiable from the context, which induces an extra 'exactly n' effect. As the *actually*-test shows, the second occurrence of *two* is even more unexpected than the first.

(51) !It's part of our heritage in a way Male speaker It's just madness. I'd come back tomorrow given the chance Voice over In a statement the W.Midlands Regional Health Authority said they needed vacant possession for the property to be handed over to a private housebuilder for development. **Two**, actually three years on nothing's

begun. The authority spent twenty thousand pounds on the eviction, half what the squatters say they'd have paid in rent over the two years.[28]

(52) !!It's part of our heritage in a way Male speaker It's just madness. I'd come back tomorrow given the chance Voice over In a statement the W.Midlands Regional Health Authority said they needed vacant possession for the property to be handed over to a private housebuilder for development. Two years on nothing's begun. The authority spent twenty thousand pounds on the eviction, half what the squatters say they'd have paid in rent over the **two**, actually three years.

Also the second instance of *two years* occurs in a temporal adverbial: these years are not presented as being in existence. In other words, it does not add entities to the universe of discourse.

Besides the fact that temporal adverbials do not present the temporal entities that they use to locate (or give the duration of) states of affairs as being in existence, they also lend themselves to focalization quite easily. The NP in (53) can easily be seen as the answer to the question "when did the Armand Hammer Museum in Los Angeles call [etc.]?", just like the one in (54) can be conceptualized as the answer to the question "when did she join UNACO?".

(53) <EBT 884> Similarly, the `Etruscans" show will cost Memphis and the other venues around $300,000 each. For many possible venues, such fees are prohibitive or contrary to policy. The lenders wish to profit from sending the shows on tour. However, because the venues are not booked sufficiently in advance, only institutions with the most flexible schedules have been able to participate. **Two** weeks before the show closed in Memphis, the Armand Hammer Museum in Los Angeles called and expressed interest in the `Catherine" show.

(54) <ECK 373> As far as her friends were concerned she worked as a translator at the United Nations. It was the perfect cover story. She had a degree in Romance languages from Wellesley and after doing her postgraduate work at the Sorbonne she had travelled extensively across Europe before returning to the States where she was recruited by the FBI, specializ- ing in the use of firearms. She had joined UNACO **two** years ago. She alighted from the train at East 74th Street and whistled softly to herself as she walked the two hundred yards down 72nd Street from the subway to her ground-floor bachelor flat.

I will elaborate on the influence of the focalization possibilities offered by the different constructions in the discussion of the subject and object phrases. At this point, it should intuitively be clear that when NPs containing *two* are in focus position (and this concept can be operationalized by constructing a "topic constituting question", cf. Van Kuppevelt 1996), the force of the exclusion of other possibilities is greater than when it is not

---

[28] Obviously, (51) becomes very odd because the second occurrence of *two* remains the same in this test. This has nothing to do with the acceptability of the first occurrence, because the focus is on the interpretation of the first occurrence *two* at the moment at which it is introduced.

in focus position. If the same utterance as in (54) is abstracted from its context, other topic-constituting questions are equally possible[29].

(55) Q: What had she joined two years ago?
       A: She had joined UNACO **two** years ago.

As has been noted by Fretheim (1992), Van Kuppevelt (1996) and Scharten (1997), in this constellation, in which *two* is not in focus position, the exclusion of other possibilities becomes less strong[30].

5.1.3.2. Two *in direct object phrases*

With the direct object phrases, the situation is totally different from the one with adverbial phrases. In 67.5% of the uses of *two* in direct object phrases, we get an 'absolute value' reading (56), while only in 21.7% an 'exactly n' interpretation is triggered (57).

(56) <CS3 925> A Second International was founded only in 1889, six years after Marx's death. It was dominated from the start by Marxism, proclaiming the industrial proletariat as saviours of the human race. But the Second International did debate **two** questions which Marx and Engels left unresolved. Could a non-violent transition to socialism take place via socialist victories in liberal democratic elections, and perhaps participation in government coalitions with `bourgeois" parties? And where would the trigger for worldwide revolution come from - advanced economies or those still in the process of industrialization?

(57) <HJ4 2166> Children were seconds away from death A SHOCKED mum wept today as she described how her two young children came within seconds of death when flames ripped through their home. Bernie O'Neill found the stairway of her home in Upper Meadow Street, north Belfast on fire - trapping her **two** young daughters in upstairs bedrooms. She could only watch in horror from the street as a local man and soldiers battled bravely to save four-year-old Stacey and two-year-old Ciara from the blaze. A third child, aged only seven months, was lifted out to safety in a carry-cot.

This is the reverse of the situation with the adverbial phrases: in this case, there is a marked preponderance of 'absolute value' readings compared to the over-all distribution of values. The corpus material suggests that the same type of explanation as the one that was used in the case of adverbials is valid here: the 'exactly n' readings are most often caused by definiteness-markers, whereas the 'absolute value' uses do not co-occur with these markers. Adverbial phrases are unlikely candidates for the introduction of new topic-prone[31] referents, while

---

[29] I do not wish to suggest that in the original context "when did she join UNACO?" is the only possible question. I do believe, however, that it is the most natural one.

[30] As already mentioned, I will discuss the differences between the accounts by Van Kuppevelt and Scharten and the account in section 1.3.6.

[31] I use this term to distinguish between newly introduced referents that are likely to become the topic of the next utterance or one of the next utterances and those that do not have this tendency.

direct object phrases are presumably much more typical candidates. This is confirmed in the literature (Dik 1989, Lambrecht 1994): direct object phrases generally appear to be the best candidates for the introduction of new topics. Hence, it is not surprising to find so many 'absolute value' uses in direct object phrases. Note that also definiteness markers other than the definite article can induce 'exactly n' interpretations, as is the case with *her* in (57).

Indirectly, (57) also provides more evidence for the 'exactly n' induction of these definiteness markers: intuitively, the mentioning of a "third child" near the end of the fragment is quite unexpected, even though it is perfectly "grammatical". What is happening here? First a mother is introduced into the discourse (by means of an indefinite article: *a shocked mum*), and then the information that she has two children has to be accommodated (no indefinite article, but that is unproblematic because the fact that a mother has a certain number of children can readily be accommodated - it is, in Lambrecht's words, "inferentially accessible"). Next, the children are identified as two daughters, and the second use of *two* (together with the second marker of definiteness, which is once again the possessive *her*) strengthens the assumption that the number of children of the mother is two ('exactly two'). Nonetheless, the final sentence mentions yet another child. This causes a feeling of surprise with the reader. It even triggers the feeling that the writer (the fragment is obviously taken from a short report from a newspaper) of the text hesitates to consider the seven-month-old baby as a full-fledged "child", but speculations as to the motivations of the author may differ. The reason why the author chose not to mention the third child at the beginning might also be that this child never was in real danger, and hence was not very interesting to write about (even though the sentence *A third child, aged only seven months, was lifted out to safety in a carry-cot* is inconclusive in this respect). In that case, it is clear that it could not be the topic of this (slightly sensationalist) piece of prose. In each case, it is clear that the reader may wonder why the third child was not mentioned from the beginning because his or her expectations as to the cardinality of the group of children are disconfirmed in the last sentence. This "surprise" can be seen as a refined, contextualized and hence less artificial variant of the *actually*-test, although in this case it is not the speaker who corrects his / her statement, but the hearer who corrects his / her "file cards" (to borrow Heim's metaphor of information-processing, cf. Heim 1983).

The following example is also remarkable, because it shows that the 'absolute value' reading is present in imperatives as well[32]. The context is clearly that of an exam or a questionnaire. The question asks for two prominent exhibits, and it can be assumed that the names of 'exactly' two exhibits are sufficient. All the same, there clearly is no explicit restriction built into the meaning of this use of *two*. If the hearer / reader names three exhibits, this will perhaps be regarded as a redundancy, but most probably not as an incorrect answer.

> (58) <HHT 46> Give the names of the BCR locomotives. (a) What is the number of the Clunbury coach? (b) What is its approximate length? (a) Name **two** prominent

---

[32] This corpus analysis is certainly guilty of what has been called the "declarative fallacy" (Belnap 1998:290-292): the tendency of logicians, philosophers but also linguists to concentrate on declarative sentences. In this case, however, the responsibility for this bias lies primarily with the sample corpus. I have not checked whether this holds for all uses of numerals, but in the *two* corpus the predominance of declarative sentences is overwhelming.

exhibits from the BCRS museum's central display case (b) What would you see on the floor of the museum in the corner opposite the door? (c) Where is the 4" gauge model coach displayed? This question and the five after it are a test on the previous two copies of the Journal.

Note also that the connection between the affirmation of existence and the 'absolute value' concept becomes less direct when the analysis is expanded to other speech acts. It is a little awkward to claim that the utterance *Name two prominent exhibits from the BCRS museum's central display case* directly conceptualizes these exhibits as being in existence. That is simply not the point of the utterance, which boils down to an examination in the guise of a request for information. Nevertheless, if the concept of "satisfaction conditions" or "felicity conditions" is assumed to have any explanatory value, it is clear that even in this imperative form the 'absolute value' use of *two* derives from the existence of the exhibits in question. Otherwise, the speaker / writer would not be cooperative (perhaps he would be pulling a prank) and this is not the default starting-point for an interpretation (cf. Chapter 2 section 2.1.2.2. for more on the Cooperative Principle, cf. Austin 1962 and Searle 1969, 1983 for the concept of felicity conditions).

5.1.3.3. Two *in subject phrases and gradations of 'absolute value'*

With respect to subject phrases, the distribution of the values of *two* is not very remarkable, as it seems to correspond rather well to the average behavior of *two*. There are slightly more 'absolute value' uses (50.4%) than normal (45.5%), but the number of 'exactly n' uses (42.2%) is more or less the same as the average number (42.6%). In (59), there is a typical example of an 'absolute value' use of *two* in a subject NP, while (60) provides an example of an 'exactly n' use.

> (59) <CBC 4141> This is the Citizen's Charter in action and we have no objection to the public being given more information. But if the Government thinks that the public is gullible enough to be happy with a table or two every now and again, it is quite wrong. There is only one good reason to issue information and that is as a basis for action. **Two** important issues emerge from today's sex crimes statistics. The first is that the figures are indeed horrifying.
>
> (60) There were those, of course, who wondered why England should be sending her brave lads across the Channel to fight against a country which seemed - the Reign of Terror notwithstanding - to be the cradle of a new and attractive democracy. Others - and the majority, no doubt - would wait anxiously for any news as a French invasion force was massing ready to launch itself against English shores. The **two** countries would be fighting each other, on and off, for 22 years; and there were those, like Benjamin Titford, born in 1786, who lived through nothing but wars and rumours of wars from the day they were born to the day they died.

Still, there is the feeling that *two* in subject NPs corresponds less well to the default 'absolute value' interpretation that is found in, e.g., adverbial phrases and direct object phrases that lack direct triggers of 'exactly n' readings (such as definiteness markers). Especially the comparison with the object phrases is illuminating - the comparison with adverbial phrases is only partly interesting because the 'exactly n' values in adverbial NPs are most often triggered by temporal adverbials, which is, by definition, not a factor in the discussion of subject NPs nor in that of object NPs.

In (59) two important issues are presented as emerging from the sex crime statistics, and because *two* is clearly part of an NP introducing new referents (constituting a new topic), the "neutrality" with respect to the value-interpretations of numerals that is inherent in 'absolute value' uses is somewhat tainted. Because *two* is part of the presentation of a new referent (which is focused) and even more because *two* is in the initial position - one of the most prominent slots of an utterance - the NP containing *two* may be doing slightly more than just presenting a group of objects as being in existence. The information contained in the numeral is brought to the fore, or at least more so than in e.g. adverbial phrases or object phrases. More specifically, the hearer would be surprised to learn that there is actually a third important issue, if that was announced later on in the discourse.

The reason why *two* in indefinite subject NPs excludes the possibility of there being more than two elements in the group denoted by the NP slightly more prominently than indefinite object NPs has by now become rather predictable. For clarity's sake, the argument will be unfolded in four steps:

1) Definite NPs imply an 'exactly n' reading of the numeral they contain, because the definiteness marker presents the entities referred to by the NP as (separately) "identifiable".
2) Object phrases are generally accepted as the best candidates for introducing new referents.
3) When a subject phrase is nonetheless used to introduce a new referent, this presents itself automatically as a marked choice. That is why indefinite subject NPs generally are excellent slots for foci.
4) This focus explains why *two* in indefinite subject NPs excludes the possibility of there being more than two elements more forcefully than if *two* were part of an indefinite object NP. Nevertheless, the exclusion is not as strong as in the case in which *two* is combined with an 'exactly' restrictor or a definiteness marker, which is why it was decided to assign it an 'absolute value' label.

This is even more blatant in passive constructions. When *two* occurs as part of a subject NP in a passive clause, it seems to tilt a little towards an 'exactly n' meaning, even if it is not combined with a definiteness-marker.

(61) <ANK 1172> Public sympathy was more inclined towards the fatherless children and widows. A massive collection was made in local towns, and **two** crosses were erected close to where the men met their tragic ends.

The hypothesis is that this is due to the markedness of the passive construction, which brings the subject of the clause even more into focus. In the unmarked active variant, this NP would have functioned as a direct object (as we have seen, a typical slot for introducing new referents in typically indefinite NPs, and hence also a good spot to find 'absolute value' readings). The fact that the speaker deemed it necessary to promote the NP to the subject-slot brings the NP more into focus than if this were a "normal" subject, i.e. a subject of an active clause.

Nevertheless, this does not mean that these uses of *two* really are instances of 'exactly n' uses: the difference between these subject NPs and the NPs or PPs containing 'exactly n' triggers is quite strong. It simply means that even if 'absolute value' interpretations are the default starting-point of an interpretation of a numeral, there may also be gradations in the extent to which these 'absolute values' leave the possibility of there being more or fewer members to a certain group unexpressed[33]. The hierarchy between these two indicators of 'absolute value' / 'exactly n' uses is clear: presence of definiteness-markers always overrules the influence of the syntactic position of the NP containing *two*. The first factor is by far the strongest: even in utterances in which the syntactic position would by default favor 'absolute value' uses (i.e., object phrases), the presence of a definiteness marker immediately induces an 'exactly n' reading.

> (62) <CEK 7678> Left 19th century Luton Hoo with its 4,000-acre estate by his grandfather - his father had been killed in the war - Mr Phillips invested heavily in an industrial project on his land. Now his executors hope that the money raised by the Constable will pay off the last of his debts and enable his wife, Austrian Countess Lucy Czernin and their **two** children, Edward, 11, and Charlotte, 15, to continue living at the house.

Without the possessive this is a very good example of an 'absolute value' use of *two* (although the additional identification of the children in question obscures this fact to a certain extent).

> (63) <CEK 7678> Left 19th century Luton Hoo with its 4,000-acre estate by his grandfather - his father had been killed in the war - Mr Phillips invested heavily in an industrial project on his land. Now his executors hope that the money raised by the Constable will pay off the last of his debts and enable his wife, Austrian Countess Lucy Czernin and **two** children, Edward, 11, and Charlotte, 15, to continue living at the house.

With the possessive, it irrevocably becomes an instance of an 'exactly n' use.

Let us try to do the same with a prepositional object, which can be turned into the subject of a clause, in order to check how the three features (definiteness-marker, focalization, passivization) compare. In (64), there is the original corpus example, yielding an 'exactly n' interpretation because of the definiteness-marker.

> (64) <CEH 2234> And two late passes a week and when you've had those you can get in through the pantry window if the front door's been locked." Although Chief Pillmoor wasn't everybody's cup of tea, Vi had discovered, at least the lady was fair

---

[33] As mentioned in the general discussion of 'absolute value' interpretations of numerals, an 'absolute value' use of a numeral naturally does imply that the possibility that the cardinality of the group is actually less than n is excluded, but, crucially, 'absolute value' uses of numerals do not explicitly encode this, as 'at least' and 'exactly' uses do.

and had no favourites. She gazed with compassion at the **two** dejected figures. Their eyes were dark-ringed, their faces pale and their hair lay dull and uncurled. Kids, that's all they were and in need of a bit of looking-after.

When the definite article is omitted, the 'exactly n' reading is lost immediately:

(65) And two late passes a week and when you've had those you can get in through the pantry window if the front door's been locked." Although Chief Pillmoor wasn't everybody's cup of tea, Vi had discovered, at least the lady was fair and had no favourites. She gazed with compassion at **two** dejected figures. Their eyes were dark-ringed, their faces pale and their hair lay dull and uncurled. Kids, that's all they were and in need of a bit of looking-after.

But when the clause is turned into a passive one, the 'absolute value' interpretation loses some of its force, to the advantage of a movement in the direction of the 'exactly n' meaning.

(66)   **Two** dejected figures were gazed at with compassion.

In other words, the "neutrality" with respect to the possibility of there being more or fewer "dejected figures" is considerably greater in (65) than in (66). In yet other words: because the emphasis on *two* in (66) is heavier than the one on *two* in (65), the use of *two* in (65) leaves more room for there being more than two dejected figures, in the sense that, alternatively, it is hardly concerned with reducing the likelihood of there being more.

5.1.3.4. Two *in predicate phrases and the "existential there"-effect*
In the general survey of the syntactic functions of NPs containing two, only subject NPs, object NPs and adverbial phrases were considered (cf. section 5.1.3. above). With respect to the determination of the value of *two* also the predicate construction is interesting. In (67), there is yet another prime example of an 'absolute value' use of *two*, and this is mainly due to the predicate function of the NP in which *two* is contained.

(67) <G33 1573> Petite protozoa One of the more common diseases caused by protozoa - microscopic amoeba-like organisms - is leishmaniasis. In Brazil, there are **two** types.

In this case, *two types* is the predicate of the sentence and *to be* functions as the copula; the construction is a typical instance of the so-called "existential *there*" construction. Of all cardinality uses of *two* under consideration ("pure" adnominal uses + pronominal uses) in which *two* occurs as part of a predicate-NP (43 instances in total), there are three times as many 'absolute value' uses (66.7%) as there are 'exactly two' uses (22.2%). This is a marked difference with the over-all distribution, in which there are nearly as many 'exactly n' (42.6%) uses as there are 'absolute value' uses (45.5%).

TABLE 6

ADNOMINAL AND PRONOMINAL *TWO* AS PART OF A PREDICATE

Absolute Value (30/45=66.7%)	At least / more than two (1/45=2.2%)	At most / less than two (4/45=8.9%)	Exactly two (10/45=22.2%)

To a very large extent, the reason for this asymmetry has to be sought in the existential meanings that at least some copula constructions generate. The "existential *there*" construction is responsible for nearly three thirds of the 'absolute value' uses as part of a predicate:

TABLE 7

ABSOLUTE VALUE *TWO* AS PART OF A PREDICATE

Existential *there* (22/30=73.3%)	"Real" predicates (8/30=26.7%)

This is of course the most straightforward existential meaning an absolute value use can have: the basic function of the "existential *there*" construction is precisely the conceptualization of the predicate as being in existence. As mentioned before, the affirmation of the existence of a group of elements (in this case with cardinality *two*) leads automatically to an 'absolute value' interpretation, on condition that no other linguistic elements (modals, restrictors, determiners, negation, etc.) interfere. The affirmation of existence is a purely positive assertion: it contains no modal elements (at least not in itself - it can of course be combined with modal elements), nor does it explicitly exclude possibilities (such as the possibility that the group of elements, the existence of which is affirmed through "existential *there*", contains more or fewer elements than indicated by the numeral itself).

The other uses of *two* in indefinite predicate NPs specify the nature of the subject and are therefore very different from the uses of *two* in "existential *there*" predicates. Nevertheless, they are also very good examples of 'absolute value' uses of *two*.

(68) <HXF 127> The specialist brochures should have a suitable front page which relates to the interests of the target group. However, brochures may be of varying kinds and history found within them in a variety of guises. The following are **two** examples from brochures in the early 1990s which were distributed to parents and local businesses, and were even to be found in doctors' and dentists' waiting rooms. They used no more than two sides of A4 to provide a basic outline of courses, being part of a large information pack.

Among the 'exactly n' uses of *two* in predicate NPs, there are the usual 'exactly' triggers: definiteness markers (69) and expressions of measurement (70) (cf. the discussion of temporal adverbials in section 5.1.3.1. above).

(69) HOW FREQUENT ARE THESE DIFFERENT TYPES OF DEMENTING CONDITIONS? This is a very difficult question to answer authoritatively as accurate diagnosis of the different types of dementia is often difficult and may not, in many cases, be confirmed without a post mortem. In both hospital and community populations Alzheimers disease and multi-infarc dementia are the **two** major causes of dementing conditions (Table 5.1). Specific causes such as tumours, drug toxicity, infection and trauma appear to be of lesser significance as causes of dementia.

(70) <B0A 1931> Otley, West Yorkshire MAP B In the churchyard of All Saints, a monument stands to the men killed during the construction of the nearby Bramhope railway tunnel in 1845-9. It consists of a scale model of the tunnel's castellated northern portal. The tunnel was built by the Leeds and Thirsk Railway, and is a little over **two** miles in length.

The question naturally arises as to the position of these existential *there* with respect to the other syntactic possibilities. The matter is quite complicated, as the differences between the force with which "the possibility of there being more than two entities" is excluded become more subtle each time a new syntactic category is added to the discussion, because each syntactic construction shows different values. In the next section, it will be discussed how they compare.

5.1.3.5. Hierarchy of syntactic functions

As argued above, the principal factor influencing the value interpretation of a numeral is not so much the nature of the syntactic construction in which the numeral occurs, but the tendency of the NP in this construction to introduce new topics (due to focalization). The preponderance of 'absolute value' uses of *two* in direct object phrases, e.g., is caused by the tendency of direct object phrases to introduce new referents, as new referents typically do not co-occur with definiteness markers. In general, the absence of definiteness markers leaves the 'absolute value' interpretation of numerals intact, and this explains the divergent distribution of the value-interpretations in direct object clauses.

A tentative hierarchy of syntactic functions with respect to their effect on the interpretation of numerals in indefinite NPs is given in figure 1. It is important to emphasize that this hierarchy is not a generalization over *all* uses of numerals - the data on all uses of *two* have already been expressed in the general table with the percentages of values per syntactic construction, at the very beginning of the section on 'at least / more than n', 'exactly n', 'at most / less than n' and 'absolute value' readings (Table 1). The hypothesis below only holds for the influence of the syntactic construction on those uses of *two* that have not yet been influenced by other factors, such as the presence of definiteness-markers, explicit focalization (by means of intonation, or when *two* is (part of) the answer to a question), or the temporal nature of the entities expressed by the NP and so on. These factors overrule every kind of influence that the syntactic constructions may have[34]. Furthermore, the influence of the syntactic construction is deemed so minimal that even the construction that is assumed to push the interpretation of the numeral most forcefully to an 'exactly n' reading (i.e., subject of a passive), is considered insufficient to turn the interpretation of *two* into that of an 'exactly n' use of *two*. In short: this hierarchy only applies to 'absolute value' uses of *two* and determines subtle meaning distinctions *within* the category of 'absolute value' uses.

FIGURE 1: HIERARCHY OF SYNTACTIC FUNCTIONS

"EXISTENTIAL *THERE*" PREDICATE < OBJECT < SUBJECT <SUBJECT OF PASSIVE (< ADVERBIAL?)

ABSOLUTE VALUE   ⟵————————⟶   EXACTLY N

Accepting the 'absolute value' interpretation of *two* as the default situation, it is clear that the fact that this numeral is part of an "existential *there*" predicate NP will change hardly anything to this interpretation. *Ceteris paribus, two* as part of an "existential *there*" predicate is the purest 'absolute value' use there is. This is caused by the fact that the existential *there* construction is the "existential" construction par excellence: no other syntactic construction expresses existence so exclusively as this one, and, as we have seen, 'absolute value' uses express existence and cardinality, nothing more. If *two* is part of a direct object NP, the 'absolute value' interpretation is still strong, but the direct object construction does not encode existence as explicitly as the existential *there* construction.

 (71) There were two, actually three janitors in this building.
 (72) He saw two, actually three janitors in this building.

Nevertheless, it is very hard to decide which syntactic construction excludes the possibility of there being more than two janitors in the building more forcefully than the other. This is not surprising since two factors, namely the conceptualization of entities as being in existence on the one hand, and focalization / stress on the other, are actually in conflict with each other here. "Existential *there*" predicate constructions are of course excellent constructions to present entities as being in existence, but most often the entities introduced by "existential *there*" constructions are also presented as "new", and hence good candidates for focalization. While the first leaves 'absolute value' readings intact as much as possible and the second moves it in the direction of the 'exactly n' value of the scale. This becomes evident when an attempt is made to imagine which topic-constituting question would fit the two utterances just mentioned. While (73) allows several WH-questions, the predicate construction in (74) allows only two.

---

[34] Not in the least because one specific syntactic construction can vary with respect to the other factors: all kinds of phrases can co-occur with definiteness markers (even the existential *there* construction - Dik 1989:178-179), all phrases can receive heavy stress, all phrases can occur at various positions in the clause.

(73)   Q: Who did he see in this building? / How many janitors did he see in this
         building? / Where did he see two janitors? Who saw two janitors?
         A: He saw two janitors in this building.
(74)   Q: Who was in this building? How many janitors were there in this
         building?
         A: There were two janitors in this building.

Moreover, as mentioned before (cf. section 5.1.3.1.), the type of referents indicated by the NP
containing *two* and the type of verb of the whole construction influences the unexpectedness
of the *actually* repair/correction phrases, and these cannot be kept perfectly constant over the
two examples[35]. But because the effect of the existence parameter is constant in the predicate
construction, and because the focus-test allows more than one possibility in the predicate
construction as well, I decided to position the predicate construction more towards the
'absolute value' point of the scale.
       The hierarchy is, however, considerably more clear with respect to the difference
between the object and the subject construction. As already mentioned, because the unmarked
way to introduce new referents is through direct object phrases, when a subject phrase is used
for this purpose, it attracts the attention of the hearer / reader. The same holds *a fortiori* for
subject NPs and subject NPs in passive constructions. Below, I will exemplify each situation,
starting from the use of *two* that leaves the 'absolute value' interpretation most intact and
ending with an example of a passivized NP, which presents itself as very prominent in
comparison to the other constructions. Of course, none of these NPs contain definiteness-
markers, as this would obscure the comparison.

       (75) <FNR 146> One step in the search consists of examining a pile of wooden blocks,
       and modifying the contents of the sets accordingly. The operator adds a property to
       one of the two sets. The goal is a state in which the set of properties common to all
       arches includes the assertions: there are **two** columns there is an extra block the extra
       block rests on both columns and the other set of properties contains the assertion: the
       two columns touch.
       (76) <B25 250> We are ready to approach these people to ask them if they will fill in
       questionnaires or be interviewed to help us with our research. At this point let us take
       stock of the limitations we have put on our research. We have decided to study just
       one area, at one particular time. That is, we have chosen **two** parishes in our particular
       town - and we cannot be sure how typical the parishes or the town are of the rest of the
       country.
       (77) <HBM 1400> **Two** colleges were receiving pilot `intensive" visits in the spring
       term, Clackmannan College and Thurso College, under the coordination of local Field
       Officers Muriel Dunbar and Chris Maythorne. Clackmannan was visited in January

---

[35] For the direct object construction, e.g. one has to choose a verb (in this case *see* was chosen), and this choice
may have an effect on the already subtle value interpretation, while in the existential *there* construction most
often *are* is used.

and Thurso in March. Further pilots in Jewel and Esk Valley, Aberdeen College of Commerce and Cumbernauld are scheduled for the summer term.
(78) <HHV 24604> Mr. Fearn About 12 months ago, I asked the Secretary of State a question about the safety of the lighting on the M6. It appears that the lighting has not been improved and that there are black holes all the way along the M6. **Two** particular spots with many accidents have been highlighted lately.

Perhaps the picture becomes clearer when using constructed examples, so that all other factors can be kept constant.

(79)   There are **two** important points with respect to government taxation.
(80)   They raised **two** important points with respect to government taxation.
(81)   **Two** points are relevant with respect to government taxation.
(82)   **Two** points were considered relevant with respect to government taxation.

The most difficult assessment is the one related to *two* in adverbial phrases. They are generally not used to introduce new topics, which suggests that when they are used as such all the same, this may be a marked choice and therefore induce focalization. But the situation with adverbials is different from the one with subjects: first of all because the indefinite NPs in adverbials often contain temporal or other measurement nouns (which refer to entities the existence of which is much less prominent - this suggests a movement towards the 'exactly n' part of the scale), second, because these new referents are often not picked up as topics of the following utterances (which suggests that they are not considered very relevant to the conversation, hence that they will not be focused on when introduced - this suggests a movement in the direction of 'absolute value' uses). To complicate things further, it is not impossible at all that adverbial phrases are in focus position anyway.

(83)   Q: Where did she raise her **two** kids?
         A: She raised her **two** kids in the slums of Bombay.

Nevertheless, the corpus analysis shows that those indefinite adverbial phrases that contain *two*, and do not contain temporal or other measurement nouns, are very often used to locate a certain activity, in which case they are generally not in focus.

(84) <J3A 238> New Scientist 3 October Energy Orimulsion application on hold The UK's Inspectorate of Pollution (HMIP) has insisted on additional environmental safeguards before it will give approval to a controversial plan to burn orimulsion at **two** power stations in Wales and Lancashire. Orimulsion, a new bitumen-based fuel from Venezuela, has been widely criticized as a "dirty" fuel because of its high sulphur content.

On the whole, it will be clear that the influence of the adverbial construction *per se* (hence, when all typical characteristics of adverbials are omitted) is difficult to gauge. The *actually* test suggests that the adverbial constructions belong to the extreme right end of the scale (i.e. the 'exactly n' end of the scale).

> (85) !!6 Roll out the remaining pink marzipan to a long strip. Mark on parallel lines with the pastry wheel and then use it to wrap round the sides of the cake. (You may find this easier to do in **two**, actually three sections.) 7 Make six small balls out of the red marzipan trimmings, each about the size of a pea, and press them gently into the red base, spacing evenly apart.
>
> (86) !!Charlemagne and Louis the Pious and their counsellors had strengthened the authority of archbishops, and promoted regular meetings of councils of one province or of several provinces: trends that continued after 840, and especially in the kingdom of Charles the Bald. The evidence lies in **two**, actually three imposing series of texts, the records of church councils, and the statutes (regulations for the performance of sacramental and pastoral duties) issued by bishops and archbishops for their lower clergy. In both cases, though some parallel texts survive from Lotharingia, from East Francia and Italy, the bulk of the evidence comes from the kingdom of Charles the Bald.

It is important to stress that this hierarchy is presented more as a plausible hypothesis than as a full-fledged result of the corpus analysis. Testing this hypothesis would ideally involve a general analysis of all sorts of NPs in syntactic constructions (and not only NPs containing *two*), but this lies beyond the scope of this study.

5.1.3.6. Comparison with Discourse Topic Theory: Van Kuppevelt (1996) and Scharten (1997)

The syntactic constructions in which *two* occurs influence the interpretation of *two* in subtle but real ways. These subtle meaning distinctions are reminiscent of the distinction between 'at least n' and 'exactly n' interpretations that many authors have perceived, but I claim that this particular distinction is really a difference between 'absolute value n' and 'exactly n' interpretations. As we have seen in Chapter 3, Van Kuppevelt (1996) and Scharten (1997) have concentrated on the meaning analysis of numerals in the "dynamic semantics" framework of Discourse Topic Theory. In this section, I will repeat some of the claims I have made concerning their analyses because I would like to emphasize the similarities and the differences between their approach and the one adopted in the analysis of the influence of syntactic structures.

The main claim of Scharten and Van Kuppevelt is that the interpretation of so-called scalar items depends to a great extent on the "topic-comment" structure of the utterance. There are genuine differences between Van Kuppevelt's and Scharten's approach, but the essence of their accounts seems to be that when numerals are in comment position (which means, in their terminology, that they can be construed as an answer to a question) the numeral receives an 'exactly n' interpretation[36].

---

[36] Actually, their accounts are a little bit more sophisticated than that, but the details are not relevant here. For a full exposition of their ideas, cf. Chapter 3 (sections 3.1.3. and 3.2.2).

(Scharten 1997:71)
(87) Q   How many sheep does John own?
      A   He owns <u>four sheep</u>.

The underlined part in (87A) is the part of the answer that is in comment position and that receives, in Scharten's terminology an "exhaustive interpretation" (which boils down to the fact that it is interpreted as an 'exactly n' use of *four*). With respect to numerals in non-comment position, Scharten and Van Kuppevelt differ in their interpretation. Van Kuppevelt notes that

> [a] quantifying term like *fourteen* thus receives a monotone increasing interpretation if it has no comment status: adding more referents than fourteen does not change the truth value of the sentence containing this expression. (Van Kuppevelt 1996:406)

As we have seen, it is not really transparent whether this statement means that Van Kuppevelt assumes numerals in non-comment position to have an 'at least' meaning (cf. also section 3.1.3. in Chapter 3 for details). Scharten is a bit ambiguous in this respect as well: she claims that newly introduced numerals that are not in comment position, such as *four* in (88A), are not interpreted exhaustively: "the interpretation that John has no more than four sheep is only the preferred interpretation" (Scharten 1997:76).

(88) Q   Who owns four sheep?
      A   <u>John</u> owns four sheep.

In each case, these accounts show that both DTT-researchers are very much aware of the fact that the meaning of numerals cannot be determined simply on the basis of the "semantics" of numerals and a general recipe of Gricean implicatures. It is the merit of Van Kuppevelt and Scharten that they have demonstrated the importance of discourse-structure on the interpretation of numerals.

The problem with their account is that they do not provide a heuristics that can decide which questions fit which sentences (i.e. sentences that become "answers" in DTT-terminology). Because they work exclusively with constructed examples, they allow themselves to formulate questions that demonstrably determine the interpretation of the numerals to a large extent. In other words, they create a linguistic laboratory in which the influence of discourse-structure becomes manifest, through careful manipulation of the data. This is of course very useful, but their account presupposes too much to reflect actual communication in an adequate way.

Of course, question-answer pairs occur regularly in everyday conversation. But it is very doubtful whether the question-answer structure can function as a model for all kinds of communication. In the corpus sample, e.g., question-answer pairs are rather rare. Scharten and Van Kuppevelt seem to realize this, because they both explicitly anticipate the situation in which the topic-constituting question is not given in the context, but has to be constructed by the analyst. As Scharten writes: "Obviously, the method of representing context by way of a question has its limitations, and these have to be taken into account" (Scharten 1997:15). She realizes that the extra-linguistic context is not captured in this question-answer pair and she also recognizes the fact that "the same question, in different contexts, may call for a different answer". Consider (89) and (90).

> (89) Two people meet each other for the first time. Both are students at an evening-school which recruits students from all over the country.
> A Where do you live?
> B In Nijmegen.
> (90) The same two people, two months later. They have agreed to work on a paper together, and are making an appointment for the following week.
> A Where do you live?
> B At 17, Oranjesingel"
> (Scharten 1997:14)

But this is not the only respect in which the question-answer method abstracts from data in actual language use. Let us exemplify this with some data from the sample corpus.

> (91) The charity has recently completed major electrical and plumbing work on a Romanian orphanage and is now waiting for the authorities to upgrade the power supply and sewerage system before volunteers complete the renovations. On the recent trip to Iasi, as well as carrying out a full survey of the children's hospital the charity also delivered more than 30 tons of aid to ten orphanages, **two** children's hospitals and the main hospital in the region. Mr Stage said: `Staff there told us that the equipment and particularly the surgical instruments and incubators would save lives. They have the skill to carry out life saving operations and treatments and now they have the equipment to do it with."

The cotext is clearly not enough to enable us to formulate one, and only one, topic-constituting question. Both (92) and (93) are possibilities.

> (92) Q: What did the charity do on the recent trip to Iasi?
> A: On the recent trip to Iasi, <u>as well as carrying out a full survey of the children's hospital</u> the charity <u>also delivered more than 30 tons of aid to ten orphanages, **two** children's hospitals and the main hospital in the region.</u>
> (93) Q: Who did the charity deliver more than 30 tons of aid to?
> A: On the recent trip to Iasi, as well as carrying out a full survey of the children's hospital the charity also delivered more than 30 tons of aid <u>to ten orphanages, **two** children's hospitals and the main hospital in the region.</u>

Actually, many more variations are possible. The point is that in the DTT-account both Van Kuppevelt and Scharten demonstrate very convincingly how the decision to opt for a specific topic-constituting question determines the interpretation of a numeral to a considerable extent, but they do this without giving criteria with respect to this choice. The linguistic analysis of numerals has to start from the empirical data at our disposal, and unfortunately these often do not include topic-constituting questions.

Therefore, it is important that an attempt is made to look for strictly linguistic manifestations of these influences. While DTT (and the strategy of turning statements into answers of questions in general, cf. R.G. Collingwood's theories in Manor 1998 and Kadmon's 2001:261-263 remarks on question-answer pairs) provides a very workable instrument for representing how discourse-structure influences interpretation, it is in a sense also too strong. More specifically, the topic-constituting question in itself already constitutes a genuine interpretive effort: it determines the speaker intention to a considerable extent. While the reconstruction of speaker intention is inevitable in this domain of research (especially in a Gricean context), the formulation of the topic-constituting question relies too much on speculations as to these intentions.

An analysis that claims to describe the behavior in actual language use should try to look for the ways in which linguistic structure supports some of the observations made by Van Kuppevelt and Scharten. One of these ways would be an investigation of how intonation contours influence the interpretation of numerals as Fretheim (1992) did. The corpus material excludes this possibility, but it does give us the opportunity to analyze what effects syntactic structures have on their meaning. The advantage of this method is that it uses real data, with pieces of linguistic interaction that are not pre-interpreted[37]. The disadvantage is that linguistic coding is typically multifunctional, especially on the syntactic level: direct object phrases are typical slots for dropping new topics in, but they are also the most likely candidates for recruiting the thematic role of "patients". Their canonical position in independent clauses seems to be right after the subject and the verb, but all sorts of movements (for the formation of questions, in topicalizations) can alter their position. These factors influence each other and blur the clear picture offered by Scharten and Van Kuppevelt. The analysis of the influence of syntactic structure on the value interpretation of numerals can be compared to what they have argued on the level of "information structure", but I focused on the linguistic (syntactic) structure. The factors "in comment position" and "in non-comment position" are rightly seen as one of the determinants of the interpretation of numerals, but these are not coded directly in the language, but only via the detour of intonation, sentence position and syntactic structure. It is the latter kind of linguistic realization of this "comment" and "non-comment" factor that I have tried to describe.

---

[37] I do of course realize that also corpus material is to a certain extent an idealization: especially the transcription of spoken discourse leaves out many of the relevant con- and cotextual features that can influence the interpretation. I do, however, believe that the DTT-methodology not only leaves out many of those features, but that it enforces an interpretation on linguistic structure. Statements that are not formulated as an answer to a question are not so explicit concerning their "point". That explains why people may sometimes wonder *why* a speaker uttered a certain statement. This indeterminacy is ruled out by DTT-methodology.

5.1.3.7. Other determinants of value interpretation

As already announced, there are some other, relatively minor factors that can influence the value interpretation of *two*. These crosscut the influence of the syntactic construction, unlike the other factors mentioned above (cf. section 5.1.2.)[38].

(1) "exhaustivity" due to presence of a superset

The first usually occurs with pronominal uses of *two* (cf. section 5.1.3.9. below for a separate discussion of the influence of pronominality on value-interpretations) and is exemplified in (94).

> (94) <A15 992> I joined a small group of three Germans, a Dutchman and an American who, with a young interpreter and a terrifyingly fit-looking guide from Kiev, set out for Europe's icy crown at four o'clock one morning last July. Before we'd gone far from the hut we had lost one of the Germans with sickness, and an hour later the Dutchman had to turn back when he had trouble with his crampons. **Two** down, six to go. It was cold that early in the morning, with a sliver of moon hanging among the stars.

In this example, the 'exactly n' interpretation is enforced by the cotext: first all eight members of the "small group" are introduced, then the fact that two of the members stayed behind is mentioned. This indicates that the *two* in *two down* has to be interpreted as referring back to the ones that are left behind. In other words, the 'exactly n' reading that is induced in this context derives from the fact that first the cardinality is determined of a set that is not the set to which *two* is attributed. This larger set, a so-called "superset", is then subdivided into two subsets ('the ones who are "down"' and 'the ones who are still in the running'), but the understanding is that these two subsets together constitute the original set. This enforces the 'exactly n' interpretation of *two*. A similar example is given in (95).

> (95) <CGB 613> JACOB'S LADDER (Guild) Freaked-out Vietnam vets get together and discover they were used as government guinea pigs during the war. Gripping if a little confusing at times HANGIN' WITH THE HOMEBOYS (Columbia TriStar) The four homeboys in question - **two** black, two hispanic - quit the Bronx for a night out of bonding and bravado in Manhattan. Sharp characterisation, fine comedy performances and spot-on dialogue. Rent it.

Another example features a partitive construction.

---

[38] One might be inclined to argue that definiteness markers also cross-cut the syntactic constructions, but we have seen that these are not entirely independent of them, at least in terms of frequency of occurrence, e.g., because certain syntactic constructions introduce new referents more easily than others.

(96) <FP2 1104> The modern law In the absence of modern authority it is possible only to speculate about how far the above account of the law represents the position today. A useful starting point is to note that **two** of the three factors just mentioned as having influenced the law's development have little application in modern conditions.

As in the previous example, the fact that a set is mentioned, which is larger than the set with cardinality two, and which is also a set that includes that smaller set, induces an 'exactly two' reading. I will call the effect of this inducing factor "exhaustivity": the 'exactly n' reading is caused by the understanding that there can be no more elements in the set under discussion since the others are part of another set that is not included in the first.[39] Here, the limits of the *actually* test are reached.

(97) !!A useful starting point is to note that **two**, actually three of the three factors just mentioned as having influenced the law's development have little application in modern conditions.

Obviously, part of the problem is caused by the fact that *three of the three* is anomalous: if the speaker wanted to correct his or her previous statement he / she should have normally gone for *all*: [...] *that two, actually all of the three factors* [...]. This is not as banal as it might seem: the fact that the relative quantifier *all* is used indicates that the presence of a "reference mass" is explicitly encoded in the *n of the m N constructions*[40]. It is precisely this comparison with a reference mass (which I have called a "superset" because this seems to fit better in the "cardinality" discussion of numerals) that induces the 'exactly n' value, if the cardinality of the superset is expressed explicitly as well[41]. The rationale is similar to the reasoning that is behind the factor of definiteness markers: the comparison with a superset indicates a heightened awareness of cardinality, just like the definiteness marker, which suggests a "separate" conceptualization of the entities denoted by the NP, brings the expression of cardinality into focus. Another variant of (96) is presented in (98), which contains a reference to a superset of four rather than three factors.

(98) A useful starting point is to note that **two** of the four factors just mentioned as having influenced the law's development have little application in modern conditions.

---

[39] Of course, the term "exhaustivity" could also apply to other 'exactly n' uses (cf. Scharten 1997), but I would like to reserve the term for 'exactly n' readings with this specific type of trigger.

[40] Where n indicates a number that is smaller than m.

[41] When the cardinality of the superset is not explicitly indicated, the effect is considerably reduced, if present at all. In the following corpus example, the pronominal use of *two* has an absolute value, even if it is compared to a reference mass (an indefinite superset):

<ARK 830> From the description Corcoran obtained I'm afraid it could be Paula Grey" `Makes sense," Newman commented. `Makes sense!" Howard's pompous manner changed, his voice went up several decibels. `If it was Paula that means I have **two** of my staff as fugitives from justice"

If the cardinality of the superset is indicated, the interpretation changes to an 'exactly n' value:

`If it was Paula that means I have **two** of my four staff as fugitives from justice.

In (98) the 'exactly n' reading is also triggered by the presence of the superset. Because the superset contains four elements, the result of the *actually* test is not influenced by the coincidental overlap of the higher numeral of the "correction" phrase and the cardinality of the superset.

(2) verbs of division or composition

A related type of trigger of 'exactly n' readings consists of predicates that denote a division or a decomposition of an entity into its constituent parts. The prominence of the 'exactly n' value is less clear than in the previous category, but it is prominent enough to group them with 'exactly n' uses.

> (99) <AMK 314> Sovereignty and EMU The fault, dear Brutus, is not in our stars But in ourselves, that we are underlings. Shakespeare, Julius Caesar . The debate over the future development of the Community has been divided into **two** topics for the purposes of the Intergovernmental Conferences, Economic and Monetary Union, and Political Union. They are intimately connected, for as this chapter will show, acceptance of monetary union implies de facto acceptance of political union.
>
> (100) <B1G 239> However, error introduced into digital map databases through the digitizing process is often ignored because the characteristics of digitizing error have not been fully defined and because no practical means of handling input data uncertainty exist within proprietary GIS software. Sources of error in the digitizing process can be broken down into **two** main streams: source map error and operational error. Source map error includes the accumulated error of the map being digitized, while operational error includes those errors propagated during the digitizing process itself.

These 'exactly n' uses resemble the previous category in that also here the feature of 'exhaustive enumeration' is clearly present, rather than a focus on 'exactness' (as in instances of *exactly two*) or 'identifiability' (when definiteness markers trigger the 'exactly n' value) or even 'non-existence' (as with temporal adverbials). Note that this exhaustive enumeration can also be argued to be part of some 'absolute value' uses. Another example of such a use is presented in (101).

> (101) <GXG 1954> James was beginning to hone his talents as a writer of fiction, and as part of a Trinidad literary circle that included such writers as Albert Gomes and Ralph de Boissière he helped found **two** important, if short-lived, literary journals as outlets for their writing: Trinidad (1929-30) and The Beacon (1931-3).

The crucial difference is, however, that in the latter example no totality is introduced: there is, strictly speaking, no *division* into two parts (the "important, if short-lived, literary journals" are not part of a whole that is explicitly mentioned), there is only the presentation of two "important, if short-lived, literary journals". The totality that delimits the possibilities with respect to the cardinality of the set (the set that in the other cases (99 and 100) is associated with the 'exactly n' reading is absent in this example). This "division" feature adds an "exhaustive" flavor to the enumeration, which is not so prominent in other examples of enumerations. While this distinction, as many others in this discussion, is a subtle one, I do consider the influence of the "division" predicates to be so strong as to justify an 'exactly n' reading. Other predicates in the sample corpus that have the same effect are: *consist of, separate into, comprises.* Another notable 'exactly n' construction is shown in (102).

> (102) <AM4 1570> The `contributing" factors hasten death. They include bark beetles, fungi, viruses and competition. While the complex of possible causes was being investigated, foresters began comparing notes on the common features of the forest decline, the `symptoms" of Waldsterben . The visible signs are of **two** main sorts. The first involve loss of leaf area, through leaves and buds not developing fully, and leaves falling early. This is particularly noticeable in conifers such as yew, spruce or fir, where it makes the canopy increasingly lace-like or transparent. The second involve changes to the branching structure of the tree.[42]

This is a copula-predicate construction, but most of the 'exactly n' uses in this "division" group belong to the adverbial group. Hence, this 'exactly n' factor crosscuts the other distinctions only to a certain extent. It is in fact one of the additional reasons why uses of *two* in adverbial phrases have 'exactly n' values so often.

I would like to emphasize that the influence of this factor is rather weak compared to other 'exactly n' inducing factors: it is the weakest factor that has been discussed so far. The *actually*-test shows this rather clearly.

> (103) !Sources of error in the digitizing process can be broken down into **two**, actually three main streams: source map error and operational error. Source map error includes the accumulated error of the map being digitized, while operational error includes those errors propagated during the digitizing process itself.

The insertion of the *actually*-phrase[43] is still very much unexpected, but it is definitely easier than with, e.g., NPs that combine *two* with a definiteness marker.

> (104) !!<A0X 1197> However, to satisfy the requirements of comfort, the back should curve (in the horizontal plane) to accommodate the back of the rib cage, and there should be no large obstruction to the positioning of the backbone. These **two** [actually three] points provide objections to the ladderback design; with sitters of different

---

[42] Actually, in this case the 'exactly n' reading is reinforced by the presence of the adjective *main* as well (cf. further on in this section). I decided to use it because this is the only example of this kind of construction I found in the sample corpus. Nevertheless, it is easy to see that even if *main* were omitted, the 'exactly n' interpretation would still be valid.

[43] Of course, the fact that only two main streams are mentioned afterwards retroactively enforces a very strong 'exactly n' reading, but that is not relevant here. If we use the *actually*-test, we should also imagine that a third "main stream" is mentioned.

heights, the cross bars can hit prominent vertebrae. The thought of producing many curved back pieces is a bit off-putting.

(3) plural attributive noun constructions

As already discussed in the section on formal properties of numerals (cf. section 4.2. in Chapter 4), *two* quite regularly occurs as a part of a construction in which it modifies a noun that is itself part of a larger nominal construction. Following Quirk et al. (1985:1333) I call these modified nouns "plural attributive nouns".

> (105) <HD4 132> I say this as and one or two others were there for only about 28 hours recently and used sixty units of electricity! Anyway, please could you thank GEORGE most sincerely for his endeavours - the fact that everyone pulls their weight up there ensures the place runs at minimal cost to all users. (I am told the **two** storey six-bed house first on left as one descends the hill rents for £350 or so, yes £350, in high summer).

These constructions also induce an 'exactly n' reading. This can be explained by referring to the meaning of the whole group: the construction *the two-storey six-bed house* introduces *one* house (which itself, incidentally, has an 'exactly n' value due to the definiteness marker) to which some properties are attributed: the fact that it has two storeys and six beds. The existence of the two storeys and the six beds in the house is not directly affirmed; precisely because it is presented as a property, the possibility that there are more (or fewer) than two storeys is more forcefully excluded than in 'absolute value' constructions. The *actually*-test shows that this correction phrase is quite unnatural.

> (106)!! I am told the **two,** actually three storey six-bed house first on left as one descends the hill rents for £350 or so, yes £350, in high summer.

This squares with some of Horn's earliest remarks with respect to numerals: "In general, lexicalization -- or morphemicization -- of cardinals strengthens their implicature" (Horn 1972:46). He does not only list nominal compounds such as *bicycle* or *trio* but also adjectives such as *two-faced* and even *ambidextrous*. Horn claims that the examples mentioned "reflect the general tendency [in this group of more or less "lexicalized" cardinals - BB] and bear the sense of *exactly n, n and only n*: there is no overlap between doubles and triples, twin births are disjoint from triplets (if not always from each other), and a bicycle doesn't have two *or more* wheels, just two" (Horn 1972:47). A similar example is given in (107).

> (107) <FR0 3372> You can't be serious about going on with this," Rosheen protested. `As far as I'm concerned, nothing has changed," he said. `There is the small matter of a splattered ship," she reminded him. He came towards her. `There is the Doctor's ship." `Sorry, but it's a **two** seater," said a familiar voice. They turned to see the Doctor and Bernice approaching. `That's all right," said Sheldukher. `I only have one bottom."

(4) presence of "ordering" numerals adjectives

The final factor I will discuss concerns the presence of "ordering" elements that occur either in front of or right after the numeral. These are of two kinds: either they indicate a sequence of entities (108 and 109), or they indicate the place of the entities in a hierarchy (of importance) (110). The influence of the first kind is hard to gauge, since *first* and *last* in this position in the NP always require a definiteness marker. Since the latter already induces an 'exactly n' interpretation, the contribution of the ordinal[44] is hard to estimate. Intuitively, however, it is certainly present: the typical understanding of *first* and *last* includes the condition that there is a restricted number of entities denoted by the construction "definiteness marker + *first* / *last* + noun". This is due to the definiteness marker which co-occurs with the 'extremity' component of the meaning of *first* and *last*.

> (108) <CGT 1088> Between 1 per cent and 5 per cent of paediatric admissions to hospital are showing failure to thrive (Berwick et al . 1982) and so it is of great concern to primary health care teams. Weight or both weight and height may be affected. It is a disorder of the first **two** years of life and is characterized by a marked deceleration of weight gain and a slowing of the acquisition of developmental milestones.
> (109) <CH3 5354> By the finish of yesterday's race he was 35 seconds ahead of second placed Gerhard Berger - and had covered the equivalent distance of London to Manchester in a little more than one hour and a half. He said: `I am dead chuffed to have got that ninth win. `I just now want to win the last **two** races in Japan and Australia and then it's a new career for me." Senna was third - just ahead of Briton Martin Brundle who was driving half blinded by oil spray over his visor.

As mentioned, it is hard to make hard-and-fast statements about the meaning contribution of *first* and *last* because when they co-occur with a numeral, they are also combined with a definiteness marker. This is different with the "hierarchy series".

> (110) This is, of course, a simplified picture of a sense-spectrum: it should be thought of as having, at least potentially, many dimensions, and as continually growing, amoeba-like. One of the points on the sense-spectrum presented above - and this is typical of the metaphorical variety - has a special status, which manifests itself in **two** principal ways. First, it is the only sense that can appear in a neutral, or minimal context, as in 69: 69. At school, we are doing a project on mouths. It seems unlikely that 69 could be taken to include river mouths.

In this example, the 'exactly n' value is much less prominent than in (108) or (109), which might suggest that the influence of these ordering elements is relatively minor. Then again, the "hierarchy" adjectives do not share the 'extremity' meaning with the ordinals. They do, however, imply that the speaker has made some kind of categorization; i.e. a decision to select

---

[44] Quirk et al. (1985:262) call items like *next* and *last* "general ordinals".

some members of a set as "major". The comparison that this involves causes the interpretation of the numeral to tilt towards the 'exactly n' end of the scale.

The influence of these "hierarchical" adjectives is hard to judge even when no definiteness markers are present. In (110), e.g., *two* is part of an adverbial phrase which refers to entities the existence of which is not really affirmed. This is reminiscent of the temporal entities that have been discussed in the analysis of adverbial phrases. One of the few other examples in the sample corpus, (111), features a similar construction, and most of the others contain definiteness markers (112).

> (111) Stokely Carmichael of the SNCC, one of the emerging radical leaders, summarized these ideas in a single phrase: "What we want," he said, is "black power", and this became the slogan of the more militant black movements from 1966. Tension between the races was increasing for **two** main reasons. First, the strain of maintaining Martin Luther King's advice to "turn the other cheek" was becoming too great to bear in the face of continued attacks and insults. Secondly, the high expectations aroused by civil rights legislation had been disappointed; the conditions of most blacks continued to show little material improvement.
>
> (112) <GX8 563> NOTES OF THE ACCOUNTS 1 Segment information For the purpose of the Companies Act 1985, the operations of the Group constitute one class of business, the exploration for and production of hydrocarbon liquids and gas. Accordingly the loss on disposal of the refining and marketing businesses acquired in 1991 is shown separately. The **two** major operations of the Group are situated in the UK and Indonesia. All other operations are shown under International, previously analysed separately as Asia Pacific/Western and Europe, Africa, Middle East [EAME].

But these constructions are not necessarily excluded from, e.g., object positions.

> (113) In France, we met **two** *extravagant* film directors.

The *actually*-test demonstrates that the influence of *extravagant* is significant. When it is left out, the *actually* phrase becomes less unexpected.

> (114) !!In France, we met **two**, actually three extravagant film directors.
> (115) !In France, we met **two**, actually three film directors.

This effect may be caused by other adjectives as well (116). Also significant is that the more adjectives you add, the stronger the 'exactly n' reading becomes (117).

> (116) In France, we met **two** good-looking film directors.
> (117) In France, we met **two** passionate, English-speaking and good-looking film directors.

The *actually*-test shows this in (117).

(118) !!In France, we met **two**, actually three passionate, English-speaking and good-looking film directors.

This suggests that the 'absolute value'-'exactly n' continuum is also influenced by the precision with which the entity is described. The more precise the description of the entities, the less likely it is that the speaker is ignorant of the exact number of entities.

In this context, it is useful to point to the influence of general "background" knowledge: the *actually*-test is not only influenced by linguistic elements, but also by information with respect to the likelihood of a situation. It is this general world knowledge that explains why, e.g., (119) is decidedly odd.

(119) !!In France, we met twenty-three, actually twenty-four passionate, English-speaking and good-looking film directors.

The reason is simply that it is very unlikely that someone should meet twenty-three passionate, English-speaking and good-looking film directors *and* would like to be precise about the number of directors *and* make a mistake concerning that cardinality judgment, which is then corrected by means of an *actually*-phrase.

5.1.3.8. Relative strength of factors influencing value interpretation

Before taking a look at the value interpretation of uses of numerals in which the expression of cardinality is not maximally prominent, I will try to arrange the factors that influence the value interpretation of fully cardinal uses in a hierarchy. First, it is evident that the strongest factor is the presence of 'exactly' restrictors such as *exactly* and *only*: when these are combined with *two*, the default 'absolute value' interpretation is radically changed to an 'exactly n' interpretation. Second, the same holds for the presence of definiteness markers: they turn the 'absolute value' meaning into an 'exactly n' meaning, but they do this slightly less directly than restrictors like *exactly*. As argued in section 1.2. definiteness markers trigger an 'exactly' interpretation only via the detour of their "identifiability" feature. Therefore, with respect to triggering 'exactly n' interpretations, the presence of these definiteness markers is less strong a factor than the presence of restrictors. Third, the 'exactly n' interpretation can also be triggered by the fact that the entities denoted by the NP containing *two* are not presented as being in existence. This seems to be the case with adverbials (cf. section 5.1.3.1.) locating a state of affairs in time and space. This factor is evidently less strong than the two previous ones: the possibility that there are more than two elements in the set denoted by the adverbial NP or PP is excluded less forcefully than by means of definiteness markers. While the latter is typically used to refer to a number of contextually identifiable entities that are presented as being in existence (so that these entities are singled out, which creates the 'exactly' reading), the former does not single out two elements that are presented as being in existence. The fact that, e.g., "temporal entities" are not singled out causes their 'exactly n' interpretation to be less strong than in combinations of *two* with definiteness markers (and *a fortiori* than combinations with restrictors); the fact that these temporal entities are not presented as being in existence accounts for the fact that they do not have a simple 'absolute value' meaning. Fourth, another factor that creates an 'exactly n' interpretation, but which is still weaker than the previous one, is the presence of verbs of division or decomposition such as *consists of*. This factor may be argued to be less strong than the previous one because it presents the elements of the set as being in existence (which is a typical characteristic of an 'absolute value' use), which temporal adverbials do not. The possibility that there are more than two elements is excluded less forcefully. Finally, there is a distinction between 'absolute value' uses of *two* as part of a subject or a direct object NP: when *two* is not combined with definiteness markers or restrictors, and is not influenced by any of the other factors that have been mentioned either, the utterance containing *two* typically does not explicitly exclude the possibility that there are more than two elements. However, when this use of *two* is part of a subject NP, its interpretation will be slightly more similar to the 'exactly n' interpretation than when it is part of an object NP (cf. section 5.1.3.5.). In other words, while I do not consider the fact that *two* belongs to either a subject or object NP as a factor that can trigger an 'exactly n' interpretation, I do contend that the interpretation of *two* in a subject NP is moved ever so slightly in the direction of the 'exactly n' endpoint of the 'absolute value'-'exactly n' continuum. If it is part of an object NP, *two* is typically simply interpreted as an 'absolute value' use.

5.1.3.9. Influence of pronominality and reduced cardinality

(1) pronominality

Before summarizing the findings, it is necessary to take a look at specific meaning contributions of pronominal uses of *two* and the uses of *two* that are not fully cardinal. I will start with pronominal uses: unproblematic examples of 'absolute value' readings of pronominal *two* can be found in (120) and (121).

> (120) <J0W 419> She admits she was outlandish in her appearance, a walking exaggeration. But she was also beautiful and had a marvellously expressive voice. She was also totally heterosexual. That was, of course, not what people automatically thought of Ken. As they walked across the square, the cobbles echoing the sound of their feet, someone threw a stone - then **two**, then three. A gang of boys were using Kenneth Williams as a mobile target. `I don't remember what he did," she told me, `so I suppose he didn't do anything."
>
> (121) <G0P 2490> She stood in the small sitting-room and ran her finger along the top of a sideboard, drawing a line in the dust that had accumulated. The room was about twelve feet square, furnished with old, antique oak merchandise they'd bought from a shop in Chichester during their first visit to the place. It had few ornaments: a vase or **two**, an ashtray and a couple of ceramic figures. The windows were leaded.

In (121), *two* is part of a larger construction, which has a general 'approximative' meaning. I will analyze this construction more closely when discussing the restrictors (section 6). Another use of *two*, which is, strictly speaking, pronominal is found in the partitive construction in (122).

(122) <B0Y 1554> CD takes this incident from the Annual Register for 1775 where it appears in the `Chronicle" under the date of 14 Mar. Prisoners in the New Gaol, Southwark, who had sawed through their leg-irons, were besieged by turnkeys and constables in the `strong-room": `the prisoners fired several pistols loaded with powder and ball at **two** of the constables: when, the balls going through their hats, and the outrages continuing, one of the constables who had a blunderbuss loaded with shot, fired through the iron gates at the window, and dangerously wounded one fellow

Among the triggers of 'exactly n' values, there is the influence of the mentioning of a superset (123) but also the influence of anaphors (124) and idiomatic expressions (125).

(123) FT2 1503 The HIV serostatus of parents was determined. One hundred and ten people infected with HIV reported 119 children, of whom 60 were dependent - that is, less than 16 years old and living with a parent. Of the HIV infected parents of dependent children, 17 had one dependent child, nine had **two**, and seven had three or more. Twenty four parents were living with partners, six were single parents, and the remainder lived with their own parents.

(124) <K20 661> Tim Russon reports Video-Taped report follows DENIS SMITH/ United Manager MALCOLM CROSBY/United Coach Voice over There was no red carpet for the new Lords of the Manor but then again Denis Smith and his right hand man Malcolm Crosby are not ones for airs and graces. They're **two** of football's straightest talkers with a record of championships cup finals and promotion Denis Smith says he likes winning and he's a football man

(125) <JYA 702> She heard him even after she had lost sight of him, those sure footsteps crunching on the stones. She stood for a long time, trying to make sense of her feelings, the words he had said tumbling around in her brain. He was nice, but he was more dangerous than she had thought. There must be no more cosy dinners for **two**. She might, heaven forbid, allow herself to fall for him, and suffer the fate of the last three nurses whom he had rejected, according to Victoria, after they had expected more from him than just mild flirtation.

In (124), *two* receives an 'exactly n' reading because of two reasons: first, the two individuals in question are mentioned explicitly, and this creates the effect that the possibility that there are more than two is excluded rather forcefully; and second, the anaphorical function of *they* induces an 'exactly n' reading, because the referents of the NP *two of football's straightest talkers* are presented as identifiable. In (125), *two* is part of an idiomatic expression *dinner for two* (cf. also *tea for two*), which excludes, on the level of coded meaning, the possibility that there are three people invited (additionally, there is also the fact that in this construction no entities are presented as being in existence).

(2) reduced cardinality

As mentioned at the very beginning of the corpus analysis of *two*, utterances that feature uses of *two* with "reduced cardinality" were not included. I will now try to analyze how they relate to the discussion concerning the values of *two*.

- *two* as a label

> (126) <HSE 944> Rate of return This method is also deceptive because it takes no account of the timing of receipts. Profit in year **two** is regarded in exactly the same way as profit in year 10. If this method is based on initial capital costs, it strongly favours long-term projects (say, over ten years) against short-term ones and those with good cash receipts in the early years.

For label uses, a discussion of *two* in terms of 'at least / more than n', 'exactly n', 'at most / less than n' or 'absolute value' uses is completely irrelevant.

- *two* in temporal indications (clock)

> (127) <FPL 304> Christine Daaé Raoul put the letter carefully into his pocket. Angry? How could he be angry with an angel? On Thursday he was in the Tuileries Gardens by **two** o'clock. At ten past three he began to feel unhappy. At half past three he wanted to die, or to kill somebody.

Also in temporal indications, the 'value' discussion loses much of its relevance. At the most, temporal indications could be said to be inherently approximative, and in that sense they can be compared with approximative uses of cardinal *two*. This is different from 'absolute value' uses of *two* in that the approximative uses also allow interpretation of *two* in terms of '(slightly) less than two'.

- *two* as the name of a symbol

> (128) <FM5 303> Two hydroxides cos they're just a single negative. Which is O H. O H now how many of those do you want? In brackets. Great. And there are two. Right right. you got the O H is the bit you want twice so write it down put the brackets round it and then the **two**. Right. Hydrogen is positive.

Since in this type of use, *two* does not have any cardinal meaning at all (it is fully nominal), a discussion in terms of "values" is out.

- *two* in mathematical contexts

(129) <KE2 2586> Now, before you right them down just tell me what they are and then we can go back and write them down. Here you've got, minus four and plus three. That's minus one. Good! Minus four and plus six? Two. Plus two, right. Yes, **two**, yeah okay. So write them down cos yo you obviously can do those alright.

In general, *two* in mathematical contexts always has an 'exactly n' value, except when it is explicitly modified by a restrictor (*close to two, approximately two, greater than two* etc.).

- discourse-structural *two*

Also discourse-structural *two* cannot be discussed in terms of the different values of *two*. Even 'approximately n' values are impossible: one cannot introduce the *approximately second* point of a discussion or a speech.

This survey makes clear that less or non-cardinal uses of *two* are generally not susceptible to the subtle value distinctions that are demonstrated by various uses of cardinal *two*. This has never been acknowledged by the neo-Gricean analysts of numerals, who have nonetheless regularly referred to (other) "special" uses of *two* (cf. Horn 1992 on numerals in lexical incorporations and numerals in mathematical statements).

5.1.4. Summary

Our analysis of the difference of 'exactly n' uses and 'absolute value' uses of *two* can be summarized as follows:

1) The 'absolute value' interpretation is the starting-point for the interpretation of *two*. It is the "coded" or "literal" meaning of *two*. By default, uses of *two* are interpreted as denoting the cardinality of a group of entities that are conceptualized as being in existence. This also means that this 'absolute value' meaning is weak: as soon as other factors come into play, the original 'absolute value' interpretation is moved up into the direction of one of the other values, or outright turns the interpretation of *two* into one of these values.

2) I have focused on the distinction between 'absolute value' interpretations and 'exactly n' interpretations and have found a number of factors that influence the interpretation: the introduction of new referents by NPs and their conceptualization as being "in existence", the syntactic function of the NP containing *two*, which was seen to be related to the presence of definiteness markers in the NP and the focal structure of the utterance. Also the fact that temporal and other measurement entities in adverbial NPs containing *two* cannot be said to be "in existence" influences the value of *two*. Finally, a number of relatively minor factors were listed. All factors were felt to be relevant for the interpretation of numerals, but they differ manifestly in the strength of their influence.

3) The existential load of NPs containing *two* is an exclusively "productive" or "positive" component: it introduces a set of referents, indicates the cardinality of this set, but does not say anything about the possibility of there being more (let alone fewer) entities of the type

defined by the noun (within the relevant domain in the universe of discourse). The difference between 'exactly n' and 'absolute value' uses is not so much a truth-conditional question as it is a question of modality: this non-'absolute value' use involves - just like two others (namely 'at least n' and 'at most n') - an expression of the attitude of the speaker with respect to the likelihood of a situation. More specifically, they indicate whether the speaker considers the possibility of there being more or fewer than two entities as explicitly included ('at least') or excluded ('at most', 'exactly')[45].

4) The strongest factor with respect to the value of *two* is the presence of a restrictor: if *exactly* or *only* co-occurs with *two*, a pure instance of 'exactly n' use of *two* is obtained. The second most important factor is the presence of a definiteness marker. When such a marker is combined with *two*, the entities denoted by the NP are usually presented as "identifiable". This correlation between definiteness and identifiability induces an 'exactly n' value of *two*, because the fact that the referents are presented as identifiable implies that each referent has been "scanned" separately. It is this that induces the conceptualization of the cardinality as excluding the possibility of there being more or fewer than two entities.

5) The factor "focus structure" could not be measured directly because of the limitations of a corpus analysis. The best indicator for focus is the intonation structure of the utterance, but as the BNC does not include information about intonation, this could not be evaluated. I decided to look for indirect influence of focus structure, namely the syntactic preferences of focalized elements. Contextual clues in specific corpus examples suggested that a correlation between focus and syntactic constructions can indeed be set up, although the material only allows to formulate general tendencies rather than hard-and-fast rules, because of the multifunctionality of syntactic constructions. There is, however, one direct manifestation of the influence of focus structure on the value of *two*. The traditional analysis of focus assumes that it can be defined as an "answer to a question". In at least one example of the sample corpus[46], *two* functioned as an answer to such a question and hence received an 'exactly n' value.

6) The relative non-existence of temporal (and some other) entities also leads to an 'exactly n' value. This is an example of a relatively weak 'exactly n' use, which means that the possibility of there being more or fewer than two elements is excluded, but not with great force. The weakest factor with respect to the induction of 'exactly n' interpretations is connected with predicates in which a totality is divided into component parts (*divide into, consist of* etc.).

7) The general behavior of *two* can be formulated as follows: if the NP containing *two* also contains an 'exactly n' restrictor or a definite article in front of the *two*, the interpretation of

---

[45] Of course, 'more than n' and 'less than n' uses, which were grouped together with 'at least n' and 'at most n' values respectively, do NOT explicitly indicate an epistemic stance of the speaker. But this does not affect the general remark

[46] In the following utterance, *two* is, by traditional definition, in focus position and receives a strong 'exactly n' value:
<KDN 4779> He's harmless like, you know but but he's harmless, that's what I mean. He just, he, I think he just tries to impress people you know. Mm. It's all army like, constant. Well how long's he been in the army? **Two** years. And it's a life like, you know.

two is always 'exactly two'. If no definiteness marker is present, then the 'exactly n' interpretation may be induced by the focal position of *two* or the presence of temporal entities in the NP. When these 'exactly n' triggers are absent, *two* is interpreted as an 'absolute value' use, but these 'absolute value' uses themselves vary in terms of the force with which they exclude the possibility of there being more than two members in the group (denoted by the NP). A hierarchy was suggested, in which the "meaning contributions" of the various syntactic constructions in which *two* figured were ordered hierarchically. The hypothesis is that if *two* is part of an existential *there* construction or in a direct object phrase, this will generally not alter the default interpretation, while if it occurs in a subject phrase or an adverbial phrase, the interpretation will gradually move up towards the 'exactly' end of the scale. But it was stressed repeatedly that the distinctions between these uses in terms of the syntactic function of the NP to which they belong are very subtle and can be overruled by very many other factors. The only distinction which is relatively transparent is the one between subject and object phrases. The first will typically exclude the possibility of there being more than two elements more forcefully than the latter. The term "'exactly n' value" remains, however, reserved for uses of *two* in which the possibility of there being more than two members is excluded more forcefully, namely when a definiteness-marker is present.[47]

8) These observations are represented in the diagram below: the left-most position on the continuum indicates "pure" 'absolute value' uses of *two*, the rightmost position indicates "pure" 'exactly value' uses of *two*.

```
(AT MOST)-----(+/- ABS VAL)-----'ABS VAL'-----A-----B-----C-----D-----E-----F-----G-----'EXACTLY'
********************************************************/////////////////////////////////////////////////////
          ABSOLUTE VALUE                                        EXACTLY N VALUE
```

(+/- Abs val) and (at most): strictly speaking, these are not part of the continuum, but I have indicated them on the continuum because in this way the diagram captures the fact that the existential component of 'absolute value' uses can be undone by adding "approximators", such as *more or less*. The same holds *a fortiori* for 'at most' uses of *two*. The capital letters stand for intermediate positions caused by the following factors: A: *two* as part of an NP in object position; B: *two* as part of an NP in subject position; C: *two* in *divide into two* and similar constructions; D: *two* in NPs denoting temporal and other entities the existence of which is

---

[47] Note that in the subject/object distinction two factors appear to come into conflict. Definiteness markers indicate "familiarity" or "givenness", and will often occur in subject phrases, which will therefore often have 'exactly n' numerals; focalization often co-occurs with "new" topics, and an extra way of emphasizing the introduction of new topics is by putting them in a subject NP. Both factors are related to the degree of "familiarity" that the hearer is assumed to have with regards to the entities referred to, but in the case of the definiteness marker a higher degree of "familiarity" leads to an 'exactly n' interpretation, while when no definiteness marker is present a lower degree of familiarity (as, e.g., in direct object phrases as opposed to subject phrases) leads to a more "pure" instance of the 'absolute value' meaning. But because the lexical factor (i.e., the presence of a definiteness-marker) is stronger than the discourse-structural factor, namely focalization (which is mediated linguistically by different syntactic constructions that blur the direct influence of focalization), the conflict is always resolved to the advantage of the 'exactly n' interpretation.

not affirmed; E: *two* combined with definiteness markers; F: *two* in combination with 'exactly' restrictors such as *exactly.*

Interestingly, the points of this continuum can also be ordered according to their degree of lexicalization: the more lexical the factor that contributes to the value of *two*, the stronger its influence. This continuum is in perfect harmony with the "value continuum" presented in the diagram: restrictors are maximally lexical and belong to the end-points of the scale (in this case, the 'exactly n' end-point, but it is clear that 'approximately' and 'at most' and 'at least' restrictors are also considerably stronger than the less lexicalized factors on the continuum). Definiteness markers are grammatical rather than lexical elements, but at the very least they are correlated with a series of written or acoustic signs: definiteness is expressed through determiners such as *the, these, those, my* etc. They are less influential than the restrictors because 'definiteness' does not directly pertain to the expression of cardinality, but only indirectly induces an 'exactly n' reading due to their 'identifiability' feature. The fact that the existence of temporal and some other entities is not affirmed as these are introduced in adverbial NPs also induces 'exactly n' interpretations, but this "non-existence" factor is clearly not lexicalized. It is only via an understanding of the function of these temporal NPs in adverbial phrases (namely, localizing a state of affairs rather than introducing new referents) that the 'exactly n' value of *two* in these constructions becomes clear. The link is real, but very indirect, certainly in comparison with the other factors that have just been mentioned. The same holds for the influence of predicates such as *divide into* or *consist of.* Finally, the influence of the syntactic construction to which the NP containing *two* belongs is minimal; it is also the least "lexical" factor. The influence of the syntactic construction can be analyzed as one of the linguistic manifestations of information structure: uses of *two* that are part of focalized NPs or that are in focus position themselves will tend more towards the 'exactly n' part of the scale than uses that are not. Needless to say, "focus" is not a lexical factor.

9) Also the effect of pronominality was analyzed and the "less cardinal" uses of *two* were assessed in terms of the four value positions. The influence of the first factor could largely be traced back to a number of specific constructions that are typical of pronominal uses of *two*. Most of the less or non-cardinal uses could not be evaluated.

5.2. 'AT LEAST / MORE THAN N' AND 'AT MOST / LESS THAN N' USES OF *TWO* IN THE CORPUS AND THE INFLUENCE OF MODALITY

Besides the 'exactly n' uses and 'absolute value' uses, two other groups of uses of *two* have been identified: 'at least n / more than n' (130) and 'at most n / less than n' (131). First, the 'at least n' and 'at most n' uses will be discussed; 'more than n' and 'less than n' uses will be focused on later. As mentioned (cf. section 5.1.1.), 'at least n' and 'at most n' uses explicitly incorporate a modal component: in (130), the possibility that there are fewer than two teams ready to screen 2-4 day old embryos is excluded explicitly; in (131) the possibility that more than two medical experts can be called is ruled out.

(130) <HSL 1107> EUGENIC SCREENING Genetic screening during pregnancy may be done on fluid or tissue samples surrounding the foetus which are obtained using amniocentesis or the newer chorion villi sampling (CVS) procedure. IVF opened the door to genetic testing of embryos in the laboratory. Such embryo screening is called embryo biopsy or preimplantation diagnosis. At least **two** teams here, one at Hammersmith Hospital in London, and one at the University of Edinburgh, are about ready to screen 2-4 day old embryos. Today, genetic screening is expanding due to genetic engineering technology.

(131) <J6V 651> Where both parties intend to rely on experts there should be mutual exchange, medical for medical and non-medical for non-medical. Unless the reports are agreed, the parties are at liberty to call experts whose reports have been disclosed, limited to **two** medical experts and one non-medical expert of any kind. In the county court there is no positive obligation to disclose expert reports but the right to adduce expert evidence is lost unless disclosure is made within 10 weeks.

Remarkably, while the meaning of 'at least n' seems primarily connected with the possibility that there are more than n elements in the set, the over-all effect is also that the lower bound is made explicit. *At least n* does two things: it explicitly opens up the possibility that there may be more than n elements and it underscores the fact that there cannot be fewer than n elements. Because the latter component is combined with the existential meaning that is inherent in NPs (excepting NPs with temporal entities in adverbial phrases etc.), the existence of the set and its cardinality is expressed so that the lower bound, which can be *inferred* from 'absolute value' uses with their existential meaning, is now explicitly confirmed. 'At most n' uses are different in this respect: rather than making the lower bound that is inferable from 'absolute value' uses of *two* explicit, they take it away. They establish an upper bound, and the underlying values ('fewer than n') are presented as a possibility.

The general table (cf. Table 1 at the very beginning of this chapter) with the interpretations of uses of *two* showed that both 'at least / more than n' uses and 'at most / less than n' uses of *two* are rather infrequent in comparison to the 'absolute value' and 'exactly n' uses: only 8% of the uses of *two* have an 'at most / less than' value and only 3.9% have an 'at least / more than' value[48]. This is devastating for the traditional neo-Gricean analysis of numerals, which starts from an 'at least' semantics for numerals. If 'at least n' is the "conventional" or "literal" meaning of cardinals, it should be possible to find many more instances of 'at least n' values of *two* in the sample corpus. More specifically, especially the uses of *two* that do not occur with explicit 'at least', 'at most' or 'exactly' markers should warrant the choice for an 'at least' semantics of numerals (of the important factors influencing the value interpretation of numerals, only those markers were acknowledged to have an influence on the value of the numeral). Of course, other influences were recognized (e.g., negation, the phenomena captured by the concept of "scale reversal", the influence of "roundedness"), but these are all very minor influences in terms of frequency. Of the many

---

[48] With respect to the investigation of the traditional 'at least' semantics of numerals, these figures are actually even more problematic, because the 'at least n / more than n' also contains 'more than n' uses, which are also incompatible with the 'at least' meaning.

linguistic elements that have a direct influence on the value interpretation of numerals (presence of definiteness markers, focus structure, (non-)existence of entities denoted by the NP), only the influence of the restrictors *at least*, *at most*, and *exactly* was considered to be important in the neo-Gricean line of research.

As argued in the theoretical part of this study, if Grice's argument that meaning ultimately has to be described in terms of speaker intentions is accepted, "conventional" meaning must ultimately be assumed to correspond with a large number of intentions that are associated with a large number of uses of *two* (which Grice himself explicitly accepted; cf. Grice 1989 [1957]). Crucially, it is this large number of uses that constitutes the backbone of the "semantics", the "conventional meaning" or even "logical form" of numerals. In true Gricean spirit, the "coded" meaning of *two* is deduced from the intentions with which *two* is used. When the corpus analysis shows that 'at least' uses of *two* are very infrequent compared to 'absolute value' and 'exactly n' uses, it would be simply wrong to adopt 'at least two' as the "coded meaning" of *two*. Nevertheless, this what has happened in the neo-Gricean history of numerals.

Two extra remarks are in order: first, it is certainly true that the corpus analysis differs from the neo-Gricean analysis in that I have opted for a "comprehensive meaning analysis". As mentioned at the beginning of the corpus analysis of *two*, I have decided to look at the interpretation of *two* as it is used together with the other linguistic elements that have an influence on the value of *two*. Only in a second step have I tried to disentangle the meaning contributions of the numeral on the one hand, and the other linguistic elements on the other. The result of this analysis was that the linguistic element *two* (its meaning contribution to the often complex expression of cardinality) can be assigned an 'absolute value' meaning as its coded meaning. This is not what Horn (1972, 1989) and his followers have done: Horn postulated an 'at least' "semantics" of numerals that was alleged to capture the coded meaning of numerals in isolation. This means that the counter-evidence to Horn's analysis cannot simply consist of the results of the "comprehensive" corpus analysis: that would leave an important escape route open. In theory, it would be possible for neo-Griceans to claim that the fact that there are surprisingly few 'at least' uses of *two* in the sample corpus is due to the fact that I have not "filtered out" the meaning contributions of other linguistic elements.

This critique would miss the point in two respects, however. One, the only empirically responsible way to arrive at a specification of the "coded" content of a linguistic element is the investigation of its meaning as it is used, i.e. with respect for the context in which it is used. This entails that the researcher will always have to disentangle the contribution of the element in question from other potential factors. The result of this "purification" is not an 'at least' semantics of *two*, but an 'absolute value' one. Two, even if the selection of uses of *two* is restricted to those and only those uses in which the other factors have minimal influence, the scarcity of 'at least' uses is even more overwhelming. If the selection of uses of *two* is restricted to those in direct object NPs which do not contain restrictors, definiteness markers or temporal or other measurement entities, in which *two* is not in focus position, and in which no supersets are mentioned, then this results in 111 uses of *two*, which all have an 'absolute value' interpretation! The few 'at least' uses that can be found in the whole of the sample corpus are all influenced by other linguistic elements, namely restrictors (the most explicit and strongest among the factors influencing the value of numerals) such as *at least (two), (two) or more* etc.

The second remark concerns the underdeterminacy thesis. If the thesis is accepted that the coded meaning of a sentence is underdetermined and usually has to be "enriched" through Gricean or other mechanisms, then it is in principle not impossible that this underdetermined meaning is so vague (skeletal) that it does not occur as such in actual language use. The evidence in favor of such a view seems rather convincing (Carston 1988, 1998a, 1998b, 1999, Récanati 1989, 1993, 1994, Bach 1994a, 1994b, Levinson 2000). With respect to the analysis of numerals, however, the corpus analysis of *two* clearly showed that this is not the case for numerals: the 'absolute value' meaning of *two* is also the "coded" content of *two*. This 'absolute value' meaning can be described accurately and was shown to be the most frequent interpretation of uses of *two*. Other linguistic elements can contribute to the meaning complex so that the 'absolute value' interpretation is abandoned in favor of an 'at least / more than n', 'at most / less than n' or 'exactly n' value, but the presence of these linguistic elements obscures the "coded" meaning of the numeral *an sich*. Whereas the underdeterminacy thesis delivers a very plausible picture for many other semantico-pragmatic phenomena, it is not necessary, nor in any way expedient, nor "theoretically economical", to adopt an underdeterminacy-analysis for English cardinals: their "coded content" is perfectly self-sustaining, in that no extra "enrichment" procedures have to be presupposed in order to arrive at "what is said", its "explicature", its "implicatures" or its "meaning".

Let us return to the 'at least' and 'at most' uses of *two* as they can be found in the sample corpus. It is clear that these uses are always caused by the presence of explicit 'at least' or 'at most' markers in the corpus[49]. Some of the triggers are exemplified below. In (132), there is a "long-distance" effect of the restrictor *at least*, which ranges over the entire list of items, while (133) provides a rather verbose synonym of *at least two* - the addition of *absolute* is yet another way to focus on the lower bound. This shows that speakers sometimes feel the need to stress the exclusion of the other possibility (i.e., that a number less than two might be meant) even more forcefully than it is already done by using *at least*. In (134), the 'at least' interpretation is also induced by a restrictor, be it one of the "interval" kind: the patients had short segment colonic interposition of the oesophagus from *two to twenty years* before undilatable peptic stricture. This induces a variety of the 'at least' interpretation of *two*: normally, 'at least' uses of *two* are open-ended in that no upper bound is indicated. This is not the case in (134): the interval restrictor clearly establishes an upper limit, namely 'twenty years'. A similar construction can be found in (135), although the 'at least' value is not as clear as in (134): the phrase *two or three Ns* also implies an approximative value. That means that the possibility of there being a small hamlet with only one farm is not excluded very forcefully (in contrast, the possibility that the patients had had short segment colonic interposition of the oesophagus less than two years before undilatable peptic stricture is excluded rather forcefully in (134)): if the speaker should make clear in the rest of his discourse that there are actually a small number of the 500+ settlements that contained only

---

[49] It is remarkable that 'at most' meanings are very rarely triggered by the restictor *at most* itself. In fact, one thousand uses of *two* did not contain a single instance of *at most two*. An extra query revealed that the whole BNC contains only eight occurrences of *at most two*.

one farm, this would not be totally unexpected. In (136), this is demonstrated by the *actually*-test[50].

> (132) <BLW 109> Here are some medically recommended guidelines from which you can plan your own menus: Every day eat at least: one helping of one of the following: lean meat, white fish, poultry, cheese, nuts one helping of: brown cereals, wholemeal bread, potatoes **two** helpings of one of the following: green vegetables, a large mixed salad, fruit one pint of fluid such as: water, soup, low calorie drink, lemon tea Remember that how you cook food is also important.
>
> (133) <BNY 845> The ferrets force the rabbits to abandon their homes and bolt to the surface, where they can be killed by a number of methods. Or the rabbits sit tight underground as they become cornered by the ferrets. They are then either killed by the ferrets or are subsequently dug out alive. A team of ferrets should number an absolute minimum of **two** and that is only sufficient if you pursue the sport only infrequently.
>
> (134) <HWS 3809> There is no information on the ambulatory motility patterns of transposed segments of colon in their new location between the oesophagus and stomach, functioning as a neo-oesophagus. Patients and methods Ten asymptomatic patients who had had short segment colonic interposition of the oesophagus **two** to 20 years previously for undilatable peptic stricture, underwent ambulatory manometric recordings in their short colonic segments. Their mean age at operation was 48 years, with a range of 21 to 67.
>
> (135) <H8U 763> In Somerset, the majority of the 500+ deserted settlements identified so far were formerly small hamlets of **two** or three farms and not large nucleated villages.
>
> (136) In Somerset, the majority of the 500+ deserted settlements identified so far were formerly small hamlets of **two** or three farms, actually in some cases only one farm, and not large nucleated villages.

The same kind of restrictors can be found with 'at most' uses of *two*: in (137) and (138), the most frequent 'at most' constructions are exemplified, namely *an N or two* and *one or two Ns*. Both combine the 'at most' meaning with an 'approximative meaning', just like *two or three* combined the 'at least' meaning with an approximative meaning. In (139), there is an 'at most' use of *two,* but from a different perspective: while *at most two* implies a view from the maximal number to anything that is less than the maximum, *up to two* conceptualizes the interval between zero and two as a rising movement with the maximal value 'two' as an endpoint of that movement.

---

[50] Admittedly, this version of the *actually* test differs from earlier applications of the test, because in this case *actually* was combined with the phrases *in some cases*. This utterance describes a very large number of settlements (500+), and this large number ranges over the number of hamlets (the total number of hamlets could be estimated by multiplying *500+* by *two or three*). This makes the application of the *actually* test considerably easier. Hence, this statement (and the result of the test) only applies to this utterance, and should not be generalized to every occurrence of *two or three*. I will come back to the meaning of this phrase when discussing the restrictors.

(137) <CL3 472> `Of course I shall, my love. I shall like it anywhere, just as long as you're with me!" It was late afternoon when they reached the hotel. It sprawled along the crest of the hill, an old house, many-gabled, curiously shaped, as if succeeding generations had added whatever took their fancy, a wing here, a chimney or **two** there. Yet the whole was harmonious, welded together beneath the vast expanse of Virginia creeper which covered the walls to the eaves.

(138) <EFT 16> Ordinary people saw him, heard him, touched him, lived with him. But we were not there ourselves. Nor can we know what Jesus was like, what he said and did by consulting the secular historians of the time. They will only tell us that a Jewish prophet called Jesus lived, preached, fell foul of the authorities and was executed. One or **two** may also suggest some knowledge of his resurrection. But that is as far as it goes.

(139) <ASB 1039> In 1957 the Birkett Committee recommended that unauthorized tapping should be a criminal offence. Some twenty-eight years later that proposal was finally implemented. Section 1 of the Act provides that it is an offence for a person intentionally to intercept a postal communication or a telecommunication. Conviction could lead to a fine or imprisonment of up to **two** years, or both. But here the progress ends.

As already mentioned, 'more than n' uses of *two*, and 'less than n' uses of *two* were grouped together with 'at least n' and 'at most n' respectively. In (140) and (141) the possibility of 'absolute value two' is excluded, which is not the case in typical 'at least' uses of *two*. In the category of 'at most n/ less than n uses' also instances of *almost two* (142) and *less than two* (143) were included. In (144), a time span is presented and the preposition *within* indicates that *two years* is the upper bound of the period in which the faults can occur.

(140) <AAU 144> Mr Simon Montgomery, administrator of the Brighton Unemployment Centre, which obtained a copy of the review, said yesterday: `We are establishing a new category of people who may have to be outside the welfare net - people with mental health problems who form part of the new underclass." The Government forecasts that the number of people out of work for more than **two** years will fall from 550,000 in April 1989 to 325,000 by April 1991. The `major constraints" of the housing market means there is no viable case for encouraging people to move home to find work, the review says.

(141) <EUU 220> Licensed dealers can be slow to deliver share certificates. One of the author's former clients is still awaiting certificates for American stocks he bought through the crashed Sheridan Securities over **two** years ago, a familiar story to clients of many licensed dealers (and many clients deal through several).

(142) <ANF 979> `Can't you work on it a little more?" he asked Modigliani. `You know we sculptors like a little more mud, a little more substance." Modigliani agreed reluctantly: `If you want me to ruin it I can continue." For almost **two** weeks Modigliani worked on the painting, an unusually long time for him and perhaps the only time when he agreed to `continue" a painting.

(143) <FD8 214> `Relevant time" is defined in similar terms to those applicable to companies so far as preferences are concerned, but a more extended period, of five years, is provided for transactions at an undervalue. The need for insolvency at the relevant time does not apply to transactions at an undervalue entered into less than **two** years before the individual is adjudged bankrupt.

(144) <K2L 900> The quality of the cabinet and its fittings is vital. If you have seen kitchens where the doors refuse to hang correctly, where shelves cannot be adjusted or where drawers refuse to open the chances are it's because `savings" have been made and lower quality materials have been used. All of these faults can occur within **two** years of the kitchen being installed and the cost of mending the damage is often more than it would be to replace all the cabinets - so it's better to check.

More interesting are the uses of *two* that are combined with modal expressions other than the restrictors that have been discussed up to now. As mentioned (cf. especially section 3.2.1. and 3.2.2. in Chapter 3), it was precisely this kind of construction that urged Carston (1985, 1998a) to introduce the 'at most' position in the cardinal debate. Unfortunately, not a single instance of this was found in the sample corpus: either the 'at most' or the 'at least' reading was already triggered by other factors (i.e. presence of restrictors), or modal expressions were simply lacking. Let us look at Carston's original examples first.

(Carston 1998a:204)

(145) She can have 2000 calories without putting on weight.

(146) The council houses are big enough for families with three kids.

(147) You may attend six courses (and must attend three).

These examples are not only important for the description of how 'at most' interpretations can arise in modal contexts, at first sight they also pose problems for the general 'absolute value' analysis of numerals. If the numeral in question is supposed to have an 'absolute value' as its "coded meaning", how can it ever result in an 'at most' reading of the same numeral? As we have seen, the 'absolute value' analysis determines the meaning of a cardinal numeral as denoting the cardinality of a set of entities, without any *explicit* commitment of the speaker with respect to the possibility of there being more or there being fewer than n entities in the set in question. In Carston's (1998a) underdeterminacy analysis, the general underlying and underspecified meaning of *two* was represented as [X [TWO]]. The X signals that this logical form is in need of enrichment; the values of X can be either 'at least', 'at most' or 'exactly'. My analysis differs in two crucial respects: one, the abstract [X [TWO]] formula is replaced by an 'absolute value' meaning of *two*; two, this 'absolute value' meaning does not *need* to be enriched. If the meaning of *two* is altered, it is not an instance of "enrichment", it is not even a pragmatic effect at all, it is simply the effect of other linguistic elements that contribute to the expression of cardinality. I have described elaborately how subtle the distinctions between 'absolute value' uses and 'exactly n' uses of *two* can be, and I have given examples of how 'at least' and 'at most' values can come about. In Carston's examples, however, at first sight there do not seem to be explicit markers of 'at least' or 'at most' interpretations; no restrictors are present at all.

The solution to the puzzle was already suggested by Scharten:

[Carston's] examples have in common that the quantities given (*2000 calories, three kids, [six courses]*[51]) function as an upper limit. Carston presents these cases as one more problem for the Radical Pragmatics theory of cardinal numbers. However, regarding the "at most" reading as a third possible interpretation for numerals is not the only possible line with respect to these examples. The possibility that the "at most" reading is forced by the semantics of other lexical items in these cases is not considered. Both *can* and *enough* are modal predicates that involve some implication of an upper bound, which may lead to the "at most" reading for the numerals. [...] The numerals are used to indicate a cardinality, and the fact that this cardinality represents an upper bound does not follow from the numeral by itself, but results from the main sentence predicate in these cases. (Scharten 1997:54)

This reasoning is supported by three other examples in Scharten's dissertation, and she draws attention to the "semantics of *criteria* or *requirements*" (Scharten 1997:55) as triggers for 'at most' readings of numerals. In fact, Scharten's analysis (which differs from ours in a number of important other respects, cf. section 3.1.3. in Chapter 3 for the discussion of focus in DTT, cf. section 5.1.3.6. below for a more general comparison) is clearly a precursor of the 'absolute value' analysis, in that it also explains some non-'absolute value' uses of numerals in terms of the meaning contribution of other linguistic elements. Carston (1998a:206-207) acknowledges this line of reasoning: "It doesn't seem implausible that the right semantics of the right modal operators operates (in some way yet to be specified) on the bilateral semantics of the cardinals to weaken them in the one direction or the other, though [Scharten] does not attempt to show this"[52]. In short, what happens in Carston's 'at most' examples is that the modals take the place of the 'at most' restrictor. As the discussion will show, the so-called "possibility / permission" modals usually trigger an 'at most' reading, while the "necessity" modals leave the 'absolute value' meaning of the numeral intact. As Scharten has stressed, the presence of a possibility modal creates a context in which an upper bound is indicated: the specification of what is allowed or possible, induces the interpretation that what is not explicitly indicated as allowed / possible is actually not allowed / possible. With necessity modals, the speaker simply indicates what is necessary, but does not explicitly mention the possibility of there being more than n elements, neither to include it, nor to exclude it. That is why the combination of necessity modals + numerals leaves the 'absolute value' of the numeral intact.

I decided to run a number of extra queries to investigate the effect of modal expressions on the interpretation of numerals. Obviously, only some of the English modal expressions were selected, more or less at random: I did queries on *may _ two* (99 solutions),

---

[51] Scharten quotes from Carston's (1985) paper, which used the utterance *You can have half the cake.* I use the 1998 version, because that version contained only examples with cardinals.

[52] In this quote, Carston seems to favor a bilateralist ('exactly n') semantics for numerals, but in the discussion of numerals a few pages later, she shows a mild preference for her own underdeterminacy thesis.

need _ two (123 solutions), *must _ two* (64 solutions). One non-verbal modal expression was
selected: *necessary _ _ two* (27 solutions)[53]. The results are presented in Table 8:

TABLE 8

VALUES OF *TWO* + MODAL EXPRESSION

	ABS VAL	AT LEAST / MORE THAN	AT MOST / LESS THAN	EXACTLY	OTHER[54]
may _ two	-	4/99 (4.0%)	75/99 (75.8%)[55]	-	20/99 (20.2%)
need two	87/123 (70.7%)	12/123 (9.8%)	11/123 (8.9%)	8/123 (6.5%)	5/123 (4.1%)
must _ two	41/64 (64.1%)	3/64 (4.7%)	-	-	20/64 (31.2%)
necessary _ two	16/27 (59.3%)	2/27 (7.4%)	1/27 (3.7%)	-	8/27 (29.6%)

The most remarkable result is undoubtedly the asymmetry between *must, need* and
necessary results for 'absolute value' uses (for all three more than fifty percent) and the
absence of 'absolute value' uses for *may*. The crucial difference between the former and the
latter is that the first are necessity modals, while the latter is a possibility modal. Let us
compare an instance of *may two* with an example of *must two*.

(148) <J2T 781> A Berlin research institute is developing a scheme by which micro-
organisms will feed on abandoned Trabant cars, large numbers of which have been
discarded by their former East German owners in favour of more modern Western
models. Disposal of the Trabants has presented problems since the chassis is
constructed of synthetic resin and Soviet cotton wool waste, which break down into
low-level toxic materials. Research on the project **may** last **two** years, but its director,
Franz Weissbach, is confident that, once the process is perfected, a Trabant chassis
could be completely consumed by the microbes in two weeks.
(149) <ABJ 2278> Unfortunately the good parts of Mr Pavlov's new plan are likely to
be overwhelmed quickly by the bad. To work, any Soviet economic plan **must** do **two**
things. First, stabilise the macroeconomy. This means cutting the budget deficit,

---

[53] In BNC queries, the underscore "_" stands for "any word", "_ _" stands for "two or more words".
[54] This category contains all sorts of uses that are not relevant for the discussion at hand: either *two* formed part
of a larger numeral, or it was not a fully cardinal use of *two*, or the scope of the modal did not include *two* as in
the following example:
<AAJ 53> Broker Maclaine Watson **must** pay **two** Shearson Lehman Hutton companies more than £55million in
damages for breach of contract after the collapse of tin prices in October 1985, a court ruled yesterday.
The constituent "£55million" could be argued to be in the scope of *must*, but *two* definitely is not.
[55] These are actually all 'at most n' uses; no 'less than n' uses were found.

freeing prices and trade, and preventing accumulated savings from causing an inflationary expansion of demand. Second, create the microeconomic conditions under which enterprises can thrive. This requires privatisation.

The instance of *two* in (148) was interpreted as an 'at most' use of *two*, the one in (149) as an 'absolute value' use. As Table 8 shows, these are the most frequent values for the two queries. What is the difference? In (148) *may* installs an upper bound on the extension of the time span and this upper bound is determined as 'two years'. In (149), there is no upper bound, which is not surprising since with a necessity modal, no upper bound is expected. If anything, a lower bound would be expected. But this is not what is found in the sample corpus: only 4.7% of the *must _ two* uses can be interpreted as 'at least / more than two'. In (149), e.g., the NP *two things* introduces 'two things' and of these two things it is said that the entity denoted by the subject NP, namely *any Soviet economic plan*, must do them. The two elements of an 'absolute value' use of *two* are present: the introduction of a set of entities that will come into existence[56] and the absence of an explicit indication of the speaker as to the possibility of there being more or fewer than two things that any Soviet economic plan must do. The *actually*-test shows that the cardinality can be changed rather easily.

(150) Unfortunately the good parts of Mr Pavlov's new plan are likely to be overwhelmed quickly by the bad. To work, any Soviet economic plan **must** do **two**, actually three, things. First, stabilise the macroeconomy. This means cutting the budget deficit, freeing prices and trade, and preventing accumulated savings from causing an inflationary expansion of demand. Second, create the microeconomic conditions under which enterprises can thrive. This requires privatisation.

This is not the case in (148): the cardinality expressed in (148) can be captured by the phrase *at most two*. This does not mean, however, that *two* in itself is changed from expressing an 'absolute value' meaning to an 'at most' meaning. The time span of the research on the project is described as an interval from an indefinite period of time to two years. The meaning contribution of *two* and the NP to which *two* belongs is the presentation of a period of two years, or, more precisely, 'absolute value' *two* years. The modal then conceptualizes this period as an upper bound, and this creates the 'at most' effect. This 'at most' reading should not be ascribed to the function of *two*, nor to the NP containing *two*, but is a direct effect of the presence of *may*. The possibility modal *may* has a similar effect on other NPs.

(151) Q: Do you have to write this paper this week?
A: The teacher told me I *may* write it this week (but I can write it next week just as well).

May explicitly opens up other possibilities; it explicitly refers to the existence of other possibilities. The fact that in combination with *two may* opens up the possibility of there being

---

[56] The fact that the entities in question are not presented as already being in existence is of course due to the presence of the modal *must*, which establishes a requirement.

fewer than two entities, and does not open up the possibility of there being more can be explained from the combined effects of *two* and *may*. The presence of *may* turns the sentence into a determination of what is possible (or allowed, in the deontic version). Since it is combined with a determination of a stretch of time the length of which is indicated by referring to a set of temporal entities the cardinality of which is two, it can readily be inferred that this stretch of time is included in what is possible / allowed. From the determination of what is allowed / possible, it is possible to infer what is not allowed, namely the semantic complement of what is possible / allowed. Hence, *may* in combination with *two* induces an upper bound, and not a lower bound. This argument is remarkably similar to the neo-Gricean explanation of how implicatures work. I will not delve into the question whether this account of *may* should be supported by a neo-Gricean reasoning (with all its presuppositions) or whether the complementarity of what is possible / allowed and what is not possible / allowed is a sufficient explanation. Important for the account of numerals is the realization that the 'at most' value of utterances in which *two* is combined with possibility modals derives from the meaning contribution of *may*, not from that of *two*.

   Must and the two other necessity modals that have been analyzed show a different situation.

> (152) <CET 1549> But, of course, all the probabilities cannot be simultaneously reified in a single Universe: while it may not seem to matter much, on the cosmic scale, if an electron is in two places at once, in fact the later consequences of that tiny discrepancy might be enormous. The obvious, although unpalatable, conclusion is that there must be **two** universes, one for each of the electrons.

This use of *two* is interpreted as an 'absolute value' use of *two*, because *must* in (152) indicates what is necessarily the case: the speaker does not mention the possibility of there being more than two universes explicitly, neither does he or she exclude it explicitly. The combination of a necessity modal and a numeral seems similar to what happens in 'at least' uses of *two*, because in both cases the lower bound is explicitly stressed: the speaker stresses that the cardinality is certainly 'not less than two'. The difference between 'at least' uses and the combination of necessity modal + numeral is that in the latter the possibility of there being more than n elements is explicitly mentioned in the first, while this is absent in the last. That is why I decided to label the combination of a necessity modal + numeral an 'absolute value' use.

   The same reasoning as the one underlying the description of *must _ two* holds for instances of *need _ two* (153) and *necessary _ _ two* (154).

> (153) <JA0 717> Of course they do Yes. but if you don't tell them that on the phone when you come it this is what I want Yes okay I yeah and it could be and if if there's two signatures if there are two signatures require on the on the cheque we **need two** on the banker's order and you need both of those people there. If they're not and left that you'd never see it again. They'll loose it they'll loose it in their system.
> (154) <EEM 965> The book of nature, he insisted, had been written in the language of mathematics. No amount of theologizing could be a substitute for mathematical

analysis. In evaluating the Copernican system, for example, mathematical criteria should take precedence over interpretations of Scripture, which may have become normative but only through ignorance. The differentiation went one stage further because Galileo found it **necessary** to distinguish **two** senses in which a biblical text could be construed.

Note that both uses of *two* are excellent examples of 'absolute value' uses: in (153), two signatures are required. This does not mean that *at least two* signatures are required: nothing is said as to the possibility of there being more than two signatures (this also means that this possibility is not explicitly excluded). The same holds for (154): Galileo is presented as having found it necessary to distinguish two senses, and nothing more than that is expressed. In this case it is indeed very doubtful whether there was a third sense in which one could construe a biblical text according to Galileo. But the fact remains that this possibility is not explicitly excluded.

The other values in these combinations of *two* with modal expressions usually come about through the presence of restrictors. In (155) *may* is combined with the phrase *two or more*, which triggers an interesting situation: *may* normally induces an 'at most' interpretation of *two*, but this is undone by the addition of *or more*. *May* indicates what is allowed: if *two* had not been modified by *or more*, this would yield an 'at most' reading, but now it is explicitly indicated that more than two deputy heads are allowed as well. The value of *two* in (155) is such that it allows 'two', 'less than two' and even 'more than two'. In (156), an 'exactly n' reading is triggered due to the presence of *only*. This shows that restrictors are stronger factors than expressions of modality with respect to the influence on the expression of cardinality.

(155) <H8D 1173> Head teachers' salaries are linked to the number of pupils in their school. Deputy head teacher The deputy head assists the head in the running of a school, often liaising between the head and the rest of the staff. Large secondary schools **may** have **two** or more deputy heads, with defined areas of responsibility (e.g. for the curriculum); primary schools normally have one. As with heads, their salaries are linked to the number of pupils in the school.

(156) <J13 3853>`What for?" asks the breadhead. He is already through the gate and starting down the slope. Even Dixie looks surprised. `I'll keep a lookout." `The Muddie's empty," the breadhead says. `Almost." The breadhead doesn't like it, but Dixie claps him on the shoulder and laughs. `We only **need two**," he says. I wait by the gate as they pick their way down to the slimy bottom of the dip.

Remarkable is the effect of the epistemic use of *may* on the modal operator *need*: in (157) *may* clearly takes scope over *need* with respect to the expression of cardinality. The over-all effect is an 'at most' reading, and this would be the effect of *may* if *need* was replaced by a non-modal expression (158).

(157) <ACX 2556> Take the frozen water bottle, remove the lid, invert and rest on the compost towards the centre of the plants. As the ice slowly melts the plants are

watered over a long period. This is particularly useful if done before leaving for work on hot days. Larger containers may **need two** water bottles.

(158)   Larger containers may contain **two** water bottles.

In general, only the presence of other markers will turn the default 'absolute value' meaning of *two* into other values. Another remarkable element, which has not yet been discussed here, is negation. In (159), negation turns the 'absolute value' meaning of *two* into a 'less than' value (which was grouped with 'at most' uses, for reasons of simplicity). I will come back to the effect of negation in a separate section.

(159) <KCD 2208> I no, but it doesn't come out scarlet, how much you need. Hey, there isn't any other magazines, there not there. What maga- oh no there aren't. Haven't got any other Early Learning Centre ones. You had them. Well I use to have, but I threw them away cos you don't really need **two** . Oh mummy . Oh I'm sorry. I didn't know you were so interested in them. You hadn't looked at them. I want to look at them .

5.3. NEO-GRICEAN ARGUMENTS IN THE CORPUS ANALYSIS OF *TWO*

Besides a general corpus analysis of uses of *two*, I also tried to test the neo-Gricean arguments in favor of a two-layered analysis of numerals. More specifically, the following two tests were implemented:

- suspension and cancellation phrases
- redundancy of restrictors

I also investigated the influence of negation on the interpretation of numerals.

5.3.1. Defeasibility: the cancellation and suspension tests

The argument in favor of a Gricean analysis that has been used most frequently is the so-called defeasibility of the 'exactly' implicature that is supposedly triggered by the Quantity 1 maxim (cf. Chapter 2). I will divide the discussion concerning defeasibility in an analysis of the suspension test and an analysis of the cancellation test, because these tests differ in certain respects.

5.3.1.1. The suspension test
I will start with the suspension test. When the discussion is restricted to fully cardinal uses of *two* (including the pronominal uses), in 823/857=96% of the cases the suspension test cannot be applied. Let us consider some examples from the sample corpus in which the suspension test cannot be implemented.

(160) <BMC 2279> What is interesting about this disc is the way in which Padilla, presumably familiar with the polyphonic style of his peers, including that of Victoria, crossed the Atlantic at a time of considerable change in European music only to uphold and preserve the traditions of Spain's musical heritage. Piers Schmidt handles the contrasts between each session of the **two** Masses on this disc with sensitivity, making the most of Padilla's double-choir writing in the Missa ego flos campi .

(161) <CB2 1181> It was a stunning performance, and certainly one of the finest that the league has ever produced. Down in the dungeon of the first division, Rosslyn Park and Nottingham are still to get off the mark. In the driving seat to replace whoever goes down are London Scottish . Their 7-6 win over previously unbeaten West Hartlepool leaves then as one of only **two** unbeaten teams in the Courage national divisions. Sale' s 16-6 win over Bedford hoists them to the second promotion slot. Liverpool St Helens' fall continues, a 9-6 defeat at Blackheath leaving them clamped to the bottom of Division Two just a year after they dropped out of the first division.

(162) <H9L 2950> 'Why should I want to remember?" Irritably, she picked up on his previous point. 'Yesterday you were the one who didn't seem to want reminding of of the whole disaster. No post-mortems, you said." 'What I want and what I'm going to get are **two** very different things." Luke paused. 'Are you trying to pick a fight? Quarrels are for lovers."

The presence of the definiteness marker *the* (163) and the restrictor *only* (164) turn the 'absolute value' meaning of *two* into an 'exactly' reading, which is incompatible with the suspension phrase.

(163) ??Piers Schmidt handles the contrasts between each session of the **two**, if not three Masses on this disc with sensitivity, making the most of Padilla's double-choir writing in the Missa ego flos campi .

(164) ??Their 7-6 win over previously unbeaten West Hartlepool leaves then as one of only **two**, if not three unbeaten teams in the Courage national divisions.

Also the introduction of two things before the NP containing *two* is mentioned (which refers back to these entities), as in (162), obstructs the suspension mechanism (165):

(165) ??'What I want and what I'm going to get are **two**, if not three very different things."

But the presence of other linguistic elements that turn the 'absolute value' meaning into 'exactly n' values is not the only factor responsible for the sabotage of the suspension test.

Two more interesting reasons are the phenomenon that is described as "scale reversal" and what I will call "unreasonable doubt". The first, "scale reversal", was already noted by Horn (1972:41-45). He said that the scales were usually reversed when ordinal numbers were used, but he also noted cases of scale reversal with cardinals as in (166).

(Example taken from Horn 1972:43)
(166) Nixon pledged to reduce the troop strength (or *ceiling*) to 30,000 if not
(to) 25,000 / *35,000.

He argued that "[s]uch instances of scale reversal generally involve implicit (if not explicit) reference to circumstances under which the normal entailment relations of sentences with cardinal numbers are permuted, and their implicatures adjusted accordingly" (Horn 1972:42). This explains why normal suspension phrases are not applicable in instances such as the following.

(167) <AR9 85> SAVE has published a whole series of reports on country houses at risk, entitled Tomorrow's Ruins, Silent Mansions and Endangered Domains , illustrating fine houses under threat. The rewarding part is that over two thirds usually find new owners or new uses within **two** years. In 1989 SAVE's Empty Quarters included every kind of listed building from cottages to a cathedral (the Roman Catholic Cathedral in Middlesbrough).
(168) <EFU 332> If it all tasted as beguiling as it looks, every dish would be a feast. **Two** courses out of the whole menu would be more than enough. Now that little meal of de Pomiane's is a feast, as a whole entity.

The suspension phrase *if not three* is clearly problematic in both examples.

(169) ??The rewarding part is that over two thirds usually find new owners or new uses within **two**, if not three years.
(170) ??If it all tasted as beguiling as it looks, every dish would be a feast. **Two**, if not three courses out of the whole menu would be more than enough.

But while the problem with (168) is easily solved by supplying a lower value instead of a higher one (171), this does not work so well for the other example.

(171) If it all tasted as beguiling as it looks, every dish would be a feast. **Two**, if not one course out of the whole menu would be more than enough.
(172) ?The rewarding part is that over two thirds usually find new owners or new uses within **two**, if not one year.

This clearly has to do with what I have called "unreasonable doubt". In order to be able to add a suspension phrase to an existing utterance in a specific context, there should be room for doubt: (167) is manifestly a part of a report on a series of reports. In that context, it is highly unlikely that the speaker (in this case probably the writer) should have doubts concerning the length of the period in which houses find new owners. Other examples of this unreasonable doubt can be found in the following excerpts.

(173) <A77 42> This container is fitted to one of the man's legs shortly before the drop, and is lowered from the body on a rope once the parachutist has left the aircraft.

This allows it to land nearby but not interfere with the descent. Using this method a full C-130 Hercules aircraft load of ninety heavily-laden troops can be dispatched from **two** parallel side doors in no more than forty-five seconds. The drop is from 800 feet, giving an individual time of descent of about forty seconds, depending on individual weights. A total of 1,280 soldiers will be deployed this way during the course of the exercise.

(174) <AM0 1332> But if you're looking for old style Cretan atmosphere as well as a place that's full of life, Ag Nik is the place to stay. A natural harbour, set between **two** rocky headlands, forms a centre point from which narrow streets wind uphill. Around the harbour, fishermen's tavernas still jostle side by side with the newer cafés and bars which have sprung up to cater for the younger market, and the main daytime activity seems to be relaxing over a quiet glass of something while watching the boats chug in and out.

Both in (173) and (174) the insertion of *if not three* would be highly problematic, not because of the presence of scale-reversing elements or circumstances, but because the respective discursive contexts simply do not allow doubt. They do allow a correction.

(175) Using this method a full C-130 Hercules aircraft load of ninety heavily-laden troops can be dispatched from **two** - excuse me - three parallel side doors in no more than forty-five seconds.

(176) A natural harbour, set between **two** - I mean three - rocky headlands, forms a centre point from which narrow streets wind uphill.

Note that the "repair" phrases are considerably stronger than the *actually*-phrases, and they must be.

(177) !Using this method a full C-130 Hercules aircraft load of ninety heavily-laden troops can be dispatched from **two,** actually three parallel side doors in no more than forty-five seconds.

With an *actually*-phrase, the correction still looks very artificial. Also in (178), the room for doubt is virtually non-existent. The "presentation" mode of the discourse is not compatible with the doubt introduced by the *if not* phrase. In this context, it is not plausible that the speaker/writer is not sure about the number of stories the building has. The "narrative" mode in (179) is not dissimilar to the presentation mode in (178) - it is very implausible that the narrator of a story (with herself as the protagonist of the story) would have doubts as to how many shocks came on the first morning[57]. In (180), it is not very plausible that the speaker / writer should leave room for doubt with respect to the number of men the plaintiff had

---

[57] Perhaps there is even more at stake than mere plausibility. I might venture the claim that the discursive script for "narrating a story with oneself as protagonist" excludes the possibility of expressing doubts as to the number of relevant events that have occurred. In that scenario, it would not merely be *implausible* that the speaker should say *On the first morning came* **two,** *if not three shocks*, it would be a "violation" of the rules of the "script" of that particular narrative act.

committed adultery with, in view of the very matter-of-fact flavor of the surrounding statements. It is in the interests of the speaker to present the facts with maximal certainty. Even considering the fact that the case against the plaintiff would be stronger if the possibility that there were not only two, but possibly also three men involved, this would reduce the persuasive power of the speaker.

(178) <HP8 30> Johnson Matthey's new technical centre at Kitsuregawa Japan, KITEC for short, is located in the rolling countryside of Tochigi prefecture some 170 kilometres to the north east of Tokyo. It is a green field development of around four acres and the centre itself has two main buildings and a number of smaller buildings for services. The main building, which has floor space of around 40,000 square feet on **two** stories, houses a pilot plant for the production of autocatalysts, a pilot plant for the production of fuel cell catalysts and a fabricated products area as well as full analytical capabilities to support these activities.

(179) <B22 12> We had also heard frightening stories about the teachers but with one exception I always found them very fair. If you stepped out of line, then look out, but you quickly learned to do as you were told at the greatest possible speed. On the first morning came **two** shocks - I found that Christian names were dropped - from now on I was Maidment. Nicknames are a favourite pastime with small boys and so during the next four years and one term I was known to my school mates as `Pavement".

(180) <HB3 541> martin and others v owen tlr 21.5.92 the likelihood of divorce can be taken into account when assessing damages for dependency . court should not shut its eyes to fact that statistically one in three marriages end in divorce. the chance would be substantially reduced if the marriage had already lasted some time and there were children. in this case the plaintiff had committed adultery with **two** different men in the space of four or five years. the multiplier was reduced from 15 years to 11 years to reflect the fact that the marriage might not have lasted for the whole of the natural life of the deceased.

While the implausibility of the addition of an *if not* phrase in the previous example can be attributed to its rhetorical drawbacks, the following example makes the insertion of a suspension phrase rather difficult because the addition *if not three* would be irrelevant. The speaker / writer is clearly engaged in the depiction of the scene and for this piece of "scene-setting", it is important that the Dobermans are mentioned, but the cardinality of the set of Dobermans does not seem very relevant.

(181) <CLD 841> Some of the gates were electronically controlled. He had to identify himself from the pavement. `I am Bill Erlich, of the Federal Bureau of Investigation in the United States of America. I would be most grateful if you could spare me a few moments of your time." One gate that he could open himself let him into a front garden patrolled by **two** Dobermans, but he was okay with dogs because there had always been dogs at his mother's home, and at his grandparents' home. He could talk his way past dogs.

These examples vary considerably in their resistance to suspension phrases. The addition of an *if not* phrase is much harder in (178) than in (180) or (181).

One may wonder whether it is fair to "test" the suspension test in this way: it is clear that the simple sentences to which Horn applied his suspension test are very different from the utterances tested here. Arguably, the cotextual, contextual and rhetorical aspects of the utterances that obstruct the suspension test in the examples mentioned above have nothing to do with what Horn tried to prove, namely that the 'exactly n' interpretation can be suspended. That allegedly shows that the upper bound component is not part of the "literal meaning" of numerals. If that line of reasoning is followed - for the sake of the argument - the fact that the suspension phrase can often not be applied due to reasons that have nothing to do with the semantics of numerals does not say anything about the meaning of numerals. The fact remains that at least some uses of numerals are compatible with suspension phrases, and in this line of reasoning this suffices to show that the 'exactly n' meaning cannot be part of the semantics of the numeral, but must be some "weaker" component of its meaning.

There are two counter-arguments against this defense of the suspension test. First, while it is true that the suspension test is to a large extent a theoretical argument, the fact that in 96% of the cases it cannot be applied is more than circumstantial evidence that there is something wrong with the premises that underlie the test. More specifically, the thesis of the 'at least' semantics of numerals and the upper bound implicature is jeopardized by this observation: if numerals indeed typically have an 'at least' semantics (and, as argued in section 2.1.1., the "semantics" of a linguistic item ultimately has to be derived from the multiple intentions with which these elements are used by multiple speakers of the same language, especially when working with Gricean mechanisms), and if this 'at least' semantics is indeed typically complemented by an implicated upper bound, then surely this suspension phrase should be able to lift the implicature in more than 4% of the cases. The results of the corpus analysis of *two* once more underscore how the neo-Gricean analysis of numerals can only be convincing when constructed, simplified, or highly artificial examples are used.

Second, the hypothesis that the factors and elements that disable the suspension test do not have anything to do with the meaning of numerals is wrong. Admittedly, as far as the pure expression of cardinality is concerned, rhetorical structure and the contextual plausibility of doubt do not influence the expression of cardinality, which is the inherent function of numerals. But the neo-Gricean project has always engaged in the question of how utterances with numerals denote more than cardinality pure and simple: the definition of the semantics of numerals in terms of 'at least n' meanings precisely incorporated the modal component of these utterances, be it only implicitly. In fact, one of the factors that directly influence the interpretation of numerals is precisely an estimation of the certainty with which the speaker is able to judge the information he or she presents. In other words, the interpretation of the numeral depends on what the hearer thinks about the speaker's knowledge of the situation.

With some utterances, the importance of this factor is considerable. More specifically, the interpretation of the numeral in the neo-Gricean example par excellence - the *children* example (182) - crucially depends on the choice of the subject of the sentence. If *I* is chosen as the subject, the usual 'absolute value' interpretation is moved to the 'exactly n' end of the scale, precisely because the subject of the sentence is the speaker of the utterance. It is part of our background knowledge that in most Western societies that normally one knows how many children one has. This is a default assumption in large parts of the English-speaking community. It is, however, not a default assumption that one knows how many children a pop star like Madonna has (183).

(182)   I have two children.
(183)   Madonna has two children.

The *actually*-test shows that these background factors are influential indeed:

(184)   !!I have two, actually three children.
(185)   !Madonna has two, actually three children.

The version with *Madonna* is much easier to correct than the one with *I*. The connection with world knowledge becomes even more manifest when the difference between a male and a female speaker is considered: for obvious reasons, if the *I* refers to a female speaker the correction phrase is harder to use than when the speaker is a man. This is an example of how contextual information structures the linguistic possibilities of speakers. It is clear that, unlike the other factors that have been discussed (presence of definiteness markers, restrictors etc.), this type of background knowledge is not part of the coded content of the sentence. But it does play a role in the hearer's assessment of the epistemic status of the speaker: can he or she be supposed to be well-informed or not?

Moreover, it is also obvious that the answer to this question will influence the modal component of utterances containing numerals: the possibility that the individual denoted by the speaker has more or fewer than two children is excluded more forcefully when the subject is the (female) speaker than when it is a third person. When a woman utters (186), there should usually be a special context licensing the use of the *at least* phrase.

(186)   I have two, if not three children.

The hearer will expect to hear a story that explains how it is possible that the speaker is not sure about the number of children she has. Hence, the influence of background knowledge on the interpretation of utterances containing numerals can be considerable, and while this influence is explicitly not part of the coded content of the sentence, it clearly is capable of disabling the suspension test. An empirically responsible analysis of the meaning of numerals should be able to explain this, and the neo-Gricean analysis certainly cannot. First, it would have to invoke the upper bound implicature in the case of the female speaker and not in the case of a third person subject. Then, it would have to find a way to explain how this implicated upper bound cannot be lifted (or only with great difficulty) in the case of the female *I*-subject, while it can be lifted in other instances. Such an analysis would have to rely on contextual influence twice: first for the triggering of the 'exactly n' value, second for the impossibility of lifting the implicature. Besides the fact that this analysis would not be theoretically economical, it is not really clear how such an account could be even minimally coherent.

A final remark concerns the first of the factors discussed here: the so-called "scale-reversals". In the corpus analysis, I have referred to it by the name of "argumentative value", a term that is borrowed from early French works on the influence of rhetorical structure (especially Ducrot 1973 and Anscombre and Ducrot 1976). Ducrot opposes the "valeur intrinsèque" of a proposition to the "valeur argumentative" of the same proposition (Ducrot 1973:232). Anscombre explains how the concept of argumentative value applies to the analysis of *même* (*even*):

> Les énonciations comportant le *même* que nous décrivons sont prononcées à des fins d'argumentation. Le locuteur cherche à prouver à l'interlocuteur la vérité d'une certaine assertion; il invoque à cet effet, explicitement ou implicitement, un certain nombre d'arguments dont l'un, qu'il met en relief à l'aide de *même*, lui paraît avoir plus de force que les autres, être la meilleure preuve de ce qu'il avance. (Anscombre quoted in Anscombre et Ducrot 1978:48)

It is clear, however, that the concept of "argumentative value" can be related to all sorts of scalar elements (as Ducrot and Anscombre have pointed out repeatedly). I prefer that concept to that of "scale reversal" (Horn 1972, Fauconnier 1975), because it explicitly relates the interpretation of the linguistic elements in question to the rhetorical function they fulfill in the clause. Let us look at two examples of how the argumentative value influences the interpretation of numerals: in (187) the clause *as they rounded corners on two wheels* is an illustration of the speed that has been mentioned in the previous part of the sentence. Rounding a corner on two wheels is a stereotypical, nearly cartoonesque way of demonstrating that a vehicle is going very fast indeed. In that context it would not make any sense to insert a suspension phrase: *There was something in the speed, as they rounded corners on* **two**, *if not three/four wheels, that shook her out of her bad mood* is almost incomprehensible. The whole point is that they rounded it on two wheels, because that shows that they went very fast. This "point" is a more mundane way of referring to the "argumentative value" of the proposition.

> (187) <JYA 1348> But now that he was here, there was no point in pretending. Her voice was cold. `Please, if you don't mind. I'd like to catch his act." `I'll do my best. Hold on." And she had never seen the jeep travel so quickly. There was something in the speed, as they rounded corners on **two** wheels, that shook her out of her bad mood, and when they drew up with a squeal of brakes in the narrow road just by Pepe's Bar, she was laughing at Miguel's uncharacteristic recklessness.

In (188), the speaker / writer is depicting the lamentable situation of a certain Mrs Farquhar and the loneliness is presented as an aspect of that situation ("the house is changed" indicates that there used to be more people in the house). In this context it would be very strange to insert a suspension phrase: *Just the old lady upstairs in her bed, and two, if not three nurses, night and day* would be a very weird thing to say.

(188) <FA5 1329> `Oh, dear." Mrs McLaren's cheerful expression changed to one of sadness and gloom. `Poor Mrs Farquhar. She had a wee stroke and she's been going downhill, by all accounts, ever since. The house is changed now, not the way it used to be with all of you running around. Just the old lady upstairs in her bed, and **two** nurses, night and day. Mary and Sandy Reekie are still there, she doing the cooking and he taking care of the garden, but Mary says it's a chilling business cooking for just the nurses, for poor Mrs Farquhar takes no more than a wee cup of baby food."

Of course, in (188) it is also the presence of the restrictor *just* that makes the addition of a suspension phrase rather difficult; as has been shown in the beginning of the discussion, the presence of restrictors is fatal for the suspension test. In (189), the argumentative value is in itself responsible for the disabling of the suspension-test. The point of the utterance containing *two* in (189) is not the length of the period in which no worse communal violence broke out than the violence in Bihar. The insertion of the suspension phrase (190) sounds contrived because the point of the utterance is the statement that a new force was deployed (and when / why it was deployed); the precise number of years that elapsed since the last outbreak of violence is of secondary importance.

(189) <HLR 1049> An 8,000-strong Rapid Action Force (RAF), under the control of the federally administered Central Reserve Police Force (CRPF), was launched on Oct. 7. The deployment of the new force, initially expected to be confined to Ahmedabad, Aligarh, Allahabad, Darbhanga, Delhi, Ghaziabad, Hyderabad, Jaipur, Meerut and Varanasi, came after the outbreak of some of the worst communal violence in **two** years between Hindus and Moslems in Bihar, which killed nearly 50 people. In September communal rioting had spread through Kerala, Maharashtra and Uttar Pradesh after renewed controversy over the disputed site of the Babri mosque at Ayodhya in Uttar Pradesh [see p. 39008].
(190) ?The deployment of the new force, initially expected to be confined to Ahmedabad, Aligarh, Allahabad, Darbhanga, Delhi, Ghaziabad, Hyderabad, Jaipur, Meerut and Varanasi, came after the outbreak of some of the worst communal violence in **two**, if not three years between Hindus and Moslems in Bihar, which killed nearly 50 people.

On the other hand, in (191) the argumentative value is precisely the reason why the suspension phrase *can* be inserted.

(191) <J11 1850> 6 Roll out the remaining pink marzipan to a long strip. Mark on parallel lines with the pastry wheel and then use it to wrap round the sides of the cake. (You may find this easier to do in **two** sections.) 7 Make six small balls out of the red marzipan trimmings, each about the size of a pea, and press them gently into the red base, spacing evenly apart.

In this example, it is perfectly possible that the suspension phrase is added.

(192)   You may find this easier to do in **two**, if not three sections.

If it is easier to wrap the pink marzipan round the sides of the cake in two sections than in one section, it might very well be even easier to do it in three sections. In some cases, the argumentative value even overrules the influence of the restrictor.

(193) <JYE 4373> Sophie hesitated and swallowed hard. Then, almost hypnotised by her godmother's steady gaze, she said, `Yes. Yes, I think I must. It can't make matters worse, anyway. Thank you for your advice." On her way back to the surgery, Sophie glanced at her watch and realised with a start that she had left Joanna on her own for nearly **two** hours. As she went in, she said apologetically, `I'm so sorry, Joanna. I had an appointment - well, I'll explain later. How have you got on?"

Even though the presence of the restrictor *nearly* would normally disable the suspension test, in this case the argumentative value is so strong that it makes the insertion of the *if not* phrase considerably easier (it still does not sound very natural, but it is certainly better than other examples with restrictors in which the expression of cardinality cannot be said to constitute the "point" or even part of the "point" of the utterance).

(194) On her way back to the surgery, Sophie glanced at her watch and realised with a start that she had left Joanna on her own for nearly **two**, if not three hours.

5.3.1.2. The cancellation test
The cancellation test was originally devised to show the defeasibility of implicatures, just like Horn's more recent suspension test. Levinson notes that Horn's distinction between suspension and cancellation is descriptively useful, but "both kinds of defeasibility can be accounted for by the same general kind of mechanism" (Levinson 1983:114). The corpus analysis shows that they are indeed comparable, but they do differ in content (suspension phrases do not commit the speaker to the falsity of what is suspended, while cancellation phrases do commit him or her to the falsity of what is canceled) and in their (very limited) range of applicability. The cancellation test is even less applicable than the suspension test: in 97.1% of the cases it was not possible to add an *in fact* phrase. The cancellation test is often disabled by factors that are similar to the factors that sabotage suspension tests, but there are some significant differences between the applicability of the two tests.

    Let us begin with some examples that illustrate problems with the cancellation test that are similar to the problems with the suspension test. In (196), the cancellation phrase cannot be inserted because it is highly unlikely, if not impossible that the speaker (probably an anchorman or -woman, cf. last sentence) should correct him- or herself by means of an *in fact* phrase. This is a case, not of "unreasonable doubt" but of something similar I would like to call "unlikely mistake". The utterances in (197) and (199) exemplify more cotextual reasons: in (198) the presence of the definiteness marker and the fact that the states in question are present in the cotext disables the cancellation test; in (200) the *in fact three* phrase cannot be inserted because the two events in question are specified immediately afterwards.

(195) <KRT 1278> President Gorbachev's been facing his worst Mayday parade and the first one not to be completely controlled by the communist party. He was jeered and booed out of Red Square by angry demonstrators demanding freedom for Lithuania and an end to communist domination elsewhere. A high court judge has halted the trial of **two** veteran peace campaigners accused of springing Soviet spy, George Blake from prison in 1966. In an unprecedented legal move, Mr Justice Hodgson ordered a a judicial view of the case to decide if Michael Randall and Pat Potell should stand trial. The weather; it'll be a warm and sunny evening.

(196) ??A high court judge has halted the trial of **two**, in fact three veteran peace campaigners accused of springing Soviet spy, George Blake from prison in 1966.

(197) <HLA 1632> The talks, originally due to be held in Pyongyang on Aug. 27-30, were postponed after the North expressed health concerns after an outbreak of cholera in the South. The postponement reflected increased tension between the **two** states during August. On Aug. 21 the South Korean authorities claimed that North Korean troops in the eastern sector of the heavily fortified border had fired upon a South Korean position.

(198) ??The postponement reflected increased tension between the **two**, if not three states during August.

(199) <J1K 739> 'Live for Sharam, Die for Izzat" 1989 2 (from the show Intimate distance , commissioned by The Photographers Gallery, London) directly precedes 'I Will always Be Here". Images of a naked young man, suspended, with cut hair scattered on his body co-exists with text framed on the wall. The text speaks of **two** parallel events: the ritualistic preparation of the body of young South Asian woman for marriage and of the memories of childhood sexual abuse, the effect on her body.

(200) ??The text speaks of **two**, if not three parallel events: the ritualistic preparation of the body of young South Asian woman for marriage and of the memories of childhood sexual abuse, the effect on her body.

Despite these similarities, (201) contains an example that allows the suspension test (202) but does not allow the insertion of an *in fact* phrase (203).

(201) <AS6 591> At the turn of the century, the very time when Pearson documents the coinage of the term 'hooligan" to portray a supposedly new breed of youthful folk-devil, there is found in other sources a mood of contemporary congratulation about the long-term conquest of the problem of order. The Criminal Registrar's Report for 1901 documents a trend for declining levels of crime and violence over more than **two** decades. The introduction comments: 'We have witnessed a great change in manners: the substitution of words without blows for blows with or without words; an approximation in the manners of different classes; a decline in the spirit of lawlessness."

(202) The Criminal Registrar's Report for 1901 documents a trend for declining levels of crime and violence over more than **two**, if not three decades.

(203) ?The Criminal Registrar's Report for 1901 documents a trend for declining levels of crime and violence over more than **two**, in fact three decades.

In (202) the suspension phrase can be added, because it is possible to construe the "point" of the discourse as one that tries to stress the duration of the "long-term conquest of the problem of order", as the previous sentence puts it. The argumentative value of the suspension phrase in (202) is in line with the general point of the discourse, and that is why it is possible to insert it. In (203), the cancellation phrase turns the utterance into an even better argument for the construed "point" of the discourse: if the point is to show how long this conquest has lasted, then three decades is better than two. But the cancellation phrase provides a better argument at the cost of a correction: whereas the suspension phrase can be used in expository prose without creating the feeling that the speaker has made a mistake, the cancellation phrase explicitly signals a mistake. While it is possible that the speaker / writer should try to strengthen his argument, in this context it is highly unlikely that he should outright correct it. The suspension phrase introduces doubt, but because the "direction" of the doubt is compatible with the argumentative value of the whole discourse, the *if not* phrase can be added. The *in fact* phrase does not introduce doubt, but simply corrects a mistake, and in the careful and manifestly premeditated discourse of (201) an insertion of the *in fact* phrase is highly unlikely, if not pragmatically impossible. A similar example is provided below.

> (204) <H9R 951> The flow method thus transforms the time-variation of concentration into a distance-variation and enables us to make an essentially static measurement (Fig. 5.47). The distance scale of the decay of this steady-state concentration depends on the ratio of the flow rate to the rate of decay. The problem with this method is that we must generate the species of interest continuously - often by mixing **two** gases or solutions - in a way that can be matched to the timescale of the measurement. Thus even here we may want to reduce the total time required to record the spectrum. In the past, much of the work with flowing gases used photographic recording of electronic emission or absorption spectra. These give only limited vibrational information, and then only for small molecules.

The point of the utterance containing *two* can be construed as the demonstration of the problematic nature of the method discussed. In that light, a suspension phrase *if not three* seems acceptable: presumably, it is harder to mix three gases or solutions than two. The *in fact* cancellation phrase, however, is ruled out due to the expository nature of the scientific discourse and to the presence of the adverb *often*[58].

---

[58] Also *often* can be said to have a specific argumentative value here. It facilitates the addition that the "generation of species of interest" is problematic because sometimes two gases have to be mixed. Given these data (that it is indeed correct that sometimes gases have to be mixed) the presence of *often* or an adverb with a similar meaning is necessary to take away the suggestion that this is *always* the case. In a sense, it is the addition of *often* that enables this parenthetic clause in this context and that explains why *often* contributes to the argumentative value of the whole utterance. Note that *sometimes* would be less appropriate here: with respect to the argumentative value, it is better to use an adverb that is slightly stronger than *sometimes*. With *sometimes*, the possibility that it happens only once or twice is left open, and this would be less compatible with the "point" of the utterance than *often*.

(205) ??The problem with this method is that we must generate the species of interest continuously - often by mixing **two**, in fact three gases or solutions - in a way that can be matched to the timescale of the measurement.

In (206), *two* is combined with a necessity modal, and hence the utterance can be interpreted as presenting a requirement, so that *two* + the modal in this context can be interpreted as an 'absolute value' use: the lower bound is stressed, but the speaker does not explicitly mention the possibility of there being more than two elements. This means, however, that this possibility is not explicitly excluded either. With necessity modals, an *if not* phrase can be expected to be relatively unproblematic, and this is indeed the case (207).

(206) <CGP 32> She has just launched Starting Out - the real beginners' workout and Fat Burning Workout - to help you burn off fat and lose weight. Both videos are now available in the UK at £10.99 each. International haircutter Terence Renati has teamed up with Japanese craftsmen to create the Terence Renati Scissor. Terence believes that every hairdresser should have **two** pairs of scissors, if they are truly professional, and is offering a free pair to each of the first five orders received from Hairflair readers.
(207) Terence believes that every hairdresser should have **two**, if not three pairs of scissors, if they are truly professional, and is offering a free pair to each of the first five orders received from Hairflair readers.

Typically, however, these necessity modals are not equally compatible with *in fact* phrases.

(208) ?Terence believes that every hairdresser should have **two**, in fact three pairs of scissors, if they are truly professional, and is offering a free pair to each of the first five orders received from Hairflair readers.

The cancellation phrase in (208) is rather odd; the hearer / reader expects the speaker / writer to give a reason why every hairdresser should have precisely three pairs of scissors. This is not true for (207): the hearer / reader can construct a rationale on his own (probably one to the effect that professionalism is associated with having plenty of equipment); no extra motivation is expected. Furthermore, (208) is once more a correction of a mistake, and this seems unlikely in the context of (206). For a final example of how suspension phrases differ from cancellation phrases, I return to an example that has been discussed before, here reproduced in (209).

(209) <J11 1850> 6 Roll out the remaining pink marzipan to a long strip. Mark on parallel lines with the pastry wheel and then use it to wrap round the sides of the cake. (You may find this easier to do in **two** sections.) 7 Make six small balls out of the red marzipan trimmings, each about the size of a pea, and press them gently into the red base, spacing evenly apart.

As mentioned, the suspension phrase is unproblematic. The cancellation phrase, however, is out, because of the discursive nature of the fragment (i.e., a recipe).

(210) ??Mark on parallel lines with the pastry wheel and then use it to wrap round the sides of the cake. (You may find this easier to do in **two**, in fact three sections.)

5.3.2. Redundancy

Another argument that is often used to defend the 'at least' semantics of numerals is the fact that if *two* really meant 'exactly two', then *exactly* in *exactly two* would be redundant. As mentioned in section 3.1.1., Horn (1972:82) first applied the redundancy argument to the analysis of numerals, in the context of the formulation of the following constraint on second conjuncts in conjunctions:

> The second conjunct Q of a conjunction *P and Q* must assert some propositional content which does not logically follow from the first conjunct P (i.e. P & Q is anomalous if P [entails] Q or, *a fortiori*, if P [presupposes] Q). (Horn 1972:79)

He also included implicated meanings in his account; his example was the following.

(211)   Three and only three Lithuanians...

This was judged to be OK, while

(212)   ??Only three and three Lithuanians...

was observed to be odd, if not ungrammatical. In Horn's account of *only*, the restrictor causes the utterance to change in meaning: the version with *only N asserts* that the predicate of the sentence applied to no one other than N, while it *presupposes* that N went. For our purposes, it is important that Horn's argument can be used for the defense of an 'at least' semantics, and this has been done repeatedly ever since Horn first brought it up.

Obviously, the general form of the redundancy argument can easily be countered: if *two* cannot mean 'exactly two' because in that case *exactly two* would be redundant, then *two* cannot mean 'at least two' either, because in that case *at least two* would be redundant as well, while it clearly is not. Horn's original *only* argument is a little trickier, but is easy to explain within the 'absolute value' analysis. Whereas (211) first introduces a set of Lithuanians the cardinality of which is three and then *only* explicitly indicates that the set contains no more than three elements, (212) introduces the set, determines its cardinality as three and no more than three, and then repeats the cardinality, but with a less exact expression than the one that was used first. It goes without saying that the second version is odd, while the first is entirely natural.

Even though the redundancy argument for the neo-Gricean analysts is not only weak but also damaging to their own 'at least' analysis, I decided to check this argument in the sample corpus, because I felt that "redundancy" could indeed tell us something about the behavior of numerals. I tried to add either an 'at least', 'at most', an 'exactly' or an 'approximately' restrictor to the utterance containing *two* in order to discover the factors that enable or disable the addition of restrictors. This will give us more insight into the meaning construction in utterances with respect to the expression of cardinality. In only 105/857 (12.3%) was it possible to add a restrictor. The proportion of the four types of restrictors are represented in Table 9:

TABLE 9

ADDITION OF RESTRICTORS: TYPES[59]

Approximative restrictors: 42/105= 40%	'Exactly' restrictors: 10/105= 9.5%	'At least' restrictors: 47/105= 44.8%	'At most' restrictors: 6/105= 5.7%

It is remarkable that 'at least' restrictors can be added much more often than 'exactly' restrictors. The neo-Gricean argument would predict the reverse. Let us take a look at some examples: in (213) *two* can be combined with an approximative restrictor without any problem (214), (215) shows how some utterances allow the addition of *exactly* (216), (217) shows an example with *at least*. Note that even though "the two respects" are enumerated immediately afterwards, this does not prohibit the addition of *at least*, due to the uncertainty introduced by *at least* (218), which, however, does not *explicitly* mention a "third respect". Finally, (219) features a use of *two* that can be combined with *at most* (220).

(213) <BNV 818> After Legrand, the aircraft lost Couvelaire, the man who had the original idea. Too bad for SuperSingle, though. This is important: an aircraft's personality is always rooted somewhere in men's minds. Trace its history back to its fathers, and you'll know how it flies. Being a close friend of Legrand and Couvelaire, I was not surprised when I first flew the prototype **two** years ago: soft and light as a feather, brilliant as a refined piece of thinking on how an ideal aircraft should fly, powerful as a civilianised fighter.
(214) Being a close friend of Legrand and Couvelaire, I was not surprised when I first flew the prototype about/approximately **two** years ago.
(215) <ASD 2600> JANET: Oh yes? GRAMPS: Fascinating young man. Property JANET: Property? GRAMPS: Abroad. Brilliant notion. They build a villa in Spain, somewhere hot and sunny. They create twenty-six different leaseholds. Each leasehold runs for two weeks of each year, at a particular time. They then sell these leaseholds to chaps like me. And chaps like me can then go down to the villa, for those two weeks, every year for the next twenty-five years, without paying a penny! We effectively own the property!
(216) Each leasehold runs for exactly two weeks of each year, at a particular time.

---

[59] When an utterance could be combined with more than one type of restrictor, it was grouped with the category of restrictor that was deemed most natural in the context of the utterance.

(217) <ABD 1718> Shifting more of the cost of training to the private sector in this way might have posed a problem, even in a buoyant economy. But the chilly economic climate has made a tricky situation desperate, in **two** respects. Falling demand and rising costs are tempting many a finance director to curb spending on his firm's in-house training, let alone its contribution to the local TEC. And TECs are having to deliver their promises, on dwindling incomes, just as the number of unemployed is rising sharply (see next page).

(218) But the chilly economic climate has made a tricky situation desperate, in at least **two** respects.

(219) <AMG 1579> The number of females with whom the male frequently interacts decreases with the size of the group. This means that in larger groups most of the interactions and mutual grooming go on between members of female pairs while the male only grooms with one or **two** of them. The male can maintain a fairly equable distribution of grooming up to a harem size of five females.

(220) This means that in larger groups most of the interactions and mutual grooming go on between members of female pairs while the male only grooms with one or at most **two** of them.

The latter example is typical in that it is very hard to find uses of *two* that could be combined with *at most* without changing the context. If it is possible to add *at most*, there usually already is a suggestion of an upper bound, which can then be made more explicit by the addition of *at most*. This is clearly the case in (221) and (222).

(221) FEJ 622 (a) £3,520.000 of 12% debenture stock 1999, secured by a fixed charge on the group's properties, was issued on 1st October 1990 at par to finance the acquisition of Model Layout Ltd and the refitting of the group's offices and factory in Coventry. (b) £550,000 (1990 - £220,000) due to subsidiary undertakings is repayable between one and **two** years. The balance of the amount due to subsidiary undertakings is repayable between two and five years. These amounts are interest free.

(222) (b) £550,000 (1990 - £220,000) due to subsidiary undertakings is repayable between one and at most **two** years.

In this context, however, the addition of *at most* already has a slight flavor of redundancy[60]. In most other contexts *at most* cannot be added due to the argumentative value of 'at most' restrictors. In (223), for instance, it is unclear why the speaker / writer should use an 'at most' restrictor (224).

(223) <EFB 381> Welsh, in a study of `The Kids", an East End teenage gang based in Bethnal Green, London, found that there were both boys and girls in the gang. In order to alleviate boredom, `The Kids" committed minor delinquencies to attract police attention and manufacture excitement. In **two** main events mentioned by Welsh it is

---

[60] Also, there is an implicit possibility / permission modal in *repayable*, i.e., 'the repayment period may last one to two years'.

girls who take the lead (Welsh, 1981). In her study of delinquent girls in a Northern city, in the UK, Wilson found that her subjects had even adopted and adapted that central mark of a successful subculture: a slum sex code.

(224) ?In at most **two** main events mentioned by Welsh it is girls who take the lead (Welsh, 1981). In her study of delinquent girls in a Northern city, in the UK, Wilson found that her subjects had even adopted and adapted that central mark of a successful subculture: a slum sex code.

The hearer / reader expects to find a reason why the speaker should explicitly impose an upper bound on the number of events in which the girls take the lead, but the context does not seem to provide one. Rather, the rest of the discourse seems to concern delinquent girls, precisely the subject that is introduced by the previous sentence. And as it is not the *scarcity* of delinquent girls that is addressed, but their characteristics (or at least one of them), the addition of *at most* is rather difficult. A similar example can be found in (225). The addition of *at most* is extremely artificial in this context (226).

(225) <CH1 6145> `Would he have gone out on a limb for anyone other than David? I fear not." PAUL FOOT COSTLY MISTAKE FOR DOROTHY LIKE thousands of others who have suffered from `tranquilliser" drugs, Dorothy King wanted to sue the drug company. **Two** years ago she got legal aid, and her case went forward. In January this year, the Legal Aid Board decided they had made a mistake, and withdrew legal aid. The deadline for suing the drug companies came and went - and she had to drop out. She is now liable for the wasted costs of her abandoned case - more than £1,000.

(226) ?PAUL FOOT COSTLY MISTAKE FOR DOROTHY LIKE thousands of others who have suffered from `tranquilliser" drugs, Dorothy King wanted to sue the drug company. At most **two** years ago she got legal aid, and her case went forward. In January this year, the Legal Aid Board decided they had made a mistake, and withdrew legal aid.

As mentioned, there are quite a few uses of *two* that can be combined with more than one type of restrictor. In (227), there is an extreme example of such a flexible use: it can be combined by 'approximately', 'exactly', 'at least' and even 'at most' restrictors (228).

(227) <A0C 167> It said the effective date of introduction will remain 1 July and has advised the BHRCA to inform all members. THE Smugglers' Kitchen, above, is being given away because its owner cannot sell it. Bill Murray spent £50,000 on setting up his restaurant at Telegraph Hill, near Exeter, Devon, **two** years ago but said the business started to go downhill when he handed it over to a manager to run. Mr Murray now wants to give away the Smugglers' Kitchen so that he can channel his efforts into another property - the Dartmoor Inn at Bovey Tracey, also in Devon. He has identified the need for a fish restaurant in the surrounding area.

(228) Bill Murray spent £50,000 on setting up his restaurant at Telegraph Hill, near Exeter, Devon, approximately / exactly / at least / at most **two** years ago but said the business started to go downhill when he handed it over to a manager to run.

What makes this use of *two* so susceptible to the addition of restrictors? The most important feature of (227) is that *two* modifies a temporal entity, more specifically it modifies *years*. There are two points that are important about this temporality: one, indications of time are usually rather "lax", in the sense that they seem to have a built-in "approximativity" (this will be discussed more extensively in the analysis of restrictors in section 5.5. below); two, the "size" of the temporal entity is utterly important here. In fact, *two years* indicates a large "quantity of time" by means of a small numeral. Unlike other uses of *two*, the "approximativity", which is already present due to the fact that it concerns a temporal entity, is enhanced by the size of *years*. In this context, the use of *two* comes very close to the use of "round numbers". As Horn put it in his neo-Gricean description:

> Returning to the question of the upper-bound implicature of cardinal numbers on positive scales, a proviso is needed to assure that the implicature will be characteristically weaker, easier to countermand, if the cardinal is "round", i.e. if the number is one which occurs freely in such approximating contexts as *about n, roughly n*, and the like. (Horn 1972:45)

As I will argue later, this reasoning is rather circular: stating that numerals occur freely in approximating contexts is simply an indication that these numerals do not express an "upper bound" (i.e. they do not express that the possibility of there being more than two elements to the set under discussion is excluded), in other words: that their original 'absolute value' meaning is not altered by any linguistic element in the context. It is not a definition. "Roundness" can be defined on independent bases (Pollmann and Jansen 1996), so that no reference to "approximating contexts" is necessary.

Important for now is that uses of *two* as in *two years* resemble the "approximativity" of round numbers because the language user who refers to two years is often assumed to be speaking somewhat loosely, just like when he is using round numbers, in particular because the degree of precision that is expected diminishes when the quantity expressed increases. That is why the addition of 'approximately' restrictors is often possible with temporal adverbs.

> (229) <H0B 524> Waste ore is a somewhat obscure term and in this context might refer to the residual sand and gravel, which did have a market of sorts. The lease was signed by Tissington and Robert Barker. On the 20th March 1757, **two** years prior to Tissington getting rights to Tilberthwaite, a spirited party of adventurers had made an agreement with Sir John Pennington.
> (230) The lease was signed by Tissington and Robert Barker. On the 20th March 1757, approximately **two** years prior to Tissington getting rights to Tilberthwaite, a spirited party of adventurers had made an agreement with Sir John Pennington.
> (231) <CBE 988> Wife No 3 for Cleese Cheryl Stonehouse JOHN CLEESE married for the third time last night and, like his previous wives, his new bride is an American. Just a few relatives and close friends were invited to watch him wed psychoanalyst Alyce-Faye Eichelberger at a beachside ceremony in Barbados. Cleese, 52, fell for her

after his divorce **two** years ago from his second wife, film director Barbara Trentham. His first wife was his co-author and co-star of Fawlty Towers, Connie Booth.
(232) Cleese, 52, fell for her after his divorce approximately **two** years ago from his second wife, film director Barbara Trentham.

However, not only 'approximately' restrictors combine freely with temporal adverbials. Because of their inherent vagueness, they combine with 'approximately' restrictors, which make this vagueness more explicit; but because of that same inherent quality they also combine with 'exactly' restrictors that take away this vagueness.

(233) <AAN 441> He has a habit of playing in at least the inaugural event held on one of his lay-outs and in December 1988 fully intended to play in the Austrian Open of 1989. He was disappointed to learn that there was no such event on last season's European Tour calendar, but seems sure to get his wish next year. **Two** days ago the organisers of the NM English Open, to be played from August 16-19 at The Belfry, announced that their prize money would be increased from £250,000 to £400,000.
(234) He was disappointed to learn that there was no such event on last season's European Tour calendar, but seems sure to get his wish next year. Exactly **two** days ago the organisers of the NM English Open, to be played from August 16-19 at The Belfry, announced that their prize money would be increased from £250,000 to £400,000.

In (227), also 'at most' and 'at least' restrictors are possible, even though the latter are slightly more problematic than 'approximately' and 'exactly' restrictors.

(235) Bill Murray spent £50,000 on setting up his restaurant at Telegraph Hill, near Exeter, Devon, at least / at most **two** years ago but said the business started to go downhill when he handed it over to a manager to run.

The addition of *at least / at most* certainly sounds a little odd, even though it is not ruled out. The slightly artificial flavor of *at least / at most* in this example can be explained by means of the concept of "argumentative" value: when *at least* is added, the utterance should be able to function as an argument that focuses on the length of the period that has elapsed since Bill Murray set up his restaurant; when *at most* is added it is usually construed as an argument to show that two years ago is *not* that long ago. But because the context of the utterance does not contain any indications for such an argumentative point, these additions are less natural (even though they are possible). In this utterance, *two* functions as part of an adverbial phrase, which locates a certain state of affairs on a time line. Moreover, it is not the focus of the utterance. The combination of the latter two factors (adverbial + non-focal position) enables the restrictors to be added more smoothly.

In general, the restrictions for 'at least' and 'at most' restrictors are the same as the restrictions that have been discussed when dealing with the suspension test. One rather banal restriction seems specific for the redundancy test: in (236) an 'at least' or 'at most' restrictor is difficult to add simply because of grammatical reasons. The other examples reiterate restrictions that are by now familiar: in (237), the presence of other linguistic material obstructs the addition of an 'at least' restrictor (in this case it is the adverb *perhaps*) and in (238) the cotext (in this case the word "couplets") disallows 'at most' and 'at least' restrictors. I will not repeat all the relevant factors, but simply exemplify some of them.

(236) <CB2 1621> They fail to realise that not everyone playing or refereeing rugby is competent, and they don't build enough safety protection into the rules". The crusader. Toks Akpata has devoted himself to changing the Laws to reduce the risk of spinal injury. Illustrating his continued love of the game, Toks has been a columnist in Rugby U.S. for the past **two** years, commenting on a wide variety of topics. He also developed an exhaustive database on U.S. rugby spinal injuries in 1990, and has tried to use the information to suggest Law changes that could help prevent catastrophic injuries.

(237) <AR9 280> The truth is that reporters are constantly swapping jobs and assignments and that your contacts may be away when you most need them. So, while it is always worth seeking out the names of journalists who have a special interest in your subject, and if appropriate sending the releases to them at home as well as to their office, always be sure to send your releases to the newsdesk and perhaps to one or **two** others on the paper too if it is appropriate. Find out which reporters on the local newspaper and radio are most likely to be interested.

(238) <F7R 422> I have not said clear away, it is not the end of the lesson and some of you have not worked hard enough to make the end of the lesson now if you don't want to make the whole poem rhyme, what you might want to do is to put **two** lines together at a time and have those rhyming, paired rhymes, rhyming couplets, you can do that.

Finally, the following examples are remarkable for the restrictors they allow or disallow: in (239), the addition of *exactly* is certainly possible (240), but the utterance then receives an additional meaning, which can once again be explained by the "argumentative value" concept: the addition of *exactly* could be used to bring into focus the surprisingly small number of corporations that control the purchase and sale of yellowfin tuna in the US. In that case, the context should give some indication that this could indeed be construed as the "point" of the utterance in (239), and the environmental issues, which seem to be at stake here certainly allow such an interpretation. It is important to note that while *exactly* is often taken to express exactness it can also be used to show the relative smallness of the cardinality of a set.

(239) <ABC 1117> Full observer coverage will undoubtedly save the lives of thousands of dolphins caught by US vessels, but a change in corporate marketing strategies and consumer preference will be the most effective way of saving the dolphins of the ETP. The purchase and sale of yellowfin tuna in the US is controlled by **two** large corporations, H.J.Heinz and Ralston-Purina, which own many of the vessels and canneries, and import most of the tuna caught by Mexican boats. Each of them has the power to decide immediately to stop purchasing tuna caught by fishing

on dolphins. Skipjack is the most abundant species of tuna in the area, and, like albacore, can be caught without killing dolphins.
(240) The purchase and sale of yellowfin tuna in the US is controlled by exactly **two** large corporations, H.J.Heinz and Ralston-Purina, which own many of the vessels and canneries, and import most of the tuna caught by Mexican boats.

In (241) the 'exactly' restrictor can be added (242) if it is construed as a coincidence or at least a remarkable or surprising situation that the school in question had beaten Cranborne two Saturdays ago. Otherwise the addition becomes much more difficult, if not impossible: there must be a reason for the insertion of the 'exactly' restrictor.

(241) <HR8 2519> He hoped the Museum had not left any priceless bits of Islamic art lying around the place. If it had, they were liable to end up in the Husayn twins' pockets. He liked his class, though. In fact he liked the school. When it had beaten Cranborne junior School by three hundred runs, **two** Saturdays ago, he had linked arms with the headmaster and sung three verses of `We Are the Champions".
(242) When it had beaten Cranborne junior School by three hundred runs, exactly **two** Saturdays ago, he had linked arms with the headmaster and sung three verses of `We Are the Champions".

Also, there is at least one special reason why 'at least' restrictors may occur: in (243), the 'at least' restrictor can be added because of the vagueness that is compatible with reports on the past (244). In (245) 'at least' is possible due to another source for "incompleteness of human knowledge", namely science.

(243) <C93 468> It was also invited to compete in the European Entente Floriale. Like most villages, Lund in past times was much more self-sufficient than it is now, with its own grocers, shoemakers, tailors and the like and, during the 19th century, a second public house, the Speed the Plough. Even in 1949 there were **two** joiners and a blacksmith, a school, post office and eight shops.
(244) Even in 1949 there were at least **two** joiners and a blacksmith, a school, post office and eight shops.
(245) <CRM 8740> These results indicate the utility of microgravity monitoring, as the precursory processes that we identify were largely undetected by seismic and ground deformation monitoring. At a late stage during the explosive activity from the southeast crater (10 September-6 October 1989), **two** prominent fissures developed, one erupting to the northeast and the second, a non-erupting fissure, extending 7km towards the south-southeast. Seismic, soil gas emanations, thermal imaging, gravity and our own deformation and gravity data indicate that magma was not emplaced within the latter fissure south of station TDF (Fig. 1).
(246) At a late stage during the explosive activity from the southeast crater (10 September-6 October 1989), at least **two** prominent fissures developed, one erupting to the northeast and the second, a non-erupting fissure, extending 7km towards the south-southeast.

A final remark concerns the difference between the applicability of the suspension test and the possibility of adding an 'at least' restrictor: (247) reproduces an example that was discussed while assessing the applicability of the suspension test. It was argued that in this example, the suspension phrase could be added only with great difficulty, because it would undermine the rhetorical power of the speaker, and the legal context of the utterance, such a reduction of rhetorical strength was considered to be unlikely (248). But, as (249) shows, the addition of *at least* is slightly more acceptable. The difference can be explained by referring to the different meaning of the two additional elements: while *if not three* explicitly introduces the possibility of a third case of adultery, the addition of *at least* could just be a rhetorical device. The former is rhetorically slightly less attractive, because in this context, the speaker clearly does not have precise information concerning a third case of adultery. If he or she were asked to make the suggestion that is implied by his suspension phrase explicit, he or she would probably be at a loss for words (at least that is what the context suggests). But the *at least* phrase does not mention a third case of adultery (not even as a possibility), and this is why the *at least* restrictor seems - given the data provided by the context of the utterance - rhetorically more attractive and therefore also slightly more acceptable.

> (247) <HB3 541> martin and others v owen tlr 21.5.92 the likelihood of divorce can be taken into account when assessing damages for dependency . court should not shut its eyes to fact that statistically one in three marriages end in divorce. the chance would be substantially reduced if the marriage had already lasted some time and there were children. in this case the plaintiff had committed adultery with **two** different men in the space of four or five years. the multiplier was reduced from 15 years to 11 years to reflect the fact that the marriage might not have lasted for the whole of the natural life of the deceased.
> (248) ?in this case the plaintiff had committed adultery with **two**, if not three different men in the space of four or five years.
> (249) in this case the plaintiff had committed adultery with at least **two** different men in the space of four or five years.

Another difference occurs when a list of two entities is announced and subsequently enumerated, as in (250). While the suspension phrase is impossible (251), the 'at least' restrictor is possible (252). In view of the fact that the two branches are named, a possible third branch would have to be named in order for the suspension phrase to be possible in this context. Even the 'at least' restrictor is difficult, because also there you would expect a third branch, but the possible argumentative value of the utterance does not exclude the 'at least' restrictor as rigorously as it excludes the suspension phrase. In fact, the rationale behind this behavior is rather similar to the situation in the previous series of examples: also here, it is the fact that a third possibility is explicitly mentioned by the suspension phrase while this third possibility is not considered anymore in the rest of the discourse that makes the addition of *if not three* unlikely. The *at least* phrase does nothing of the kind, and can therefore be added rather more easily.

(250) <GT9 293> He also worked on economics, encouraged by his friend John Maynard (later Baron) Keynes [q.v.], and his papers, `A Contribution to the Theory of Taxation" (1927) and `A Mathematical Theory of Saving" (1928), started **two** flourishing branches of the subject: optimal taxation and optimal accumulation.

(251) ??He also worked on economics, encouraged by his friend John Maynard (later Baron) Keynes [q.v.], and his papers, `A Contribution to the Theory of Taxation" (1927) and `A Mathematical Theory of Saving" (1928), started **two**, if not three flourishing branches of the subject: optimal taxation and optimal accumulation.

(252) He also worked on economics, encouraged by his friend John Maynard (later Baron) Keynes [q.v.], and his papers, `A Contribution to the Theory of Taxation" (1927) and `A Mathematical Theory of Saving" (1928), started at least **two** flourishing branches of the subject: optimal taxation and optimal accumulation.

This leads to the following conclusions with respect to the redundancy test:

1) All phenomena can be captured by the 'absolute value' analysis, in the sense that by default a numeral can be combined with any type of restrictor, be it an 'at least', 'at most', 'exactly' or 'approximately' one. This can be predicted from the coded meaning of numerals like *two*: an 'absolute value' semantics allows the semantics of the numeral to be changed by linguistic and non-linguistic, co- and contextual factors. When the addition of a restrictor in a specific context is not possible (as is often the case, especially with 'at least' and 'at most' restrictors), this is due to the presence of other linguistic elements in the context that prohibit the addition, or because of rhetorical reasons, which make the addition very unlikely, if not impossible.

2) Some phenomena are difficult to explain within a neo-Gricean account. As mentioned above (see, e.g. section 3.4. of Chapter 3), it is possible to claim that numerals cannot have an 'exactly n' semantics because otherwise the addition of *exactly* would be redundant, while it certainly is not. But researchers who use this type of argument, should be aware of the fact that the same argument yields an important problem for an 'at least' analysis of numerals as well. How could *at least* be added to a numeral without being redundant if the semantics of the numeral are determined as 'at least n'? The 'absolute value' analysis does not exclude any combination with any type of restrictor on the basis of the semantics of numerals.

3) The various types of redundancy tests underscore the influence of other linguistic elements and the influence of rhetorical structure on the interpretation of expressions of cardinality.

5.3.3. Negation

Besides the suspension test, the cancellation test and the redundancy test, another recurring argument in the neo-Gricean account of numerals is the behavior of numerals under negation (I refer once again to Horn 1972 for the first application of this idea to a Gricean account of numerals). I have discussed the roots of this argument in section 3.1.1.; now the way in which the influence of negation is manifested in the sample corpus will be tackled. I will quote Jespersen's remark concerning the "B-class terms" in his proto-scalar account (terms that are intermediate between two extremes, such as *something* is in between *everything* and *nothing*) once again, to make the issue clear:

Here the general rule is that *not* means 'less than', or in other words 'between the term qualified and nothing'. Thus *not good* means 'inferior', but does not comprise 'excellent'; *not lukewarm* indicates a lower temperature than *lukewarm*, something between lukewarm and icy, not something between lukewarm and hot. This is especially obvious if we consider the ordinary meaning of negatived numerals: *He does not read three books in a year / the hill is not two hundred feet high / his income is not £200 a year / he does not see her once in a week / the bottle is not half full* - all these expressions mean less than three, etc. [...] But the same expressions may also exceptionally mean 'more than', only the word following *not* then has to be strongly stressed (with the particular intonation indicative of contradiction), and then the whole combination has generally to be followed by a more exact indication: *not lukewarm but really hot / his income is not* two *hundred a year, but at least three hundred* [...] (Jespersen 1948 [1924]:325-26)

This long quote contains all information that is necessary, except for the connection with the neo-Gricean 'at least' line, which is easy to pinpoint. The fact that "unmarked" negation induces a 'less than' reading of a numeral is, at least at first sight, an excellent argument for an 'at least n' analysis for numerals. If the "coded meaning" of a numeral is 'at least n' ("lower bound") and if it is combined with an expression of negation, all values that are equal to n or that are higher than n are excluded: this is the definition of 'less than n'. That is Horn's basic point with respect to the 'at least' semantics of numerals and negation: numeral + negation creates a 'less than' effect; if the numeral has to be interpreted as 'more than n', it must be a special kind of negation, called "metalinguistic" negation. I will not repeat the theoretical discussion on negation in Chapter 3, but simply look at the data in the corpus, summed up in Table 10. I decided to do four separate queries: one on "not two", one on "not _ two", one on "don't _ two" and one on "don't _ _ two".

TABLE 10

TWO + NEGATION

	'Less than'	'More than'	'Less/more than'	Irrelevant
NOT TWO	29/123=23.6%	-	40/123=32.5%	54/123=43.9%
NOT _ TWO	60/200=30.0%	35/200=17.5%	9/200=4.5%	96/200=48.0%
DON'T _ TWO	14/53=26.4%	-	15/53=28.3%	24/53=45.3%
DON'T _ _ TWO	5/59= 8.5%	-	-	54/59=91.5%

The least interesting category is the one with the tokens of *don't __ two*, because most of the data were not relevant for the discussion at hand: too much material was allowed in between *don't* and *two* so that the negation did not influence the interpretation of the numeral at all, as in (253).

(253) <CBS 250> But the curtains were drawn, warm thick flowered curtains. `You know," said Dorothy, `I've been thinking about you two." David put down his spoon to listen as he would never have done for his unworldly mother, or his worldly father. `I don't believe you **two** ought to rush into everything - no, let me have my say. Harriet is only twenty-four - not twenty-five yet.

Nevertheless, in this category Jespersen's remarks are confirmed: if the distinction between so-called "descriptive" negation and "metalinguistic" negation is ignored, the 'less than' interpretation is the most frequent one. The situation is different for the instances of *don't __ two*, in the sense that the difference between the number of instances of 'less than' and those of 'less than / more than' is relatively small. Let us take a look at some examples of each. In (254) and (255) negation induces a 'less than' understanding of the numeral. In (256), (257) and (258), however, the expression of cardinality, at least when interpreted in isolation from the surrounding cotext, leaves two options open: either the cardinality expressed is lower than two, or it is higher than two. In this case the context (and more specifically the "rectification phrase") will usually steer the over-all interpretation in one of the two directions.

(254) <FY9 462> The first thing to do is forget about the six for a minute. Right It's not six women, it's one gang. Right one gang take eight hours. So how many gangs are you going to need, to get this job done in six hours? Well two gangs are gonna get it done in four hours. Right two gangs in four hours, so we don't need **two** whole gangs. Yeah. So that'd be too many. So one gang takes eight hours. How many gangs would take six hours? This is where it's the inverse proportion. It's going to take eight over six. Right? Eight over six which comes to? One and one and a bit gangs.
(255) <G1D 2724>`You're just a spoil-sport," said Sam. `You got no sense of adventure." `It was I who broke in," Tim reminded her. `I think that was very brave and daring, considering my conscience and my reputation as a law-abiding person." `And people don't have **two** lots of make-up," said Sam. `She's left all her moisturizers and her rejuvenating creams and her eye-liner and everything. She might have her lip-gloss in her handbag, but she wouldn't go off without her Estée Lauder. And you only broke in to show how smart you are, not because you're so brave."
(256) <FXR 1559> Have two. I spoke to them, Well I think that would be a bit naughty Yes, so do I. I I think if we get one of them we'll be doing very well, and to get two would be perhaps a bit naughty . We don't want **two** dancers , but one one set of dancers . But erm I I would like to suggest that the er the morris ones are er possibly our better bet, partly because I I I know one of them, er and er
(257) <KPY 1068> Then you should move any obstacles before. We're going. Oh, stop making fun of me. We'd better empty the whole kitchen then hadn't we? Oh shut up you. There you go. Where would you put my How much is there? I weighed you

two ounces. I don't want **two** ounces. Well put some back. I won't, I'll just eat them. Two ounces is a lot to have of cereal. Is it? For me, it is because I only have half of that. How many, how many are you supposed to have?

(258) <KB1 5398> Have you eat them all now? Oh! Have they all gone? No. One left? The trouble is if you get her boxfuls she won't stop until you eat the lot! Ah! Don't put too many in. Two in at once. Don't put **two** in. She's had five in her mouth at once! Thank you! Oh! Bang! She likes them friendship rings you know. Like jelly things? Like a, they're like a jelly. There's one look. This bloke looks like Len .

In the latter two examples, the eventual interpretation of *two* is also 'less than two'. In (256), however, not the number of dancers as such is negated, but the fact that *two dancers* is interpreted as two individual dancers (who do not form one group). The speaker asserts that he or she does not want two individual dancers, but a group of dancers. In (256), *we don't want two dancers* is interpreted as 'we do not want two individual dancers', or, more technically, 'we do not want two singleton sets of dancers', while *but one set of dancers* means 'we want one set of dancers, the cardinality of which is not specified'. Also (257) is not a typical instance of so-called metalinguistic negation, in that there is no rectification clause present. In the context, there is some sort of rectification clause further on, namely *Two ounces is a lot to have of cereal. Is it? For me, it is because I only have half of that*, which does replace the value 'two' with 'only half of that'. But it is clear that (257) could be classified with the 'less than' uses as well, because the rectification clause is rather far removed from the original expression of cardinality. Consequently, the combination of numeral + negation will be, by default, interpreted as 'less than two' (ounces). The same holds for the use of *two* in (258): the speaker is probably a parent talking to his / her child who has just tried to put two pieces of candy in her mouth. It is this - 'putting two in' - which is prohibited by the mother by the negative imperative clause. The context, however, makes clear that also in this case the combination of the numeral with the negation has to be interpreted as 'less than two'.

The difference between (254) and (255) on the one hand, and (256), (257) and (258) on the other, is relatively small: the latter are grouped with the 'less / more than' group simply because the context yields a "rectification". The presence of the rectification phrase makes clear that the over-all expression of cardinality should be interpreted in the direction of the rectification phrase: rectification wins out over the 'less than' interpretation, which is the default interpretation of the combination of *two* + negation. The 'less than' group is distinct from the other group in that in those instances no rectification is given; the hearer/reader is, as it were, left to his own devices. No further clues with respect to the interpretation of the numeral are given. In this situation the effect of negation on the numeral will usually be a 'less than' reading, which confirms Jespersen's and Horn's observation.

The general rule is that if *two* is combined with a negative particle it will always be interpreted as 'less than', unless special circumstances obtain. These special circumstances include the traditional Jespersenian ones: contrastive stress on the numeral, presence of a rectification phrase, but also some of the familiar 'exactly n' inducing factors, such as the presence of definiteness markers, as in (259), a constructed variant of (256).

(259)   We don't want the **two** dancers , but one one set of dancers .

Let us also take a look at another type of expression of negation, one in which *not* is not attached to the supporting *do*. In (260), there is an instance of *not two* (without intervening material), in (261) one of *not _ two*. Both examples show 'less than' uses of *two*.

(260) <H9V 256> Sighing, wishing she felt more confident, more able to cope, she madre her way slowly downstairs. Reluctant to face Leo, she idled to admire Colonel Newman's family portraits. He hadn't said he was going away and renting his house, which was odd because they'd been chatting in the village **not** two days before he'd disappeared and Leo taken up residence.

(261) <HP0 2702>`He wanted twelve shillings. I said we'd sooner sleep under the hedges. But I shall leave at the end of this week, Lord John. I can't pay a third of the wage in lodgings." All the while the coal merchant looked on, smiling. `Why do you charge so much?" John asked him. `You know the room is not worth **two** shillings, much less ten." `It's worth what it will fetch, see," the man said, unruffled. `Who says only two shillings? You. I say twelve, and I let it for less because I'm soft-hearted. Rooms is scarce in Rhyll, see. Demand and supply. I do both, see."

There is a remarkable number of 'more than' interpretations of *not _ two* (17.5% - while other queries did not yield a single instance of 'more than' uses), but that is nearly always the effect of an intervening 'exactly' or 'at most' restrictor.

(262) <ATA 957> The study of women and film involves, as in the subtitle of Kaplan's book, at least `both sides of the camera": women as film-makers, and women as cinematic objects, viewed through the camera eye. In my attempt at a wide-angled overview, however, I shall argue that the camera has not just **two** but many sides, and that feminist film criticism and theory can only benefit from casting its eye outside a field of vision in which the theory of the gaze and questions of representation and power have been dominant for too long.

(263) CD9 n=377> The last is important. Niki is an Austrian and, at that, an Austrian in the full sense of the word, and Austrians, at least after the collapse of their empire in 1918, are a little bit aslant to the world. As an Austrian, Niki is divided against himself, and there are not just **two** Nikis but several dozen of them. The job of keeping them together has been entrusted to a series of `confidants" who write his books, churn out his articles, furnish his quotes, capture his image and sweeten the sour, and when I once asked Niki why he wouldn't ever do a serious - and in consequence, a truthful - book about himself, he replied, why should he?

In these uses of *two*, first an 'exactly' restrictor is added to turn the 'absolute value' into an 'exactly n' value of the *only*-type, only to change it again, this time into a 'more than n' value of the numeral, due to the presence of negation. The negative particle does not directly affect the numeral, but affects the 'only'-restrictor: it removes the restriction, and the rectification phrase makes clear that the expression of cardinality has to be reanalyzed as having a 'more than' value. When this rectification phrase is left out, or replaced by a different one, the scope of *only* may change, so that it is not the cardinality of one set of one type of entities that changes, but the number of types of entities that the predicate applies to.

(264) In my attempt at a wide-angled overview, however, I shall argue that the camera has not just **two** sides, [but also two subject positions for the director] and that feminist film criticism and theory can only benefit from casting its eye outside a field of vision in which the theory of the gaze and questions of representation and power have been dominant for too long.

(265) As an Austrian, Niki is divided against himself, and there are not just **two** Nikis but [there are also two sides to each Nikki]

In (264) and (265), the rectification phrase does not change the cardinality of the original sets (the set of "sides") but indicates that, apart from these sets, there are also other types of things that deserve to be mentioned. These constructed variants make clear that the combination of negation + *just* + *two* does not necessarily lead to a change in the value of *two*, let alone a change to a 'more than' value. The type and content of the rectification phrase is crucial for the determination of the eventual value of the expression of cardinality, and so is the focal stress: in (262) and (263) the stress is on *two*, which creates the expectation that a different numeral will be provided (which indeed happens); in (264) and (265) the stress is on the nouns *sides* and *Nikis*. I will not go into the specifics of the combination of *only*, negation and numerals here, but I would like to point out that the phenomena in (262) and (263) are entirely predictable from the 'absolute value' analysis of numerals. *Two* is focalized, which turns the numeral into an 'exactly n' use of *two*, and an 'exactly' restrictor is added to make that interpretation even stronger, but the negation negates this 'exactly n' value, and hence both a 'more than n' and a 'less than n' interpretation are allowed. Eventually, however, this interpretation is replaced with an expression of a higher cardinality, which turns the entire expression of cardinality into a 'more than n' use. This is clearly a case of "echoic use" (Sperber and Wilson 1995 [1986], Carston 1996), and the context in (262) and (263) explicitly supports such a characterization. An "echoic use" can be defined as a representation of a representation: it is not a *description* of a state of affairs; it is an *interpretation* of a propositional form (e.g. a thought). As Sperber and Wilson put it: "[...] an utterance used as an interpretation of someone else's thought is always, in the first place, an interpretation of one's understanding of that other person's thought" (Sperber and Wilson 1995 [1986]:238). In relevance-theoretic terminology, an echoically used representation attributes some aspect of its form or content to someone other than the speaker and expresses an attitude to that aspect. In (262) the phrase *both sides of the camera* is mentioned (and it is attributed to a certain Kaplan), and the later phrase *not just two sides* explicitly reiterates the assertion contained in the first phrase that the camera has two sides, only to rectify it. In (263), it can be seen that the requirement that the "represented" thought (the one that is echoed) originally should not belong to the speaker is not a very strong requirement. I would argue that also (263) contains an instance of echoic use, but the proposition that is echoed is one that is suggested by the speaker himself. First, the speaker says that *Niki is divided against himself.* This implicitly suggests that there are "two Nikis" (*Niki* and *himself,* which are portrayed as being two constituents of the same person, who is divided against himself). But the speaker wants to correct this suggestion, echoes his own proposition and states that *there are not just two Nikis but several dozen of them.*

But why is it that such a construction will typically be interpreted as 'more than two', even when a rectification phrase is absent?

(266) As an Austrian, Niki is divided against himself, and there are not just **two** Nikis.

The hearer would expect a rectification phrase, and would expect this phrase to express a higher cardinality than two. Indeed, the reverse is very difficult.

(267) ??As an Austrian, Niki is divided against himself, and there are not just **two** Nikis, there is only one.

The combination of negation + *just* + *two* clearly calls for a higher value, because *not* + *just* encodes an announcement to the hearer that an even better / stronger argument for the utterance in question will follow, in this case a higher numeral. But I will come back to this construction in the discussion of the restrictors.

Less problematic cases of *not _ two* with 'more than' values are caused by the presence of the restrictor 'not less than' (268) or, in a temporal adverbial, *for* (269). Just like in earlier sections, I grouped 'at least' uses together with 'more than' uses.

(268) <FAG 341> The enclosure of heaths and commons reduced the extent of natural gorse patches where a fox could hide. Good arable farmers grubbed them up. To get more foxes and to get them distributed more evenly over the country, gorse covers and spinneys were started by hunting landlords in well-chosen spots. These were not less than **two** acres in size, and rarely more than twenty acres. Some of these covers were actually odd pieces of common land, old cow-pastures that had been allowed to get out of hand, taken over by the fox-hunters for fencing and preservation, in return for a money payment to the holders of the common rights.
(269) H82 n=406>`It would be unwise to try to move her back to the Rectory," Tom Horrocks was saying. `Not for **two** or three days, I think. There is some risk of infection, of fever." Henry Agnew cleared his throat and nodded. Louisa saw that some further response was required. `Of course, she must stay here," she answered. `I will care for her myself."

The latter examples are easier because the combination of negation + restrictor is transparent: 'not less than two' necessarily equals 'two or more', 'not for two or three days' equals 'at the earliest in two or three days' or 'after at least two or three days'.

Finally, let us take a look at the results of *not two*. Remarkably, the number of 'less / more than' readings of *not two* is higher than the 'less than' interpretations. As we have seen, the difference between the two interpretations basically hinges on the presence vs. absence of a rectification phrase. In (270) there is a clear 'less than' use; in (271), the 'less than / more than' option is exemplified.

(270) <H9V 256> Sighing, wishing she felt more confident, more able to cope, she madre her way slowly downstairs. Reluctant to face Leo, she idled to admire Colonel Newman's family portraits. He hadn't said he was going away and renting his house, which was odd because they'd been chatting in the village not **two** days before he'd disappeared and Leo taken up residence. When she reached the bottom of the rather ornate staircase she hovered uncertainly for a moment, then with a defiant toss of her head she marched into the shabby splendour of the lounge before coming to a lame halt.

(271) <G1N 1141> One wonders why Lacan's narrative of the genesis of the subject has to pass `through" this flaw in the female anatomy - a flaw in the `proper" functioning of the female body. This leads to the second main characteristic of the retrovizor in Thru : unlike the Lacanian mirror, it is flawed, causing it to reflect not **two** but four eyes, two in their correct position and two further up the brow (1-3/579-81). The rectangular figure which this creates provides a frame for the Greimassian narrative chiasmus in which the four eyes become four `I" s or ` actants ".

As has been emphasized in the literature, in these 'less than/more than' uses, the rectification can go in two directions. In (271) the over-all expression of cardinality is to be interpreted eventually as 'more than', but in (272), the over-all expression of cardinality has to be interpreted as 'less than'.

(272) CK1 952> One of the philosophers he may have had in mind is Joseph Butler. In his dissertation, Of Personal Identity , Butler says that `by reflecting upon that, which is my self now, and that, which was my self twenty years ago, I discern they are not **two**, but one and the same self". This presupposes that a person (a) is now conscious of the self he is now; (b) is now conscious of the self he was at some time in the past; and (c) can discern the identity of the self he is now and the self he was at some time in the past.

It is important to stress that it is not so much *two* or *not two* that is interpreted as 'less than' or 'more than' in these cases. The eventual value is determined on the basis of all information that is found in the context and that can be assumed to affect the expression of cardinality. The crucial question is now: can we explain these data on the basis of the 'absolute value' analysis of numerals?

First of all, the difference between the two groups is, I repeat, not linked to an inherent characteristic of the two different possibilities. In both cases, it is the same type of negation: the ambiguity analysis for negation that, among others, Horn (1989, 1992) seems to defend does not seem to be an empirically motivated description, at least not in the case of numerals. I will not go into the debate on the analysis of negation (cf. Carston 1996, 1998a for an extensive discussion), but I will limit myself to a discussion of how negation and *two* can be seen to interact in the sample corpus and how these data can be explained from an 'absolute value' analysis of numerals.

Table 10 is clear: the various versions of the combination of *two* + negation that have been tested typically yield either 'less than' or 'less than/more than' values; the cases in which the expression of cardinality is 'more than two' (in the *not _ two* group) are due to the presence of intervening material in between the negative particle, most often the restrictors *just* or *only*. In terms of frequency, the straightforward 'less than' uses are similar to the 'less than / more than' instances, but there is an important *caveat* here: of the latter combinations of negation + *two*, a large part is eventually *also* interpreted as 'less than'. Of the 40 instances of 'less than / more than' interpretation of negation + *two*, 26/40 (65%) eventually were rectified in the direction of 'less than two' (most often the correction phrase included *one*), and only 14/40 (35%) got a 'more than' reading when the rectification phrase was taken into account. A special extra query was done to check this with a different (higher) numeral, namely *ten*, and also there both eventual interpretations were present, with a slight advantage of the 'less than' readings (6/11=54.5%) over the 'more than' readings (5/11=45.5%). Of course, the latter sample is much too small to be conclusive with respect to this issue, but the data on *two* together with the data on *ten* suggest at the very least that 'less than' readings are well represented in the 'less than / more than' group, i.e., the group in which the original cardinal is rectified explicitly by another cardinal. On the whole, then, it transpires that negation + *two* most often results in a 'less than' value.

This was originally used as an argument in favor of the 'at least' semantics of numerals, but an 'absolute value' analysis is compatible with these data as well, at least if one extra assumption is taken aboard, namely that it is an epistemological[61] truth that, if n>m then if you have n instances of X, then you also have m instances of X. I will refer to this type of reasoning, in which inferences are based on background knowledge of reality and not on linguistic knowledge, by the term "epistemological principle". This is clearly different from a linguistic entailment relation: the entailment-relationship between *bachelor* --> *unmarried* is a linguistic phenomenon. The fact that if you have three cookies, you also have two cookies relies on a basic fact about our knowledge of reality, i.e. it is part of the way we structure reality, and this is not totally dependent on the language we use to capture or represent this structure. Together with the 'absolute value' analysis of the numeral itself, it is predominantly the epistemological nature of this principle that makes my account of the interpretation of utterances in which numerals and negation are combined different from the classical neo-Gricean account.

Let us see what happens in a variety of cases. Let us first take the canonical *children* example.

(273) Mary doesn't have **two** children.

As has been emphasized in the literature, this may mean that Mary has more than two children, or it may mean that she has less than two children. It has also been remarked that if (273) occurs in isolation, without contrastive stress on *two* or the addition of a rectification phrase, the default interpretation is 'less than two', not 'more than two'. Within the 'at least' analysis of numerals, this was easy to explain: the negation was assumed to yield the

---

[61] With "epistemological" I mean that this principle is one of the principles that guide our knowledge of reality.

contradictory value of 'at least n', namely 'less than n'. Within the 'absolute value' analysis, *two* in (273) has an 'absolute value', which is combined with a negation. Through the "epistemological principle", a 'less than' interpretation is arrived at: general knowledge of the world tells us that if Mary has two children, she necessarily also has one child, but not necessarily three. The possibility that she has three children is not explicitly mentioned; it is not explicitly considered. The possibility that she has less than two children is not explicitly considered either; but the mentioning of *two* allows us to think that she may perhaps have less than two -- the existence of two children (including the consequence that there is also one child) functions as a reference point for the interpretation of the cardinal. The default interpretation of the combination of a numeral with negation will concentrate on what *has* been explicitly mentioned. The possibility of there being more than two children is, by default, of no concern -- it is *two* that functions as the reference point, not, e.g., *three*. Since the possibility of there being 'absolute value' two children is negated, and the possibility of there being more than two children is not considered, the only remaining interpretation is 'less than two'. This is compatible with our knowledge of the world: if someone does not have two children, it may still be the case that she has less than two children.

An apparently more problematic example for the 'absolute value' analysis is the following.

> (274) <FAB 430> She sighed heavily. `He's right, you know, Kate. She's not a child any more." `Oh, Mum, don't you jump on the bandwagon. She's so grown up that she shouted herself hoarse through a bloody pantomime not **two** hours ago. I saw a girl not much older than her battered and dying in a hospital bed, not twenty-four hours since. There's a bloody maniac on the loose and you tell me that she's grown up!" Evelyn put her hand on her daughter's arm. That's not all that's bothering you, is it? Now is it?

I argued earlier that this type of adverbial NPs, in which *two* modifies temporal entities, induces an 'exactly n' reading of the cardinal. The combination of 'exactly two' and negation leaves two options open: 'less than two' and 'more than two'. Nevertheless, it is clear that the default reading of this combination is 'less than two hours ago'. Therefore, I need to refer to the epistemological principle again. If something happened two hours ago, the event necessarily happened also at least one hour ago, but it is not true that in that case it happened three hours ago. Because the possibility that it happened more than two hours ago is not considered, while the possibility that it happened less than two hours ago is in a sense "covered" by the mentioning of the fact that it happened two hours ago (this "covering" is what is expressed by the epistemological principle), the latter will be considered when the numeral is combined with negation. 'More than two' is not considered, 'absolute value' / 'exactly n' two is negated, hence the default interpretation will be 'less than two'. That is what explains the default 'less than' reading of combinations of *two* + negation. Some extra examples of this phenomenon are listed below. In (275), the gathering of the group of 200 men is less than two years ago, in (276) fewer than two houses were communicable for whole winters round, in (277) the mansion is less than two miles from the bell tower.

(275) <CRA 3110> The defence ministry is pursuing what it calls `administrative" control over them, and is trying to win the loyalty of the troops serving at the missile sites. But even were Ukraine to get real control, its nuclear weapons would still be a questionable means of defence. For the time being, arguably an unneeded one anyway. It is not **two** years since a rag-tag group of about 200 men, few of them daring to wear their Soviet uniforms, gathered in the Kiev building that housed a short-lived nationalist government in 1917-18, to found the Ukrainian Officers Union.

(276) <AS4 571> If such is the character of these places now, what must they have been like when both men and livestock could only get around them by boat, and parishes such as Dogdyke in Lincolnshire had in the eighteenth century `not **two** houses communicable for whole winters round". For all their imperfections, the old wetland commons had a certain self-sufficiency and self-containment which provide a standard against which to judge the enthusiastic, never-satisfied ambitions of the agriculturalists and drainage men who set out to exploit them. Traditional management of the marshes was tuned to the finest nuances of the local water-table.

(277) <CN3 474> They seem to be buying up half Europe" The observation seemed irrelevant, but Tweed doubted whether the man from the Yard ever said anything without a purpose. He kept silent, forcing Buchanan to continue. `An odd coincidence is the fact that Franklin D. Hauser, chief executive of INCUBUS, has his English home in a mansion not **two** miles from that bell tower." `Probably just a coincidence," Tweed remarked, `as you suggested." `I paid a call at Livingstone Manor, Hauser's place. A butler, very English, the old school, told me Hauser was abroad.

It will be clear that this solution is in some respects a resuscitation of Horn's concept of "scales": in Horn's scale of numerals, *two* is entailed by *three*. The crucial difference, however, is that Horn's scales are representations of entailment relationships between *linguistic* elements. In the 'absolute value' analysis, it is not the case that *three* entails *two*, but it is argued that there is an epistemological principle that states that if you are certain that you have three objects, you may also be certain that you have at least two objects. This principle can be transposed from "possession" to other domains in which numerals are used to represent (our knowledge of) reality: if something is two miles away, it is necessarily also always one mile away; if something happened two years ago, it also happened at least one year ago.

This means that these inferences cannot be tied to the linguistic category of numerals (and certainly not as part of their semantics), but that they are associated with empirically verifiable phenomena, which are verified through "measurements" of reality such as counting elements of a set, counting time, counting distances etc. The 'less than' interpretation is overruled, however, if a rectification clause corrects the cardinality in the direction of a higher number of elements.

(278) CS7 922> Central government was not prepared to take that gamble, but was happy to see the localities take it. When looking at the local underbelly of the centre initiative at Powick, it was seen that the provision of more than one psychiatric hospital within a district, after 1982, meant certain death for one or other institution. In

Exeter, there were not **two**, but three, psychiatric hospitals. It would have been remarkable if no closures had been planned.

In (278), the over-all expression of cardinality is eventually interpreted as 'more than two', due to the rectification *but three*. As was to be expected, the default 'less than' reading of negation (which is based on an epistemological "inference", an indirect influence of background knowledge) + *two* can be overruled by explicit linguistic material. The epistemological principle is part of our general world knowledge, often called "background", and is relatively weak, not in the sense that the principle itself can be contradicted, but in the sense that the default reading it provides of the combination of the linguistic elements "negation" + *two* will not survive when another reading is supplied explicitly, by means of a rectification clause. This does not mean that the numeral itself receives another value - the rectification phrase does not turn *two* into a 'less than' or 'more than' value, it simply indicates that the statement that the cardinality is not two has to be (re)interpreted as leaving two possibilities open: it is either 'less than' or 'more than'.

This fits very well into the analysis of the factors that turn the default 'absolute value' semantics of *two* into an 'exactly n' interpretation: as other researchers have suggested (Van Kuppevelt 1996, Scharten 1997), and as was confirmed in the corpus analysis, when numerals are stressed, e.g. because they are in focus position, they receive an 'exactly n' interpretation. The cases of *two* that were collected in the 'less than / more than' group all seem to be in focus position, so they are turned into 'exactly n' uses. The negation of 'exactly two', with an upper and a lower bound, only negates what is within these bounds, which means that 'not exactly two' can be represented as 'less than two' OR 'more than two'. This is exactly what can be found in the uses of *two* that are combined with a negative particle. Note also that the simpler *children* example is also based on this type of epistemological reasoning: the inference from negation of existence to a 'less than' interpretation of the numeral is also based on this more general type of reasoning: if it is not the case that two instances of something exist, it is also the case that there do not exist three instances of the same thing, but there may exist less than two instances of that thing.

A final note concerning so-called cases of scale-reversals. What happens if these utterances are negated? Let us take a look at one of Horn's original examples.

(279)   Kipchoge can run a mile in 4 minutes, if not 3:58.
(adapted from Horn 1972:43)

With negation:

(280)   Kipchoge cannot run a mile in 4 minutes. [It takes him 4:30]

In the 'absolute value' analysis of numerals, negation + numeral normally induces a 'less than' interpretation. In this case, however, *four* is interpreted as 'exactly four' due to the fact that it modifies a temporal entity in an adverbial phrase. Negation + 'exactly four' normally leaves open two possibilities: 'less than four' and 'more than four', but because of the general epistemological principle, the default 'less than' reading is preferred. This is the opposite of the situation in (280), because the reading of the numeral is clearly 'more than four'.

The example in (280) is rather complicated, due to two special characteristics. One, it contains a modal operator, and it has been demonstrated that these operators interact with the expression of cardinality. Two, the epistemological principle is not only different from the entailment relationship that Horn uses with respect to the level at which it is supposed to hold (epistemological versus linguistic), but in this case their consequences do not overlap either. While it is generally true that if you have three apples, you also have two, it is not true that if you can run a mile in four minutes, you can do it in three minutes, but rather the reverse. The latter shows that the entailment from *three* to *two* is not valid. Horn had to resort to the concept of "scale reversal" to explain what was going on, without really providing a clear indication of what triggered this reversal. The epistemological principle links the interpretation of the numeral directly to our knowledge of the world.

It also shows that the epistemological principle has to be related to a specific type of measurement. For each type of measurement, the epistemological consequences must be checked: if the utterance is about the counting of entities, the epistemological principle says that for m>n, if you have m instances of that entity, you also have at least n instances. With respect to the 'ability to run a mile in X minutes', our knowledge of reality tells us that if you can run a mile in three minutes, you can also run it in four minutes, but not necessarily in two minutes. That is because people can run slower than their maximum speed, but not faster. Another way of saying this is that people can always run a shorter distance in the same time period, but not necessarily a longer distance. The association with a specific type of measurement is absolutely crucial: another way of measuring speed is expressed in the phrase *x miles an hour*. But if someone can run at 60 miles an hour, it does not follow that she can run at 70 miles an hour, but it does follow that she can run at 50 miles an hour. Returning to the example, it is clear that this knowledge tells us that if Kipchoge can run a mile in four minutes, he can also do it in more than four minutes, but not necessarily in less than four minutes. This can be paraphrased by saying that on the basis of the information in (279) - namely that Kipchoge can run a mile in four minutes - it is certain that he can run a mile in more than four minutes. Crucially, however, this certainty is NOT an explicit part of the coded meaning of *four*, whether it is part of reversed scale or not. Note that this is not the same as saying that he can do it in *at least* four minutes, because the latter encodes an epistemic component, namely 'possibly more than four'. It is clear that this is not what is meant in (279): if anything, the hearer may conclude on the basis of (279) that Kipchoge can *certainly* run a mile in more than four minutes, even if also this is not encoded by the speaker. The speaker certainly does not express the *possibility* that he can do it in more than four minutes.

But there is yet another complicating factor: the negative particle. The crucial mistake one could make here is interpreting (280) as an utterance in which negation acts directly on the numeral. In this case, it actually acts on the modal, which is also clear from its position in the clause. First, the effect of negation on the modal has to be interpreted and this is the "input" of the "epistemological principle". If an attempt is made to ascertain the conclusions that can be drawn from (280) in terms of longer and shorter periods of time, it transpires that they are different from the ones described in the previous paragraph. While our general knowledge of the world tells us that if someone can run a mile in four minutes, he can certainly run a mile in five minutes, but not necessarily in three minutes, the opposite holds for "inabilities". If someone is not able to run a mile in four minutes, he is certainly unable to run a mile in three minutes, but he is not necessarily unable to run a mile in five minutes. It is this background knowledge that takes care of the interpretation of (280), not the semantics of the numeral, nor the concept of scale reversal. The fact that the modal has to be taken into account first is also clear from the fact that it is impossible to paraphrase (280) without the negative particle without changing the modal. The correct paraphrase is not (281), but (282).

> (281) Kipchoge can run a mile in more than 4 minutes.
> (282) Kipchoge needs more than 4 minutes to run a mile.

It would be wrong to interpret (280) as an instance of negation interacting with a numeral. In (280), the negation interacts with the modal, and it is the combination of the negative + modal that forms the basis of the epistemological consequences that can be drawn from (280) with respect to the capacities of Kipchoge. If negation could be applied directly to the numeral, as in (283), the usual 'less than' interpretation would return.

> (283) Kipchoge can run a mile in not (even) 4 minutes.

In (283), the epistemological consequences only concern 'four minutes', because *not* acts on the NP *four minutes*, and not on the whole predicate (*can run a mile in 4 minutes*): a time span of 'four minutes' is always also a time span of 'three minutes', but not one of 'five minutes'. This explains the 'less than' interpretation in (283).

5.3.4. Conclusion

The conclusion of the implementation of three classical neo-Gricean tests in the sample corpus is that an 'absolute value' analysis is more adequate than the classical neo-Gricean account of numerals in terms of 'at least' semantics. With respect to the concept of "defeasibility", it became clear that in an overwhelming number of cases, neither the suspension, nor the ·cancellation test can be applied. Nevertheless, the attempt at implementation of these tests into the sample corpus was not useless: it brought a number of factors to the fore that influence the applicability and interpretation of *if not* and *in fact* phrases. While these can almost never be used to test the values of numerals in actual tokens of language use, they are often used as part of (the correction of) expressions of cardinality, and therefore deserve to be analyzed here.

The applicability of the redundancy test is considerably better, but it is remarkable that 'at least' as well as 'exactly' restrictors could be added to the expression of cardinality. Even more surprising from the neo-Gricean point of view is that 'at least' restrictors could be added much more often than 'exactly' or 'at most' restrictors: the neo-Griceans' redundancy argument was based on the redundancy effect that the addition of *exactly* would create if the semantics of the numeral were 'exactly n'. Within their 'at least' analysis, the addition of an 'at least' restrictor should create a similar redundancy-effect, but the corpus analysis showed that this was definitely not the case. In fact, in nearly half of the uses of *two*, 'at least' could be added without creating this redundancy effect, or any artificial "flavor" at all. Only in less than ten percent, the same result was achieved with the addition of an 'exactly' restrictor.

Finally, the effect of "negation" on the expression of cardinality was tested. In the neo-Gricean analysis, the fact that "negation" + a numeral usually triggers a 'less than' interpretation of the numeral follows naturally from the 'at least' semantics of the numeral. In this section I did not delve into the theoretical niceties of this argument (cf. Chapter 3), but I directly confronted the argument with four extra queries in the sample corpus. The tendency that Horn and other neo-Griceans discovered was confirmed: in most cases, the combination of negation and *two* yielded 'less than' values for *two*. But while neo-Griceans tended to attribute the other readings, namely the 'more than' interpretations of the combination 'negation + two' to a special type of negation, called "metalinguistic negation", I opted for the Relevance-theoretic approach in terms of an "echoic use", which only requires one meaning for the negative particle. The eventual interpretation of 'negation + two' depends on two factors: the so-called "epistemological principle" which reanalyzes the neo-Gricean linguistic "entailments" from higher numerals to lower numerals as consequences of the ways in which we structure reality, and the presence of a rectification clause, which had been interpreted by neo-Griceans as a signal for the metalinguistic character of negation. In the analysis, the 'less than' value of the combination of negation + *two* is explained via the basic 'absolute value' meaning of *two* in an NP, which introduces a set of referents and presents them as being in existence. The 'less than' value is considered to be an effect of the interaction of 'negation' on this existential meaning, and only in a second stage on the cardinal, and not directly on the cardinal as such. The denial of existence then leads automatically to a 'less than' interpretation: if it is not the case that two instances of something exist, it is necessarily so that it is not the case that three instances of the thing exist, but it may be the case that fewer than two instances of the thing exist.

The second factor, the presence of a rectification clause, which contains a lower or a higher "replacement numeral", is much stronger than any influence of inferences based on the "epistemological principle". If *two* is combined with a numeral, the default interpretation is 'less than two' as long as no replacement numeral is given. As soon as a rectification of the expression of cardinality is uttered, the over-all expression of cardinality is changed in the direction of the replacing numeral. This does not mean that the original interpretation of *two* itself is altered by the presence of the rectification clause: rather, in these uses of *two*, the presence of a rectification clause usually co-occurs with a focus on *two*. This focus turns *two* into an 'exactly n' value, and the combination of this meaning + negation results automatically in the disjunction of 'less than' and 'more than' values. The rectification clause pushes the interpretation in one of these two directions. When this rectification phrase is absent, the focus on *two* is often also absent, which leaves the 'absolute value' meaning unaltered. The combination of negation + this 'absolute value' meaning then results in a 'less than' value, through the "epistemology principle". The reasoning that is behind this principle is fully compatible with the existential meaning that is typical of 'absolute value' uses of *two*: typically, the denial of existence reduces the cardinality of a set, rather than increasing it. When the negated *two* is stressed without there being a rectification phrase in the context, the interpretation of the expression of cardinality can normally not be completed: the hearer is presented with two possibilities - either 'less than two' or 'more than two' - and is not given any clue to resolve the dilemma. My hypothesis would be that this situation does not normally occur in communication: either the speaker does provide a rectification phrase, or the hearer will ask for it.

5.4. SMALL NUMBERS, LARGE NUMBERS, ROUND NUMBERS AND NON-ROUND NUMBERS

I have based the analysis of numerals on the corpus data provided by one thousand instances of *two* in the BNC. The general principles and factors that have been derived from that corpus analysis hold for other cardinals as well, but some other numerals have characteristics that *two* does not have. Especially high numerals and the roundness of numerals seem interesting; a number of extra queries show how these two factors, magnitude and roundness, influence the interpretation of numerals. I looked at the small round numeral *ten*, the larger non-round numeral *twenty-two* and the large round number *one thousand*. Since the focus is on the effects of magnitude and roundness on the value interpretation of the numeral, I have limited myself to the discussion of the uses that demonstrate full cardinality (hence, the adnominal, fully cardinal uses and the pronominal uses).

5.4.1. *Ten*

Let us start with a "round number", namely *ten*, which is the "base" of our decimal counting system. I will not go into the discussion concerning the exact definition of what constitutes a round number (Channell 1980, Pollmann and Jansen 1996), but I will simply take two non-controversial examples of "round numbers", namely "ten" and, in a separate section "one thousand".

I compiled 100 utterances containing *ten* from the BNC, in order to check whether the behavior of *ten* is significantly different from that of *two*. Seventy-three of these one hundred instances turned out to be fully cardinal uses of *ten* (adnominal or pronominal). The results do not suggest that *ten* is very different from *two*, and in general, the observations that were made concerning *two* also hold for *ten*. Some minor differences include the frequency of the occurrences in adverbial phrases, the results of the redundancy test (especially concerning the 'approximately' restrictors) and some qualifications with respect to the suspension test. Table 11 shows the distribution of the value-interpretations in the sample corpus of *ten*.

TABLE 11

VALUES OF *TEN* AND *TWO* COMPARED

	Absolute value	Exactly n	At least / more than n	At most / less than n
TEN	27/73=37%	33/73=45.2%	9/73=12.3%	4/73=5.5%
TWO	390/857=45.5%	365/857=42.6%	33/857=3.9%	69/857=8%

Compared to the distribution of *two*, the most remarkable result is that with *ten* there are more 'exactly n' uses than 'absolute value' uses, while the opposite holds for *two*. Nevertheless, just like with *two*, the 'absolute value' uses and the 'exactly n' uses are by far the most important groups; the 'at least / more than n' and the 'at most / less than n' interpretations are rather marginal.

Table 12 describes the distribution of *ten* with respect to the syntactic function of the NP they form part of.

TABLE 12

SYNTACTIC FUNCTION OF NP CONTAINING *TEN* COMPARED TO *TWO*

	Adverbial	Subject	Direct Object	Adjunct
TEN	42/73=57.6%	13/73=17.8%	12/73=16.4%	6/73=8.2%
TWO	249/857=29.1%	244/857=28.4%	166/857=19.4%	117/857=13.7%

This table suggests the explanation of the mysterious abundance of 'exactly n' readings, compared to the values of *two*: *ten* occurs much more frequently in adverbial clauses than *two*. Whereas the adverbial clauses take up 57.6% of the uses of *ten*, they only cover 29.1% of the uses of *two* (cf. Table 4). As we have seen in the discussion of the influence of the syntactic nature of the NP on the value interpretation of numerals, adverbial NPs containing numerals often serve to locate a state of affairs. Therefore, the entities they introduce are often temporal or spatial entities that give the coordinates of a certain state of affairs, rather than introducing entities that form part of this state of affairs. Therefore, these entities are not presented as being "in existence", and it is the latter feature that is the hallmark of 'absolute value' interpretations. That is why *ten* often receives an 'exactly n' interpretation in adverbial NPs.

With respect to the redundancy test, I expect to find more uses of *ten* that are compatible with the addition of a restrictor than there are uses of *two* compatible with the addition of a restrictor. As has been mentioned before (see, e.g., the discussion of Horn 1972 in section 3.1.1.), it is widely believed that round numbers can be characterized by an inherent degree of "inexactness". The difference between *two* and *ten* with respect to the redundancy test can be explained by the fact that this inexactness, which is implicit in *ten*, is made explicit by means of an 'approximately' restrictor. With respect to the other restrictors, no differences are expected between *two* and *ten*. This is confirmed by the data in the sample corpus: in 26/73 instances of *ten* a restrictor could be added (compare: the uses of *two* only allowed the addition of restrictors in 12.3% of the cases). The distribution of these additions is schematized in Table 13.

TABLE 13

ADDITION OF RESTRICTORS TO USES OF *TEN* COMPARED WITH TWO: TYPES[62]

	Approximative restrictors	'Exactly' restrictors	'At least' restrictors	'At most' restrictors
TEN	18/26=69.3%	1/26=3.8%	6/26=23.1%	1/26=3.8%
TWO	42/105= 40%	10/105= 9.5%	47/105= 44.8%	6/105= 5.7%

Finally, I also checked whether the suspension test and the cancellation test could be applied more easily than with *two*: only in 8/73=11% of the instances could the suspension test be applied and in 4/73=5.5% cases the cancellation test could be applied. With *two*, the suspension test could be applied in 4% of the cases and the cancellation test in 2.9% of the cases. It is not fully clear what explains the difference between *two* and *ten*, but the presence of definiteness markers is certainly an important factor: *two* combines with a definiteness marker more often than *ten*. In the sample corpus of *two*, 252/857=29.4% of the utterances contain a definiteness marker, whereas with *ten* only 10/73=13.7% contain a definiteness marker.

This confirms the general trend (cf. also the remarks concerning adverbials in section 5.1.3.1.): *ten* is not often used to introduce or refer back to referents that are part of the state of affairs. This is the indirect reason why they have a higher rate of 'exactly n' values (i.e., they are most often used in adverbial NPs that refer to temporal entities), but it also explains why there are fewer definiteness markers in NPs containing *ten*: people do not often refer back to a set of ten identifiable elements. At any rate, they do it less often than referring back to a set containing two identifiable referents. But people easily locate a state of affairs as being "ten years ago", as happening "within ten minutes", as being "ten miles away". Some examples are given below: (284) exemplifies the typical use of *ten* (as part of an adverbial phrase referring to temporal entities, and, consequently, with an 'exactly n' value), (285) is one of the less frequent 'absolute value' uses of *ten* and (286) shows that also with *ten* 'at most' interpretations can only be triggered by the presence of special features (modal operators or, as in this case, a restrictor).

(284) <AC2 110>Very generous financial assistance would be given by the Government, in the form of a grant of up to thirty per cent of capital and remission of all taxation on export sales for **ten** years. The fact that in the whole of South West

---

[62] When an utterance could be combined with more than one type of restrictor, it was grouped with the category of restrictor that was deemed most natural in the context of the utterance.

Ireland there was not sufficient labour to man a new United Motors plant was not seen by the Minister as any kind of problem; simply as a little local difficulty.

(285) <A0G 390> Strawberry taste on trial This month we're starting a trial to discover the best-tasting strawberries. We've asked Ken Muir, of the famous fruit nursery, to select eight varieties of strawberry for the test. He's chosen Royal Sovereign, Tenira (his own favourite), Elsanta, Cambridge Favourite, Honeoye, Korona, Bounty and a new variety, Pegasus. We're looking for **ten** volunteers to take part, each of whom will be sent five plants of each of the eight varieties to grow. The plants will be despatched at the end of September, with full cultural instructions.

(286) <EBW 475> The approval of the Spanish Government will be required for both the Architectural Project and the final acceptance of the refurbishment. Third - A Loan Agreement for a period of up to **ten** years shall be executed between the Foundation and the owners of the category `A" and `B+" paintings. The Foundation shall pay to the owners of the paintings as consideration for the loan an annual sum to be determined.

At the beginning of the discussion of *ten*, I also referred to a difference between *two* and *ten* with respect to the suspension test. In (287) there is an example that demonstrates this difference.

(287) <AT4 288>`Did you achieve something, sir?" Bean asked. `Very good, Bean! I did indeed! I'll tell you all about it on Monday, in class events. Something to look forward to." They weren't so sure, but made no comment. On Monday morning Sam came to class events with dark shadows under his eyes, looking **ten** years older over a weekend. He came to the door with Foggerty the games master, who was grinning like an ape. Nutty, coming in late, heard Sam say, `Look, I made a bet and I'm going through with it. We attempt nothing in this school, and even if I've bitten off more than we can chew here, it's better to try -"

While the suspension test generally applies to this type of utterance due to its argumentative value, the magnitude of the replacement numeral is very important. If a suspension phrase is inserted with the next numeral in line, *eleven*, it does not work.

(288) ?On Monday morning Sam came to class events with dark shadows under his eyes, looking **ten**, if not eleven years older over a weekend.

In (288) the suspension phrase is odd because we live with the assumption that you cannot estimate how much older someone looks in a very accurate way. The promise or even guarantee that is inherent in the suspension phrase *if not eleven* is not compatible with what we believe about estimations of how old someone looks. Also, besides being imprecise, or vague (the typical characteristics of utterances that make use of round numbers), the phrase *looking ten years older* might also be an exaggeration, a hyperbole. Those two factors also explain why the addition of the suspension phrase *if not eleven* creates a mildly humorous effect: it suggests that the speaker pretends to be able to estimate very accurately "how much older someone looks", while such estimations can only be vague and are normally used only "in a manner of speaking". The suspension test can, however, be applied to the example, provided that a round numeral is used as replacement numeral, such as *fifteen* or *twenty*.

> (289) On Monday morning Sam came to class events with dark shadows under his eyes, looking **ten**, if not fifteen / twenty years older over a weekend.

A similar example is provided in (290).

> (290) <CGH 413> It works, I don't know how, or why, and I certainly don't understand why they are not advertised, but these things are incredible. They remove ammonia, nitrates to a small extent, nitrates, copper and God-knows what else. It does all that carbon will do about **ten** times over, can visually be checked for when it is fully loaded, and will NOT release the lot back into the water even when fully charged. (Oh, and it can be used in marine systems too). So, with all systems working, the choice of fish can be taken from the categories listed in the final table.

The problem in this example is not so much that people cannot really estimate the relative strength of "these things" in comparison with carbon (they certainly can), but that the phrase *ten times* is clearly a hyperbole, which turns it into a "vague" estimation. The addition of *if not eleven* would suggest a high degree of precision, which is not in tune with the cotext.

> (291) ?It does all that carbon will do about **ten**, if not eleven times over, can visually be checked for when it is fully loaded, and will NOT release the lot back into the water even when fully charged.

Again, a suspension phrase with a round numeral is unproblematic[63].

> (292) It does all that carbon will do about **ten**, if not twenty times over, can visually be checked for when it is fully loaded, and will NOT release the lot back into the water even when fully charged.

5.4.2. *Twenty-two*

Of the 100 instances of *twenty-two* that have been compiled from the BNC, only 67 could be classified as "fully cardinal". Of those 67 instances, most uses had an 'absolute value' meaning, as in (293).

---

[63] Another phenomenon that deserves attention is the fact that the replacement value of *if not* phrases should not be too far removed from the original value: ??*It does all that carbon will do about ten, if not five hundred and thirty times over* is very odd indeed. I will not go into this problem here.

(293) <C9M 369> This is a headstock shape that works, I think; it's functional and not overly indebted to its forbears - modern, without being moderne , if you see what I mean. The New York has a rosewood fingerboard which is well up to usual Eggle standards; they really do seem to be consistently good across the entire range. It has **twenty-two** quite chunky and well-seated frets, and a low, buzz-free action testifies to quality of workmanship in this area, too.

The general distribution can be found in Table 14.

TABLE 14

VALUES OF *TWENTY-TWO* AND *TWO* COMPARED

	Absolute value	Exactly n	At least / more than n	At most / less than n
TWENTY-TWO	32/67=47.8%	27/67=40.3%	5/67=7.4%	3/67=4.5%
TWO	390/857=45.5%	365/857=42.6%	33/857=3.9%	69/857=8%

Generally speaking, *twenty-two* is also quite similar to *two*. With respect to the distribution of its values, it is even more similar to *two* than *ten*, as the 'absolute value' uses form the largest group, just like with the uses of *two*. Nevertheless, with respect to the syntactic nature of the NPs to which the numeral belongs, *twenty-two* resembles *ten* much more than it resembles *two*. Especially the high rate of adverbial NPs is striking: whereas with *two* these adverbial NPs constituted only 26% of the total instances, with *ten* (57.6%) and *twenty-two* (41.8%) they are much more prominent.

TABLE 15

SYNTACTIC FUNCTION OF NP CONTAINING *TWENTY-TWO*

	Adverbial	Subject	Direct Object	Adjunct
TWENTY-TWO[64]	28/67=41.8%	12/67=17.9%	13/67=19.4%	12/67=17.9%
TWO	249/857=29.1%	244/857=28.4%	166/857 =19.4%	117/857 =13.7%

In (294), there is an example of *twenty-two* as part of an adverbial phrase.

(294) <EBP 901> Between 1254 and 1272, moreover, the position had been made more complex by clashes between Henry III and the Lord Edward. There were

---

[64] Two out of the 67 (3%) instances featured *twenty-two* in a predicate NP.

fourteen changes of seneschal in Gascony during these eighteen years, while under Edward, as king, only six changes took place in the **twenty-two** years from 1272 to 1294. It has recently been pointed out by Dr J. R. Studd that 'one of [the Lord] Edward's greatest problems was his inability to settle lands from his appanage [of Gascony and the isle of Oléron] on those who gave him loyal service in a traditional way".

This abundance of adverbial NPs suggests that language users do not often refer to sets of ten or twenty-two members, even though they may use these numerals in locating states of affairs in terms of time or place. Even when *twenty-two* is part of other syntactic constituents, it often does not directly indicate the cardinality of the set the NP refers to, but only quantifies the noun through a mediating concept, such as 'percentage'.

> (295) <AD2 787> The interesting competition was between Paisley and the Official Unionists for the title of spokesman for the Protestant people, and it was a contest which Paisley won comfortably. He took 29.8 per cent of the first preference votes, Hume took 24.6 per cent and John Taylor did not pass the quota until West was eliminated and he collected his transfers. Together both the Officials took only **twenty-two** per cent of the first preferences. In an opinion poll conducted in 1967, ninety per cent of the people asked said they preferred Terence O'Neill to Ian Paisley as premier.
> (296) <ECB 272> Unemployment insurance and wage levels The great depression of the 1930s during which unemployment never fell below nine per cent and at one point exceeded **twenty-two** per cent, meant that a large section of the population was dependent on insurance and assistance benefits. It became increasingly difficult to pay insurance and assistance benefits and at the same time keep them below the level of wages.

Of course, "regular" adnominal uses of *twenty-two* in non-adverbial NPs do occur.

> (297) <AN9 1806> The researchers had gone through the medical records for the whole period from 1959, when Hinkley A was still being built, right through to 1986. They had used exactly the same methodology as that employed to reach the results at Dounreay and Sellafield. And their findings were decisively similar. Over the entire period, there were **twenty-two** cases of under-25 leukaemia, when only eleven would be expected, and in one critical period - from 1964 to 1978 - there had been fifteen cases where six would have been normal. The probability of this occurring by chance was 1,700 to 1.

Finally, I also checked whether restrictors could be added. Only 11 of the 67 instances were compatible with the addition of a restrictor. Table 16 shows the distribution (I have omitted the percentages, as the number of instances is too low).

TABLE 16

ADDITION OF RESTRICTORS TO USES OF *TWENTY-TWO* COMPARED TO *TWO* AND
TEN: TYPES[65]

	Approximative restrictors	'Exactly' restrictors	'At least' restrictors	'At most' restrictors
TWENTY-TWO	8/11	1/11	2/11	-
TWO	42/105= 40%	10/105= 9.5%	47/105= 44.8%	6/105= 5.7%

No instance of *twenty-two* could be exclusively combined with an 'at most' restrictor (but
some uses that are compatible with an 'approximately' restrictor could also be combined with
an 'at most' restrictor). This mainly demonstrates that *twenty-two* does not combine very well
with any type of restrictor. Especially the difference with *ten* with respect to the
'approximately' restrictors is striking: whereas with *ten* this type of restrictor could be added
in a relatively high number of cases (18/73=24.7%)[66], with *twenty-two* this percentage
diminishes to 8/67=11.9%. This could be expected on the basis of the inherent "vagueness" of
round numbers, a feature that (especially higher) non-round values lack. In (298), the addition
of an 'approximately' restrictor would be rather odd (299): if the speaker makes the effort to
be precise in terms of the number of years, he or she will normally not import vagueness by
means of an 'approximately' restrictor. The speaker could have used *twenty* in (298) without
really having to "lie", precisely because the expectations with regard to precision of numerals
diminish as the numeral becomes larger. If he does decide to use the more precise numeral
twenty-two, the fact that the speaker has made an extra effort to provide this extra information
will often preclude the addition of a restrictor making the statement vaguer again.

> (298) <CMP 1547> Sharpe rolled right again, this time plunging deeper into the rye
> stalks before reloading the rifle. He pushed the pistol into his belt. French muskets
> banged. He heard the heavy lead balls flicking through the stalks of rye, though none
> went near him. Sharpe was loading fast, going through the drill he had first learned
> **twenty-two** years before. Another volley of musketry hammered from the French who
> were firing blind into the tall crops. Sharpe did the same, simply aiming the rifle in the
> direction of the column, and pulling the trigger so that the bullet whipped off through
> the stalks.
> (299) ?Sharpe was loading fast, going through the drill he had first learned
> about/approximately **twenty-two** years before.

This explanation holds for the addition of 'approximately' restrictors in as far as they
are interpreted as making the number of years differ a few *units*: *approximately* can hardly be

---

[65] When an utterance could be combined with more than one type of restrictor, it was grouped with the category
of restrictor that was deemed most natural in the context of the utterance.
[66] These figures refer to the instances in which an 'approximately' restrictor could be added, compared to the
total number of instances (and not relative to the addition of other restrictors).

used to introduce that type of vagueness that would allow 'twenty-four' and certainly not 'twenty'. It can, however, be used to introduce another type of vagueness, namely when *approximately twenty-two years ago* is understood as 'twenty-two years, seven months and three days ago', in other words, when divisions within one *unit* (in this case: a year) are meant. In that case, however, the speaker would have to have a special reason for being so careful with respect to the expression of cardinality. Whereas the first type of vagueness (at the level of the units) would be odd due to the fact that the introduction of vagueness would undo the precision inherent in *twenty-two*, the second type (below the level of the units) would require a very specific type of context, namely one in which precision will be considered to be of high importance. Nevertheless, 'approximately' restrictors *can* be used with some specific utterances containing *twenty-two*.

(300) <CBN 50> The Borinage, desolate and impoverished, was a coalfield in the south-west of Belgium near, a region of flat blasted lands surmounted by slag heaps of waste, One assumes that his father financed this latest venture. He probably thought it would be short-lived. In fact Vincent spent **twenty-two** months in this terrible black country, a period nearly as long as his stay in France. For thirty Belgian francs a month he lodged with a pedlar by the name of van der Haegen who lived at Paturages, not far from Mons (the house was demolished in the early 1960s to allow for road widening).

(301) In fact Vincent spent about **twenty-two** months in this terrible black country, a period nearly as long as his stay in France.

(302) ECH n=612> Projet de Gauche and Projet de Droite (e1 and E2 5b respectively) push the grade up a bit and, like the excellent Excelsior (E25c,5c), both finish with tricky walls. RUSSAN **Twenty-two** kilometres upstream, above a huge meander in the Gardon, are the newer cliffs of Russan. With development starting in 1984, the first guidebook not appearing until 1989, and comparatively more difficult access than the virtually roadside Collias, even the easiest routes here are still unpolished.

(303) Approximately **twenty-two** kilometres upstream, above a huge meander in the Gardon, are the newer cliffs of Russan.

Finally, a short note about the relatively high number of non-cardinal uses of *twenty-two* (33%): no less than 23 of the 100 instances of *twenty-two* were indications of the *age* of persons, such as in (304). This is no doubt caused by the fact that *twenty-two* is relatively seldom used to indicate the cardinality of sets of entities, which causes the relative prominence of indications of age to be higher. Also, *twenty-two* is definitely within the range of "possible ages" of a human being, and may even be one of the more popular "ages".

(304) AC3 n=2298>Viola was cold and distant and seemed determined to get rid of him. He put the phone down and had a violent coughing fit. He spat what looked like bloody phlegm into his paper hanky. `TB," he muttered, `I must be dying of love." Then he remembered the red lozenges he'd sucked all the way in the car. At **twenty-two**, it seemed, Viola was too set in her ways for him. She looked like a beautiful young girl, but she had the hardness of an old woman. He wouldn't bother with her any

more. She wasn't worth the effort, he decided. Perhaps he could pick up someone new today. He didn't often have the chance of meeting schoolgirls.

5.4.3. *One thousand*

Finally, I will also discuss a still larger and round numeral, namely *one thousand*. In order to get an acceptable number of utterances, I had to extract 200 instances from the BNC, as in very many of the solutions provided by the BNC, *one thousand* was part of a larger non-round numeral, as in (305).

(305) <JT3 405> The friendly doctor. You have to be off for a while to receive that, or straight away. Yes. Depending on we look for details, as we go through it. Teacher, March eighty-seven, low premiums. Lower risk. September ninety-two, through stress and depression My God. that one, **one thousand six hundred and ninety-five** pounds. That's cos she wanted paid. We've got a brick-layer. August eighty-nine, took the policy out. March ninety Here we go.

Even within this larger sample corpus, only 53 instances of *one thousand* could be found. Table 17 shows the distribution of the values of *one thousand*.

TABLE 17

VALUES OF *ONE THOUSAND* COMPARED TO *TWO*

	Absolute value	Exactly n	At least / more than n	At most / less than n
ONE THOUSAND	26/53=49.1%	12/53=22.6%	10/53=18.9%	5/53=9.4%
TWO	390/857 =45.5%	365/857 =42.6%	33/857=3.9%	69/857=8%

The large number of 'absolute value' uses of *one thousand* is rather remarkable. The sample corpus suggests two reasons: *one thousand* hardly ever co-occurs with definiteness markers, and it does not function very often as part of an adverbial clause. In (306), there is an example of such an 'absolute value' use, while (307) exemplifies the much less frequent 'exactly n' use, in this case triggered by the "non-existence" of the "times" it is bigger than the "million".

(306) <CD8 117> How to attempt this? It was out of the question to consider attacking or besieging Roxburgh Castle, of course, without heavy cannon. Would it be best to wait, hidden, and seek to ambush Balliol's party on their return to their main army - as surely they must intend? The difficulty there would be to achieve surprise. **One**

thousand men could not enter and remain in the vicinity for any time without being discovered. Balliol would undoubtedly soon learn of their presence, however heedfully they hid.

(307) <ANX 2589> After all, spread around, that's what it would buy. From this Pperspective, our hypothetical generous increase in NHS funding amounts to roughly one Ppint of beer. It really does bring everything down to earth. The fabulous MILL ION becomes a paltry 2.5 Ppence. The equally fabulous (equal because equally incomprehensible) BILL ION becomes **one thousand** times as big, as it should be: P£25. It's not a sum you'd throw away; but you'd be happy if it bought a new handbag, a train fare to London or a tankful of petrol.

Table 18 shows the distribution of *one thousand* in terms of the syntactic nature of the NP to which it belongs:

TABLE 18

SYNTACTIC FUNCTION OF NP CONTAINING *ONE THOUSAND* COMPARED TO *TWO*

	Adverbial	Subject	Direct Object	Adjunct
ONE THOUSAND[67]	8/53=15.1%	14/53=26.4%	19/53=35.8%	10/53=18.9%
TWO	249/857 =29.1%	244/857 =28.4%	166/857 =19.4%	117/857 =13.7%

As mentioned already, especially the relatively low number of adverbial phrases is striking, together with the result for direct object NPs, an instance of which is presented in (308).

(308) <JNB 308> When we get to the jobs erm side of it the jobs I I I'm accused outside this afternoon of of putting in jeopardy **one thousand** something jobs erm, this authority got rid of seven hundred jobs, education jobs er only a few months ago and there's many more, something on the region of two thousand jobs will be lost in this authority without a protest.

I do not see any specific reasons for the remarkably high number of direct object NPs, but it should be emphasized that also the subject NPs are relatively frequent, compared to *two, ten* and *twenty-two*. This suggests that the high frequency of direct or subject NPs is not caused by a preference of *one thousand* for subject or object NPs, but rather that it is caused by the fact that *one thousand* seems to avoid adverbial NPs more than, e.g., *ten* or *twenty-two*. In (309) there is an instance of *one thousand* in a subject NP, in (310) an example of an adverbial NP containing *twenty-two* is given.

---

[67] Two out of the 53 (3.8%) instances featured *one thousand* in a predicate NP.

(309) <K8T 1324> He knelt down by a familiar mound and after a moment's hesitation yanked out the cross that he had placed at the head of the grave. Charlie unclipped a knife that hung from his belt and beside the name Tommy Prescott he carved the letters MM. *** A fortnight later **one thousand** men, with a thousand legs, a thousand arms and a thousand eyes between them, were ordered home. Sergeant Charles Trumper of the Royal Fusiliers was detailed to accompany them, perhaps because no man had been known to survive three charges on the enemy's lines.

(310) <HA3 1869> The stone really was uncomfortable. Twoflower looked down and, for the first time, noticed the strange carving. It looked like a spider. Or was it a squid? Moss and lichens rather blurred the precise details. But they didn't blur the runes carved below it. Twoflower could read them clearly, and they said: Traveller, the hospitable temple of Bel-Shamharoth lies **one thousand** paces Hubwards. Now this was strange, Twoflower realised, because although he could read the message the actual letters were completely unknown to him.

Finally, in 19/53=35.8% of the instances, a restrictor could be added to the numeral. This is a rather high number compared to *two* (12.3%) or *twenty*-two (11.9%). It is even higher than the percentage of additions to the other round number that has been discussed, *ten* (24.7%). Not surprisingly, most restrictors are 'approximately' restrictors such as in (311).

(311) <HL8 1650> Five hundred sports grounds would be built in 18 months; young people would be offered training courses with the army, fire brigades and charities and would be encouraged to join the police. **One thousand** police would be posted to the suburbs that summer and 12 more "houses of justice" would be built as centres for dispute settlement and advisory services.

(312) Approximately **one thousand** police would be posted to the suburbs that summer and 12 more "houses of justice" would be built as centres for dispute settlement and advisory services.

This confirms the generalization concerning round numerals: they are often compatible with 'approximately' restrictors due to their inherent vagueness. The restrictor merely makes explicit what was already contained in the numeral itself. A good example of this inherent vagueness can be found in (313).

(313) <J1L 267> An enormous public storm ensued - both internally and externally. But he stuck to his guns. And the audience for Woman's Hour is now larger than it was. We've gone back and looked at the correspondence we've had about the News Network. And we've found that so far, we've had **one thousand** letters of concern since the network was announced. Since the campaign was launched on `Feedback", the BBC has received thirty-nine critical calls. Compare that to one day recently when there were more than seventy calls about a schedule change. Of course we take all of these worries seriously - but I want you to get the scale of the complaints in perspective.

Most probably *one thousand letters of concern* should not be taken as indicating 'exactly 1000' letters. When it is not possible to add an 'approximately' restrictor, it is often because definiteness markers or other restrictors are present.

> (314) <BMC 2400> She also has the advantage of an outstanding recording. Very strongly recommended - even to those who don't usually like guitar albums. [RMW] `THOMAS HARDY AND LOVE" An Anthology with music, compiled and presented by Bernard Palmer From a corpus of almost **one thousand** poems this anthology is well selected and presented. `Love" (in all its aspects) is the theme of most of Hardy's fiction and poetry, and the well known poems To Lisbie Browne , and The Dark-Eyed Gentleman are excellent contrasting examples.

Table 19 shows the relative frequencies of the different types of restrictors.

TABLE 19

ADDITION OF RESTRICTORS TO USES OF *ONE THOUSAND*: TYPES[68]

	Approximative restrictors	'Exactly' restrictors	'At least' restrictors	'At most' restrictors
ONE THOUSAND	14/19 =73.7%	3/19=15.8%	2/19=10.5%	-
TWO	42/105= 40%	10/105= 9.5%	47/105 = 44.8%	6/105= 5.7%

Often, *one thousand* can be combined with more than one restrictor. Especially uses of *one thousand* that allow an additional 'approximately' restrictor are often compatible with an 'exactly' restrictor as well. With an 'approximately' restrictor the inherent vagueness of round (and especially large and round) numerals is underscored; with an 'exactly' restrictor this inherent characteristic is overruled by the exactness expressed by the restrictor. Just like with the 'absolute value'-'exactly' continuum, the influence of explicit linguistic material (such as definiteness markers of restrictors) is stronger than more or less implicit characteristics (such as the "non-existence" of temporal entities or the inherent vagueness of large round numerals). This is exemplified in (315), (316) and (317).

> (315) <HL9 2221> As well as the USA, Belgium, France, Italy, the Netherlands and the United Kingdom, were to participate in the operation - initially entitled "Poised Hammer" but now rechristened "Provide Comfort - II". **One thousand** Turkish troops

---

[68] When an utterance could be combined with more than one type of restrictor, it was grouped with the category of restrictor that was deemed most natural in the context of the utterance.

were also to be stationed at Silopi as part of the operation. Talks with Turkish and Iraqi Kurdish leaders In the week July 22-28 US Maj.-Gen. Jay Garner, head of the coalition forces, met with representatives of the (Turkish) Kurdistan Workers' Party (PKK).

(316) Approximately **one thousand** Turkish troops were also to be stationed at Silopi as part of the operation.

(317) Exactly **one thousand** Turkish troops were also to be stationed at Silopi as part of the operation.

5.5. RESTRICTORS

In the corpus analyses of *two, ten, twenty-two, one thousand* and *zero* I have often emphasized the importance of the influence of restrictors on the interpretation of expressions of cardinality. To conclude the corpus analysis, I will take a closer look at these elements. I will deal with them only to the extent that they are important for the corpus analysis of numerals. The relationship between the 'cardinality' uses of these restrictors and their other uses (as in, e.g., *at least, he was willing to drive me to the party*) will not be discussed here. I will primarily concentrate on a survey of the restrictors that are used in the sample corpora and I will single out two special cases: the relationship between 'exactly' and 'approximately' restrictors and a short discussion of how 'only' restrictors influence the meaning of numerals.

5.5.1. Survey of restrictors: from 'more than' to 'less than'

The starting point of the analysis of every combination of a restrictor and a numeral is always the 'absolute value' of the numeral. The restrictors may change the cardinality and the epistemic load of the expression of cardinality in various ways, but the 'absolute value' meaning expressed by the numeral itself always forms the basis of the whole construction. Stretching the meaning of the term a little, it could be called the "topic" of the expression of cardinality. The expression containing n as numeral is always "about" 'n' - it may contain other numerals, but it is always also about n. The 'absolute value' is also the middle value of all the values that can be expressed by means of the combination of a numeral and a restrictor. The relationship between how restrictors change the expression of cardinality itself and how they stage the speaker's epistemic attitude towards that expression is interesting as well.

In general, all meanings expressed by the "restrictor + numeral" combination can be situated on the continuum schematized below:

---------(N-x)---------(N-2)---------(N-1)---------(|N|)---------(N+1)---------(N+2)---------(N+x)---------

The combination of restrictor+numeral can be characterized by means of three features: cardinality, epistemic load and orientation. The first, cardinality, simply refers to the kind of sets that can be denoted by means of the combination with respect to the cardinality of those sets (e.g., only those sets that contain two elements, or also the sets that contain three elements etc.). The second feature, the epistemic load, has been elaborated upon in the discussion of 'absolute value'-'exactly n' uses: it refers to that component of the expression of cardinality that indicates the speaker's estimation of the likelihood of his or her statement being true or false. The third feature refers to the orientation of the whole expression of cardinality: if the expression refers to sets with cardinalities higher or lower than n, does it take the latter as the conceptual starting point or does it start from *n* itself? On the basis of the cardinality feature and the orientation feature alone, eight categories can be formed, which are presented below. I will also provide the "range" of the expression by indicating what section of the continuum is captured by the expression. I will once again work with instances of *two*, which means that this survey is organized in terms of *two*. This has consequences for the description of these combinations. I will deal with the epistemic load of the restrictors in a separate section.

1) 'exactly n'

```
---------(N-x)---------(N-2)---------(N-1)---------(|N|)---------(N+1)---------(N+2)---------(N+x)---------
                                         |X|
```

The "X" indicates the range of 'exactly n', and two instances of this type of combination of restrictor+numeral are given below.

> (318) <G00 1443> Turning the clock back to the point immediately before computers got involved in the publishing business there were **only two** real technologies at work; hot metal and cold metal. In the former, each character was cast on demand and the composed page was built up either from lines of individual characters (Monotype's method) or from complete lines cast as a single element (Linotype's approach).
> (319) <HR3 1206> Without the absolute power of an Egyptian Pharaoh one could scarcely test the consequences of an experiment involving the manipulation of people's lives, for example forcing a percentage of the population to emigrate or insisting that each fertile married couple produce **exactly two** offspring.

As has been mentioned before, the meaning of this combination is quite clear: it denotes sets with exactly two elements (cardinality) and it explicitly excludes the possibility of there being more or fewer elements in the set denoted by the NP that is modified by *exactly two* (epistemic). It is a purely 'n-oriented' expression. Besides *exactly n* and *only n* also *just n* belongs here.

2) 'from n --> more than n'

```
---------(N-x)---------(N-2)---------(N-1)---------(|N|)---------(N+1)---------(N+2)---------(N+x)---------
                                   _____
                                                        ------>
```

The arrow indicates the orientation of the combination.

(320) <B19 822> A sort of boarding house where the food was "wholefood"? A form of hospital where the predominant smell was dettol? Or, as **at least two** people suggested, a place where one learned to die?

(321) Of course, the models of analysis are metaphors too, and it is the recognition of this unavoidable fact that points to the linkage of isomorphism across the reading experience. By this I mean any process or phenomenon that involves a mapping of **two or more** elements.

(322) <CT8 44> ICL SHOWS UP CONTINENTAL SIBLINGS WITH £39m FOR 1991; LIKE-FOR-LIKE SALES UP 2% ICL Plc has pushed back the timeframe for its stock market flotation, saying that it will most likely be towards the back end of the **two to five** year target it set when Fujitsu Ltd took its 80% stake.

(323) <EA2 605> Although capsule distribution could be linked to other programmes such as immunisation, it must be given **two to three** times a year to achieve continuous coverage, and the risk of toxicity also needs consideration.

'From n to more than n' expressions include all sets with n elements and all sets with more than n elements - it is in principle open-ended on one side of the continuum (e.g., *at least* and *two or more* have no upper bound), but some restrictors explicitly provide an upper bound, such as *two to five* (322) or *two to three* (323). Other 'from n --> more than n' restrictors include *an absolute minimum of two* and *within two to five N*, in which N often denotes a temporal entity.

3) 'from n --> less than n'

---------(N-x)---------(N-2)---------(N-1)---------(|N|)---------(N+1)---------(N+2)---------(N+x)---------

◄——

These combinations are rather hard to find, and I did not find examples of them in the sample corpus. It is, however, possible to provide a list of combinations that yield the meaning schematized above: *two or less than two, two if not only one, two or maybe even less than two*. These combinations require specific contexts: the argumentative value must be such that there being 'less than two' elements is actually a better argument for the point the speaker is trying to make than the argument that the set contains 'absolute value' two elements. Typically, these combinations co-occur with *only* or *even*, which indicate this argumentative value (Anscombre and Ducrot 1978:48). A constructed example can be found in (324).

(324) He did not stay very long. He stayed for **two or maybe even less than two** hours.

4) 'from less than n --> n'

---------(N-x)---------(N-2)---------(N-1)---------(|N|)---------(N+1)---------(N+2)---------(N+x)---------

——►

With respect to "cardinality", this is the same as the previous category, but the orientation is different: here, the speaker conceptualizes the cardinality of the set starting from 'less than n'. Examples can be found in the following utterances.

(325) <J6V 651> Where both parties intend to rely on experts there should be mutual exchange, medical for medical and non-medical for non-medical. Unless the reports are agreed, the parties are at liberty to call experts whose reports have been disclosed, **limited to two** medical experts and one non-medical expert of any kind.

(326) <K35 2001> Familiar After Brian's murder, the couple could not bear to stay in their home in Well Street and **within two** months had moved to Tullycarnett.

(327) <CBP 828> Once again, the best way to open the sequence is to establish the location with a wide shot which shows the character of the setting: maybe it's one of those idyllic places which the crowds have not yet discovered, or perhaps it is crammed with people and overlooked by tourist hotels. Either way, the audience likes to know. Follow this with **one or two** closer shots which show the family against this background: the adults might be sunning themselves while the younger members of the family amuse themselves in more active ways - paddling, or playing beach football.

(328) <K55 9236> `I'm rather lame people in the village say you've caught arthritis, and I caught it **a year or two** ago but my brain hasn't entirely given out.

(329) <C97 1011> The decision as to how many fry the brichardi would allow to grow on to adulthood is in their hands, not yours. Some pairs will not tolerate any other adults, others will tolerate another pair, **or maybe even two** pairs.

Of course also *at most* belongs here.

The orientation becomes clear when, e.g., *limited to two medical experts* is compared with *two or less than two experts* or *I caught it a year or two ago* with *I caught it two years ago, or maybe slightly less than two years ago*. With combinations in which first a lower numeral is mentioned, as in *one or two* (327), the orientation is manifest, but for *at most two* or *up to two* this orientation is less explicit. In the latter expressions it is contained in the inherent orientation of the counting sequence; it is the fact that we count from one to ten and not from ten to one that gives these expressions their orientation. Only if the higher numeral is mentioned first and the restrictor links the higher numeral with the lower numeral the orientation can be said to be reversed. Often this orientation is linked to upwards or downwards movement: *from one up to two* or *from six down to one*. Because of the approximativity inherent in *an X or two* or *one or two X* constructions the upper bound of these combinations is rather flexible. For these combinations the continuum may extend slightly beyond the 'absolute value' denotation of *two*: if something is reported as having happened *a year or two* ago, it might have happened two years and a couple of months ago and maybe even three years ago. Likewise, the *one or two* construction in (327) may allow the possibility of there being "three closer shots" (instead of one or two). Moreover, there is a difference between *one or two* and *an X or two* in that the latter suggests that the possibility of there being only one element in the set is less likely than in the former: *an x or two* is much closer to *two* in its 'absolute value' meaning than *one or two*.

5) 'from more than n --> n'

---------(N-x)---------(N-2)---------(N-1)---------(|N|)---------(N+1)--------(N+2)---------(N+x)--------

This is a category of restrictors that occur rather infrequently, just like the 'from n to less than n' category described in 3). The orientation of this type of combination is from a higher numeral to n. Examples of this group include *three, possibly only two* and *from five to two days*, as in the constructed examples (330) and (331).

> (330) Spring break is reduced **from five to two** days.
> (331) John promises quite a show, but there are going to be hardly any celebrities present. There would be **three, possibly only two** movie stars, a TV producer and a journalist.

6) 'from less than n --> more than n'

---------(N-x)---------(N-2)---------(N-1)---------(|N|)---------(N+1)--------(N+2)---------(N+x)--------

This category includes the 'approximately' restrictors. The orientation is bidirectional, and, typically, the end-points of the continuum defy exact determination. One example is given below.

> (332) <G09 1238> On the feet were home-made boots with double tongues: `They were made by the village cobbler and cost fourteen shillings: they'd last **about two** years if you got them clumped at the end of the first year."

Other examples include: *approximately n* and *some n* (typically combined with round numbers as in *I found some fifty different shoes*).

7) 'less than n'

---------(N-x)---------(N-2)---------(N-1)---------(|N|)---------(N+1)--------(N+2)---------(N+x)--------

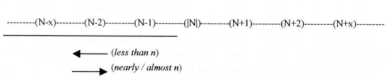

(less than n)
(nearly / almost n)

These combinations include all the sets with less than two elements: the sets that contain two elements are explicitly excluded. Examples are provided in the following utterances.

> (333) The need for insolvency at the relevant time does not apply to transactions at an undervalue entered into **less than two** years before the individual is adjudged bankrupt.
> (334) South Africa demonstrably adjusted better to the more disciplined requirements of the longer game after **almost two** months of the uninterrupted frenzy of the World Cup.
> (335) On her way back to the surgery, Sophie glanced at her watch and realised with a start that she had left Joanna on her own for **nearly two** hours.

Actually, there is an important difference in orientation between the combination in (333) and the combinations in (334) and (335): *less than n* conceptualizes the cardinality in terms of n, and everything less than n ("downwards movement"), while *almost n* and *nearly n* start from the "absolute" starting point of the counting sequence ('zero') and "move up" to just before 'n'. (I decided to group them together in one category for reasons of symmetry: the next category is exactly the reverse of this one in terms of cardinality, but has only one type of orientation). The upper bound of these combinations is rather vague and will depend on the numeral that is used: 'one hour' would probably not be captured by the phrase *nearly two hours*, but *999 miles* would be covered by *nearly 1000 miles*.

8) 'more than n'

---------(N-x)---------(N-2)---------(N-1)---------(|N|)---------(N+1)---------(N+2)---------(N+x)---------

$$\longrightarrow$$

This is the mirror image of the previous group, although this group only seems to contain combinations with an orientation from 'slightly more than n' to 'much more than n', and not the other way around. Examples can be found in the following utterances.

> (336) <ABC 98> THE MONKEY MIA DOLPHINS Monkey Mia, on the remote western coastline of Australia, has for **more than two** decades been visited by wild dolphins.
> (337) <EUU 220> One of the author's former clients is still awaiting certificates for American stocks he bought through the crashed Sheridan Securities **over two** years ago, a familiar story to clients of many licensed dealers (and many clients deal through several).

Of course, one could always think of constructions that capture the same cardinality with an inverted orientation, such as *five, but possibly only slightly more than two* but these sound rather artificial, even if they could indeed be used in certain very specific contexts (namely, contexts in which 'five' functions as the maximal cardinality and 'slightly more than two' as the absolute minimum).

5.5.2. "Epistemic load"

Besides cardinality and orientation, there is a third factor that is important in the discussion of restrictors, namely the "epistemic load" of the combinations of restrictor+numeral, which crosscuts the other distinctions. As I have devoted a considerable part of the 'absolute value'-'exactly n' continuum discussion of *two* to this component of expressions of cardinality, I will limit myself to an exemplification of how other restrictors may also encode the attitude of the speaker with respect to the veracity of his or her own statement. Let us take three combinations from the 'from n to more than n' group, namely *at least two, two to three* and *two or three*, exemplified below.

> (338) <KE2 6426> Yeah! About twenty six years. That's oh I thought they were very old. No. Where have you lived in? Would you a hou the house did you live into it when it was new? No. No? No. I don't know ho certainly I know there had been **at least two** peo different lots of people living in ours before we moved in, and I would think there were probably more than that.
> (339) <CAM 292> The committee rose. Odell had to see the President over at the Mansion. `Fast as you can, Morton," he said. `We want to be talking **two to three** days here. Tops." In fact it would take another seven.
> (340) <J18 1525> At Turrialba in Costa Rica, the mineralization of nitrogen is higher in secondary forest there than in most forests so far measured elsewhere. With disturbance the rate is further increased by **two or three** times and then decreased to comparable levels after 6 months or so, the short-lived increase representing 300-400kg nitrogen released to the site.

Whereas the first includes an explicit modal component by means of which the speaker indicates his or her relative uncertainty, the speaker presents him- or herself as more confident in the latter two examples. *At least* in (338) encodes the fact that the speaker is certain that two people have lived in their house before they moved and explicitly includes the possibility that there might be even more than two people that have lived in their house. In (339) the time period under discussion is presented as ranging from two to three days and nothing is coded with respect to the possibility of it taking more or less than 'two or three' days (actually, the next phrase *tops* does indicate an upper bound and as such explicitly excludes the possibility of it taking more than two to three days, but I will concentrate on the meaning of *two to three* before the expression of cardinality is influenced by the restrictor *tops*). Arguably, in (339) and (340) the speaker commits himself to a statement of possibility as well: in (339) the expression of cardinality can be paraphrased as 'the time period is possibly two, possibly three' days and (340) can be paraphrased as 'the rate is further increased by possibly two, possibly three times'. Nevertheless, there is a crucial difference: whereas in the *at least* example the speaker explicitly indicates that he is not certain of the upper bound of the expression of cardinality, with *two to three* or *two or three* an upper bound is explicitly encoded. With respect to the values in the range from 'two to three' the speaker may be uncertain: *two to three* encodes that the speaker's estimation is situated between two and three days, hence (339) encodes that he or she is not sure whether it is going to last two or three days, but he or she does not commit him- or herself to the possibility of it taking more days. In fact, the function of the suspension phrase *if not more* is exactly the addition of an epistemic component, by explicitly indicating that the speaker does not commit him- or herself to an upper bound.

(341) We want to be talking **two to three** days here, if not more.

Crucially, the difference between *at least two* on the one hand and *two to three* or *two or three* on the other is that in the latter an upper bound is provided while in the former this is not the case. Whereas *at least two* encodes that the speaker is only certain with respect to one end of the range of possibilities (namely he or she is certain that it is not less than two, but he or she does say what the upper bound is, or, indeed, if there even is an upper bound), *two or three* indicates that the speaker is certain that the range of possibilities lies between two and three, and does not indicate anything concerning the possibility of there being more than three elements to the set denoted by the NP. The only expression of possibility the speaker commits him- or herself to concerns the possibilities *within* that range. The following example demonstrates the importance of the indication of an upper bound.

(342) With disturbance the rate is further increased by **two** times **or more** and then decreased to comparable levels after 6 months or so, the short-lived increase representing 300-400kg nitrogen released to the site.

The only difference with (340) is that **or three** is replaced by **or more**, but this has an important effect on the epistemic load of the expression of cardinality: the speaker of (340) presents the multiplication factor as two or three, while the speaker of (342) also indicates that it is at least two, but does not indicate an upper bound.

The same line of reasoning holds for the difference between *at most two* and *one or two*: the first explicitly includes an indication of the epistemic stance of the speaker with respect to the possibility that the set in question contains more or fewer than two elements, while the second does not. A special case is the suspension phrase *one, if not two,* which differs from both of the other constructions: it differs from *at most two* in that *one, if not two* presents the situation in which the set denoted by the NP contains one element (in the 'absolute value' meaning of *one,* i.e., not explicitly excluding the possibility that the set contains more than one element) as a factual one, while it explicitly adds the possibility that the set contains more than one element by means of the suspension phrase. *At most two* does not represent the state of affairs in which the set contains one ('absolute value' one) element as factual. This is partly a difference with respect to the pure expression of cardinality, not so much in terms of epistemic attitude: if the set in question is an empty one, *at most two* can capture this fact, while *one, if not two* cannot. But there is a clear difference with respect to the epistemic stance too: while *at most two* explicitly excludes the possibility of the set containing more than two elements, *one, if not two* does not. Moreover, the latter construction explicitly encodes the possibility that the set contains two elements, while in the *at most two* construction this possibility is not singled out compared to the other two possibilities (namely that the set is empty or contains only one element). In the *at most two* construction the three possibilities 'zero', 'one' or 'two' elements are all presented as possible; none of the three possibilities is presented as more or less likely than the others. With the *one, if not two* construction, the possibility 'zero' is ruled out (although this is not made explicit - it is a consequence of the 'absolute value' use of *one*), the possibility that the set contains one element is presented as the actual state of affairs, and the situation in which the set contains two elements is explicitly presented as a possibility.

5.5.3. Approximativity and exactness

With respect to the indication of vagueness, or "approximativity", it is important that two ways in which an approximative construction may differ from an "exact" description are distinguished. There is the "inherent" approximativity or vagueness of round numerals, which is different from the encoded approximativity. The latter has been discussed in group 6 of the survey of the restrictors, the 'from less than n to more than n' group.

In between those two kinds of approximativity, there is a class of combinations of restrictors + numerals that can be considered to be encoding approximativity, but less explicitly than the canonical 'approximately' restrictors such as *about* or *approximately*. More specifically, expressions such as *an x or two* or *two or three*, as in (343) or (344), which have been placed in the 'from less than n to n' group or the 'from n to more than n' group, also suggest that the cardinality indicated is an approximation of the actual cardinality.

> (343) <K63 240> I knew one of the girls and er she never got right properly again. She got injured in her back somewhere, but er it was national news, I mean it was in The Mirror and all the papers and it became a, for a day or **two** it was er it was in everywhere, and the theory is that er it was this erm very very dry summer and a very very wet autumn and a bit of dry rot in the timbers somewhere, but it was it was another How long did it actually take you to get out of there?
>
> (344) <KE3 3789> I wouldn't be able to use my car No. so, I'd have to pay bus fare Mm. so I'd be paying, we'd be paying for our petrol which wouldn't be a lot different to what it is now really No , a bit, **two** or three pounds a week perhaps mm. and I'd be paying a lot more in bus fare Mm. plus you haven't got the convenience of being able to go and get in your car.

In (343), the utterance suggests that the accident may have been in all the papers for two days, but possibly also for three days or maybe even longer, and in (344) the speaker suggests that what he or she has to pay will be two or three pounds, but possibly even four pounds or more. Naturally, the possibility that it is more than what is indicated by the numerals themselves is less forcefully present than the possibilities presented by the numerals themselves: in (343) the utterance suggests that it is considerably less likely that the accident was in the papers for three days than it was in the papers for two days; in (344) the state of affairs in which four pounds per week have to be paid is presented as less likely than the one in which two or three pounds have to paid. Typically, this intermediate category (between explicitly encoding approximativity by means of 'approximately' restrictors and expressing it as an inherent quality through the roundness of the numeral used) does not only differ from the pure and explicit approximative expressions in terms of the force with which other states of affairs are presented as possible, but also with respect to their orientation. Restrictors such as *about* or *approximately* turn the expression of cardinality into a vaguer expression in both directions: *I saw about seven cars* means that the set of cars seen by the speaker may have six or eight elements. No preference with respect to 'less than seven' or 'more than seven' is suggested by these restrictors. With combinations such as *an x or two* or *one or two* there is only one direction in which the range of possible cardinalities can be extended, namely the 'more than' direction: *I saw a car or two* excludes the possibility that the set of cars seen by the speaker is empty.

A final remark concerns the status of the opposite of "approximativity", namely "exactness". While it is true that 'exactly' uses of numerals and 'exactly' restrictors indicate that the possibility of there being more or fewer than n elements in the set denoted by the NP is excluded, this is only one interpretation of "exactness". Besides this epistemic interpretation, the term "exactness" may also indicate the precision of an expression of cardinality. In the first interpretation of "exactness" an 'exactly n' use of a numeral indicates that the speaker encodes the possibility of there being more or fewer than n elements, in the second interpretation the "exactness" of an expression of cardinality refers to the "granularity" of the description (to use a Langackerian metaphor): the more fine-grained an expression is, the more "exact" it is. This has nothing to do with the speaker's estimation of the likelihood of his utterance corresponding to the language-external state of affairs. While (345) is more exact than (346) in this sense, they do not differ with respect to the epistemic reading of the term "exactness".

> (345)   This stick is 1.03 meter long.
> (346)   This stick is one meter long.

These two interpretations need to be distinguished, because they have very different consequences: clearly, as the examples show, an utterance can be more exact in the "precision" sense of the term, without being "exact" in the epistemic sense. Nevertheless, there is a connection between the two uses in the sense that in the "precision" use of the term an "exact" expression of cardinality excludes more possibilities than one that is less "exact": (345) excludes the possibility that the stick is 1.01 meter long more forcefully than (346). In this way, the connection between the epistemic load of "exactness" and that of "approximativity" can be underscored once again: it is the "roundness" of (346), and hence its inherent "approximativity", that is responsible for the fact that the possibility that the stick is 1.01 meter long is excluded less forcefully than in (345).

5.5.4. *Only* and *just*

There is a long history of logical and linguistic research on various types of constructions with *only* (e.g. the combination of *only* with a proper name, or constructions of the type *Only Fs are Gs*) (cf. Atlas 1996 and Horn 1996 for complementary surveys). I will not participate in this discussion, but I will try to determine the effect of *only* and *just* (which I will assume to be identical) on the interpretation of numerals. Three examples are provided below.

> (347) <K4W 8693> Mrs Duffy's son Lee, 26, of Durham Road, Eston, a former boxer and nightclub bouncer, was the victim of an alleged attempted murder in The Commercial pub, Middlesbrough on April 26 last year. It was the second time witnesses had failed to turn up for Tapping's trial. The family claim all the witnesses to the incident live locally. Only **two** of the seven civilian witnesses needed for the trial had been traced and witness summonses served. Prosecutor Andrew Robertson said: `Although I can't put forward a proper evidential basis for this, there is a feeling they are extremely reluctant to give evidence and don't wish to attend court."
>
> (348) <K4P 782> Sometimes they may even become directly involved in helping to set things up. Mr Chettle, who lives in Saltburn and who has led workshops and lectured in Amsterdam, recalled how Cleveland Arts was once asked to paint a mural for a hospital. Having had only **two** weeks in which to complete the work, Mr Chettle burned more than the midnight oil to finish it in time. The last brush stroke was put in by 3am on the day it was unveiled in the children's ward at South Cleveland Hospital! In his spare time, Mr Chettle enjoys looking for fossils and regards the east coast as `a brilliant area" for his hobby.
>
> (349) <J15 395> Banks and the transmission of payments: the clearing system The clearing banks are so called because they operate a central clearing house in London. This is a means of settling banks' debts with each other on a daily basis. It enables cheques, standing orders and other means of payment to be cleared rapidly. But how does it work? Let us examine the case of just **two** banks, say Lloyds and Midland. Each day all the cheques written by Midland customers that Lloyds customers have received and paid into their accounts are sent by Lloyds branches to its head-office clearing department and are added up. Likewise all the cheques that Lloyds customers have written and have been deposited in Midland accounts are sent to Midland head office and are added up.

According to Horn (1996), one thing is clear with respect to the meaning of *only Gs are Fs*: the expression *entails* the negative assertion that nothing other than Gs are F[69], while the positive component, namely that G is F is implicated / presupposed / accommodated. Atlas' view is that *only a is F* (with *a* standing for a proper name) entails *a is F*, i.e., *exactly one individual, and at most a, is F*, which entails *a is F*. But Atlas distinguishes this use of *only* (in which it is combined with a proper name) from constructions like *only Gs are Fs.*

---

[69] Actually, as Atlas (1996:274) notes, Horn uses what is - in Horn's opinion - a paraphrase of the assertion *nothing other than Gs are Fs*, namely "All Fs are Gs".

More important for this discussion is that Atlas also stresses the fact that the combination of *only* and a numeral in an NP is not negative at all (Atlas 1996:289, 304-305). For Atlas, *only n CN* is equivalent to *exactly n CN* with respect to "negativity"[70].

What is the relevance of this for the corpus analysis? If Horn's analysis of *only Gs are Fs* is expanded to combinations of *only* and numerals, it can be predicted that *only two weeks* in (348) entails that 'nothing other than two weeks' was available for completing the work, which can be paraphrased as an explicit exclusion of the possibility that the time period denoted by *only two weeks* should be longer than two weeks. Also, this extrapolation of Horn's *only* account implies that *only two weeks* implicates / presupposes that Mr Chettle indeed had two weeks to complete the work. In Atlas' account it is not entirely clear whether his assertion that *only n CN* combinations are non-negative also implies that the negative component, which is in the extrapolation of Horn's account a semantic entailment to the effect that 'no more than n Gs are Fs', is excluded from the meaning of the *only* + numeral + common noun construction altogether. In other words it is not clear whether Atlas considers the meaning 'no more than n CNs' as being part of the meaning of *only n CN*, or not?

Would Horn allow this extrapolation of his (1996) account of *only*? There does not seem to be a direct answer to this question, but in each case Horn (1972:37-38) strongly suggests that at the time he thought that *only three children* entails a negative assertion, namely *no more than three children*, and presupposes the positive assertion *three children*.

On the basis of the data in the sample corpus and the 'absolute value' analysis of numerals, the negativity of Horn's account can be retained, while also explaining the similarity between *only two CN* and *exactly two CN* as Atlas would have it. In view of the generally attested "exclusionary" effect of *only*, it seems obvious to retain this negative component in *only* + numeral constructions: *only two weeks* encodes the fact that no more than two weeks were available to Mr Chettle. I agree with Horn that this is the only thing that is entailed by *only*. But *only two weeks* does indeed mean that Mr Chettle did get two weeks to do the job. Unlike Horn, I do not consider the latter component of the meaning of *only two weeks* as a "weaker" element (be it a presupposition, an accommodated presupposition or an implicature), but as a full-fledged part of the coded content of *only two weeks*. Crucially, however, I do not ascribe this meaning to the coded content of *only*, but to the 'absolute value' meaning of the numeral, in this case *two*. This explains the similarity between the meaning of *exactly two* and *only two*. While the first explicitly excludes the possibility of there being more or less than two elements in the set denoted by the NP, the latter only explicitly excludes the possibility of there being *more* than two elements. Nevertheless, as we have seen, the 'absolute value' meaning of a numeral n entails that there are indeed n entities in existence, which amounts to installing a lower bound, even if the possibility that there are fewer than n elements is not explicitly excluded.

The final problem is the combination of *only* + numeral + CN and negation. As argued above (cf. 5.3.3. Negation), this combination calls for a higher value, because *not* + *just* encodes an announcement to the hearer that an even better/stronger argument for the utterance in question will follow, in this case a higher numeral. I will repeat the examples provided.

---

[70] Atlas refers to Zwarts's (1998) typology for negative quantifiers, but for our purposes it suffices to note that *only n CN* is not negative at all.

(350) <ATA 957> The study of women and film involves, as in the subtitle of Kaplan's book, at least `both sides of the camera": women as film-makers, and women as cinematic objects, viewed through the camera eye. In my attempt at a wide-angled overview, however, I shall argue that the camera has not just **two** but many sides, and that feminist film criticism and theory can only benefit from casting its eye outside a field of vision in which the theory of the gaze and questions of representation and power have been dominant for too long.

(351) CD9 n=377> The last is important. Niki is an Austrian and, at that, an Austrian in the full sense of the word, and Austrians, at least after the collapse of their empire in 1918, are a little bit aslant to the world. As an Austrian, Niki is divided against himself, and there are not just **two** Nikis but several dozen of them. The job of keeping them together has been entrusted to a series of `confidants" who write his books, churn out his articles, furnish his quotes, capture his image and sweeten the sour, and when I once asked Niki why he wouldn't ever do a serious - and in consequence, a truthful - book about himself, he replied, why should he?

In both examples, the original numeral is corrected by a quantifier whose cardinality is higher than two. This can be explained rather easily in my account of *only*: the negation does not operate on the numeral itself, but exclusively interacts with the restrictor *only*: the negation of *only* takes away the exclusion normally installed by *only*. *Only* explicitly excludes the possibility of there being more than two elements, *not only* takes this restriction away, and the road to a higher cardinality lies open. This explains why *not only/just two* constructions are followed by an expression indicating a higher cardinality. In the discussion of the effects of negation, it was even argued that *not only/not just* constructions can often not be completed by an expression indicating a lower cardinality. The effort involved in first establishing an upper bound (*just/only*) and then negating it (*not*) can only be relevant as the preparation for the affirmation of a higher cardinality.

6

CONCLUSION

In this study, I have analyzed the different meanings of English cardinals by means of a corpus analysis. The corpus data make clear that English numerals are primarily used to indicate the cardinality of the set denoted by the NP they modify. I have concentrated on the specific interpretations that these fully cardinal uses of numerals have in the light of the neo-Gricean debate on the conventional meaning of numerals and the implicatures they trigger. I have also argued, however, that "cardinality" is not a binary notion and I have tried to determine the formal characteristics and the function of less than fully cardinal uses, which have often been ignored in the neo-Gricean discussions of numerals. In addition, I have devoted much attention to the influence of other linguistic elements on the interpretation of numerals. Finally, I have also investigated the interpretation of numerals denoting "round" numbers and large numbers.

In order to emphasize the importance and the complexities of the neo-Gricean debate concerning the semantics and pragmatics of cardinals, I have started the study with a reconstruction of Grice's original program. It was argued that Grice's lectures on logic and conversation provide a plausible picture of how language users bridge the gap between the conventional meanings of words and sentences and the meanings that can be expressed by using them. Moreover, the conversational maxims that Grice proposes to explain the interpretation of *uses* of linguistic elements allow him to simplify semantics. His principle of parsimony, called "Modified Occam's Razor", implies that senses of an item that can be explained by reference to these maxims should not be seen as parts of the conventional meaning of that item.

Crucially, however, the acceptance of this principle does not mean that the meaning that best fits the Gricean schema should be considered as the conventional meaning of that item. As I have argued, Grice's attempt to reconcile logic and language has led to highly questionable meaning postulates. Especially in his discussion of the natural language counterparts of logical operators, such as *therefore, or* and *if ... then*, Grice seems to sacrifice firm intuitions concerning the conventional meanings of these items in order to be able to bridge the gap between the way in which logic uses logical operators and the ways in which alleged natural language counterparts of these operators function. Even though his more general work on the intentionalist conception of meaning clearly states that the "conventional" meaning of linguistic elements eventually should be reduced to what speakers standardly mean by these elements, he ignores the need for a methodological foundation of the determination of this conventional meaning when he investigates specific words and constructions. It is this methodological consideration that motivates the decision to investigate the English cardinals by means of a corpus analysis. Conventional meanings are "familiar" meanings, and a good indication of the familiarity of a certain meaning is the frequency with which a certain item expresses that meaning.

The neo-Gricean development of Grice's original theory of conversation is interesting in that it lays bare some of the fundamental problems of the theory. The various reformulations of the original maxims, for instance, are an attempt to constrain the explanatory power of the theory. It has been said that Grice's principles are so flexible that they can explain everything, and I have argued that this indeterminacy indeed weakens the explanatory value of such an explanation to a considerable extent. Nevertheless, the different redefinitions of these principles hardly offer more rigidity. The so-called "bucket theory", which is supposed to regulate the order in which entailments and implicatures are added to the "background", and the related principles that have been proposed to guide the "clashes" between different maxims, are also insufficient to constrain the theory.

Moreover, as various researchers have stressed, Horn's concept of "scalar implicatures", one of the most successful attempts at formalizing Grice's original insights, is flawed in a number of respects. It is clear that the entailment criterion, on which the original scales are based, counter-intuitively excludes a number of phenomena that are very similar to uncontroversially scalar elements. In addition, it is evident that numerous counterexamples can be provided to show that even the supposedly more precise concept of Horn scales is too broad. Levinson's amendments to Horn's concept at first sight seem to solve a number of the problems introduced by the broadness of its definition. However, whereas Horn's entailment requirement sometimes allows elements to form scales that generate implicatures that do not in reality occur, Levinson's rather rigid formal requirements seem too strict: phenomena that are rightfully considered to be similar to the original canon of scalar phenomena are excluded. Even more important for the analysis of the English cardinals, which are traditionally used as one of the showcases of scalar implicatures, is the fact that the success of the concept of "scales" has established the practice of deriving the lexical meaning of an allegedly scalar item from its position on the scale. I contend that this explains why counter-intuitive meaning postulates have mushroomed ever since: they range from the statement that the meaning of a numeral n is 'at least n' to the assertion that the meaning of the proper name *Russell* is 'at least Russell'. Especially the combination of this trend with the progressively more outspoken emphasis on the Generalized Conversational Implicature (GCI) as the essentially *linguistic* subcategory of the Gricean implicatures has been detrimental to the semantic description of specific lexical items.

A related and equally problematic aspect of the original theory of conversation is its emphasis on truth-conditional meaning as the input of the pragmatic "working-out schema" that derives the conversational implicatures on the basis of this input. In Grice's original texts, but also, and more emphatically so, in many neo-Gricean texts, it has been emphasized that the "conventional" meaning of a sentence can be identified with its truth conditions. Especially during the last ten years, researchers have demonstrated that these truth conditions cannot serve as the input of the working-out schema, since the propositions expressed by the utterances that generate the implicatures often need to be enriched before they become truth-evaluable. Other propositions need to be pragmatically enhanced before the implicatures are calculated, because otherwise the theory will predict implicatures that do not correspond with intuitions. The phenomenon of "pragmatic intrusion" into truth conditions has led to a radical reduction of "semantics": the "logical form" of a sentence is typically subpropositional in the sense that it is not sufficient to determine its truth conditions; the "literal meaning" of linguistic elements is often presumed to be as "skeletal" as possible. This separation of the investigation of the truth-conditional content of lexical items and sentences from their semantic analysis is crucial for empirically verifiable analyses of linguistic items and constructions.

I have zoomed in on the implicature analysis of English numerals, which constitutes one of the most hotly debated topics in neo-Gricean history. The so-called 'at least' analysis of cardinals has become very influential, but it has also been one of the most vividly contested examples of scalar implicatures. Many arguments have been proposed in favor of the 'at least' analysis, which starts from the observation that sentences containing a higher numeral entail the same sentence with a lower numeral. This means that if a sentence containing an NP with a numeral n is judged to be true, this truth-value judgment will generally not change when in reality the set denoted by the NP turns out to have more than n elements. Another important argument refers to the fact that it is possible to correct a sentence that identifies a set as having n members by adding a phrase that makes clear that the speaker thinks that the set actually has more than n elements, while it is much harder to correct it by saying that the set has less than n elements. This phenomenon has given rise to the formulation of two "tests": the "cancellation test" (with *in fact* introducing the correction phrase) and the "suspension test" (with *if not* introducing the correction phrase). Also the default 'less than' interpretation of the combination of a numeral with negation has often been used as an argument in favor of the 'at least' analysis.

Inspired by a number of dispersed remarks and arguments in the existing literature on neo-Gricean analyses of cardinals, it has been argued that none of the arguments in favor of the 'at least' analysis are convincing. As mentioned, the confusion between the semantic content of a lexical item and the entailments that are inferable from sentences containing that item leads to counter-intuitive meaning postulates with respect to that item. More than one researcher has argued that the neo-Gricean Radical Pragmatics program, which intends to reduce the "semantics" of items and constructions as much as possible, often ends up with semantic descriptions that are too poor to function as input for the pragmatic calculation of implicatures. In the case of numerals, it is rather the opposite: 'at least n' not only captures the fact that a numeral n indicates the cardinality of a set, it also indicates that it is possible that the set contains more than n elements. The latter, however, is not encoded by the numeral. The principal argument against the 'at least' analysis of cardinals is that cardinals most often do not have an 'at least' meaning. This is also demonstrated by the fact that 'at least' meanings make it impossible to calculate with numerals. Other arguments against the 'at least' analysis have emphasized the fact that if a numeral n meant 'at least n', *at least* in the phrase *at least n* would be redundant, which it clearly is not.

The main alternatives that have been proposed to the 'at least' analysis are an 'exactly' analysis of numerals and an underdeterminacy analysis. The first solves a specific problem with mathematical uses of numerals and also captures the intuition that cardinals hardly ever have an 'at least' meaning. As Kadmon and Carston (among others) have argued, however, the problem with an 'exactly' analysis is that it is not easy to derive the 'at least' and 'at most' interpretations of numerals without having recourse to *ad hoc* explanations. Moreover, the 'exactly' analysis runs into the same problem as the 'at least' analysis: if *n* means 'exactly n', *exactly* in *exactly n* should be redundant, while it clearly is not. The second important alternative, the underdeterminacy analysis, is inspired by the discussion concerning pragmatic intrusion and the reduction of semantics to a level below that of the truth-conditional content of utterances. The analysis of the meaning of a numeral as being "underdetermined" implies that the coded content of a numeral is in need of pragmatic enrichment before the utterance containing the numeral becomes truth-evaluable. One of the obvious advantages of the underdeterminacy analysis is that it covers all the meanings that can be expressed by numerals: the underdetermined semantic content can be enriched to an 'at least', 'at most', 'exactly' and even 'approximately' value. This analysis is not unproblematic either, because numerals often do not seem to be in need of enrichment. Whereas typical examples of enrichment indeed signal that the proposition expressed needs to be completed pragmatically, this is usually not the case with numerals. Moreover, the corpus analysis shows that 'at least', 'at most' and 'exactly' values of numerals are most often triggered by *linguistic* elements in the immediate cotext of the numeral.

Before embarking on the corpus analysis of *two, zero, ten, twenty-two* and *one thousand*, the word class status of numerals in general was investigated. Traditional grammars are rather inconsistent with respect to the classification of numerals: often they are put in a separate lexical category, but sometimes they have been grouped together with either "pronouns and determiners", "quantifiers" or "noun adjuncts". I have argued that numerals indeed can be separated from other word classes on the basis of a number of formal and functional characteristics.

The corpus analysis of English numerals is to a large extent devoted to an investigation of the meanings of *two*. With respect to the formal characteristics, it was noted that *two* occurs in a large variety of syntactic positions. The majority of the uses of *two* are adnominal (either pre- or postnominal). A second significant subgroup collects pronominal and elliptical uses of *two*: in these uses the numeral does not modify a noun and functions as the head of the noun phrase. Third, *two* can also function nominally and even as a proper name, or in a counting sequence, as well as in a number of idiosyncratic constructions. I have also looked at the syntactic function of the NP containing *two* and it transpired that it occurs most often in adverbials, but the differences in terms of frequency with, e.g., the groups with uses of *two* in subject and object NPs are rather small.

With respect to the functions of *two*, seven distinct types have been distinguished: *two* is very often used to indicate pure cardinality; it sometimes functions as a "label" of a certain entity; it can be used for the indication of time, it is often used pronominally (which, in my broad conception of "pronominal" refers to the fact that it is often used anaphorically), it can be the name of a symbol, it is used in mathematical discourse (in which the numeral usually functions as a proper name) and it may have a discourse-structural function. Typical examples of each category have been discussed and divergent uses within each group have been analyzed. In this way, the many intricate ways in which *two* can be used have been emphasized, and each time an attempt was made to determine the degree of cardinality that the specific uses of *two* evoke. I have also looked at the numeral *zero*, which is in many respects an oddity in the word class of numerals. Especially the fact that it is very often used as the head of an NP is striking.

The major part of the corpus analysis is devoted to the neo-Gricean question of the different "values" of cardinals. Despite the gradual nature of the cardinality concept, the uses of numerals that I have called "pure cardinal" uses can be separated from the other more complex uses. The pronominal uses of *two* have been grouped together with the fully cardinal adnominal uses because the pronominal uses also express full cardinality, although this function is less prominent due to their additional anaphorical function. First, the number of positions that could be taken with respect to the value interpretation of these numerals were extended: not only can numerals have 'at least n', 'exactly n', or 'at most n' meanings, they can also have an 'absolute value' meaning. These labels have been defined in terms of their constituent parts: 'at least n' can be defined as the combination of 'necessarily n' and 'possibly more than n'; 'at most n' is 'possibly n' and 'not possible more than n'; 'exactly n' is the combination of 'necessarily n', 'not possible more than n' and 'not possible less than n'. The difference with the 'absolute value' meaning is that in the latter there are no modal components: 'absolute value' uses do not involve any explicit commitment with respect to the possibility of there being more or less than n elements in the set denoted by the NP. Naturally, being part of an NP, an 'absolute value' use of a numeral asserts the existence of n elements, which implies that the speaker asserts that the cardinality of the set will not be less than 'n'. However, this fact is not emphasized by the speaker: the possibility that there are less than n elements is excluded by virtue of the assertion of existence through the use of the NP containing the numeral, but this possibility is not excluded explicitly. This is one of the crucial differences with respect to the 'at least n' and the 'exactly n' uses: in the latter the possibility that there are less than n elements *is* explicitly excluded. 'At least n' and 'exactly n' uses of *two* are also different in that the first explicitly includes the possibility that there are more than n elements in the set, while the second explicitly excludes both the possibility that there are more than n, as well as less than n elements in the set. Unlike 'at most n', 'at least n' or 'exactly n' uses, 'absolute value' uses do not focus on the epistemic stance of the speaker towards his or her expression of cardinality. It is important to emphasize that the 'at least', 'at most', 'exactly' and 'absolute value' uses of numerals are indications of the values of numerals as they are triggered by the *whole* utterance: the material in the cotext and the context that influences the interpretation of the numeral has not been filtered. Only in a second stage have I tried to disentangle the "meaning complex" caused by the combination of the numeral and the other elements that happen to have an effect on the value of the numeral. Moreover, the positions concerning the value interpretation of the numeral should not be considered to be the only possibilities: I have especially focused on the gradual distinction between 'exactly n' and 'absolute value' interpretations.

Taking these considerations into account, it was found that the majority of the utterances containing *two* could be classified as having either an 'absolute value' meaning or an 'exactly n' meaning, with the 'absolute value' group being the largest. Crucially, however, the 'exactly n' interpretation of the "meaning complex" including the numeral could always be reduced to a combination of an 'absolute value' meaning as the coded meaning of *two* and other factors inducing 'exactly n' interpretations. Therefore, the conventional meaning (the "coded content") of *two* is the 'absolute value' meaning.

With respect to the factors influencing the value interpretation of numerals, it was found that the presence of restrictors (whose primary function is precisely to specify the expression of cardinality) and the presence of definiteness markers are important parameters. I have also investigated the influence of the syntactic nature of the NP containing the numeral. This influence turns out to be rather weak, but the analysis demonstrates the importance of information-structural characteristics of the utterances containing numerals. Especially the correlation between syntactic structures and the focalization of certain elements has been brought to the fore. Moreover, it transpired that the primary function of certain adverbially used NPs and PPs containing numerals is to locate a state of affairs in time and space. The entities denoted by these constructions do not inherit the assertion of existence that is by default related to NPs in subject or direct object position, and this causes the value interpretation of the numeral to move in the direction of the 'exactly' end-point of the continuum between 'absolute value' and 'exactly n' meanings. Most often these NPs and PPs denote so-called temporal entities, but also NPs and PPs denoting spatial entities trigger this 'exactly' effect. Finally, a number of other determinants of the value interpretation of numerals have been discussed. The presence of a superset, of verbs of division or composition, and of "ordering" numeral adjectives in the cotext, as well as the integration of the numeral in a plural attributive noun construction move the interpretation of the numeral in the direction of the 'exactly n' interpretation.

In general, the distinction between the 'exactly n' and the 'absolute value' interpretation of *two* can be sketched as follows. The coded content of *two* is its 'absolute value' meaning. If the NP containing *two* also contains an 'exactly n' restrictor or a definiteness marker, the interpretation of the "meaning complex" of *two* together with the surrounding material is always 'exactly two'. If these are not present, and if *two* is part of an adverbial, it will acquire an 'exactly n' interpretation if the NP or PP denote entities the existence of which is not asserted. When these 'exactly' triggers are absent, *two* will have its default 'absolute value' meaning. However, within the category of 'absolute value' uses, it is possible to make still further and progressively more subtle distinctions. These distinctions are based on the syntactic function of the NP containing the numeral: in general, if *two* is part of an "existential *there*" construction or a direct object phrase, the 'absolute value' interpretation is not altered, while if it occurs in a subject phrase or an adverbial phrase the interpretation will gradually move up towards the 'exactly' end of the continuum. Nevertheless, the distinctions between these various 'absolute value' uses of *two* can be overruled by many other factors. The only distinction that is relatively clear is the one between subject and object phrases: the first will typically exclude the possibility of there being more than two elements more forcefully than the latter. This discussion of the influence of syntax on the value interpretation of numerals can be compared to the information-structural analysis of the meaning of numerals by researchers such as Van Kuppevelt and Scharten, but there are important differences: whereas the latter analysts work with constructed examples to show the influence of the position of the numeral, I have investigated how these influences can be realized on a linguistic level. The fact that an NP containing a numeral can be construed as the answer to a question or not is indeed one of the determinants of the interpretation of numerals, but this "comment" / "non-comment" position is often not directly coded in linguistic structure, but only manifests itself via the detour of intonation, position in the sentence and syntactic structure. It is the latter kind of realization that I have tried to describe.

With respect to the 'at least' and 'at most' meanings of numerals, it was argued that these have to be realized through the presence of extra linguistic material in the cotext. Occasionally, also the presence of special contextual conditions will trigger these interpretations. For the description of the latter I have often referred to Ducrot's concept of "argumentative value", which captures the intuition that an utterance normally has a "point", i.e. can be related to a "conversational goal". The corpus analysis has demonstrated that 'at least' and 'at most' interpretations are much less frequent than 'exactly n' and 'absolute value' interpretations. When they do occur, these interpretations are usually triggered by restrictors such as *only, merely* or *at least* or by the presence of modal elements (be it modal verbs or other elements). The influence of a number of necessity modals and one possibility modal on the interpretation of numerals has been analyzed.

Next, I have also tested a number of classical neo-Gricean arguments in favor of the 'at least' analysis of numerals in the corpus. First, I have looked at the alleged "defeasibility" of the 'exactly n' meanings of numerals. The corpus analysis has shown that the cancellation test and the suspension test can very often not be applied because of contextual elements that do not allow the insertion of *in fact* or *if not* phrases. Moreover, the function of these cancellation and suspension phrases themselves have been analyzed, because they contribute to the expression of cardinality in their own distinct ways. The concept "argumentative value" has been used to point out subtle differences in the ways in which both phrases function. Second, I have checked the Hornian redundancy argument in the corpus: the corpus analysis showed that 'at least' restrictors could be added much more frequently than 'exactly' restrictors. 'At most' and 'exactly' restrictors are rather difficult to add to *two* without creating a redundancy effect, or without changing the argumentative value of the utterance to such an extent that it is no longer compatible with the context. Besides the 'at least' restrictors, also 'approximately" restrictors could be added rather freely. Rather than providing an argument for the 'at least' analysis of numerals, the redundancy test demonstrates that the conventional meaning of *two* is its 'absolute value' meaning. Third, also the interpretation of the combination of numerals and negation has been analyzed: the 'less than' reading, as predicted by the neo-Gricean account, indeed turned out to be the default interpretation. Rather than explaining this interpretation by accepting the 'at least' meaning of numerals as their conventional meaning, I have formulated an "epistemological principle", which relates the default 'less than' interpretation to world knowledge: if the state of affairs is such that it is true that a certain set contains n elements, it will also be true that it contains less than n elements. The interpretation of this combination will often also be steered by the presence of a so-called "rectification clause", in which another numeral is supplied to replace the negated expression of cardinality.

I have also investigated the influence of "roundness" and "magnitude" on the interpretation of numerals in a number of separate corpus analyses. As expected, round numerals can be used approximatively, at least more often than lower numerals like *two*, and larger, non-round numerals (*twenty-two*) are characterized by an inherently higher degree of exactness. With an even larger - but round - numeral (*one thousand*), the same pattern as with *ten* is found.

Finally, the various linguistic elements that explicitly modify the expression of cardinality have been looked at. These restrictors come in a wide variety of forms, and may have an epistemic component or not, which once again demonstrates that the English language user disposes of numerous lexical means to turn the coded 'absolute value' meaning of numerals into the specific expression of cardinality that he or she wants to use.

REFERENCES

Allan, K. (2000). "Quantity implicatures and the lexicon", in Bert Peeters (ed), *The lexicon-encyclopedia interface*. Amsterdam, Lausanne, New York: Elsevier, 169-218.

Allan, K. (2001). *Natural language semantics*. Oxford, Malden: Blackwell.

Anscombre, J.-C. (1975). "Il était une fois une princesse aussi belle que bonne", *Semantikos* 1:1-28.

Anscombre, J.-C. and O. Ducrot. (1976). "L'argumentation dans la langue", *Langages* 42:5-27.

Anscombre, J.-C. and O. Ducrot. (1978). "Échelles argumentatives, échelles implicatives, et lois de discours", *Semantikos* 2: 43-68.

Anscombre, J.-C. and O. Ducrot. (1983). *L'argumentation dans la langue*. Bruxelles: Pierre Mardaga.

Anward, J. (2000). "A dynamic model of part-of-speech differentiation", in P. M. Vogel and B. Comrie, *Approaches to the typology of word classes*. Berlin, New York: Mouton de Gruyter, 3-45.

Atlas, J. D. (1979). "How linguistics matters to philosophy: presupposition, truth, and meaning", in C.-K. Oh and D. A. Dinneen (eds), *Syntax and semantics. Volume 11. Presupposition*. New York, San Francisco: Academic Press, 265-281.

Atlas, J. D. (1989). *Philosophy without ambiguity*. Oxford: Clarendon Press.

Atlas, J. D. (1996). "'Only' noun phrases, pseudo-negative generalized quantifiers, negative polarity items, and monotonicity", *Journal of Semantics* 13:265-328.

Atlas, J. D. and S. C. Levinson. (1981). "It-clefts, informativeness, and logical form: Radical Pragmatics (revised standard version)", in P. Cole (ed), *Radical Pragmatics*. New York, London: Academic Press, 1-61.

Austin, J. L. (1962). *How to do things with words*. Oxford: Oxford University Press.

Auwera, J. van der. (1985). *Language and logic. A speculative and condition-theoretic study*. Amsterdam, Philadelphia: John Benjamins.

Auwera, J. van der. (1996). "Modality: the three-layered square", *Journal of Semantics* 13:181-195.

Auwera, J. van der. (1997). "Pragmatics in the last quarter century: the case of conditional perfection", *Journal of Pragmatics* 27:261-274.

Auwera, J. van der. (1999). "On the semantic and pragmatic polyfunctionality of modal verbs", in K. Turner (ed), *The semantics/pragmatics interface from different points of view*. Oxford, Amsterdam: Elsevier, 49-64.

Auwera, J. van der. (2001). "On the typology of negative modals", in J. Hoeksema, H. Rullmann, V. Sanchez-Valencia and T. Van der Wouden (eds), *Perspectives on negation and polarity items*. Amsterdam, Philadelphia: John Benjamins, 23-48.

Auwera, J. van der, and B. Bultinck. (2001). "On the lexical typology of modals, quantifiers, and connectives", in I. Kenesei and R. M. Harnish (eds), *Perspectives on semantics, pragmatics, and discourse. A Festschrift for Ferenc Kiefer*. Amsterdam, Philadelphia: John Benjamins, 173-186.

Bach, K. (1982). "Semantic nonspecificity and mixed quantifiers", *Linguistics and Philosophy* 4:593-605.

Bach, K. (1994a). "Conversational impliciture", *Mind and Language* 9:124-162.

Bach, K. (1994b). "Semantic slack. What is said and more", in S. L. Tsohatzidis (ed), *Foundations of speech act theory. Philosophical and linguistic perspectives*. London and New York: Routledge, 267-291.

Baker, C. L. (1995). *English syntax*. Cambridge, London: MIT Press.

Barwise, J. and R. Cooper. (1981). "Generalized quantifiers and natural language", *Linguistics and Philosophy* 4:159-219.

Belnap, N. (1998). "Declaratives are not enough", in A. Kasher (ed), *Pragmatics. Critical concepts. Volume II: Speech act theory and particular speech acts*. London and New York: Routledge, 290-315.

Benacerraf, P. (1965). "What numbers could not be", *Philosophical Review* 74:47-73.

Bloomfield, L. (1970 [1933]). *Language*. London: George Allen & Unwin.

Brainerd, C. J. (1979). *The origins of the number concept*. New York, London: Praeger.

Brainerd, C. J. (1982). *Children's logical and mathematical cognition. Progress in cognitive development research*. New York, Heidelberg, Berlin: Springer.

Brandt Corstius, H. (ed). (1968). *Grammars for number names*. Dordrecht: D. Reidel Publishing Company.

Brisard, F. (1999). *A critique in and about tense theory*. Ph.D. Thesis, Universitaire Instelling Antwerpen.

Brown, P. and S. Levinson. (1978). "Universals in language use: politeness phenomena", in E. Goody (ed), *Questions and politeness: Strategies in social interaction*. Cambridge: Cambridge University Press, 56-311.

Brysbaert, M., W. Fias and M.-P. Noël. (1998). "The Whorfian hypothesis and numerical cognition: is 'twenty-four' processed in the same way as 'four-and-twenty'?", *Cognition* 66:51-77.

Bultinck, B. (2001). "English numerals as a lexical category: the case of zero", *SKY Journal of Linguistics* 14:43-73.

Burnard, L. (ed). (1995). *User reference guide for the British National Corpus*. Oxford: Oxford Computing Services.

Burton-Roberts, N. (1984). "Modality and implicature", *Linguistics and Philosophy* 7:181-206.

Campbell, R. (1981). "Language acquisition, psychological dualism and the definition of pragmatics", in H. Parret et al. (eds), *Possibilities and limitations of pragmatics*. Amsterdam: John Benjamins, 93-103.

Carston, R. (1985). "A reanalysis of some 'quantity implicatures'". Ms., University College London.

Carston, R. (1988). "Implicature, explicature, and truth-theoretic semantics", in R. Kempson (ed), *Mental representations: The interface between language and reality.* Cambridge: Cambridge University Press, 155-181.

Carston, R. (1995). "Quantity maxims and generalised implicature", *Lingua* 96:213-244.

Carston, R. (1996). "Metalinguistic negation and echoic use", *Journal of Pragmatics* 25:309-330.

Carston, R. (1998a). "Informativeness, relevance and scalar implicature", in R. Carston and S. Uchida (eds), *Relevance Theory: applications and implications.* Amsterdam: John Benjamins, 179-236.

Carston, R. (1998b). *Pragmatics and the explicit-implicit distinction.* Ph.D. Thesis, University College London.

Carston, R. (1999). "The semantics/pragmatics distinction: a view from Relevance Theory", in K. Turner (ed), *The semantics/pragmatics interface from different points of view.* Oxford, Amsterdam: Elsevier, 85-125.

Chafe, W. (1987). "Cognitive constraints on information flow", in R. Tomlin (ed), *Coherence and grounding in discourse.* Typological studies in language vol XI. Amsterdam: John Benjamins: 21-52.

Channell, J. (1980). "More on approximations: a reply to Wachtel", *Journal of Pragmatics* 4:461-476.

Chomsky, N. (1972). *Studies on semantics in generative grammar.* The Hague: Mouton.

Christophersen, P. and A. O. Sandved. (1970 [1969]). *An advanced English grammar.* Houndmills Basingstoke Hampshire: Macmillan.

Clark, H. H. (1977). "Bridging", in P. N. Johnson-Laird and P. C. Wason (eds.), *Thinking: Readings in cognitive science.* Cambridge: Cambridge University Press, 411-420.

Cohen, J. L. (1971). "Some remarks on Grice's views about the logical particles of natural language", in Y. Bar-Hillel (ed), *Pragmatics of natural languages.* Dordrecht, Boston: Reidel Publishing Company, 50-68.

Cohen, J. L. (1977). "Can the conversationalist hypothesis be defended?", *Philosophical Studies* 31:81-90.

Corbett, G. G. (1978). "Universals in the syntax of cardinal numerals", *Lingua* 46: 355-368.

Cornulier, B. de. (1984). "Pour l'analyse minimaliste de certaines expressions de quantité", *Journal of Pragmatics* 8:661-691.

Croft, W. (2000). "Parts of speech as language universals and as language-particular categories", in P. M. Vogel and B. Comrie (eds), *Approaches to the typology of word classes.* Berlin, New York: Mouton de Gruyter, 65-102.

Crystal, D. (1967). "Word classes in English", *Lingua* 17:24-56.

Davis, W. A. (1998). *Implicature. Intention, convention, and principle in the failure of Gricean theory.* Cambridge: Cambridge University Press.

Dehaene, S. (1992). "Varieties of numerical abilities", *Cognition* 44:1-42.

Dehaene, S. and J. Mehler. (1992). "Cross-linguistic regularities in the frequency of number words", *Cognition* 43:1-29.

Dik, Simon C. (1989). *The theory of functional grammar. Part I: The structure of the clause.* Dordrecht: Foris.

Doyle, J. J. (1951). "In defense of the square of opposition", *The New Scholasticism* 25: 367-396.

Ducrot, O. (1972). *Dire et ne pas dire. Principes de sémantique linguistique.* Paris: Hermann.

Ducrot, O. (1973). *La preuve et le dire. Langage et logique.* Paris: Maison Mame.

Eco, U. (1995). *The search for the perfect language.* Trans. James Fentress. Oxford, Cambridge: Blackwell.

Erteschik-Shir, N. (1986). "Wh-questions and focus", *Linguistics and Philosophy* 9:117-149.

Fauconnier, G. (1975). "Pragmatic scales and logical structure", *Linguistic Inquiry* 6:353-375.

Fauconnier, G. (1976). "Remarque sur la théorie des phénomènes scalaires", *Semantikos* 1:13-36.

Fogelin, R. J. (1967). *Evidence and meaning.* New York: Humanities Press.

Fraser, N. M., G. G. Corbett and S. McGlashan. (1993). "Introduction", in G. G. Corbett, N. M. Fraser and S. McGlashan (eds), *Heads in grammatical theory.* Cambridge, New York: Cambridge University Press, 1-10.

Frege, G. (1990 [1884]). *Die Grundlagen der Arithmetik. Ein logisch-mathematische Untersuchung über den Begriff der Zahl.* Hildesheim, Zürich, New York: Georg Olms Verlag.

Fretheim, T. (1992). "The effect of intonation on a type of scalar implicature", *Journal of Pragmatics* 18:1-30.

Fuson, K. C. and J. W. Hall. (1983). "The acquisition of early number word meanings: a conceptual analysis and review", in H. P. Ginsburg (ed), *The development of mathematical thinking.* New York, London: Academic Press, 49-107.

Gazdar, G. (1979). *Pragmatics. Implicature, presupposition and logical form.* New York, London: Academic Press.

Geeraerts, D. (1988). "Cognitive Grammar and the history of lexical semantics", in B. Rudzka-Ostyn (ed), *Topics in Cognitive Linguistics.* Amsterdam: John Benjamins, 647-677.

Geeraerts, D. (1993). "Vagueness's puzzles, polysemy's vagaries", *Cognitive Linguistics* 4:223-272.

Gelman, R. and C. R. Gallistel. (1978). *The child's understanding of number.* Cambridge: Harvard University Press.

Giering, D., G. Graustein, A. Hoffmann et al. (1987 [1986]). *English grammar. A university handbook.* Leipzig: VEB Verlag Enzyklopädie.

Ginsburg, H. P. (ed). (1983). *The development of mathematical thinking.* New York, London: Academic Press.

Givón, T.. (1993). *English grammar. A function-based introduction.* Vol. I. Amsterdam, Philadelphia: John Benjamins.

Grandy, R. E. and R. Warner. (eds). (1986). *Philosophical grounds of rationality.*

Intentions, categories, ends. Oxford: Clarendon Press.

Green, M. (1995). "Quantity, volubility, and some varieties of discourse", *Linguistics and Philosophy* 18:83-112.

Greenbaum, S. (1996). *The Oxford English Grammar.* Oxford: Oxford University Press.

Greenberg, J. H. (1978). "Generalizations about numeral systems", in J. H. Greenberg (ed), *Universals of human language: word structure.* Stanford: Stanford University Press, 249-295.

Grice, P. H. (1975). "Logic and conversation", in P. Cole and J.L. Morgan (eds), *Syntax and semantics 3: Speech acts.* New York: Academic Press, 41-58.

Grice, P. H. (1989 [1967]). "Logic and conversation". Unpublished. William James lectures at Harvard University.

Grice, P. H. (1989). *Studies in the way of words.* Cambridge: Harvard University Press.

Gvozdanovic, J. (1992). *Indo-European numerals.* Berlin, New York: Mouton de Gruyter.

Hamblin, C. L. (1971). "Mathematical models of dialogue", *Theoria* 37:130-155.

Hammerich, L. (1966). *Zahlwörter und Zahlbegriff.* Mannheim: Dudenverlag.

Harnish, R. M. (1976). "Logical form and implicature", in T. G. Bever, J. J. Katz and D. T. Langendoen (eds), *An integrated theory of linguistic ability.* Sussex: The Harvester Press: 313-391.

Hatcher, A.G. (1956). "Syntax and the sentence", *Word* 12:234-250.

Heim, I. (1983). "File change semantics and the familiarity theory of definiteness", in R. Bäuerle, C. Schwarze and A. von Stechow (eds), *Meaning, use and interpretation of language.* Berlin, New York: Walter de Gruyter, 164-189.

Hengeveld, K. (1992). *Non-verbal predication: theory, typology, diachrony.* Berlin: Mouton de Gruyter.

Himmelmann, N. P. and J. U. Wolff. (1999). *Toratán (Ratahan).* München, Newcastle: Lincom Europa.

Hirschberg, J. (1991 [1985]). *A theory of scalar implicature.* New York: Garland.

Horn, L. R. (1972). *On the semantic properties of logical operators in English.* Ph.D. Thesis, UCLA.

Horn, L. R. (1984). "Toward a new taxonomy for pragmatic inference: Q-based and R-based implicature", in D. Schiffrin (ed), *Meaning, form, and use in context: Linguistic application.* Washington: Georgetown University Press, 11-42.

Horn, L. R. (1985). "Metalinguistic negation and pragmatic ambiguity", *Language* 61:121-174.

Horn, L. R. (1989). *A natural history of negation.* Chicago: University of Chicago Press.

Horn, L. R. (1990). "Hamburgers and truth: why Gricean explanation is Gricean", in K. Hall, J.-P. Koenig et al. (eds), *Proceedings of the sixteenth annual meeting of the Berkeley Linguistics Society.* Berkeley: Berkeley Linguistics Society, 454-471.

Horn, L. R. (1992). "The said and the unsaid", in C. Barker and D. Dowty (eds), *Salt II: Proceedings of the second conference on semantics and linguistic theory.* Columbus: Ohio State University Linguistics Department, 163-192.

Horn, L. R. (1996). "Exclusive company: *only* and the dynamics of vertical inference", *Journal of Semantics* 13:1-40.

Horn, L. R. and S. Bayer. (1984). "Short-circuited implicature: a negative contribution", *Linguistics and Philosophy* 7:397-414.

Huang, Y. (2000). *Anaphora. A cross-linguistic approach.* Oxford, New York: Oxford University Press.

Huddleston, R. (1984). *Introduction to the grammar of English.* Cambridge, London: Cambridge University Press.

Hurford, J. R. (1975). *The linguistic theory of numerals.* Cambridge: Cambridge University Press.

Hurford, J. R. (1987). *Language and number. The emergence of a cognitive system.* Oxford, New York: Basil Blackwell.

Ifrah, G. (1998 [1994]). *The universal history of numbers. From prehistory to the invention of the computer.* Trans. D. Bellos, E.F. Harding, S. Wood, and I. Monk. London: The Harvill Press.

Jackendoff, R. S. (1972). *Semantic interpretation in generative grammar.* Cambridge: MIT Press.

Jackendoff, R. S. (1997). *The architecture of the language faculty.* Cambridge: MIT Press.

Jespersen, O. (1948 [1924]). *The Philosophy of Grammar.* London: Allen and Unwin.

Jespersen, O. (1972 [1933]). *Essentials of English Grammar.* London: George Allen & Unwin.

Jespersen, O. (1970 [1949]). *A modern English grammar on historical principles.* London: George Allen & Unwin.

Kadmon, N. (1987). *On unique and non-unique reference and asymmetric quantification.* Ph.D. Thesis, University of Massachusetts.

Kadmon, N. (2001). *Formal pragmatics. Semantics, pragmatics, presupposition, and focus.* Malden, Oxford: Blackwell.

Kamp, H. and U. Reyle. (1993). *From discourse to logic. Introduction to modeltheoretic semantics of natural language, formal logic and Discourse Representation Theory.* Dordrecht, Boston, London: Kluwer Academic Publishers.

Kaplan, R. (1999). *The nothing that is. A natural history of zero.* New York, Oxford: Oxford University Press.

Kasher, A. (ed) (1998). *Pragmatics. Critical concepts. Volume IV: Presupposition, implicatures, and indirect speech acts.* London and New York: Routledge.

Katz, J. J. (1977). *Propositional structure and illocutionary force.* New York: Crowell.

Katz, J. J. (1981). "Literal meaning and logical theory", *The Journal of Philosophy* 78:203-234.

Keenan, E. Ochs. (1976). "The universality of conversational postulates", *Language in Society* 5:67-80.

Kempson, R. (1986). "Ambiguity and the semantics-pragmatics distinction", in C. Travis (ed), *Meaning and interpretation.* Oxford: Blackwell, 77-103.

Kempson, R. and A. Cormack. (1981). "Ambiguity and quantification", *Linguistics and Philosophy* 4:259-309.

Kempson, R. and A. Cormack. (1982). "Quantification and pragmatics", *Linguistics and Philosophy* 4:607-618.

Kiefer, F. (1979). "What do conversational maxims explain?", *Lingvisticae Investigationes* 3:51-74.

Kiss, K. É. (1998). "Identification focus versus information focus", *Language* 74:245-273.

Kitcher, P. (1984). *The nature of mathematical knowledge*. Oxford: Oxford University Press.

Koenig, J. (1991). "Scalar predicates and negation: punctual semantics and interval interpretations", *Chicago Linguistic Society 27, Part 2: Parasession on negation*, 140-155.

Krifka, M. (1999). "At least some determiners aren't determiners", in K. Turner (ed), *The semantics/pragmatics interface from different points of view*. Oxford, Amsterdam, Lausanne: Elsevier, 257-291.

Kuroda, S.-Y. (1977). "Description of presuppositional phenomena from a non-presuppositionist point of view", *Lingvisticae Investigationes* 1:63-162.

Lakoff, G. (1986). "The meanings of literal", *Metaphor and Symbolic Activity* 1:291-296.

Lakoff, G. (1987). *Women, fire and dangerous things*. Chicago: University of Chicago Press.

Lakoff, G. and M. Johnson. (1980). *Metaphors we live by*. Chicago, London: University of Chicago Press.

Lakoff, G. and M. Johnson. (1999). *Philosophy in the flesh. The embodied mind and its challenge to Western thought*. New York: Basic Books.

Lambrecht, K. (1994). *Information structure and sentence form. Topic, focus, and the mental representations of discourse referents*. Cambridge, New York, Melbourne: Cambridge University Press.

Landman, F. (1998). "Plurals and maximalization", in S. Rothstein (ed), *Events and grammar*. Dordrecht, Boston, London: Kluwer Academic Publishers, 237-271.

Langacker, R. (1987). *Foundations of cognitive grammar*. Vol. I: Theoretical Prerequisites. Stanford: Stanford University Press.

Langacker, R. (1991). *Foundations of cognitive grammar*. Vol. II: Descriptive application. Stanford: Stanford University Press.

Leech, G. N. (1983). *Principles of pragmatics*. London, New York: Longman.

Leezenberg, M. M. (1995). *Contexts of metaphor. Semantic and conceptual aspects of figurative language interpretation*. Ph.D. Thesis, Universiteit van Amsterdam.

Levinson, S. C. (1983). *Pragmatics*. Cambridge: Cambridge University Press.

Levinson, S. C. (1987). "Minimization and conversational inference", in J. Verschueren and M. Bertuccelli-Papi (eds), *The pragmatic perspective. Selected papers from the 1985 international pragmatics conference*. Amsterdam, Philadelphia: John Benjamins, 61-129.

Levinson, S. C. (1989). "A review of Relevance", *Journal of Linguistics* 25:455-472.

Levinson, S. C. (2000). *Presumptive meanings. The theory of generalized conversational implicature*. Cambridge, London: MIT Press.

Lewis, D.. (1979). "Scorekeeping in a language game", in R. Bäuerle, U. Egli and A. von Stechow (eds), *Semantics from different points of view*. Berlin: Springer Verlag, 172-187.

Löbner, S. (1985). "Drei ist drei. Zur Bedeutung der Zahlwörter", in W. Kürschner and R. Vogt (eds), *Akten des 19. Linguistischen Kolloquiums Vechta 1984.* Band I, 311- 317.

Lyons, C. (1999). *Definiteness.* Cambridge: Cambridge University Press.

Mackie, J.L. (1973). *Truth, probability and paradox. Studies in philosophical logic.* Oxford: At the Clarendon Press.

Manor, R. (1998). "Pragmatics and the logic of questions and assertions", in A. Kasher (ed), *Pragmatics. Critical concepts. Volume II: Speech act theory and particular speech acts.* London and New York: Routledge, 334-365.

Matsumoto, Y. (1995). "The conversational condition on Horn scales", *Linguistics and Philosophy* 18:21-60.

Menninger, K. (1970 [1958]). *Number words and number symbols. A cultural history of numbers.* Cambridge, London: MIT Press.

Morgan, J.L. (1978). "Two types of convention in indirect speech acts", in P. Cole (ed), *Syntax and semantics. Volume 9. Pragmatics.* New York, San Francisco: Academic Press: 261-280.

Neale, S. (1992). "Paul Grice and the philosophy of language", *Linguistics and Philosophy* 15:509-559.

Nunberg, G. (1978). *The pragmatics of reference.* Bloomington: Indiana University Linguistics Club.

Nunberg, G. (1995). "Transfers of meaning", *Journal of Semantics* 12:109-132.

Peirce, C. S. (1991 [1867]). "On a new list of categories", in J. Hoopes (ed), *Peirce on signs. Writings on semiotic by Charles Sanders Peirce.* Chapel Hill and London: The University of North Carolina Press, 23-33.

Peters, F.J.J. (1980). "Phrasing rules for complex number sequences in English", *Studia Linguistica* 34:124-134.

Piaget, J. (1952). *The child's conception of number.* London: Routledge and Kegan Paul.

Pollmann, T. and C. Jansen. (1996). "The language-user as an arithmetician", *Cognition* 59:219-237.

Poutsma, H. (1916). *A grammar of late modern English.* Part II: The Parts of Speech. Groningen: P. Noordhoff.

Powell, M. J. (1992). "Folk theories of meaning and principles of conventionality: Encoding literal attitude via stance adverb", in A. Lehrer and E. F. Kittay (eds), *Frames, fields, and contrasts. New essays in semantics and lexical organization.* Hillsdale, London: Lawrence Erlbaum Associates, 333-353.

Pustejovsky, J. (1991). "The generative lexicon", *Computational Linguistics* 4:409-441.

Pustejovsky, J. (1995). *The generative lexicon.* Cambridge: MIT Press.

Pustejovsky, J and P. Bouillon. (1996). "Aspectual coercion and logical polysemy", in J. Pustejovsky and B. Boguraev (eds), *Lexical semantics. The problem of polysemy.* Oxford: Clarendon Press, 133-162.

Quirk, R., S. Greenbaum, G. Leech and J. Svartvik. (1985). *A comprehensive grammar of the English language.* London and New York: Longman.

Récanati, F. (1979). "La langue universelle et son 'inconsistance'", *Critique* 387-388:778-789.

Récanati, F. (1989). "The pragmatics of what is said", *Mind and Language* 4: 295-329.

Récanati, F. (1993). *Direct reference. From language to thought.* Oxford, Cambridge: Blackwell.

Récanati, F. (1994). "Contextualism and anti-contextualism in the philosophy of language", in S. L. Tsohatzidis (ed), *Foundations of speech act theory. Philosophical and linguistic perspectives.* London and New York: Routledge, 156-166.

Reinhardt, M. (1991). "The word-class character of English numerals", *Zeitschrift für Phonetik, Sprachwissenschaft und Kommunikationsforschung* 44:196-202.

Richardson, J.F. and A.W. Richardson. (1990). "On predicting pragmatic relations", *Proceedings of the sixteenth annual meeting of the Berkeley Linguistics Society. General session and parasession on the legacy of Grice.* Berkeley: Berkeley Linguistics Society, 498-508.

Rooth, M. (1996). "Focus", in S. Lappin (ed), *Handbook of contemporary semantics theory.* Oxford: Blackwell, 271-297.

Sadock, J. M. (1977). "Truth and approximations", in *Proceedings of the third annual meeting of the Berkeley Linguistics Society.* Berkeley: Berkeley Linguistics Society, 430-439.

Sadock, J M. (1978). "On testing for conversational implicature", in Peter Cole (ed), *Syntax and semantics. Volume 9: Pragmatics.* New York, San Francisco: Academic Press: 281-297.

Sadock, J. M. (1984). "Whither radical pragmatics?", in D. Schiffrin (ed), *Meaning, form and use in context.* Washington: Georgetown University Press, 139-149.

Sasse, H.-J. (1993). "Syntactic categories and subcategories", in J. Jacobs, A. von Stechow, W. Sternefeld, T. Venneman (eds), *Syntax: Ein internationales Handbuch zeitgenössischer Forschung / An international handbook of contemporary research,* pp. (Handbücher zur Sprach- und Kommunikationstheorie/Handbooks of Linguistic and Communication Science 9.1.). Berlin: Walter de Gruyter, 646-686.

Saxe, G. B. (1982). "Culture and development of numerical cognition: studies among the Oksapmin of Papua New Guinea", in Charles J. Brainerd (ed), *Children's logical and mathematical cognition. Progress in development research.* New York, Heidelberg, Berlin: Springer, 157-176.

Saxe, G. B. and J. Posner. (1983). "The development of numerical cognition: cross-cultural perspectives", in H. P. Ginsburg (ed), *The development of mathematical thinking.* New York, London, Paris: Academic Press, 291-317.

Schachter, P. (1985). "Parts-of-speech systems", in T. Shopen (ed), *Language typology and syntactic description.* Vol.1. Cambridge: Cambridge University Press, 3-61.

Scharten, R. (1997). *Exhaustive interpretation: A discourse-semantic account.* Ph.D. Thesis, Katholieke Universiteit Nijmegen.

Scott F. S., C.S. Bowley, C.S. Brockett, J.G. Brown, and P.R. Goddard. (1973 [1968]). *English grammar. A linguistic study of its classes and structures.* London: Heinemann Educational Books.

Searle, J. (1969). *Speech acts.* Cambridge: Cambridge University Press.

Searle, J. (1981). *Expression and meaning. Studies in the theory of speech acts.*

Cambridge, London: Cambridge University Press.

Searle, J. (1983). *Intentionality*. Cambridge, London, New York: Cambridge University Press.

Sgall, P., E. Hajicová, and J. Panevová. (1986). *The meaning of the sentence in its semantic and pragmatic aspects*. Prague: Academia and Dordrecht: Reidel.

Smith, S. (1970). *Meaning and negation*. Ph.D. Thesis, UCLA.

Sperber, D. and D. Wilson. (1995 [1986]). *Relevance: Communication and cognition*. Oxford: Blackwell.

Stalnaker, R. (1972). "Pragmatics", in D. Davidson and G. Harman (eds), *Semantics of natural language*. Dordrecht: Reidel, 380-397.

Stalnaker, R. (1978). "Assertion", in P. Cole (ed), *Syntax and semantics. Volume 9. Pragmatics*. New York, San Francisco: Academic Press, 315-332.

Stassen, L. (1997). *Intransitive predication*. Oxford: Clarendon Press.

Strawson, P.F. (1952). *Introduction to logical theory*. London: Methuen.

Szemerényi, O. (1960). *Studies in the Indo-European system of numerals*. Heidelberg: Winter.

Thomason, R. H. (1990). "Accommodation, meaning, and implicature: interdisciplinary foundations for pragmatics", in P. R. Cohen, J. Morgan and M. E. Pollack (eds), *Intentions in communication*. Cambridge, London: MIT Press, 325-363.

Thomson, A.J. and A.V. Martinet. (1980). *A practical English grammar*. 3rd edition. Oxford, London, New York: Oxford University Press.

Van Kuppevelt, J. (1995). "Discourse structure, topicality and questioning", *Journal of Linguistics* 31:109-147.

Van Kuppevelt, J. (1996). "Inferring from topics: scalar implicatures as topic-dependent inferences", *Linguistics and Philosophy* 19:393-443.

Van Roey, J. (1982). *English grammar. Advanced level*. S.l.: Didier Hatier.

Verschueren, J. (1999). *Understanding pragmatics*. London, New York: Arnold.

Walker, R. C. S. (1975). "Conversational implicatures", in S. Blackburn (ed), *Meaning, reference and necessity. New studies in semantics*. Cambridge, London: Cambridge University Press, 133-181.

Wilson, D. and D. Sperber. (1988). "Representation and relevance", in R. M. Kempson (ed), *Mental representations. The interface between language and reality*. Cambridge, New York: Cambridge University Press, 133-153.

Wilson, D. and D. Sperber. (1992). "On verbal irony", *Lingua* 87: 53-76.

Wittgenstein, L. (1972 [1953]). *Philosophical investigations*. Trans. G.E.M. Anscombe. Oxford: Basil Blackwell.

Wynn, Karen. (1992). "Children's acquisition of the number words and the counting system", *Cognitive Psychology* 24:220-251.

Zipf, G.K. (1949). *Human behavior and the principle of least effort*. Cambridge: Addison-Wesley.

Zwarts, F. (1998). "Three types of polarity", in E. Hinrichs and F. Hamm (eds), *Plurality and quantification*. Dordrecht: Kluwer, 177-238.

INDEX